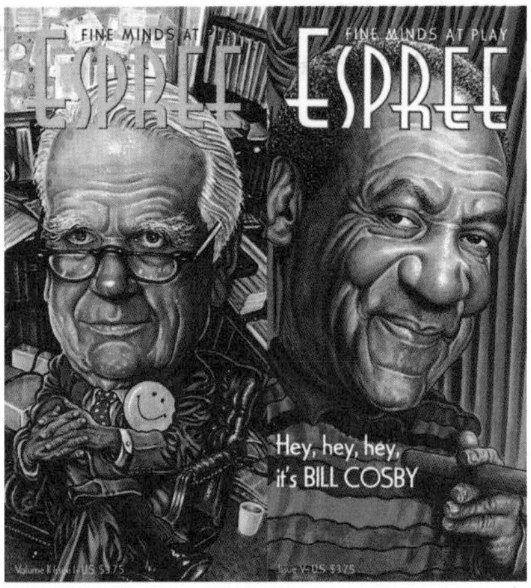
FINE MINDS AT PLAY
ESPREE
FINE MINDS AT PLAY
ESPREE
Hey, hey, hey,
it's BILL COSBY

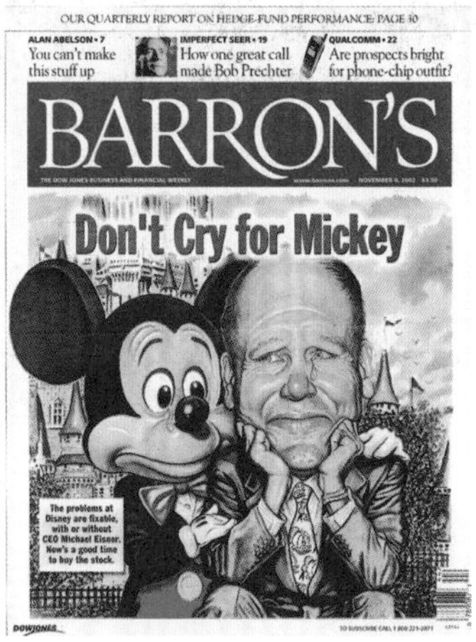
OUR QUARTERLY REPORT ON HEDGE-FUND PERFORMANCE: PAGE 40
ALAN ABELSON • 7
You can't make this stuff up
IMPERFECT SEER • 19
How one great call made Bob Prechter
QUALCOMM • 22
Are prospects bright for phone-chip outfit?
BARRON'S
Don't Cry for Mickey
The problems at Disney are fixable, with or without CEO Michael Eisner. Now's a good time to buy the stock.

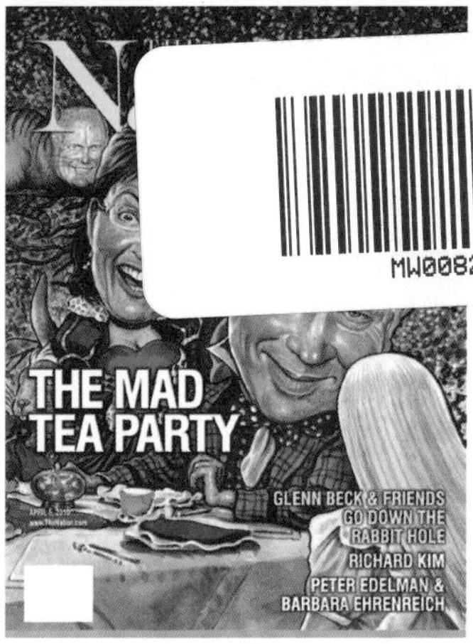
THE MAD TEA PARTY
GLENN BECK & FRIENDS GO DOWN THE RABBIT HOLE
RICHARD KIM
PETER EDELMAN & BARBARA EHRENREICH

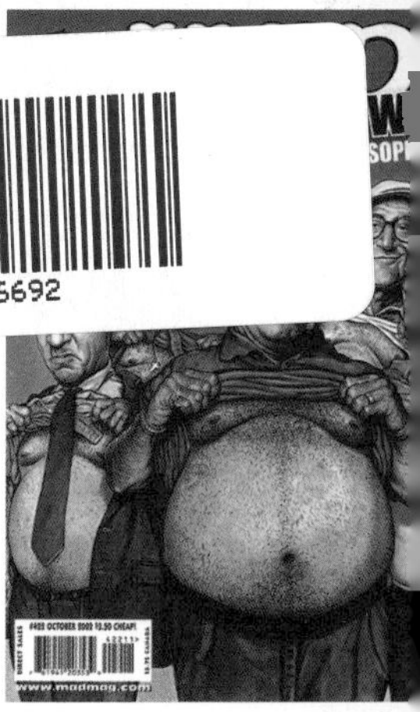
www.madmag.com

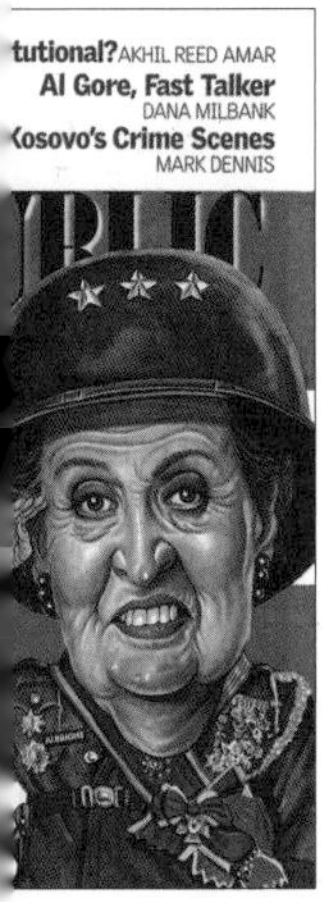
tutional? AKHIL REED AMAR
Al Gore, Fast Talker
DANA MILBANK
Kosovo's Crime Scenes
MARK DENNIS

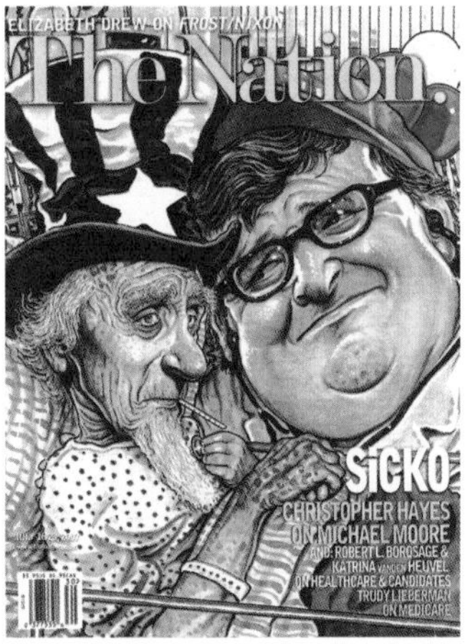
ELIZABETH DREW ON FROST/NIXON
The Nation.
SiCKO
CHRISTOPHER HAYES ON MICHAEL MOORE
AND: ROBERT L. BOROSAGE & KATRINA VANDEN HEUVEL ON HEALTHCARE & CANDIDATES
TRUDY LIEBERMAN ON MEDICARE

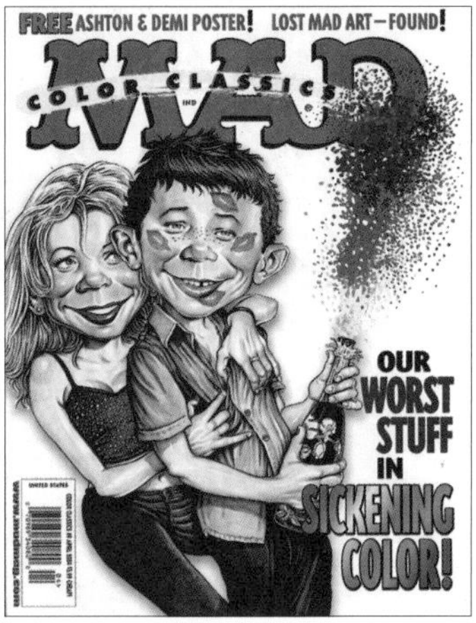
FREE ASHTON & DEMI POSTER! LOST MAD ART—FOUND!
COLOR CLASSICS
MAD
OUR WORST STUFF IN SICKENING COLOR!

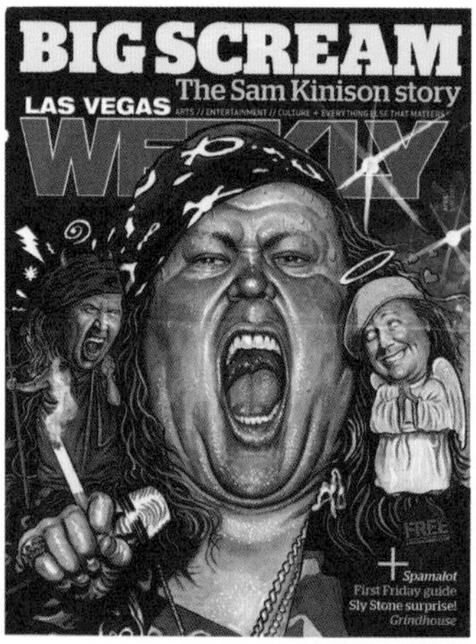
BIG SCREAM
The Sam Kinison story
LAS VEGAS WEEKLY
Spamalot
First Friday guide
Sly Stone surprise!
Grindhouse

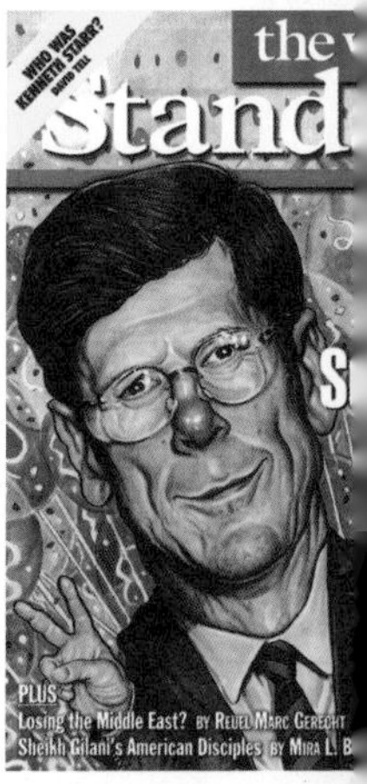
the
Standard
PLUS
Losing the Middle East? BY REUEL MARC GERECHT
Sheikh Gilani's American Disciples

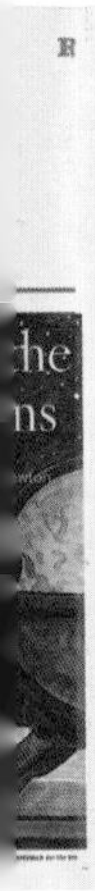

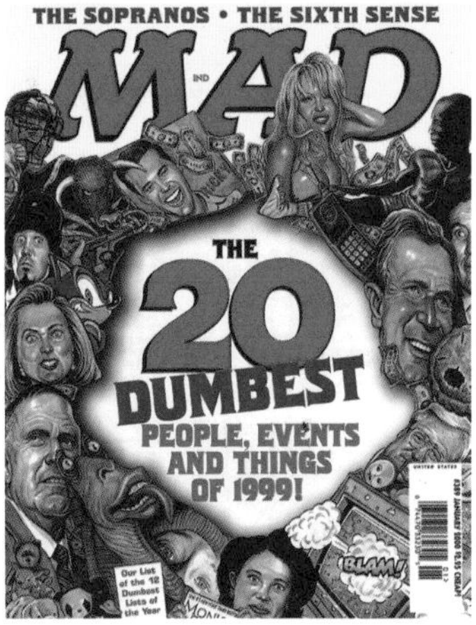
THE SOPRANOS • THE SIXTH SENSE
MAD
THE 20 DUMBEST PEOPLE, EVENTS AND THINGS OF 1999!

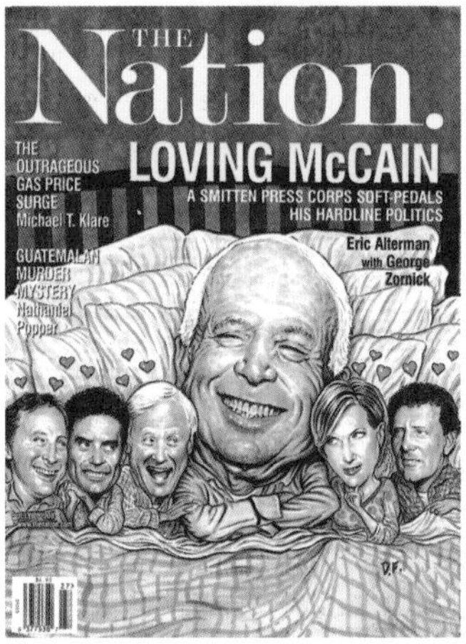
THE Nation.
THE OUTRAGEOUS GAS PRICE SURGE
Michael T. Klare
LOVING McCAIN
A SMITTEN PRESS CORPS SOFT-PEDALS HIS HARDLINE POLITICS
GUATEMALAN MURDER MYSTERY
Nathaniel Popper
Eric Alterman with George Zornick

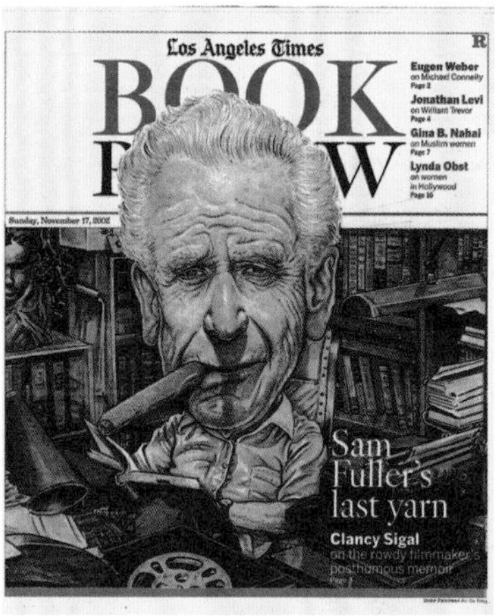
Los Angeles Times
BOOK REVIEW
Eugen Weber
Jonathan Levi
Gina B. Nahai
Lynda Obst
Sunday, November 17, 2002
Sam Fuller's last yarn
Clancy Sigal

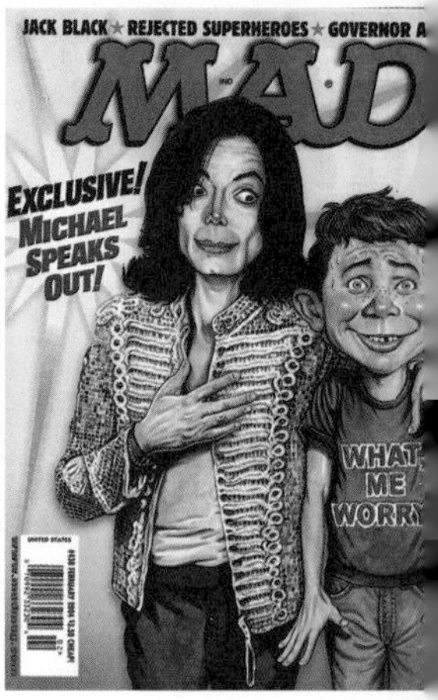
JACK BLACK ★ REJECTED SUPERHEROES ★ GOVERNOR A
MAD
EXCLUSIVE! MICHAEL SPEAKS OUT!
WHAT, ME WORRY

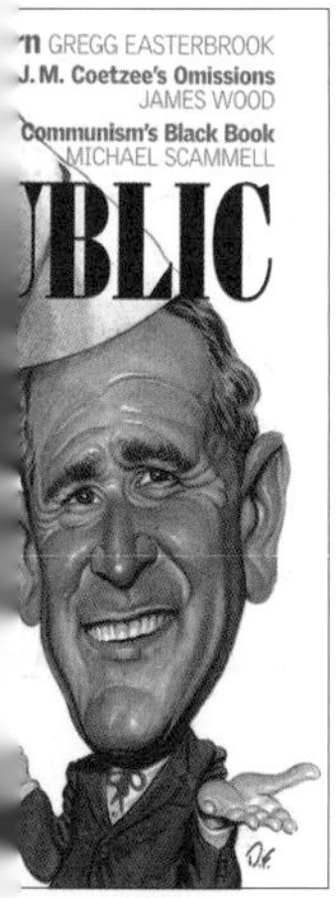
GREGG EASTERBROOK
J. M. Coetzee's Omissions
JAMES WOOD
Communism's Black Book
MICHAEL SCAMMELL
UBLIC

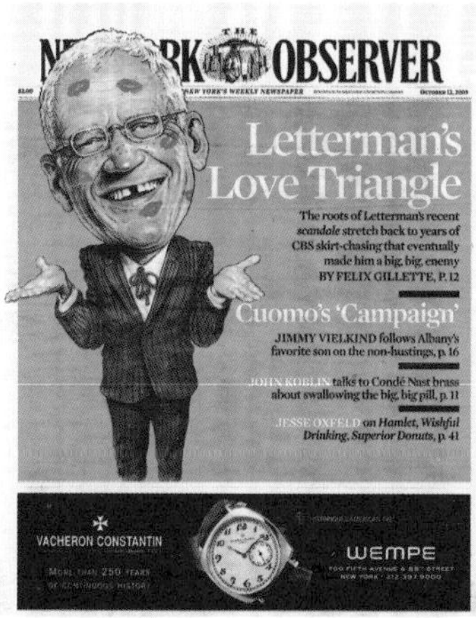
NEW YORK OBSERVER
Letterman's Love Triangle
The roots of Letterman's recent scandale stretch back to years of CBS skirt-chasing that eventually made him a big, big, enemy
BY FELIX GILLETTE, P. 12
Cuomo's 'Campaign'
JIMMY VIELKIND follows Albany's favorite son on the non-hustings, p. 16
JOHN KOBLIN talks to Condé Nast brass about swallowing the big, big pill, p. 11
JESSE OXFELD on Hamlet, Wishful Drinking, Superior Donuts, p. 41
VACHERON CONSTANTIN
WEMPE

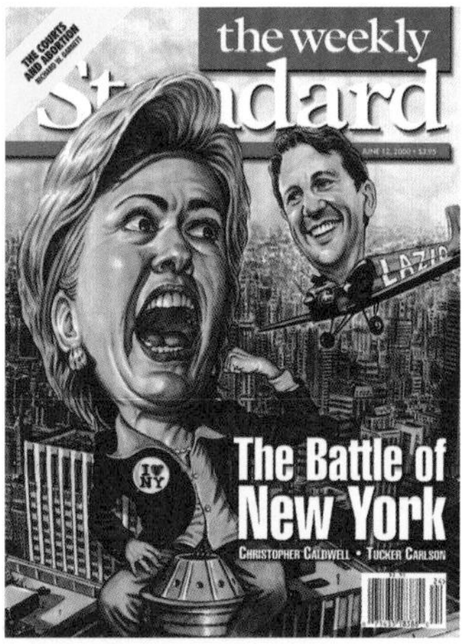
the weekly Standard
The Battle of New York
CHRISTOPHER CALDWELL • TUCKER CARLSON

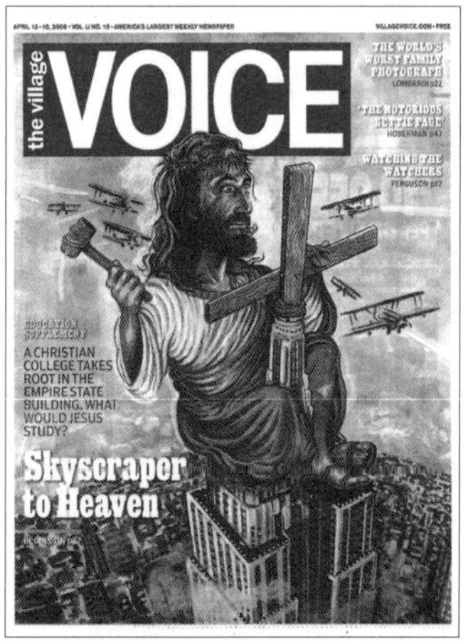
the village VOICE
A CHRISTIAN COLLEGE TAKES ROOT IN THE EMPIRE STATE BUILDING. WHAT WOULD JESUS STUDY?
Skyscraper to Heaven

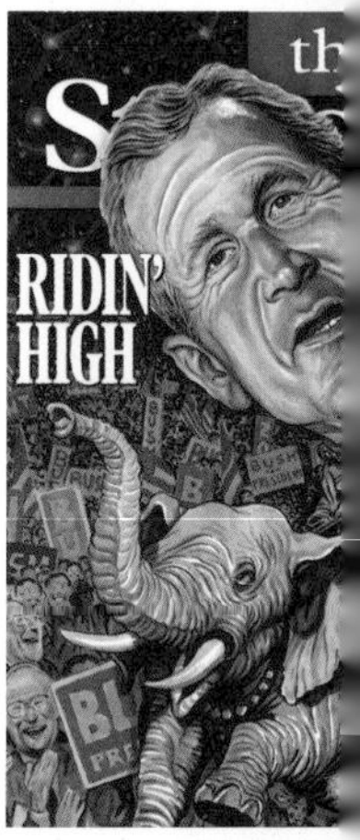
RIDIN' HIGH

TOO SOON?
___

FANTAGRAPHICS BOOKS
7563 Lake City Way NE
Seattle WA 98115

EDITED by Drew Friedman and Kim Thompson
DESIGN AND PRODUCTION Alexa Koenings
PRODUCTION Paul Baresh
ASSOCIATE PUBLISHER Eric Reynolds
PUBLISHED by Gary Groth and Kim Thompson

To receive a free catalog of comics,
call 1-800-657-1100 or write us at:

Fantagraphics Books,
7563 Lake City Way NE
Seattle, WA 98115.

Distributed in the U.S. by W.W. Norton and
Company, Inc. (212-354-5500)
Distributed in Canada by Canadian Manda Group
(416-516-0911)
Distributed in the United Kingdom by Turnaround
Distribution (208-829-3009)

Visit the Fantagraphics website: www.fantagraphics.com

First printing: July, 2010

ISBN: 978-1-60699-357-6

Printed in China

TOO SOON?

FAMOUS/INFAMOUS FACES 1995–2010

by Drew Friedman

Dedicated to my cousins,

CHUCK AND SCOTT MESSING

the first to expose me to *MAD* and *Famous Monsters of Filmland.*

New Jersey winners of the
"Master Monster Maker Contest."
Famous Monsters of Filmland
Magazine #32, 1964

FOREWORD

by JIMMY KIMMEL

When I was a kid, most every night, I sat at my desk drawing Spidermen, Batmen, Hulks, and dozens of unflattering caricatures of my neighbors and schoolmates. When my parents finally upgraded from the twelve-inch black-and-white TV around which our living room was organized to a full-sized color set, I claimed the little Magnavox for my bedroom.

I never saw my family again.

The TV went on my desk and I stayed up watching it later than any junior high school student should. Every night, for hours uninterrupted, I would draw in the glow of the *Tonight Show with Johnny Carson,* followed by *Late Night with David Letterman.* It became a ritual, one my parents allowed because we all knew that one day, it would pay off when I became a great artist!

Instead, I became a mediocre talk show host.

I got lucky. Drew Friedman makes me glad I drifted from the black ink pens I still covet to a career inside the television I loved because, if I had pursued a career in cartooning and illustration, his greatness would torment me. I marvel at his work and I am not much of a marveller. His wildly ridiculous, funhouse mirror-like takes on the human face are matched by startling technical skill.

Drew's portraits capture his subjects' best and worst qualities at once. His work is both beautiful and grotesque, brilliant and cruel.

As a long-time fan, I must admit I was as horrified as I was thrilled when Drew got around to drawing me. He finds flaws flawlessly and imperfections perfectly. Drew sees the things we choose not to see. He is merciless.

Enjoy this book slowly. Don't rush through it. Study it—and while we're at it, chew your food. What are you, an animal?

Drew Friedman is the artist I wanted to be when I was a kid. I am honored that he asked me to open for him and hope that doing so wins me a little less fat on my neck and hook in my nose.

"LIVER SPOTS ARE MY NINAS."

INTRODUCTION BY DREW FRIEDMAN.

"Lose the stipple, Friedman"… "It lacks sophistication"… "You really don't need the dots." That was just some of the sage advice I received from several very esteemed gentlemen back in the day — advice I would ignore, at least for the time being.

The funny thing was, I wasn't necessarily an admirer or fan of the "stipple" or "pointillistic" style of drawing ("thousands of tiny dots") which I was then employing. My parents had always encouraged my two brothers and me to pursue our artistic interests, be they music, writing, or, in my case, drawing. I was taken (sometimes, um, dragged) to art museum shows in Manhattan, indulged with art books, cartoon and comics anthologies, *MAD* magazine, and countless comic books. My father, the author Bruce Jay Friedman, whose day job was editing men's adventure magazines at "Magazine Management" (the company that also included Marvel Comics under its umbrella), would shower us with stacks of *Spider-Man*, *Fantastic Four* and *Millie The Model* comics every week. Inspired by all this and more, I "drew" constantly, covering my bedroom walls, school desks, textbooks, copy books, blackboards, bathroom stalls, etc., with twisted, sometimes lewd, magic-marker drawings of monster faces, freaks, unfortunate fellow students, teachers (naked), faculty members (naked), President Nixon (naked), or any random ugly, horrific face that popped into my head. On more than one occasion, this charming activity led to my mother "politely" being invited to school to bail me out of the assistant principal's office. Mom was always more annoyed with the school staff for not recognizing her child prodigy's brilliance than she ever was with me. One solution to my naughty obsession was to send me to after-school art classes, and eventually I attended the High School of Music & Art in upper Manhattan, and, finally, The School of Visual Arts (SVA) on E. 23rd St.

When I was younger, I sort of liked the whimsical work of pulp science fiction artist Virgil Finlay, who illustrated for decades in a stipple style, and the French pointillist painter, Georges Seurat, but other than them, my favorites were the great humor illustrators, caricaturists and cartoonists of the era, mainly *MAD* contributors, the "Idiot" legends: Will Elder, Jack Davis, Wally Wood, Don Martin, Dave Berg, Mort Drucker, Al Jaffee, and cover artist Norman Mingo, among many others. I consumed and adored Topps Bubblegum cards (and the cheap bubblegum), especially "Ugly Stickers," "Wanted Posters," and the more subversive "Wacky Packs," featuring the art of the great Norm Saunders. The insanely detailed art of Basil Wolverton "blew my mind." My (totally unrealistic) dream was to actually work for *MAD* and Topps one day.

Other favorites included the great *New Yorker* artists, especially the darkly humorous Chas. Addams, the sophisticated Peter Arno, and the intricate George Price. I was mesmerized by Maurice Sendak's beautifully crosshatched children's books, and by Edward Gorey's detailed, obsessively grim illustrations, the incredible airbrushing of Robert Grossman, the brilliant theatrical caricaturist Al Hirschfeld (like every other lemming, I'd gravitate to the Sunday *NY Times*, just to count the "Ninas") and fearless political caricaturist David Levine, who first introduced me to the beauty of the Liver Spot—and, inevitably, I was drawn to the pioneering underground cartoonist Robert Crumb. When I first saw *Zap* #0 in 1967, I was shocked and mesmerized, and I knew at that moment where my path in life would lead. I never looked back.

By the late '70s, I was entrenched as a "cartoon major" at SVA, a school I chose to attend simply because I was surprised to see *MAD* founder Harvey Kurtzman's name listed as an instructor in their catalog. I was shuttling back and forth between the upper East and West Sides, living with one or the other of my (by then) divorced parents. My older brother, Josh, was beginning to establish himself as a writer, and submitted a comic strip script to a new, raunchier, *National Lampoon*-type humor magazine being published by *Hustler* called *SLAM*. The script detailed a lone black man innocently driving into Andy Griffith's fictional southern TV town of Mayberry, circa the mid-'60s, and the inevitable, terrifying aftermath. Josh asked me if I would like to draw it, and liking the script, I agreed to, even though I was busy with class assignments. I worked on it off and on over the next week, mainly at night, trying to give it a semi-realistic, EC Comics feel, while still attempting to keep the art somewhat funny. The results, I felt, were slightly awkward, and the crack editorial board at *SLAM* wisely decided to pass on it (sadly, *SLAM* would last all of two issues). That seemed to be that, perhaps the end of my comics career, but it kept nagging at me. I was convinced that I should take another stab at it, that my first version had been too rushed, had not achieved the feel for the material I had originally imagined. This time out, I slowed myself way down, and spent over two months on the strip, intensely rendering it, sometimes during my SVA classes, using a Croquill pen with a "Hunt" #4 nib, and employing the "stipple" style, which achieved a photo-realistic, Weegee-like effect for the strip, which was simply titled "The Andy Griffith Show."

Josh was happy with the second version, as were the friends and fellow travelers we shared it with. When I showed the newly completed two-page comic strip to my new instructor Harvey Kurtzman after class, he adjusted his glasses and stared at if for some time, saying nothing. I'm not even sure he read it, as Harvey (nicknamed "Harvey the Vague" by those who knew him well) was a man of few, yet always choice, words. Eventually, he looked up at me, rubbed his eyes and moaned: "Friedman, you're nuts!… I can't believe the goddamn detail you put into this! Not since Wally Wood… dot's incredible!" He decided there and then to feature the strip prominently in his annual class magazine, *Kar-tunz*. Not nearly so impressed,

though, was another of my SVA instructors, the legendary creator of "The Spirit," the bombastic Will Eisner. While acknowledging my dedication, he was completely dismissive of my new style, sniffing, "Lose the stipple, Friedman, you can buy it by the barrel," a reference to sheets of readily available "Zip-A-Tone." Not so dismissive was underground cartoonist Art Spiegelman, also an instructor at SVA, then teaching a class on "the Language of Comics." He had seen the strip in Kurtzman's class magazine, was duly impressed, and chose to include it in the new comix/graphics anthology he was planning to launch with his wife, Françoise Mouly, at the dawn of the '80s, to be called *RAW*.

RAW was quickly the talk of the comics world, or at least of the "alternative comix" world, where it became known as the flagship publication of the movement. *RAW* featured early work by artists who would go on to be some of the comics scene's leading lights, including Spiegelman himself (introducing chapters of his graphic-novel-in-progress, *Maus*), Gary Panter, Sue Coe, Ben Katchor, Charles Burns, Chris Ware, and my fellow SVA classmates, Mark Newgarden and Kaz. My comics, scripted either by Josh or myself (as I was pushing myself to write more), were getting printed more frequently, in publications such as *Screw*, *High Times*, the Peter Bagge-edited *Comical Funnies*, and in all the early issues of *RAW*.

In Winters, California, Robert Crumb had just started his own counterpart magazine to *RAW* called *Weirdo*, following a format closer to the late underground comics magazine *Arcade*, but like *RAW*, also featuring work by newer artists. Trying not to get my hopes up, I sent him some samples of my work, assuming he wouldn't think much of them. On the contrary, to my surprise, he sent an effusive hand-written note telling me he had been following my stuff and he'd love it if I sent him some new comic strips for *Weirdo*. I was thrilled. Having just graduated from SVA, and living on my own in my new walk-up apartment in possibly the crappiest building in the hip, punk-infused East Village (I'd live at 341 E. 6th St., a block with 30 Indian restaurants, for the next decade, where it became a sort of meeting place/clubhouse for many fellow cartoonist and comedian friends), I sat right down and got to work on two pieces, the first detailing a day in the life of 400-lb. Swedish wrestler/movie zombie Tor Johnson, and a comic page chronicling people's reactions on hearing the news that long-retired NBC anchorman Chet Huntley had just died. Crumb was pleased with both pieces (while admitting he had never heard of Tor Johnson), and put them into the next issue (#4), paying me the then handsome sum of $50 per page. He continued to run everything I sent him, but more importantly, sent me the following advice: "I wouldn't be surprised if you someday loosened up stylistically. I hope you're not ruining your eyesight doing that detail work... think about the future a little bit, EH??"

Back in the '70s, it had been my goal to contribute to "The Funny Pages," the comics section of *The National Lampoon.* It was a bit tricky at that time, though, as I was but a teenager during their golden era. By the early '80s, they had fallen onto harder times, but still it remained a goal, and Josh and I made several attempts to get in the door, coming close, but ultimately to no avail. Feeling pretty dejected by this, and with nothing to lose, I dropped off a portfolio of my published comics with their sister publication upstairs, the fantasy/sci-fi oriented comics magazine *Heavy Metal.* To my surprise, the editor, Julie Simmons, hired me on the spot to create a new page for them, with the stipulation that the piece have a "science fiction" theme. I got right to work, writing and drawing a comic strip about all the citizens of Baltimore in the year 2040 looking exactly like Ernest Borgnine. She was delighted, and hired me to create a regular (sci-fi oriented) strip, which I'd go on to contribute for the next several years. Along the way, the magazine and I were sued for 40 million dollars by seminal NY talk show host/nostalgia king, Joe Franklin, over the strip "The Incredible Shrinking Joe Franklin" (seems Joe was touchy about his height). Although I thought it a reasonable sum, the suit was finally dismissed. Eventually, a new Friedman-friendly regime took over at *National Lampoon* and Josh and I were invited to become regular contributors. By the mid-'80s, we had enough material to fill our first (Shemp-covered) anthology which I titled *Any Similarity to Persons Living or Dead is Purely Coincidental*, published by Fantagraphics. (It's out of print. Please get on their asses!)

In 1986, I got a call from E. Graydon Carter, who invited me to draw a regular cartoon for a new New York-based humor magazine he was starting up with fellow editor Kurt Andersen, to be called *Spy.*

They had seen my work and thought I was perfect to draw "Private Lives of Public Figures," a feature they imagined as humorously depicting a behind-the-scenes peek at the ridiculous and bawdy personal lives of self-satisfied celebrities. *Spy* became possibly the most influential magazine of the excess-driven 1980s. It was notorious, taking no prisoners with its regular features, pranks, and investigative journalism. *Spy* also helped get my work far greater exposure, resulting in magazine assignments coming in on a more frequent basis. I was starting to cut way back on the time-consuming (and low-paying) comic strip work, although I still did my regular work for *Heavy Metal* and the *Lampoon,* occasionally illustrating strips for Harvey Pekar's *American Splendor,* and creating new comics for *RAW,* which was then being published by Penguin Books. I was still illustrating Josh's now more elaborate comic scripts, leading to our second and final anthology, *Warts & All,* edited and designed by Art Spiegelman and Françoise Mouly, and this time published by Penguin.

At the time, Mark Newgarden was working with Spiegelman in the product development department at Topps, where they had just created the phenomenally successful sticker series "Garbage Pail Kids." Mark invited me to help him develop and draw concepts for a new card series he had in mind depicting fictional high school insanity called "Toxic High." For the next several years, co-creating "Toxic High," as well as penciling concepts for Wacky Packs, drawing an updated version of "Ugly Stickers" ("America's Ugliest"), and designing new products and packages (including "Barfo Candy" and "Sneaky Snacks"), became almost a full-time job, and more importantly, forced me to draw at a much faster pace. Several times a week, I would head out to Topps' large, old, industrial waterfront warehouse offices in Brooklyn and, for the first time, was actually making good money at what I'd always loved to do. The timing was perfect, as my soon-to-be wife Kathy and I were making plans to move from the tiny East Village flat (the tap-tap-tapping of my stippling was slowly driving her insane, not to mention the nightly crackhouse-induced fires that were creeping closer and closer to our building) to the country, which we would finally achieve in 1990.

Kathy and I were married, living in a large log house in the mountains of PA, far from the distractions of the city, and my main focus, aside from my continuing work for Topps and briefly editing "The

Funny Pages" for the *Lampoon* (and trying to humanely rescue the flying squirrels that would constantly fly through the house each evening), were the magazine assignments which were escalating, thanks to the attention I was getting from *Spy*. After the *NY Times Magazine* assigned me a full-page comic strip about the bizarre behaviors of Congressman Jack Kemp, the floodgates completely opened and I was inundated with calls. A new magazine focusing on show business called *Entertainment Weekly* (*EW*) published my work practically on a weekly basis. I finally parted ways with *Spy* and *Lampoon*, as they both had shifted staffs and now firmly entered their "unfunny" years.

At that same time, I was invited to contribute to *MAD*, a magazine that had been off my radar for decades, but had once been my childhood goal. Soon, I proudly joined the ranks of the "Usual Gang of Idiots," and received the following advice from co-editor Nick Meglin: "Ya, know Drew, you don't really need the dots." Happily, I was still able to find time to do work of a more personal nature, for graphics/comics anthology *BLAB!*, comics for *Details*, animation work for MTV's Liquid Television, and the particularly gratifying experience of illustrating the great Howard Stern's two best-selling books *Private Parts* and *Miss America*. Yet, as Robert Crumb had once predicted, my eyes were beginning to show signs of fatigue.

By the mid-'90s, I instituted some changes. The stipple style which I had never particularly liked yet had pursued for over a decade had become an albatross, so I decided to phase it out, slowly, over the course of a year. I began rendering dots more sparingly, finally using them only in faces, hoping no one would notice. I was also determined to teach myself to paint with a brush, and work with watercolor exclusively, as many of my past artistic idols had. Art Directors were now asking for color more often than not, so I started to

"Friedman Family 1966, Glen Cove, NY"
This was originally printed in the *Saturday Evening Post*, in 1966.
Clockwise from Left: Ginger, Josh, Drew, Kipp, Bruce Jay.

practice between assignments, attempting to become proficient with color. In 1994, I stippled my last dot for a small spot drawing for *Premiere* magazine.

Another decision I made was to try to loosen up stylistically. I had moved away from the photorealism and was trying to give my work a more lighthearted, whimsical, yet at the same time distorted look, sometimes stretching figures to nightmarish extremes (see the Drew Barrymore image, page 120). Color proved to be trickier than I anticipated, and my early attempts now look somewhat garish to me, as though I was overcompensating by using extremely bright colors (see the Ross Perot image from *The New Yorker*, page 9), but with practice, I was finally able to "tone it down," achieving the more subtle affect I strove for.

This was a particularly potent, exciting time for magazine illustration, perhaps the last "Golden Era," and I was proud to see my work appear alongside so many new, young, talented artists who had seemingly grown up on the same diet of pop culture and in many cases shared the same artistic influences as me. There was also an abundance of innovative, risk-taking art directors I was fortunate enough to work for, many who would pass through *EW* over the years. About that time, I began contributing a monthly cover to the salmon-colored weekly newspaper *The New York Observer*, alternating with fellow illustrators Philip Burke, Victor Juhasz, and one of my boyhood favorites, Robert Grossman. (My covers for the *Observer* are not included in this collection, the lone exception being the cover image of Michael Jackson.)

My wife Kathy (K. Bidus) has been and continues to be my essential work partner and BFF, and is instrumental in helping me with almost each and every assignment or project I take on. Whether it be reading through reams and reams of text on my behalf (my eyes would normally glaze over after the first paragraph), hashing out concepts, collaborating on scripts, copy-editing (e.g. this introduction), coming up with or suggesting brilliant or semi-brilliant ideas, finding solutions, printing reference photos, etc. I couldn't get by without her, then or now. Nor could the beagles.

After several decades of assignments, some dealing with subjects I had little passion for (Wall Street, golf, hunting, fishing) I decided to reel it in a bit, and am now far more selective about which jobs I take on. I had already instituted a "NO FRIENDS" policy with *EW*, after being asked to draw the actors portraying the "Friends" one too many times. Sadly, the magazine and newspaper industry appears to be in flux, cutting way back on their budgets for illustration, affording me more time to concentrate on work which I have a personal passion for: portraits of beloved, famous and obscure Old Jewish Comedians, carnival sideshow freaks, and the subjects I've been rendering for my series of limited-edition prints: showbiz icons such as Frank Sinatra, Dean Martin, Bob & Ray, and Groucho Marx, and the sometimes overlooked, under-appreciated fringe-players such as Vernon Dent, Tiny Tim and Judson Fountain.

This anthology includes selections from the last fifteen years of magazine and newspaper illustrations, covers, caricatures/silhouettes, book and CD covers, and many of my recent print portraits. Overall, it's been a wacky, slightly stressful, long, strange, fulfilling trip. I hope you enjoy the results.

And don't forget to count the liver spots.

Drew Friedman, April 2010

For a comprehensive overview of my first 25 years of work, check out the excellent article "We Can't All Be Movie Stars, Friedman," by Ben Schwartz, in *Comic Art Magazine* #8, also reprinted in *The Fun Never Stops!* (Fantagraphics), Unless of course, you're completely sick of me by now.

I'D LIKE TO THANK THE FOLLOWING PEOPLE FOR THEIR GENEROUS HELP, SUPPORT AND SUGGESTIONS IN PRODUCING THIS NEW ANTHOLOGY OF WORK:

The majority of the illustrations included in this book represent 15 years of magazine and newspaper assignments and would not be possible without the many Art Directors, Designers, Editors, Writers, Front Desk Secretaries and FedEx drivers who I've had the pleasure to know and work with and are too numerous to mention by name.

My wife and BF Kathy, my Family, Fiona, Mary, Hugh, Glenn Bray, Mark Newgarden, Irwin Chusid, Phil Felix, Ben Schwartz, Eddie Gorodetsky, Frank Santopadre, Tom Leopold, Tyler Rush, Mark G. Parker, and Lorrie Davis.

Chip Kidd, Kurt Andersen, Howard Stern and that "big, fat idiot" Rush Limbaugh, for their thoughtful blurbs, and special thanks to Jimmy Kimmel for his more-than-funny Foreword.

My old friends at Fantagraphics Books, Kim, Gary, Eric, Mike, Janice, Paul, etc. Special thanks to Alexa Koenings for her brilliant design work.

My fellow illustrators at DRAWGER for their always supportive comments, and all my Facebook "Friends," and their generous "Likes." I live for "Likes."

POLITICS

"Politicians are a notch below child molester." — Woody Allen

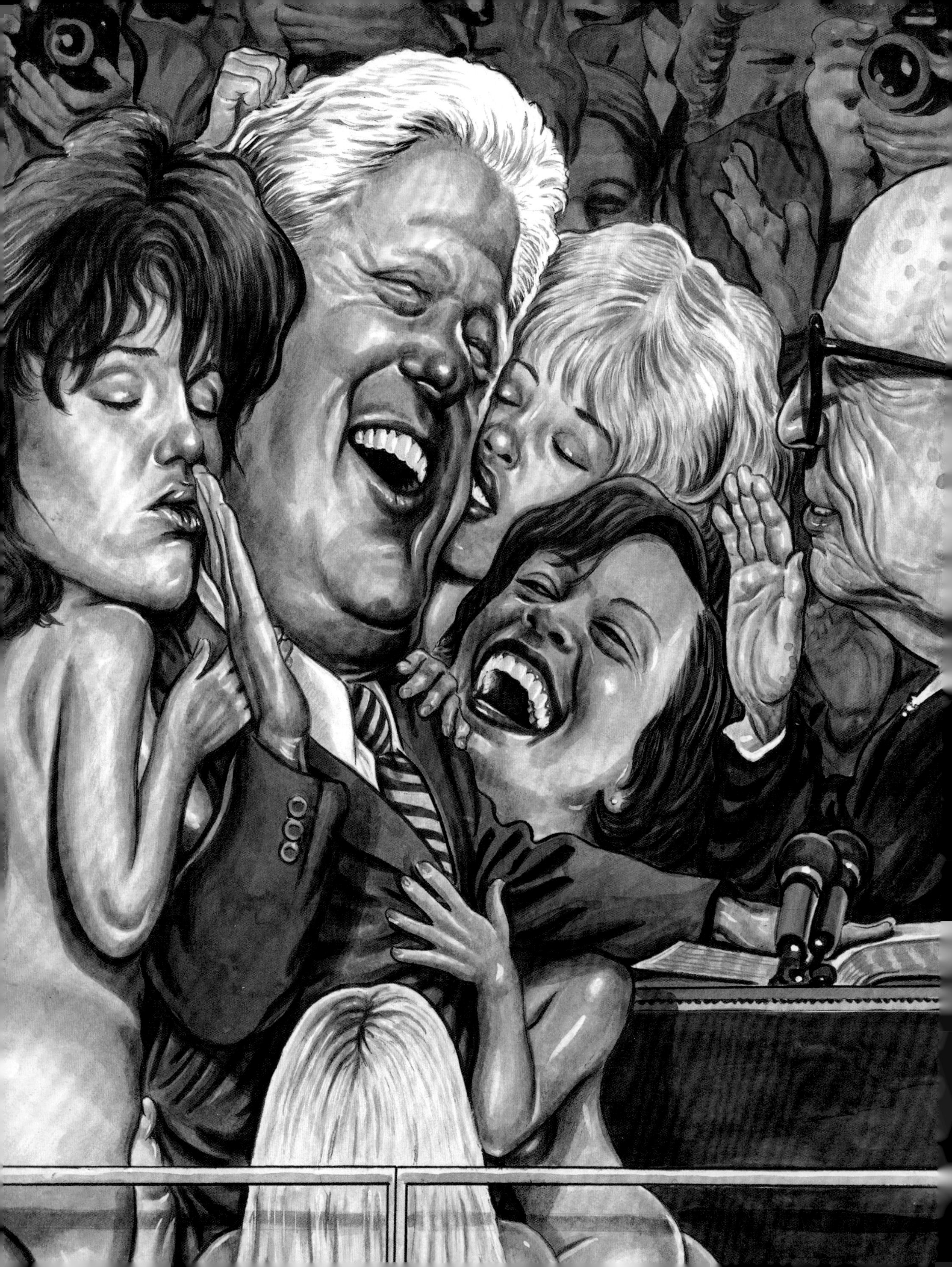

"THE BUBBA CHRONICLES."

GQ MAGAZINE

Imagining **Bill Clinton's** Third Inauguration (for a piece written by Tony Hendra).

"NOW, THIS MIGHT HURT."

TIME

Inquisition counsel **Kenneth Starr** with his pincushions of choice.

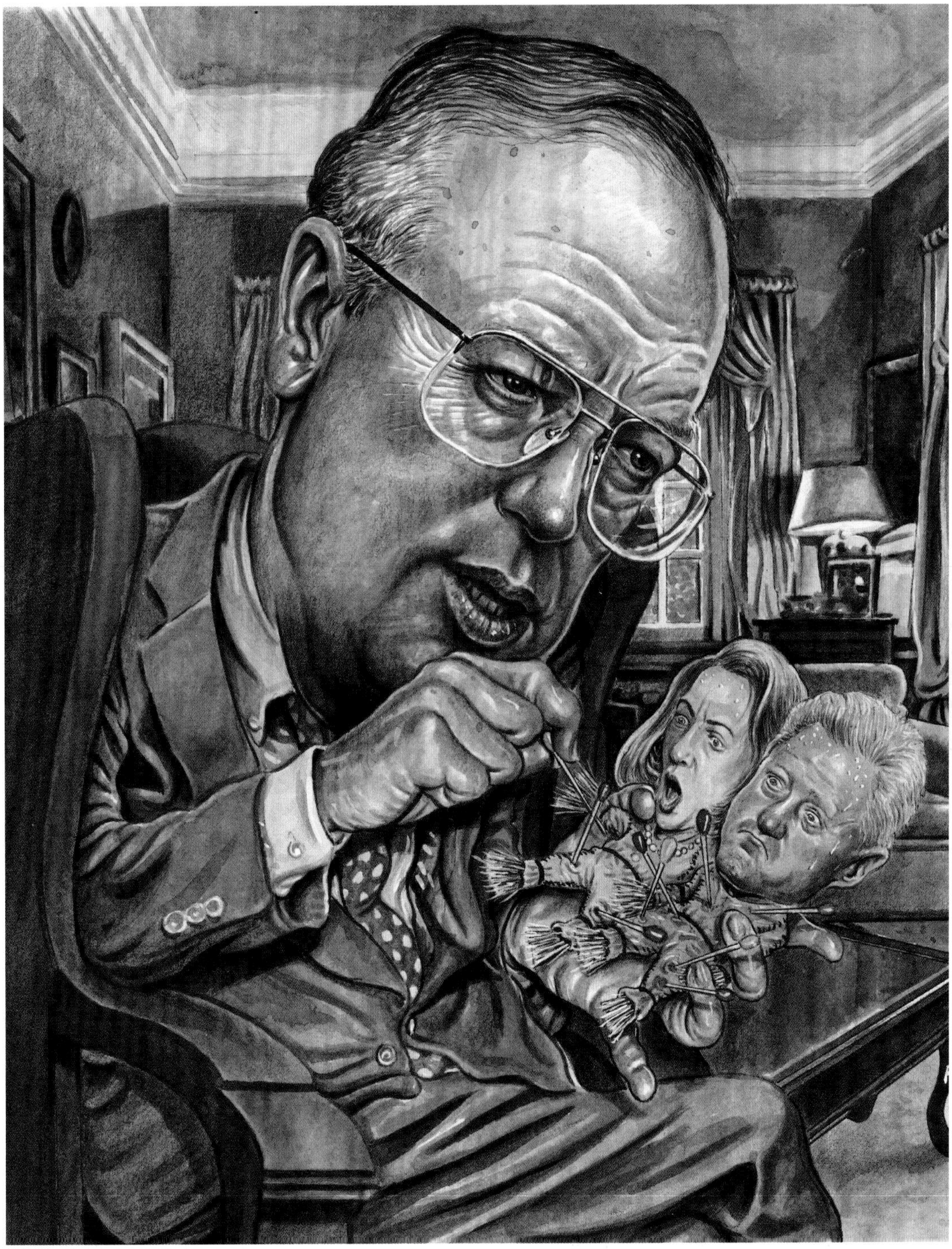

"STARR WITNESS."

TIME

With her claim to immunity apparently rejected, the president's bimbo **Monica Lewinsky** nears her day of reckoning with prosecutor **Ken Starr.** Will she talk? Plead the fifth? Or coyly pose again for photographers on the beach at Malibu?

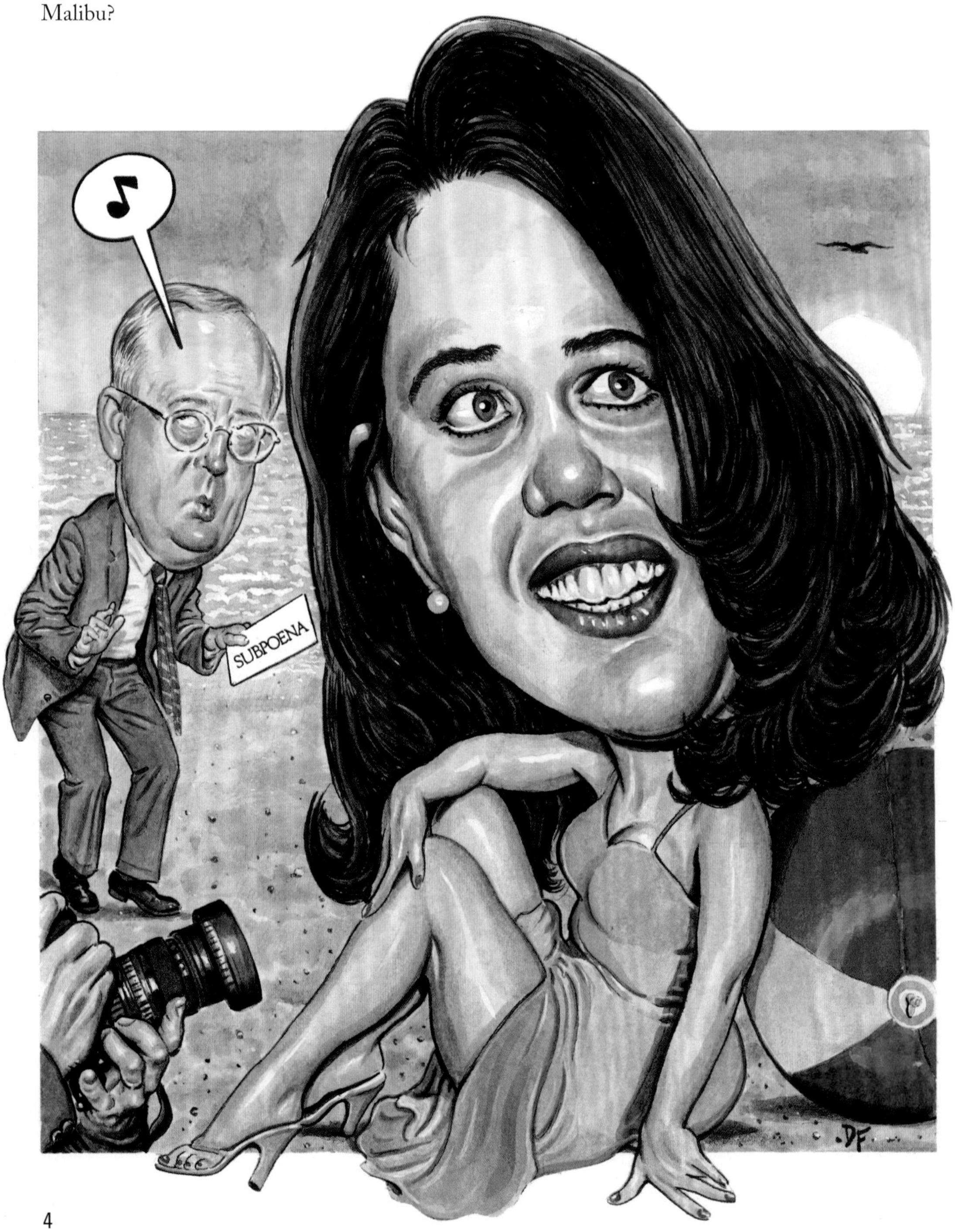

SUBPOENA
DF

"MONICA, WHITE HOUSE SEDUCTRESS."

ROLLING STONE

JFK had Marilyn Monroe. Bill Clinton had **Monica Lewinsky**.

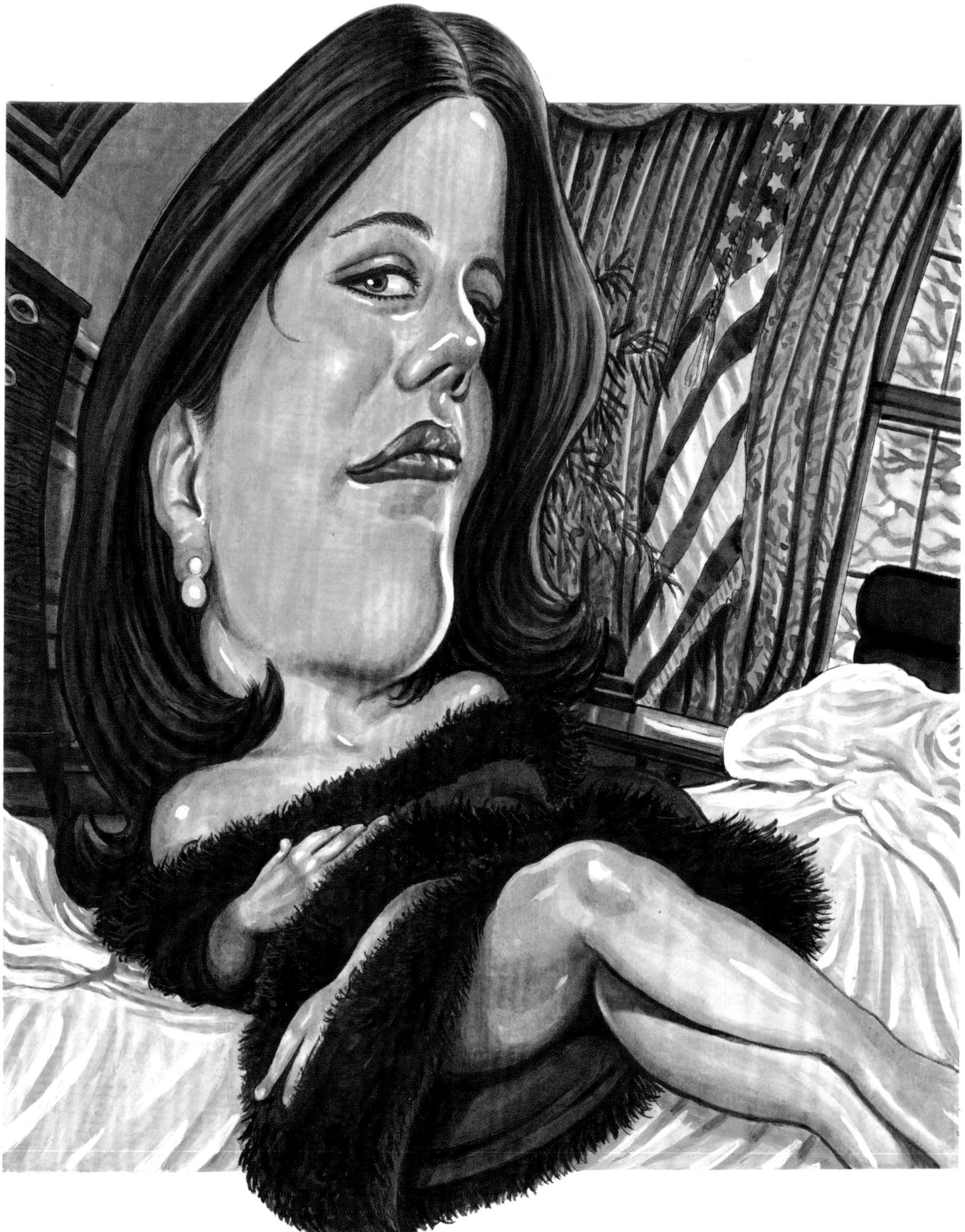

"STANDING BY HER MAN."

TIME

Hillary Clinton as Tammy Wynette, standing by her cheatin' man, **Bill**.

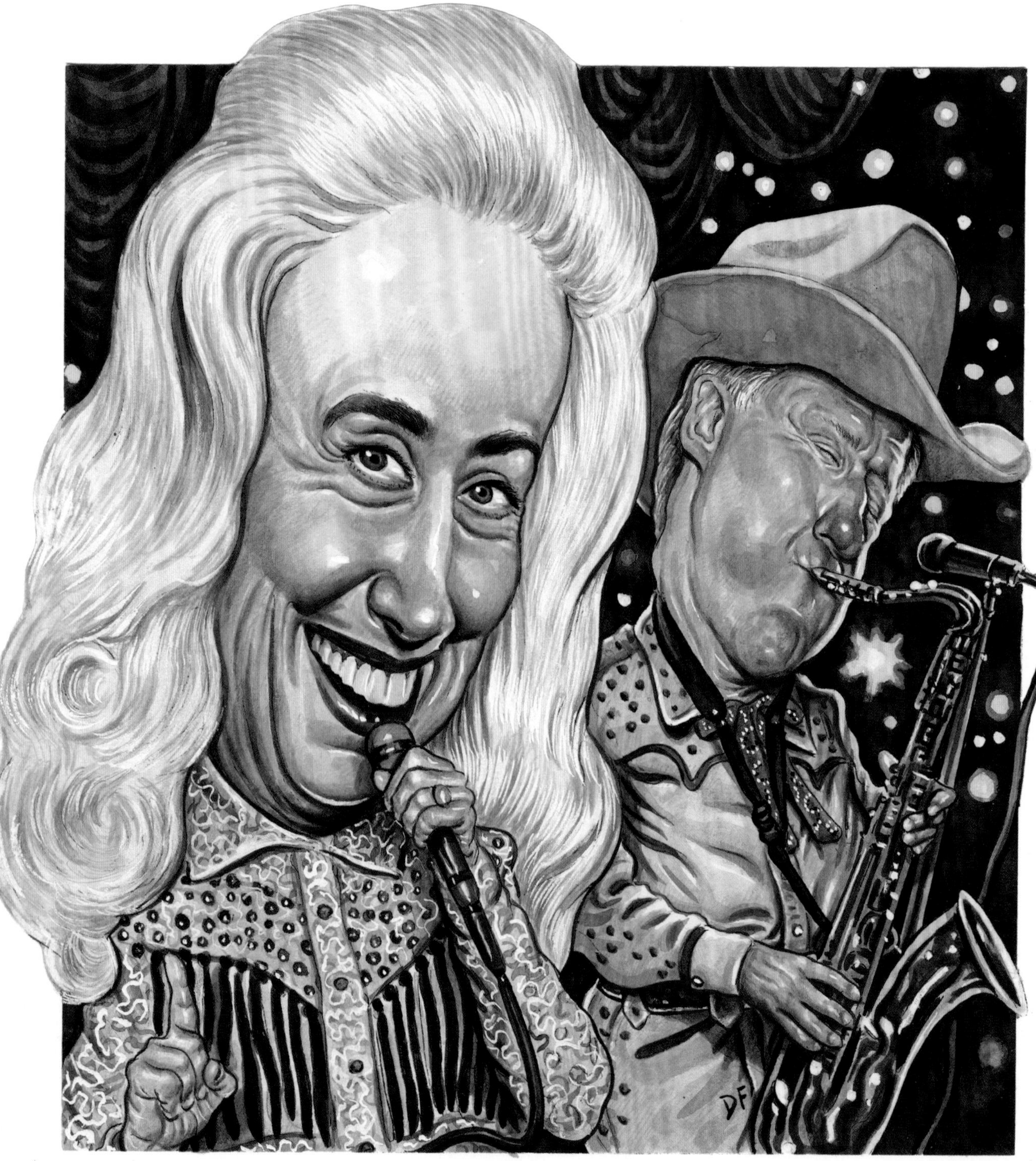

"THAT'S A GOOD BOY— ON THE NEWSPAPERS."

TIME

The President instructs his new pup where to relieve himself.

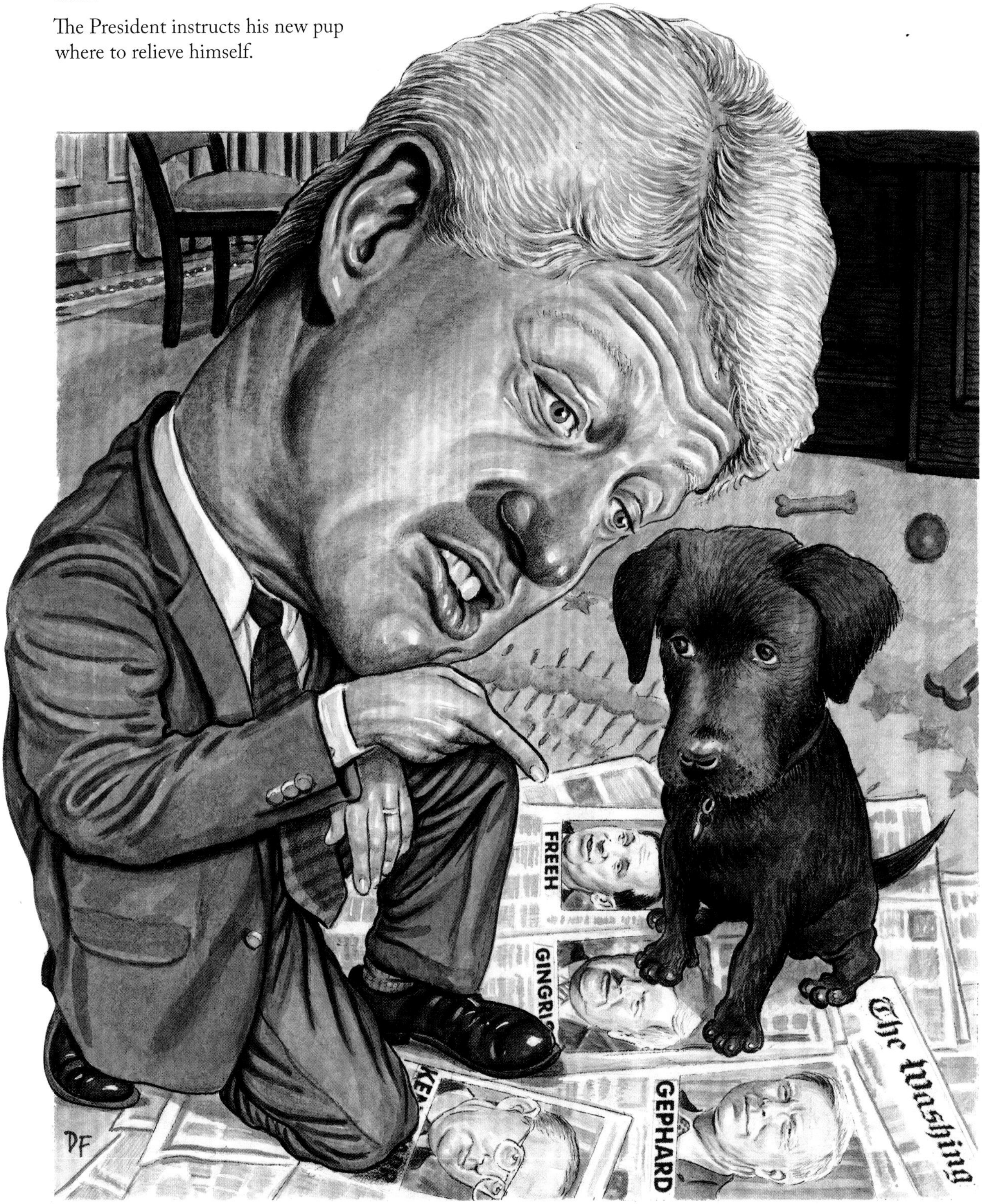
FREEH
GEPHARD
The Washing
DF

"GENERAL ALBRIGHT."

THE NEW REPUBLIC (cover)

Secretary of State **Madeleine Albright** channels General George Patton. This image was hijacked by Middle Eastern protesters, enlarged to gigantic proportions and broadcast on CNN.

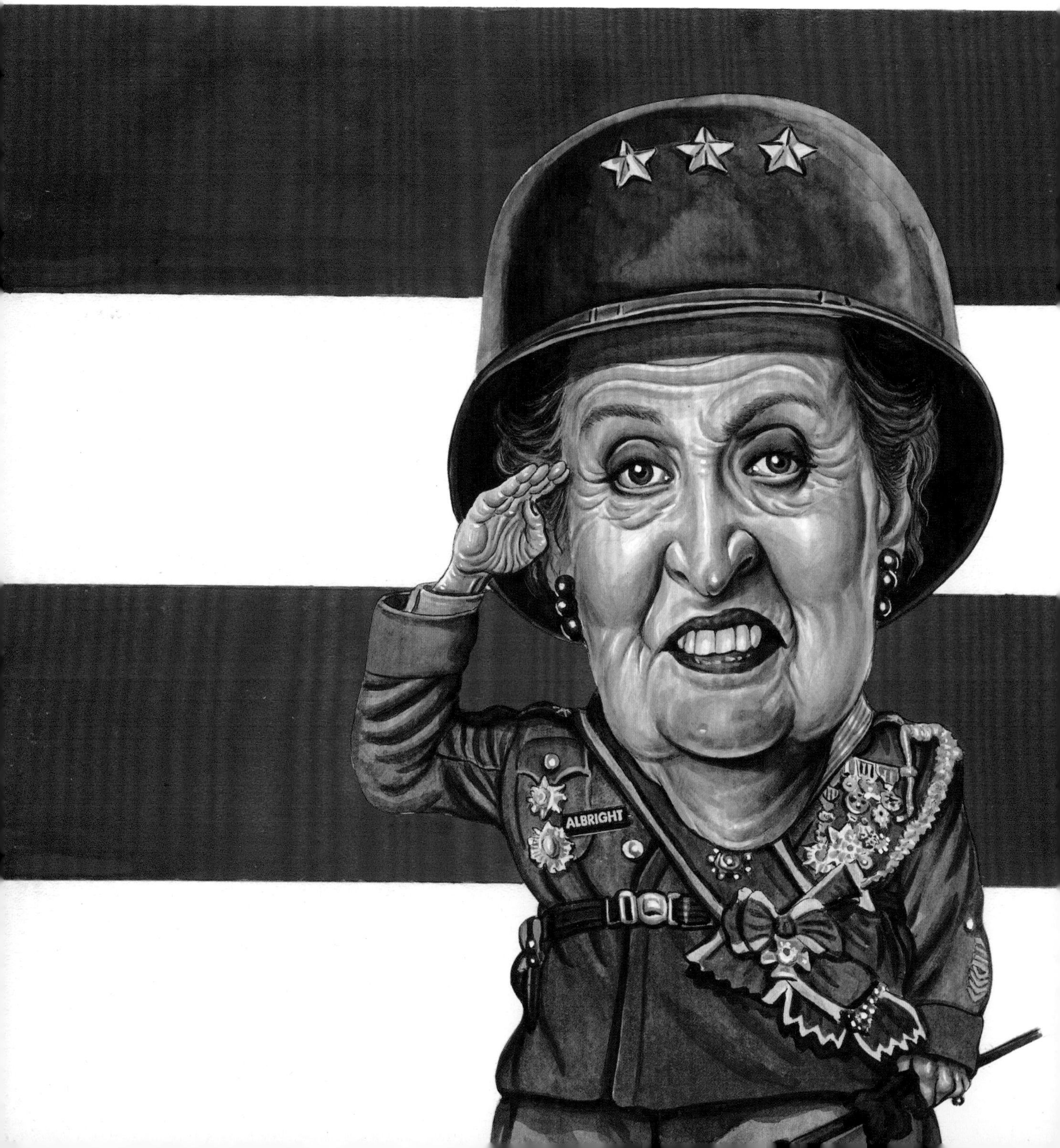
ALBRIGHT

"NUTS TO THE NUT."

THE NEW YORKER

Wacky, big-eared billionaire/dwarf **Ross Perot**, leader of the "Reform Party," throws a convention all for himself, and is poised to take the stage.

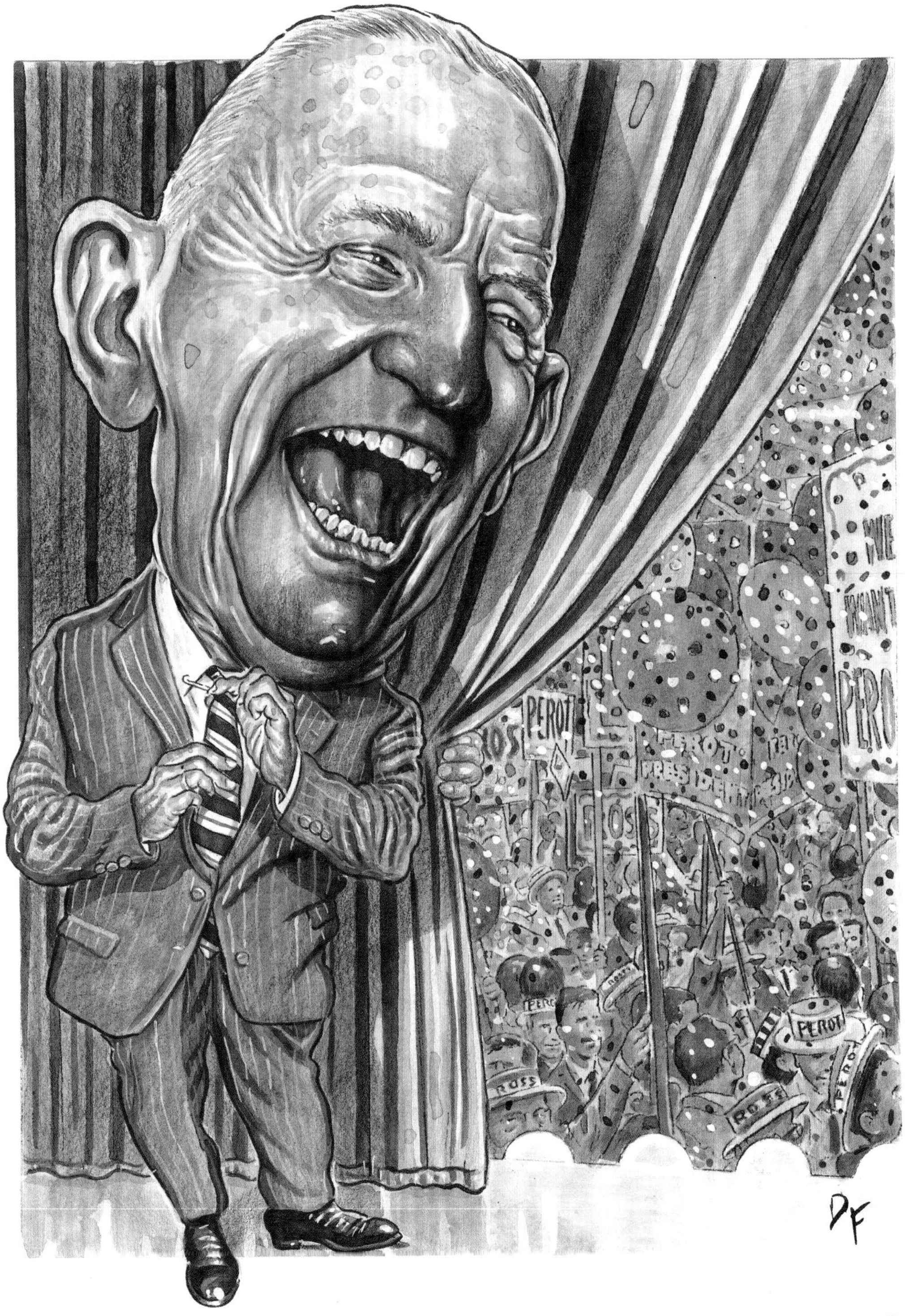
ROSS
PEROT
PEROT
ROSS
PEROT
ROSS
DF

"CATCH ME IF YOU CAN."

NEW YORK PRESS (cover)

Republicans **Dick Armey, Henry Hyde**, and **Trent Lott** can't seem to catch that bad boy.

TIME (cover)

German candidates for president.

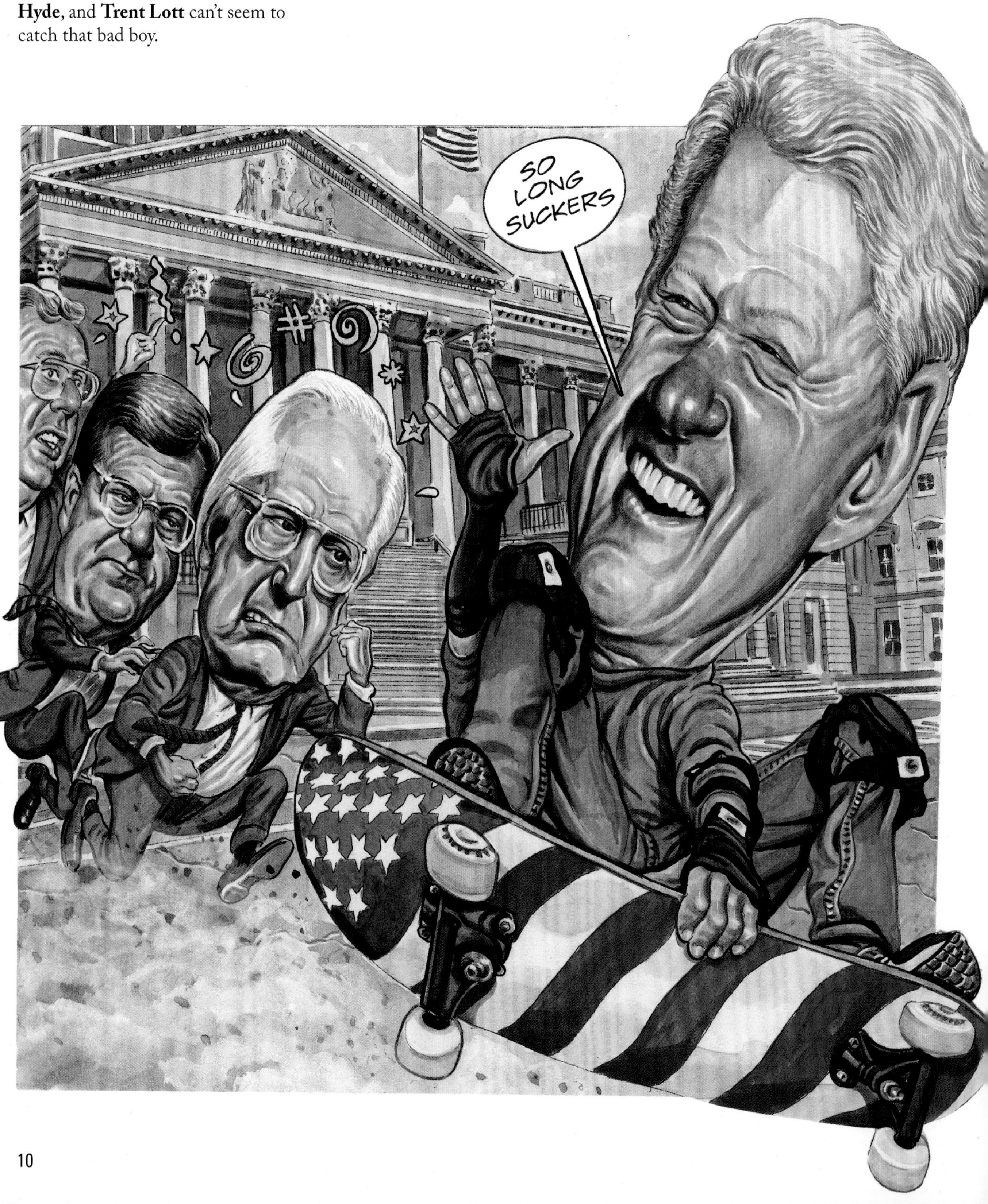
SO LONG SUCKERS

SEPTEMBER 28, 1998

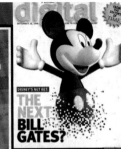

THE CLINTON TAPES ■ TIME DIGITAL

TIME

digital

DISNEY'S NET BET.

THE NEXT BILL GATES?

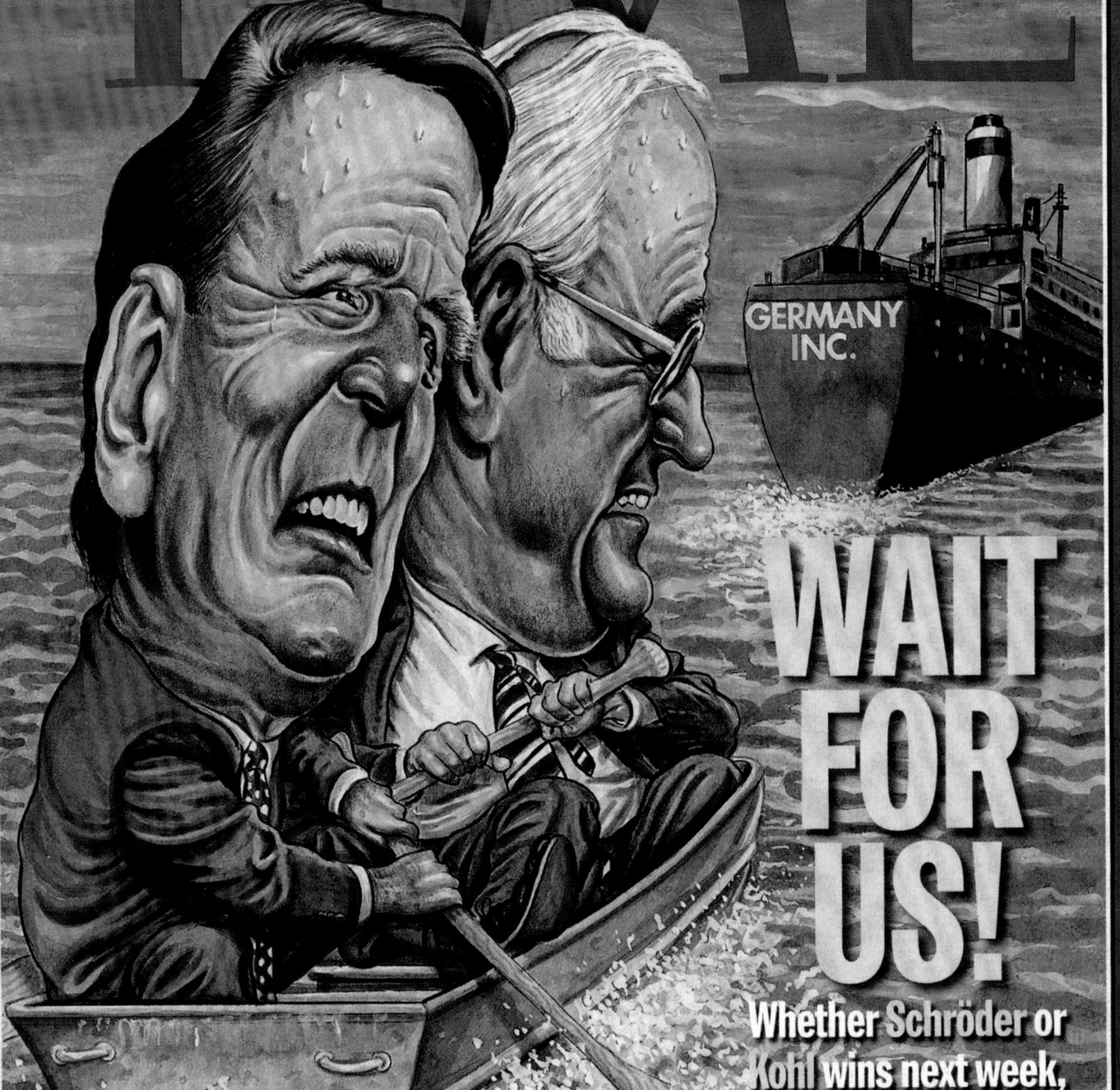

GERMANY INC.

WAIT FOR US!

Whether Schröder or Kohl wins next week, Germany's global firms will steam ahead

9 770928 843003 39

www.time.com

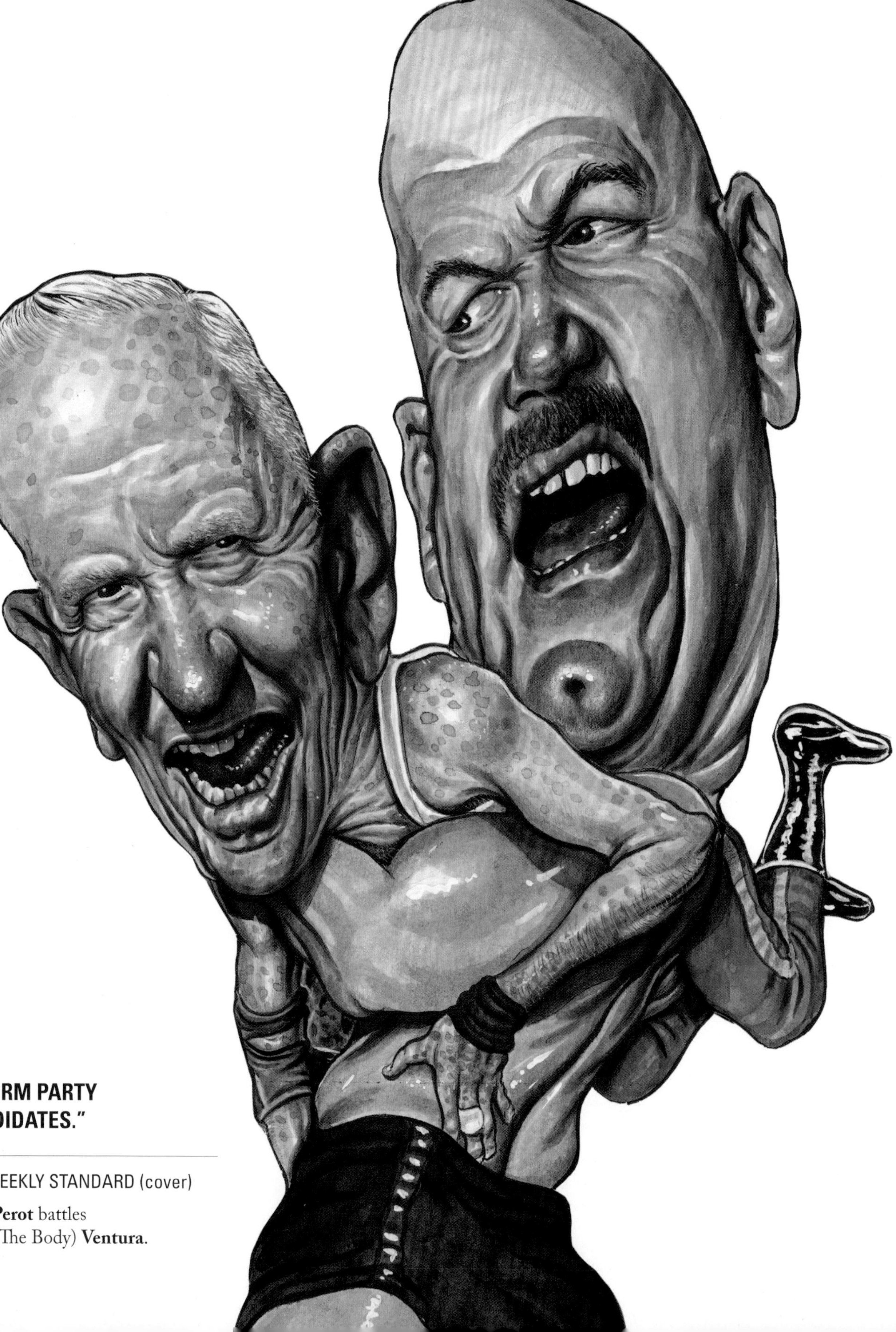

“REFORM PARTY CANDIDATES.”

THE WEEKLY STANDARD (cover)

Ross Perot battles
Jesse (The Body) **Ventura**.

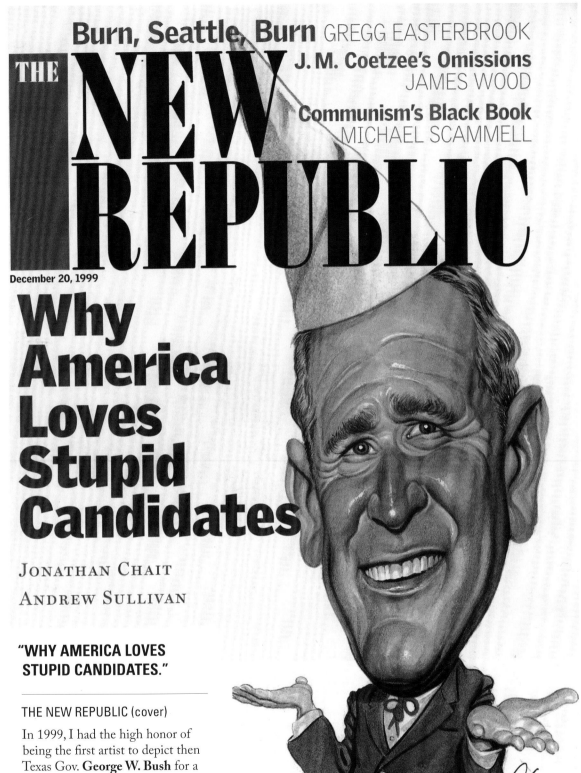

THE NEW REPUBLIC

Burn, Seattle, Burn GREGG EASTERBROOK

J. M. Coetzee's Omissions
JAMES WOOD

Communism's Black Book
MICHAEL SCAMMELL

December 20, 1999

Why America Loves Stupid Candidates

JONATHAN CHAIT

ANDREW SULLIVAN

"WHY AMERICA LOVES STUPID CANDIDATES."

THE NEW REPUBLIC (cover)

In 1999, I had the high honor of being the first artist to depict then Texas Gov. **George W. Bush** for a cover of a national magazine. He had just announced his candidacy for President, but was still largely unknown, aside from his familiar name, which wasn't even mentioned on the cover.

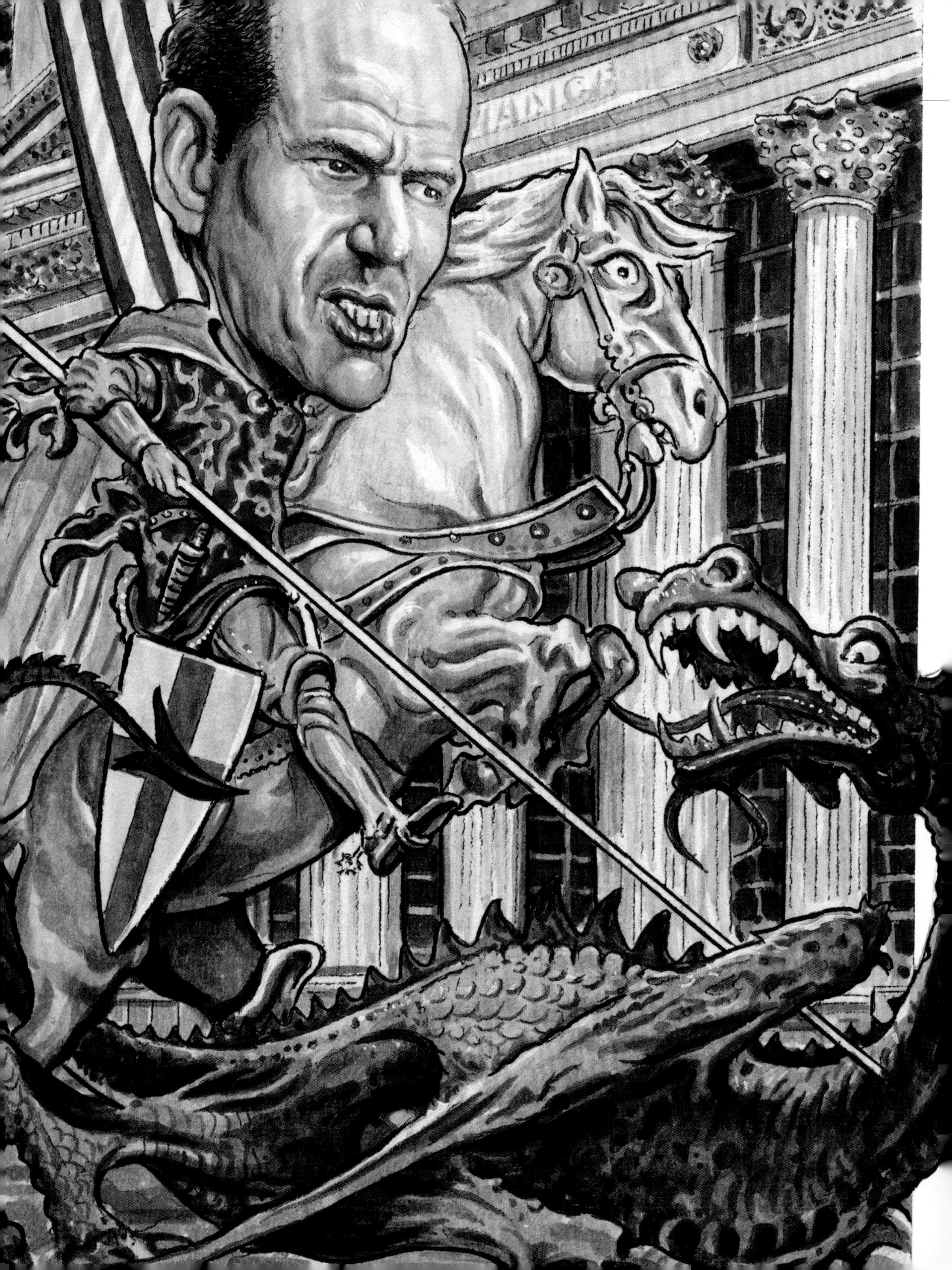

"ST. ELIOT."

THE WALL STREET JOURNAL

N.Y. Attorney General **Eliot Spitzer**, pictured as St. George, slays Wall St. dragons.

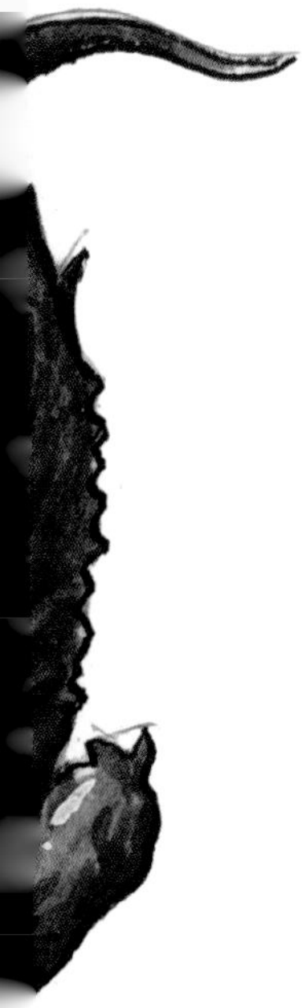

"MAYOR MIKE."

NEW YORK MAGAZINE

N.Y.'s new billionaire Mayor, **Michael Bloomberg**.

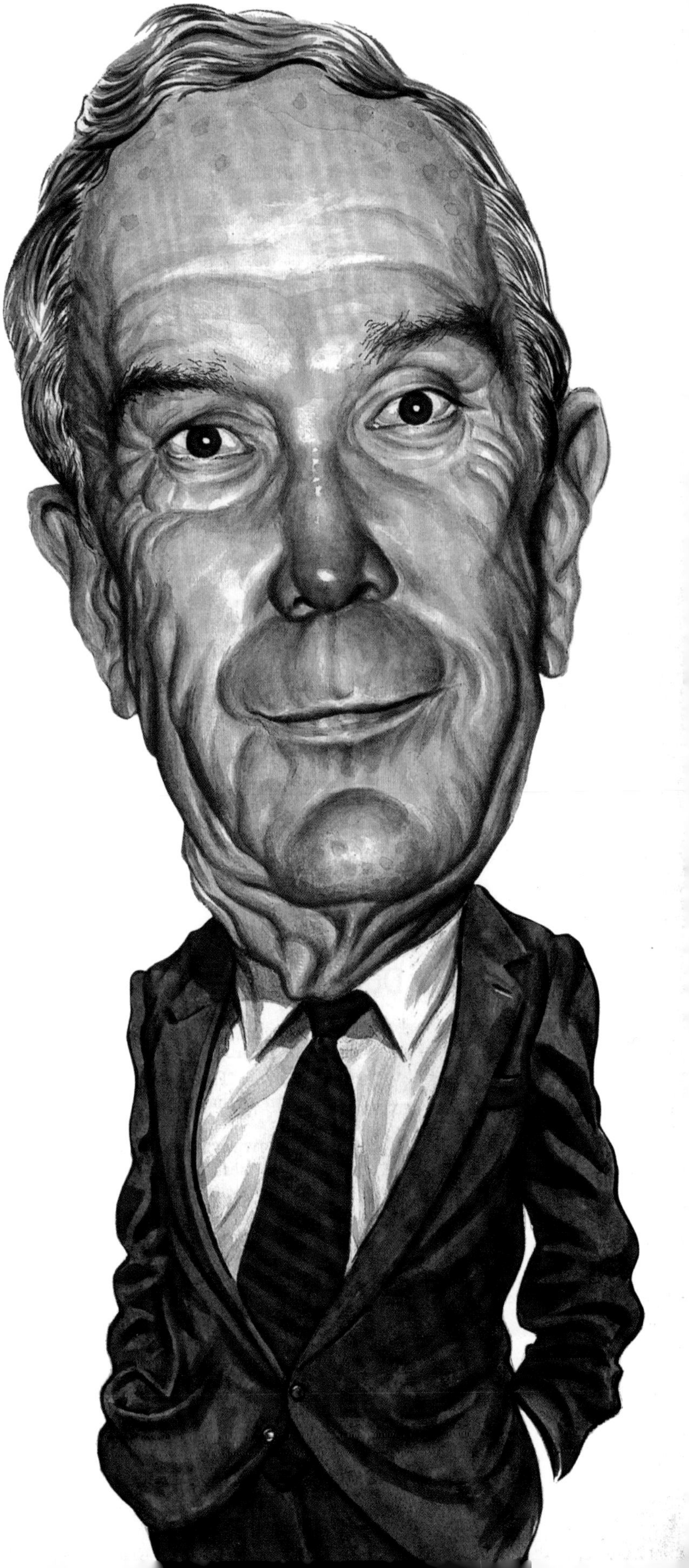

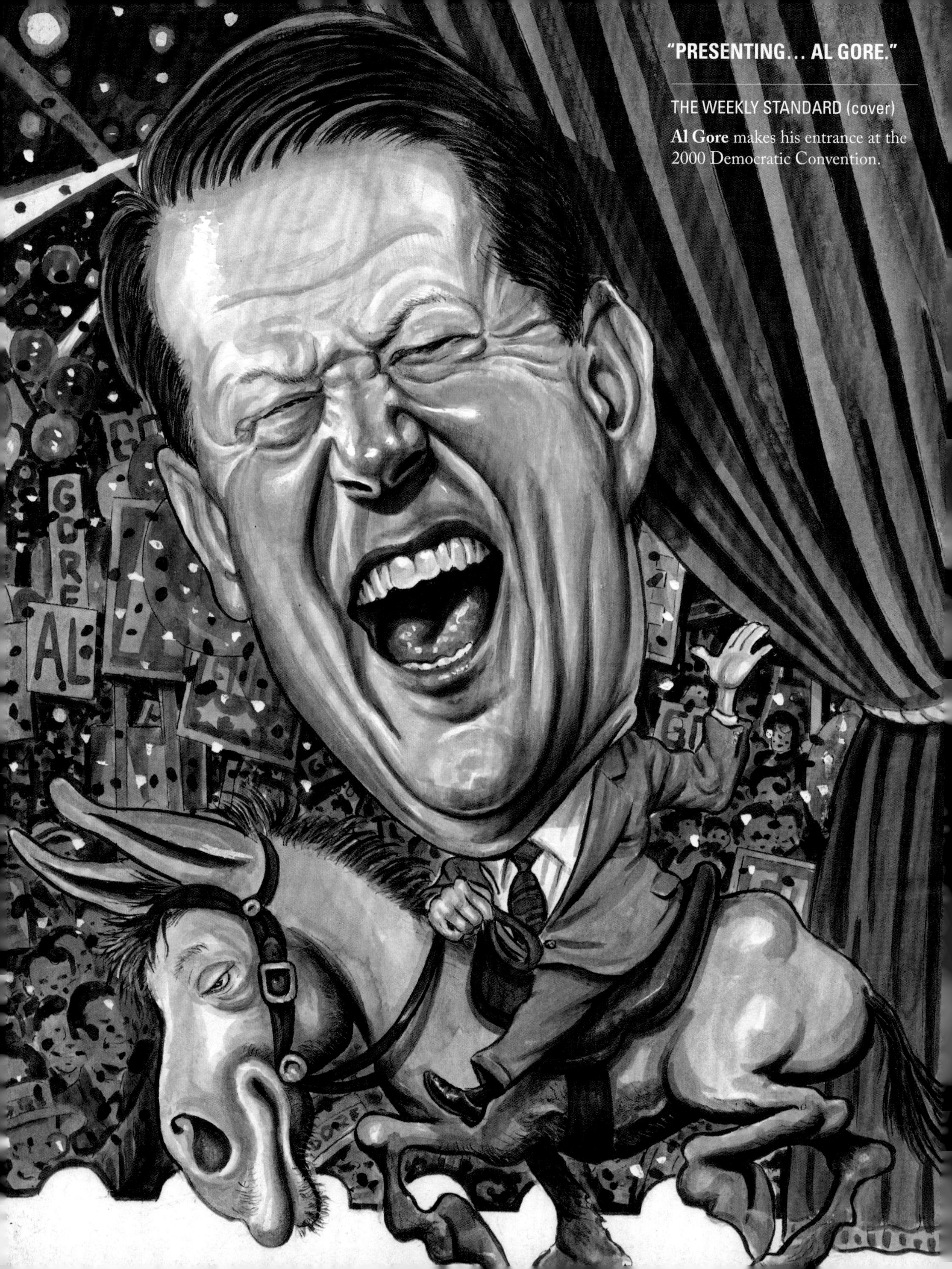
GORE
AL

"PRESENTING… AL GORE."

THE WEEKLY STANDARD (cover)

Al Gore makes his entrance at the 2000 Democratic Convention.

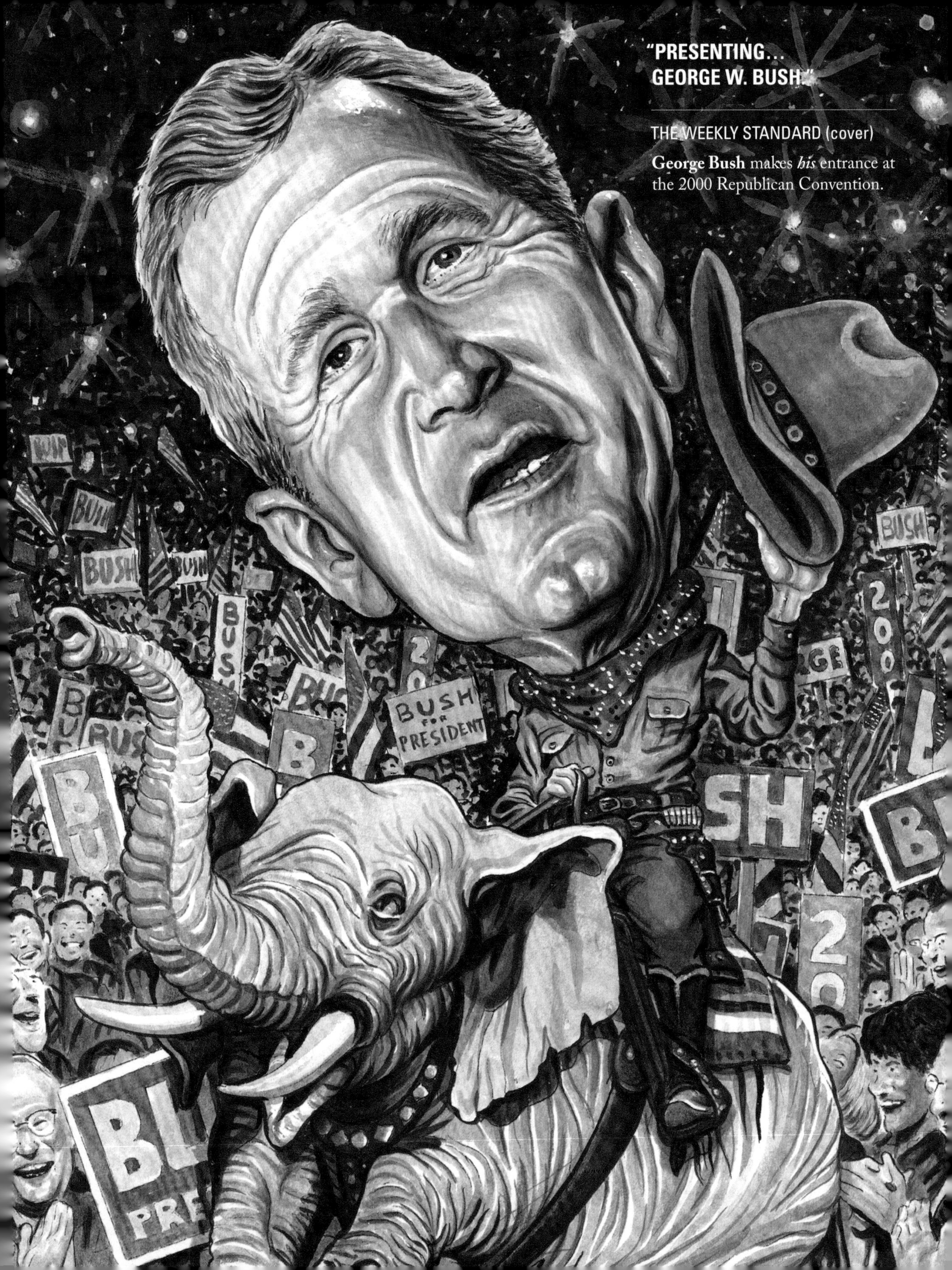
BUSH
FOR
PRESIDENT
BUSH
BUSH
SH
2000

"PRESENTING… GEORGE W. BUSH."

THE WEEKLY STANDARD (cover)

George Bush makes *his* entrance at the 2000 Republican Convention.

THE WEEKLY STANDARD

I did hundreds of these silhouettes, for *The Weekly Standard*, over the last few years.

The Weekly Standard is basically a right-wing political magazine, but I was never asked to make Democrats look any less attractive than Republicans.

JOE LIEBERMAN   RALPH NADER   AL GORE

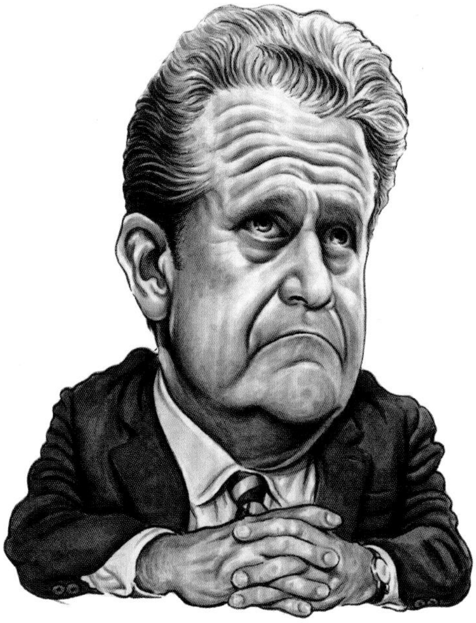

LAURENCE TRIBE

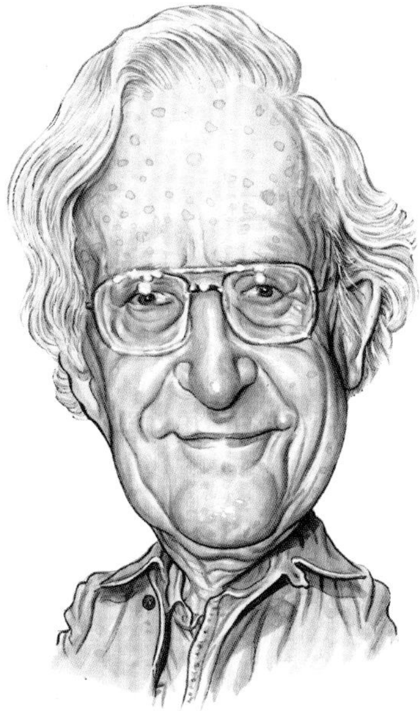

NOAM CHOMSKY

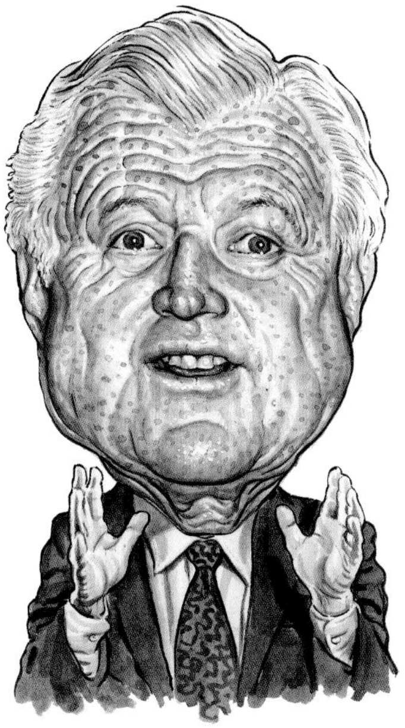

SEN. TED KENNEDY

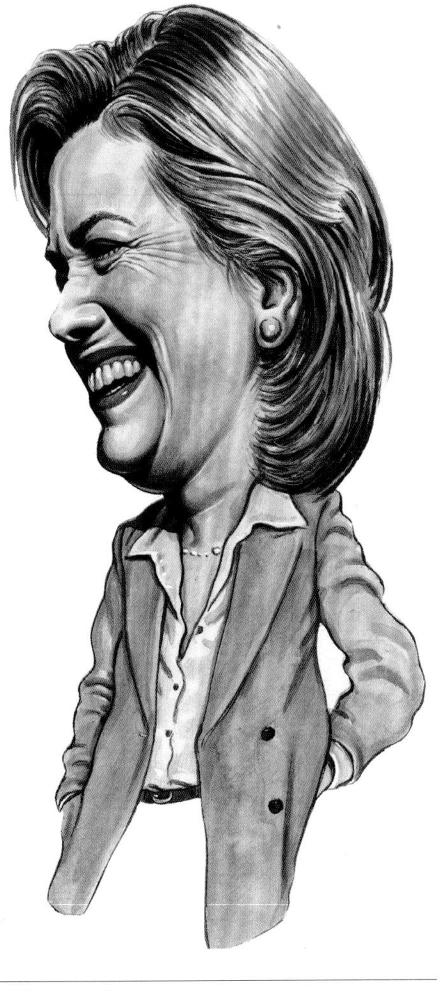

HILLARY CLINTON

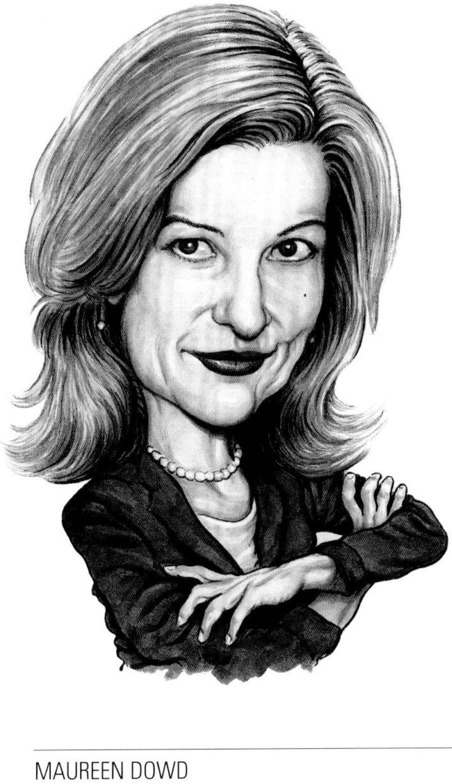

MAUREEN DOWD

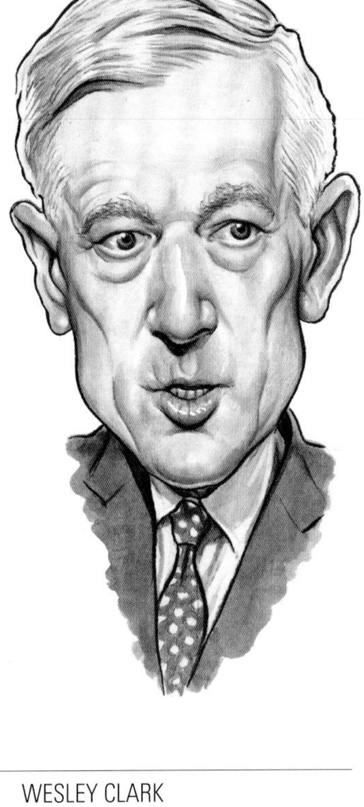

WESLEY CLARK

"MEATY ISSUES."

TIME

As Foot and Mouth Disease ravages Britain, PM **Tony Blair** encourages the British people to eat more fish.

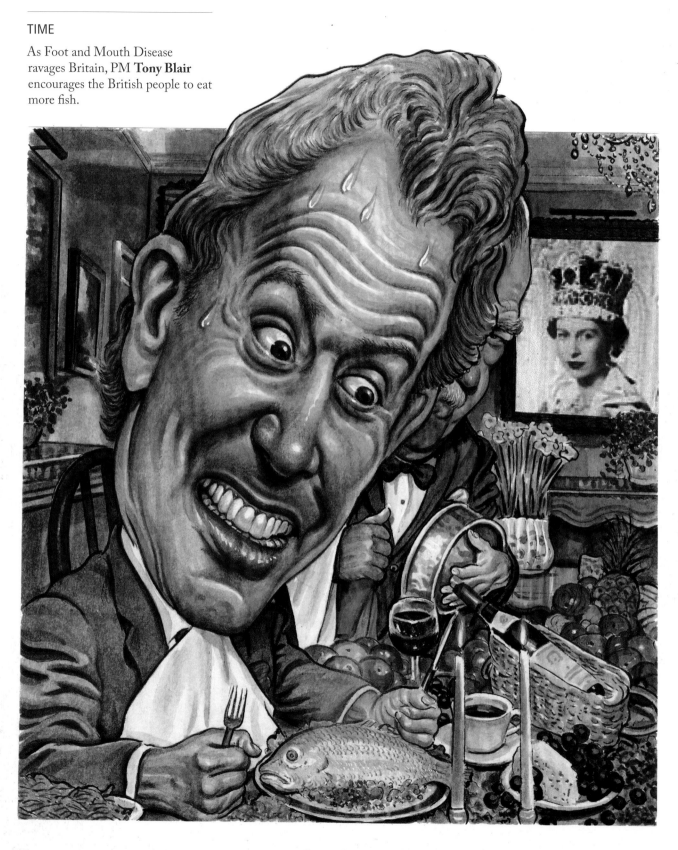

"NOW, WHAT THE HECK IS THIS."

THE NEW YORK TIMES MAGAZINE

Brand new President **George W. Bush**, who has rarely traveled out of the country, has things explained to him by pals, **Condi** and **Colin**.

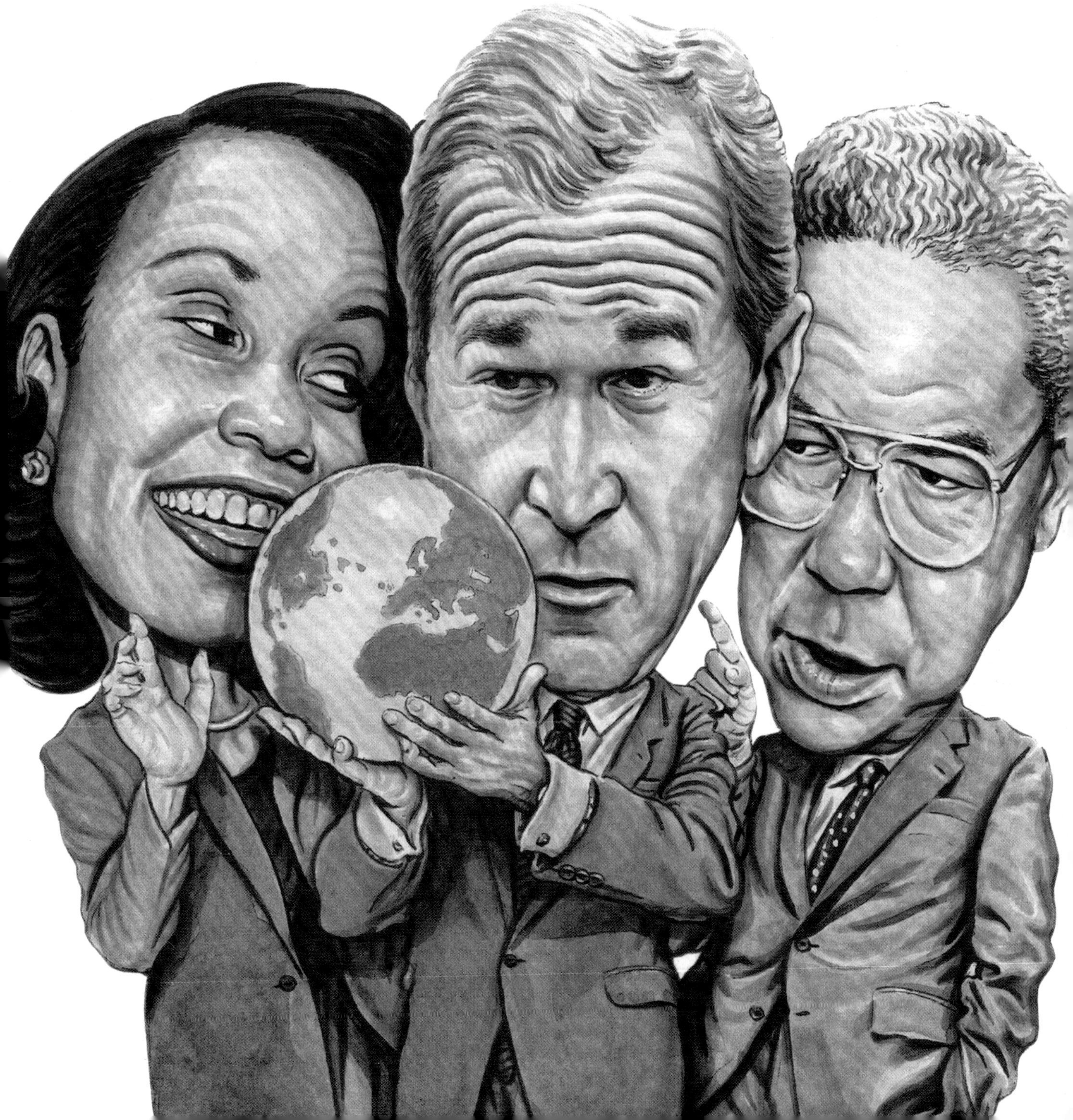

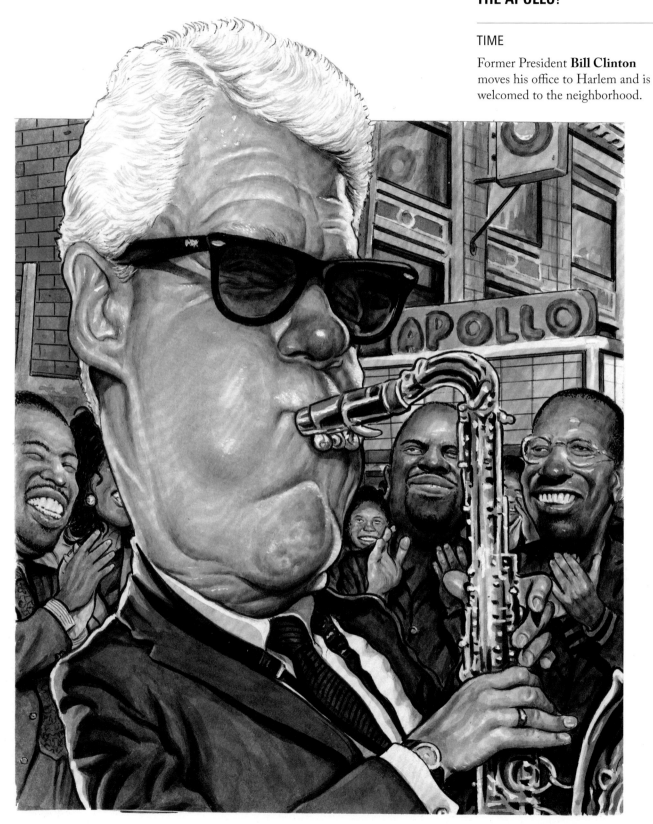

"BILL CLINTON, LIVE AT THE APOLLO!"

TIME

Former President **Bill Clinton** moves his office to Harlem and is welcomed to the neighborhood.

22

"KING OF THE HILLARY."

THE WEEKLY STANDARD (cover)

Hillary Clinton runs for N.Y. senator and makes herself known to the city.

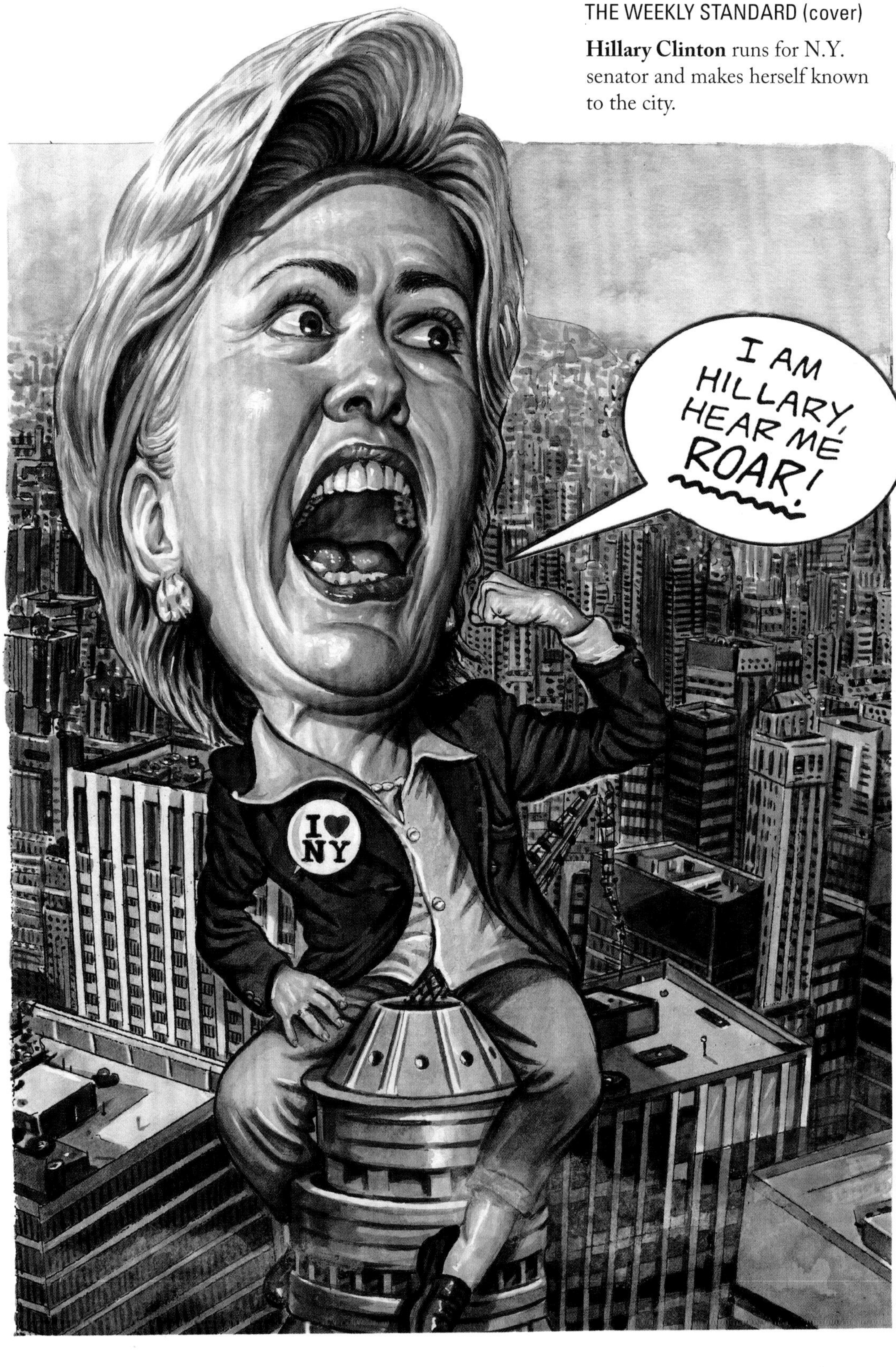
I AM HILLARY, HEAR ME ROAR!
I ♥ NY

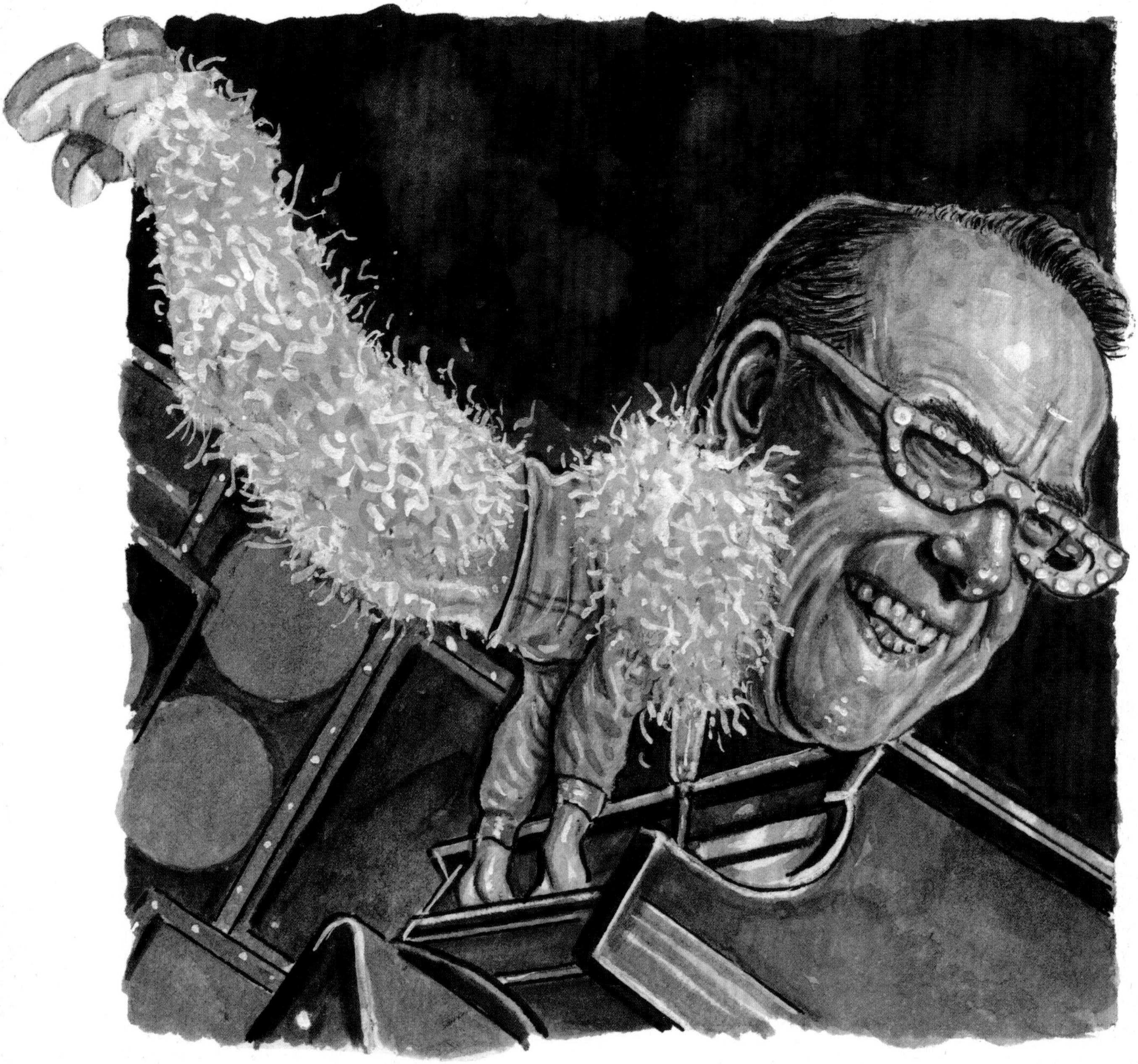

"BOB DOLE IS *STILL STANDING*."

ENTERTAINMENT WEEKLY

"LAUGHING BEN FRANKLIN."

TIME

I was asked to play up his "ribald" sense of humor for a special Ben Franklin issue.

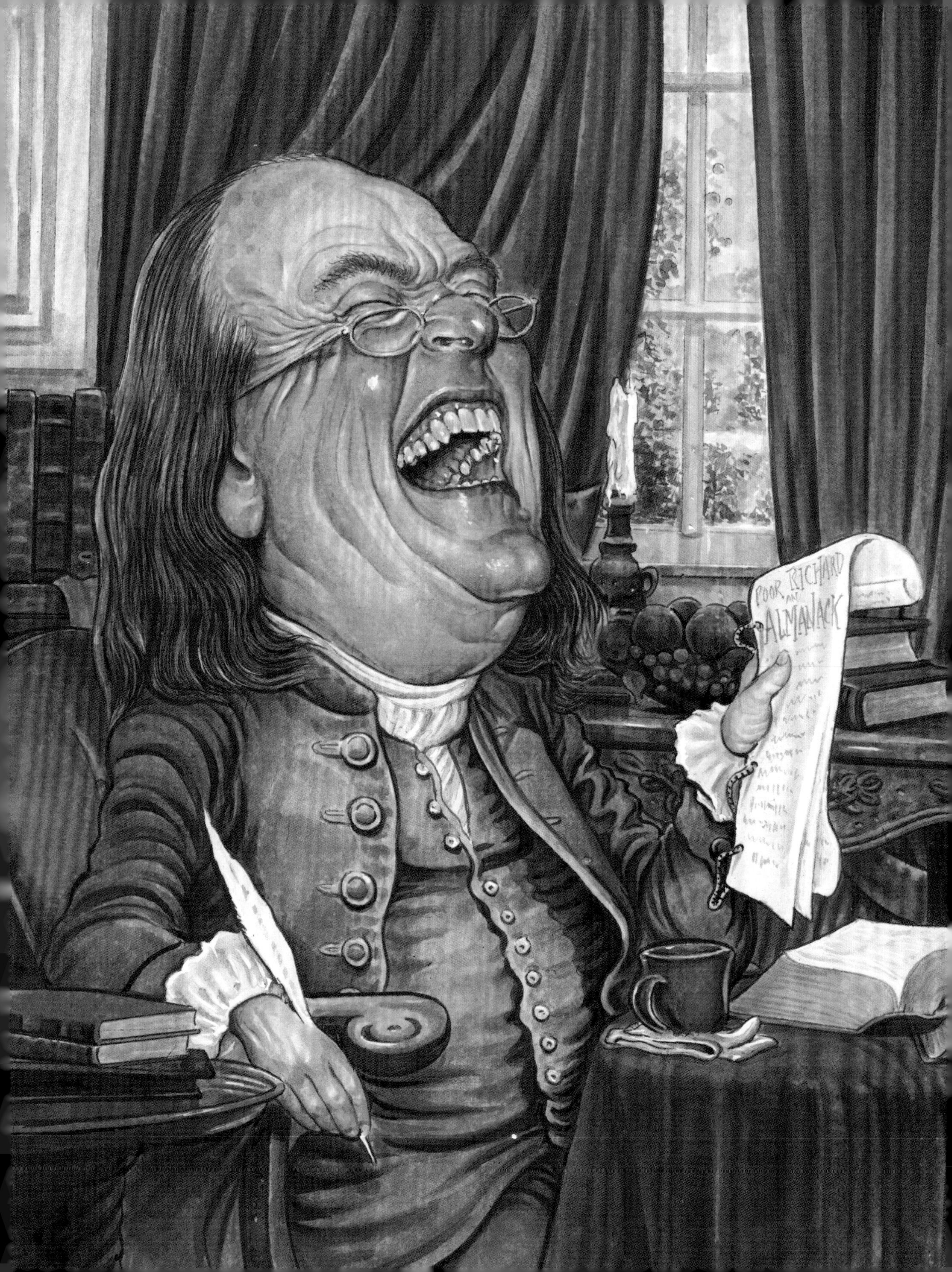
POOR RICHARD, AN ALMANACK

**“REPUBLICANS,
TERRORISTS,
A SAINT AND A KING.”**

THE WEEKLY STANDARD

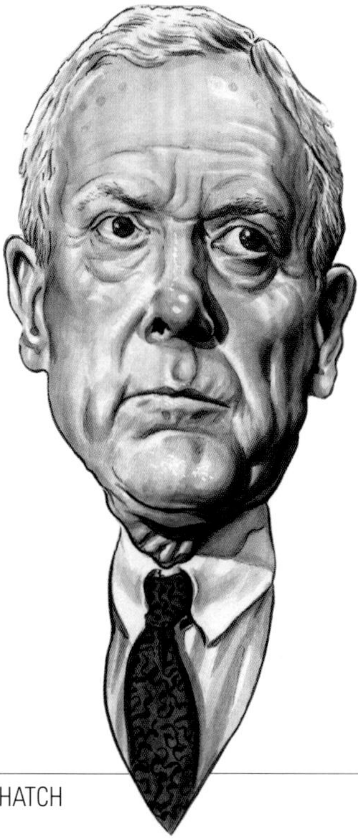

ORRIN HATCH

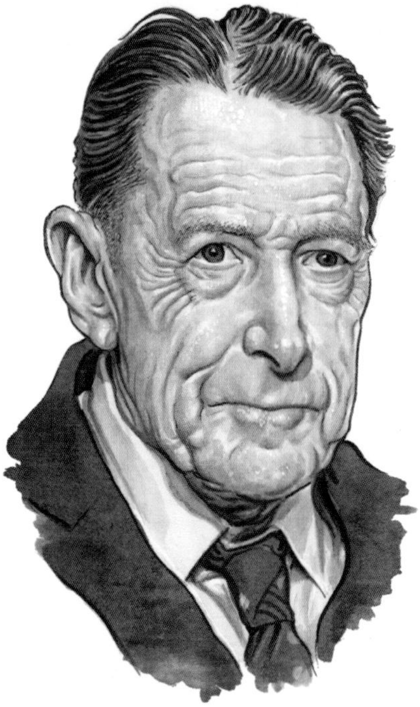

CASPAR WEINBERGER

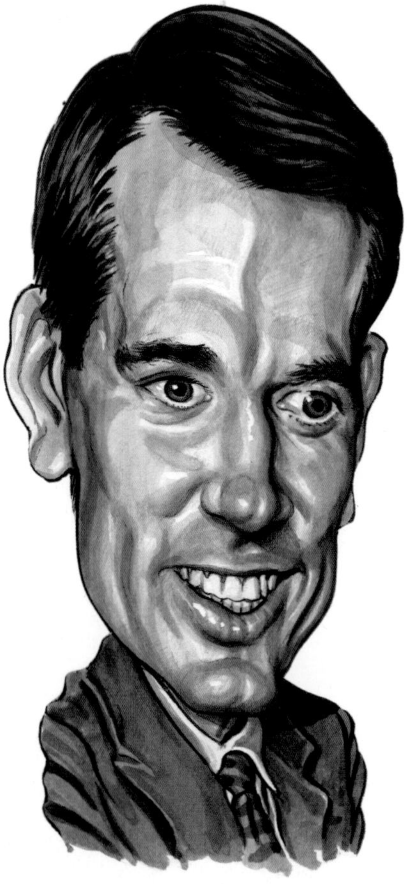

BOB PORTMAN

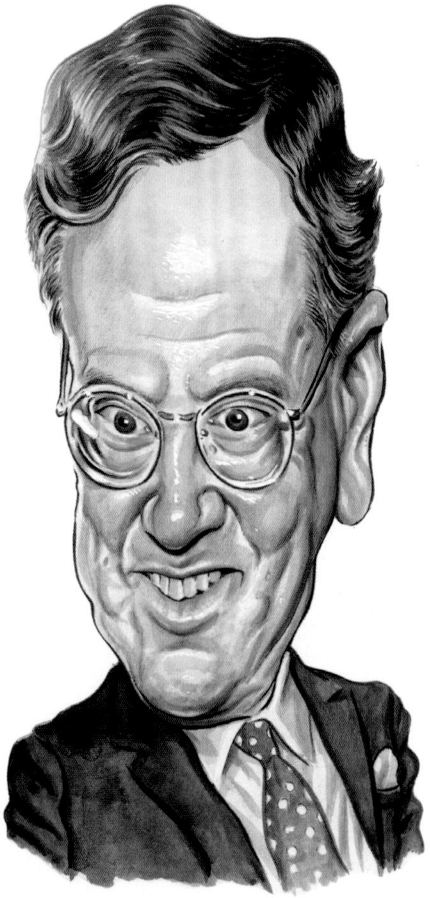

STEVE FORBES

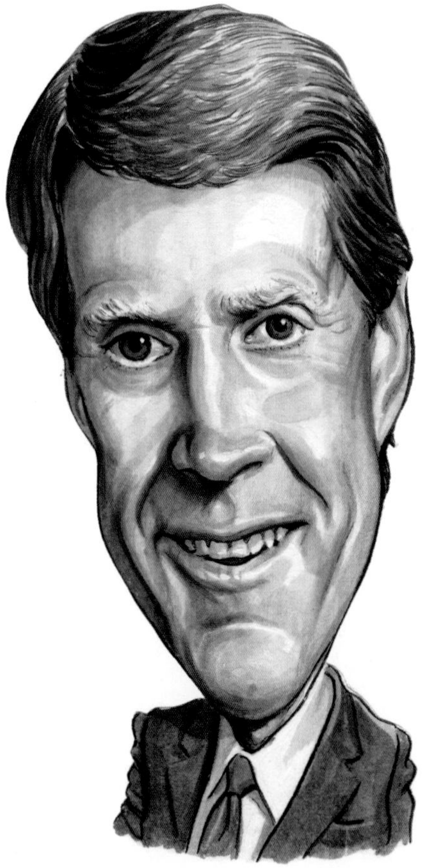

BILL FRIST

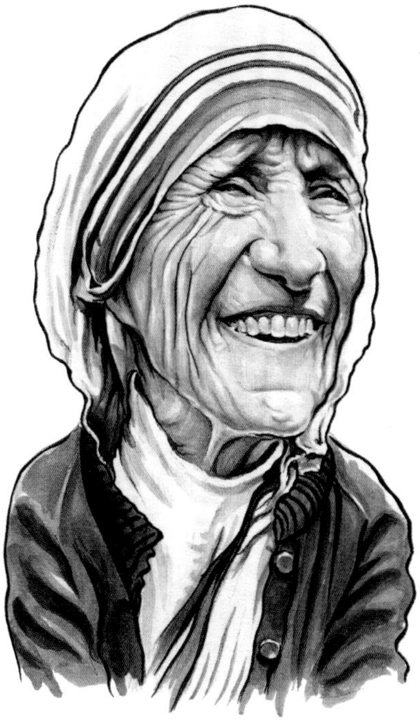

MOTHER TERESA

OSAMA BIN LADEN

The flies were removed from this portrait of Osama Bin Laden before publication a few days after 9/11. I was confused as to who might be offended. The flies?

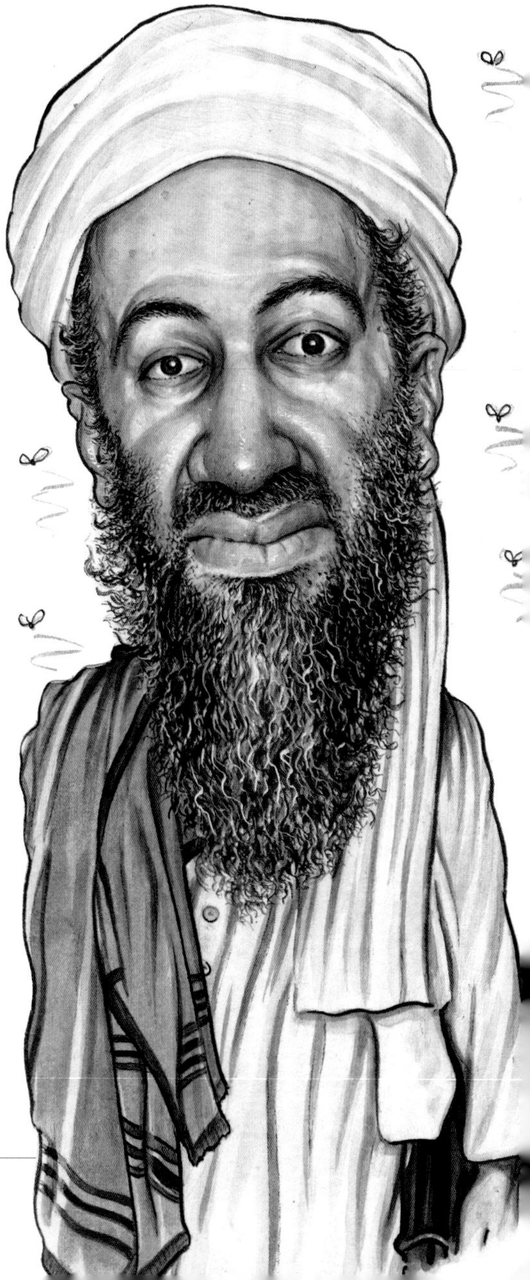

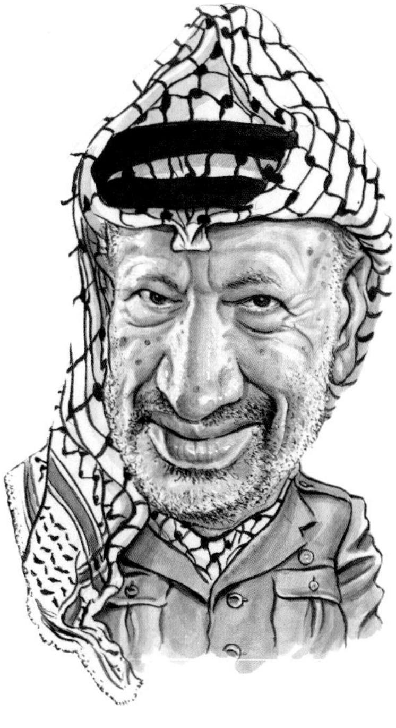

YASSER ARAFAT

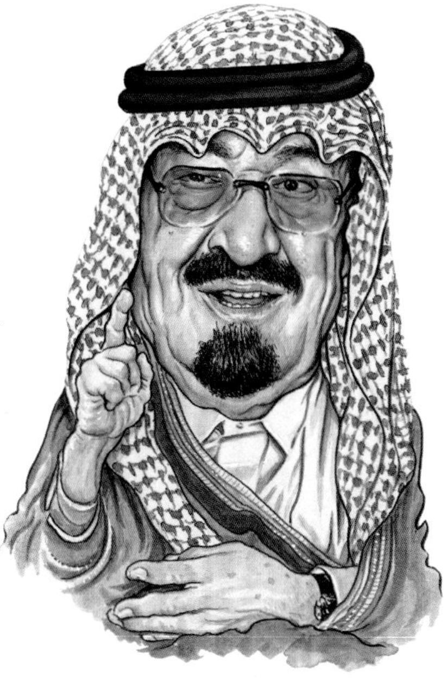

KING ABDULLAH

"FILL 'ER UP, MAHATMA."

MOTHER JONES

Senator Clinton had recently blurted about **Gandhi**: "You know, he ran a gas station down in St. Louis for two years?"

"THE DEER HUNTERS."

FIELD AND STREAM

Despite being a Jewish, anti-hunting vegetarian, I did a few illustrations for ***F+S. Until*** the editors finally caught on to the fact that I was drawing the animals heroically and the hunters as stupid-looking as possible.

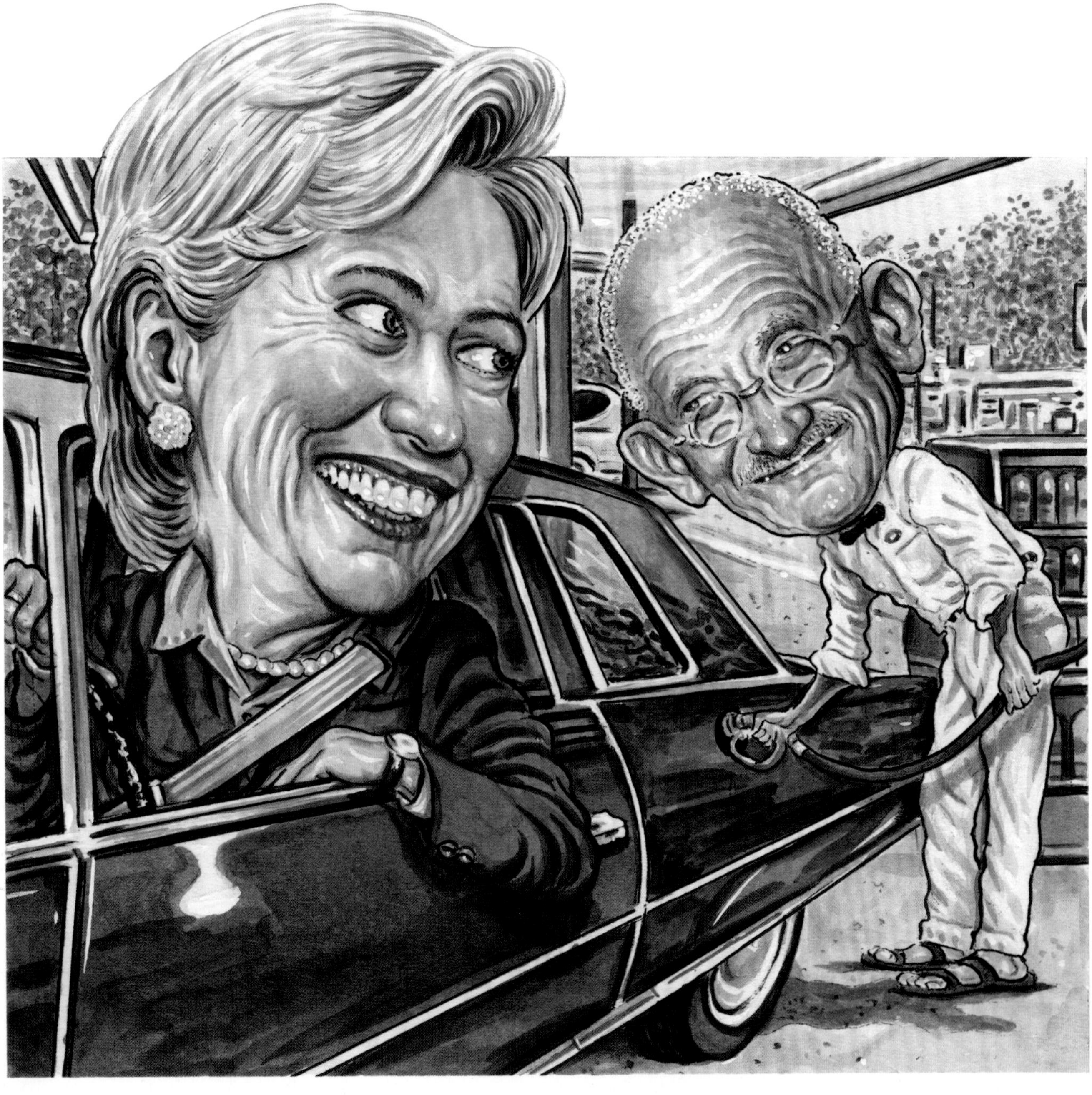

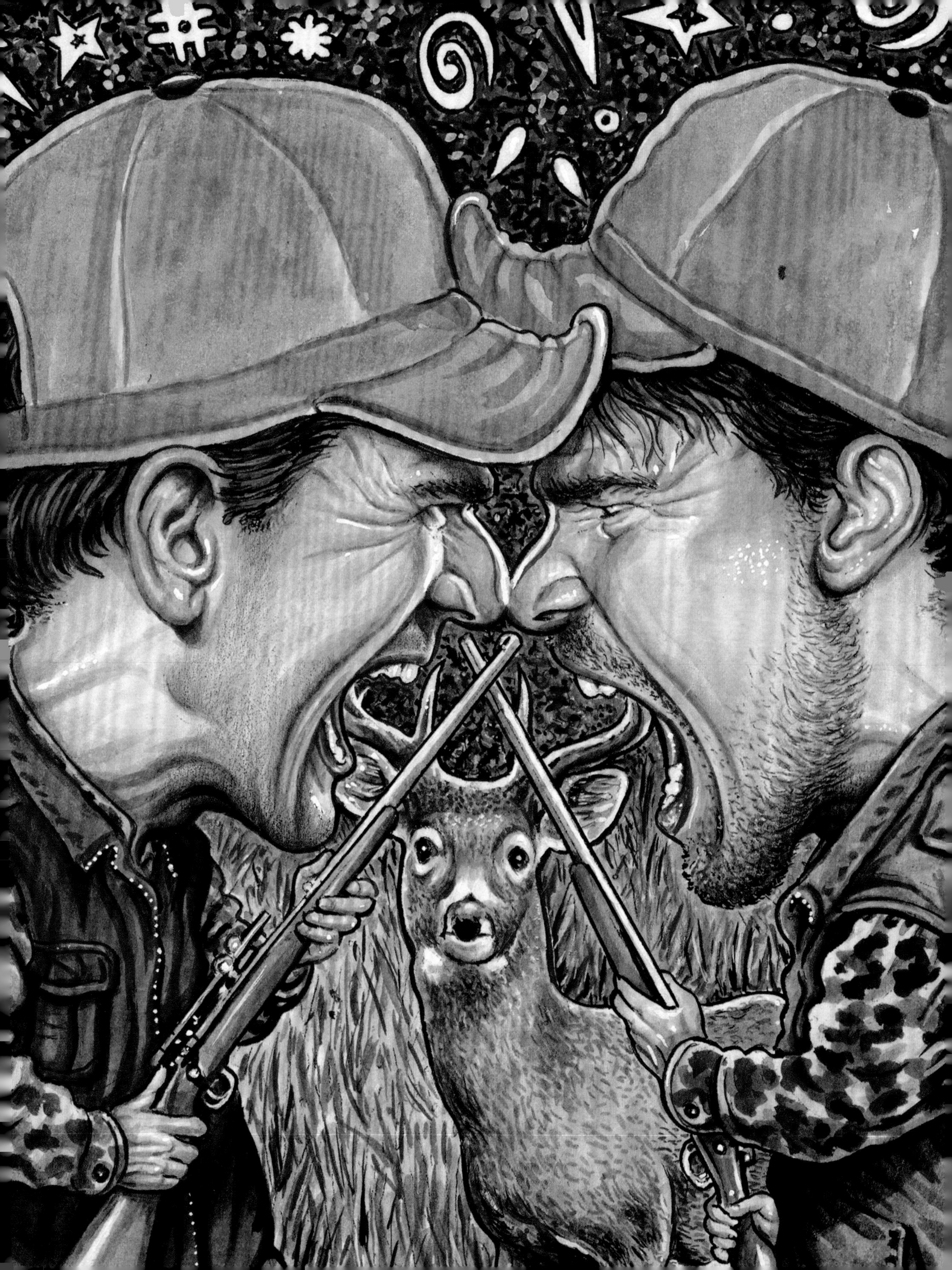

"MY FAIR CITY."

CHICAGO MAGAZINE

Hizzoner Mayor **Daley** welcomes you to his fair city.

"LONE STAR CANDIDATES."

TEXAS MONTHLY

Candidates for Governor of Texas, including, at the bottom, the "Texas Jewboy" (and eventual loser) **Kinky Friedman**. From bottom to top, the others were Democrat **Chris Bell**, Independent **Carole Keeton Strayhorn**, and the winner, Republican **Rick** "maybe Texas ought to secede" **Perry**.

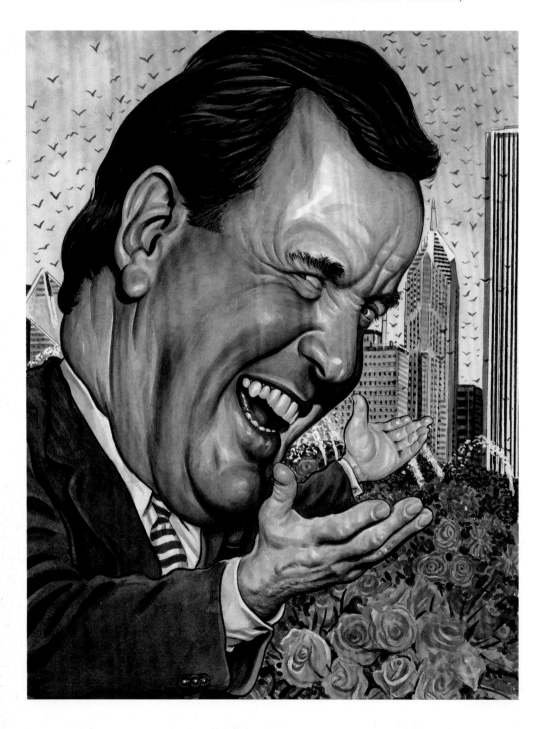

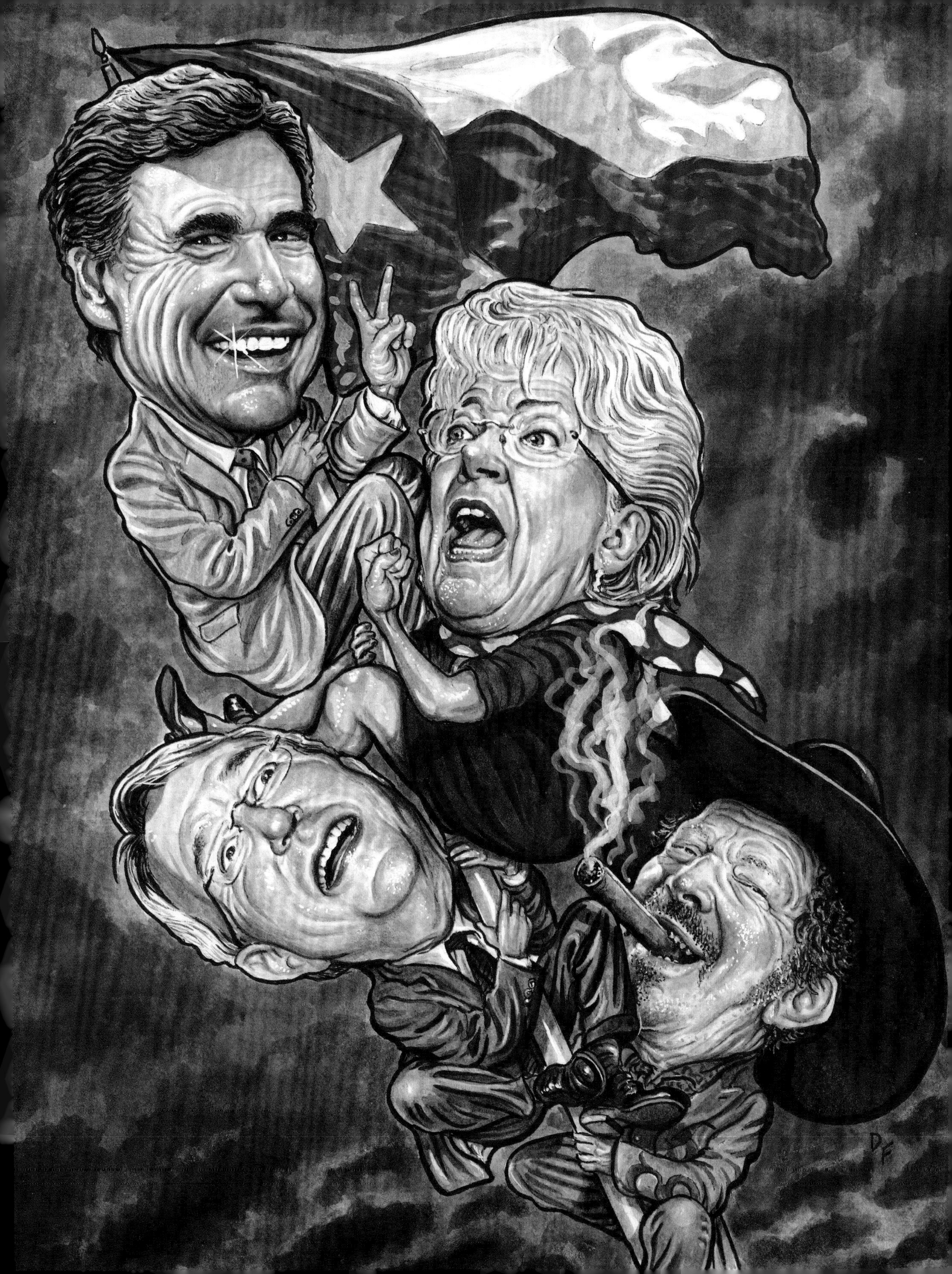

"GREENSPAN FOR THE PASS."

THE WALL ST. JOURNAL

Alan Greenspan attempts to make a pass.

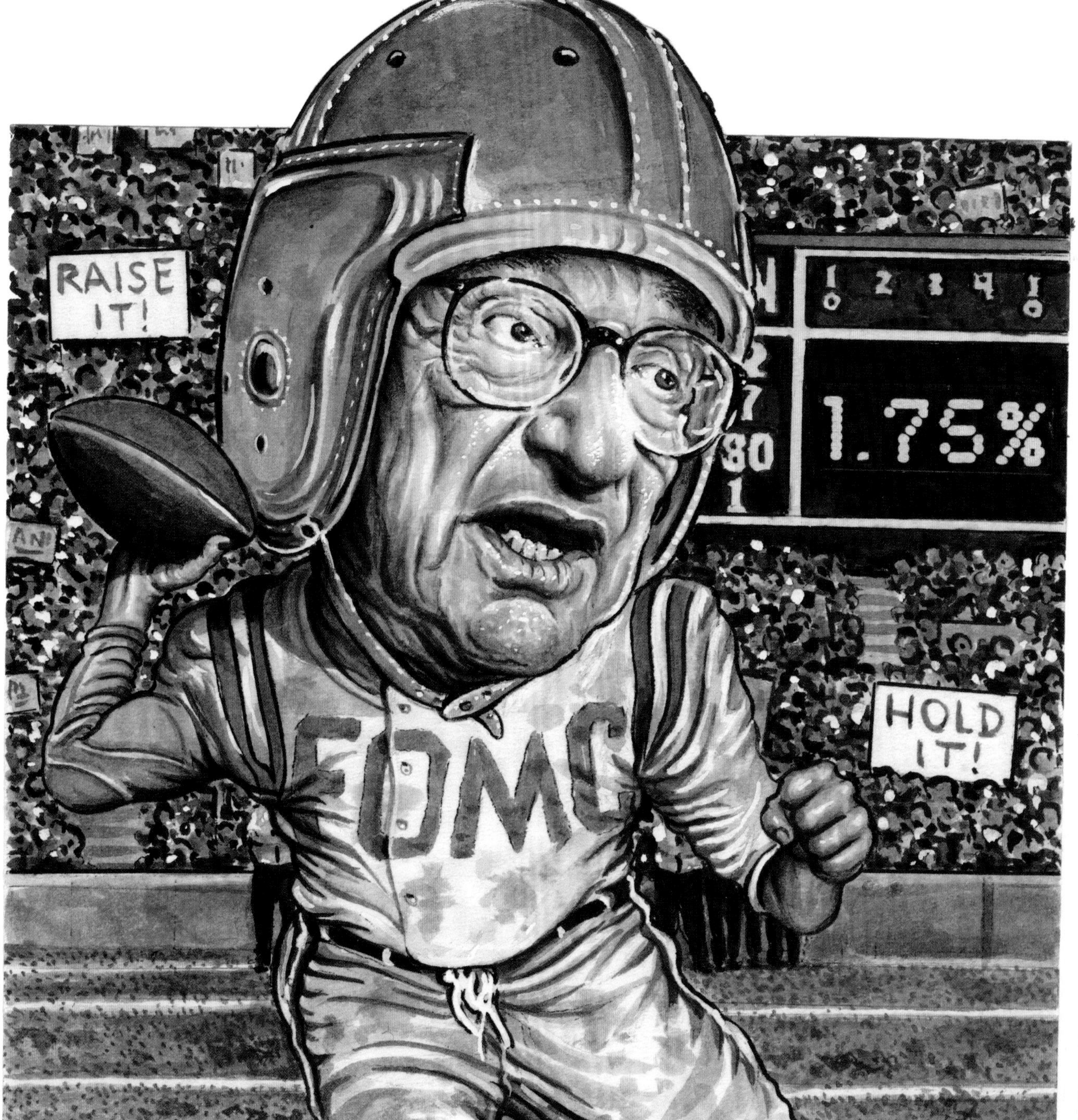
RAISE IT!
1.75%
FOMC
HOLD IT!

"BESTEST FRIENDS."

THE WASHINGTON POST

Alan Greenspan and wife **Andrea Mitchell** enjoy a Washington Nationals game with pundit **Al Hunt** and wife **Judy Woodruff**.

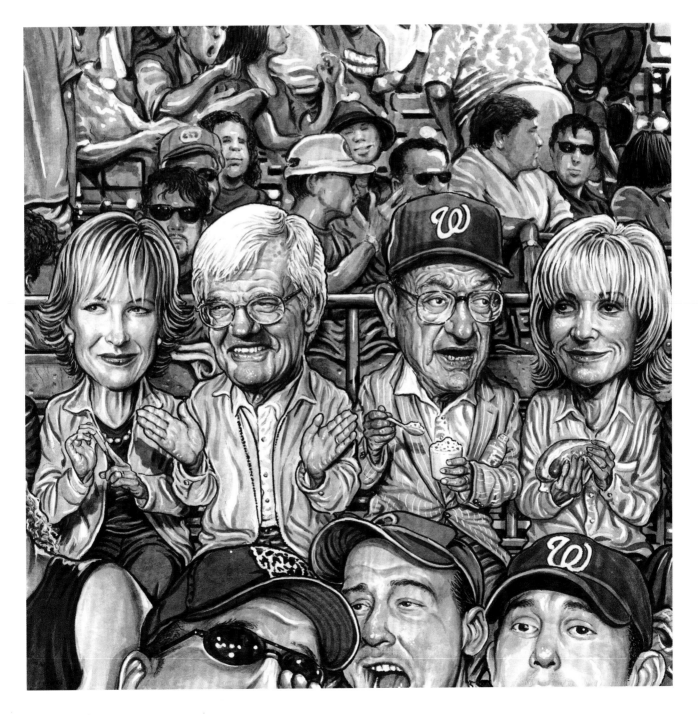

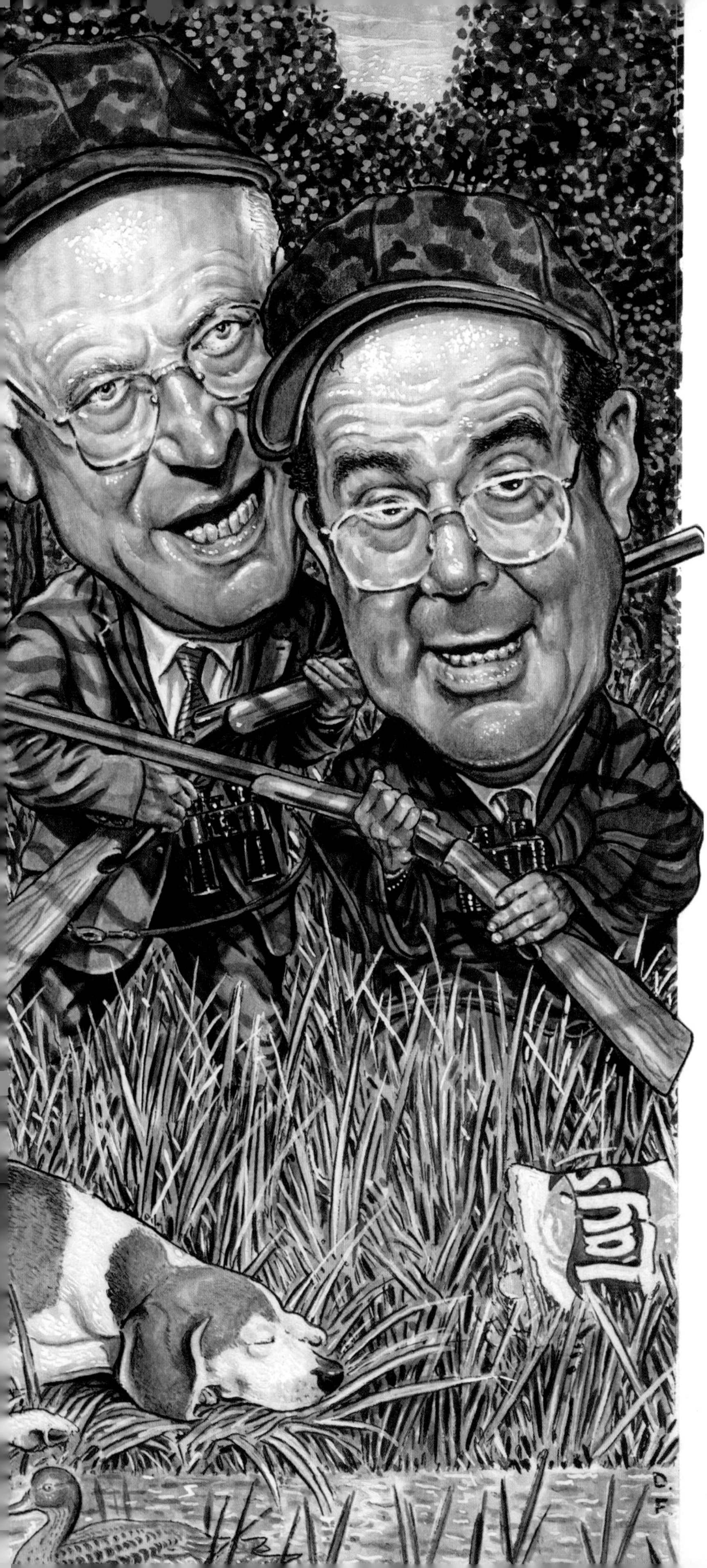

"DICK AND ANTONIN."

THE LOS ANGELES TIMES

Best buds **Dick Cheney** and **Antonin Scalia** bond on their hunting trip. Our beagle Roy posed for this (while asleep).

"THEY WANT TO BE PART OF IT."

THE NEW YORK OBSERVER

Welcome, Republicans, to New York City!

Co-written with K. Bidus.

"WHAT COULD HAVE/ SHOULD HAVE BEEN?"

FOLLOWING SPREAD

THE BOSTON GLOBE

John Kerry takes the Presidential oath in 2005 as friends and enemies relish the moment. Clockwise from bottom center: **Teresa Heinz Kerry,** John Kerry, **Vanessa** and **Alexandra Kerry**, **Edward Kennedy**, **Osama Bin Laden**, **Hillary Clinton**, **Bruce Springsteen**, **Bill Clinton**, **Michael Moore**, **Condoleezza Rice**, **George W. Bush**, **Dick Cheney**, **Colin Powell**, **Laura Bush**, **George H. W. Bush**, **Karl Rove**, **Barbara Pierce Bush**, **Barbara** and **Jenna Bush**, and **William Rehnquist**.

They Want to Be Part of It ...

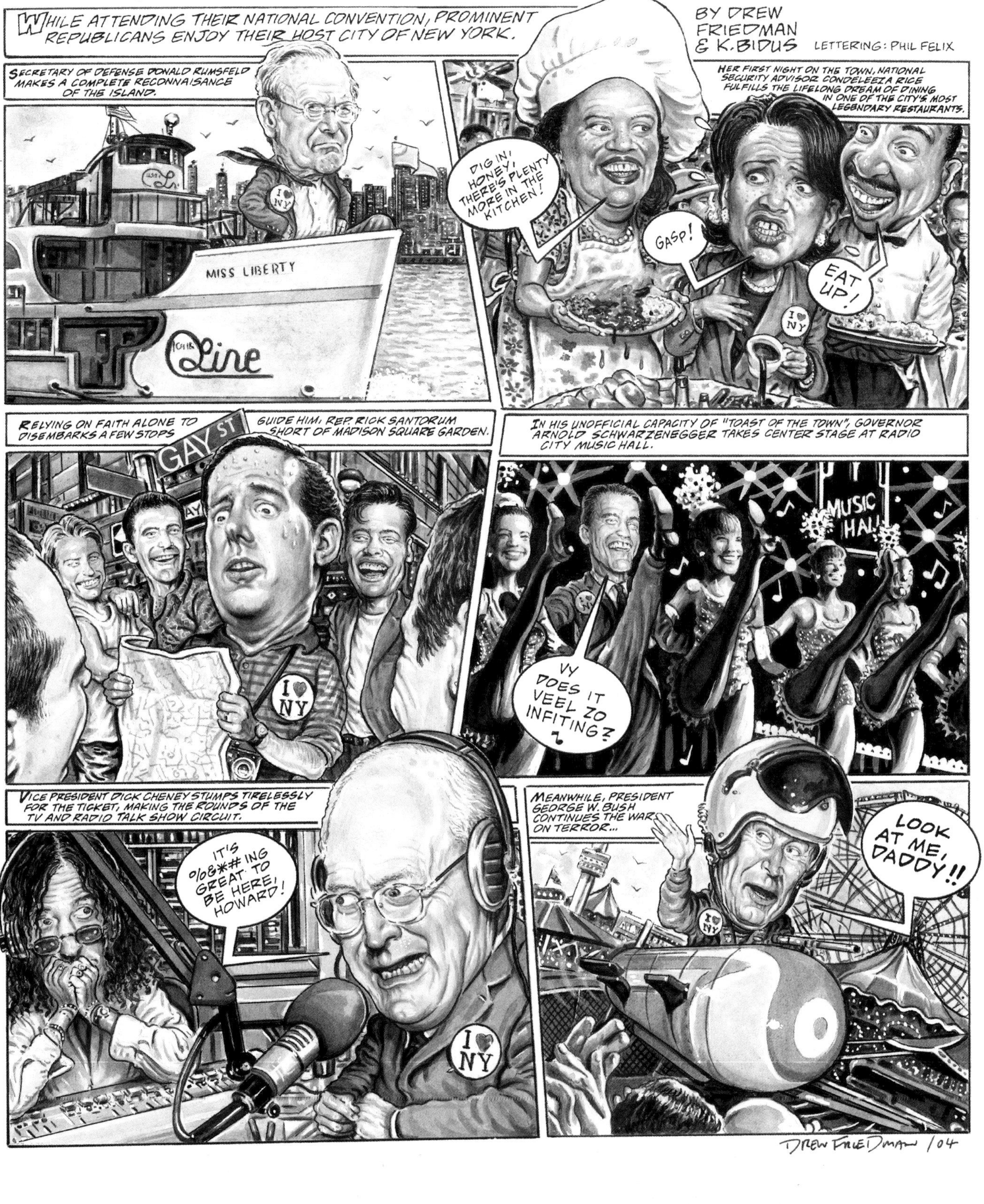

WHILE ATTENDING THEIR NATIONAL CONVENTION, PROMINENT REPUBLICANS ENJOY THEIR HOST CITY OF NEW YORK.
BY DREW FRIEDMAN & K. BIDUS
LETTERING: PHIL FELIX
SECRETARY OF DEFENSE DONALD RUMSFELD MAKES A COMPLETE RECONNAISANCE OF THE ISLAND.
I ♥ NY
MISS LIBERTY
Line
HER FIRST NIGHT ON THE TOWN, NATIONAL SECURITY ADVISOR CONDELEEZA RICE FULFILLS THE LIFELONG DREAM OF DINING IN ONE OF THE CITY'S MOST LEGENDARY RESTAURANTS.
DIG IN, HONEY, THERE'S PLENTY MORE IN THE KITCHEN!
GASP!
EAT UP!
I ♥ NY
RELYING ON FAITH ALONE TO GUIDE HIM, REP. RICK SANTORUM DISEMBARKS A FEW STOPS SHORT OF MADISON SQUARE GARDEN.
GAY ST
I ♥ NY
IN HIS UNOFFICIAL CAPACITY OF "TOAST OF THE TOWN", GOVERNOR ARNOLD SCHWARZENEGGER TAKES CENTER STAGE AT RADIO CITY MUSIC HALL.
MUSIC HALL
VY DOES IT VEEL ZO INFITING?
VICE PRESIDENT DICK CHENEY STUMPS TIRELESSLY FOR THE TICKET, MAKING THE ROUNDS OF THE TV AND RADIO TALK SHOW CIRCUIT.
IT'S %@&*#ING GREAT TO BE HERE, HOWARD!
I ♥ NY
MEANWHILE, PRESIDENT GEORGE W. BUSH CONTINUES THE WAR ON TERROR...
LOOK AT ME, DADDY!!
I ♥ NY
DREW FRIEDMAN /04

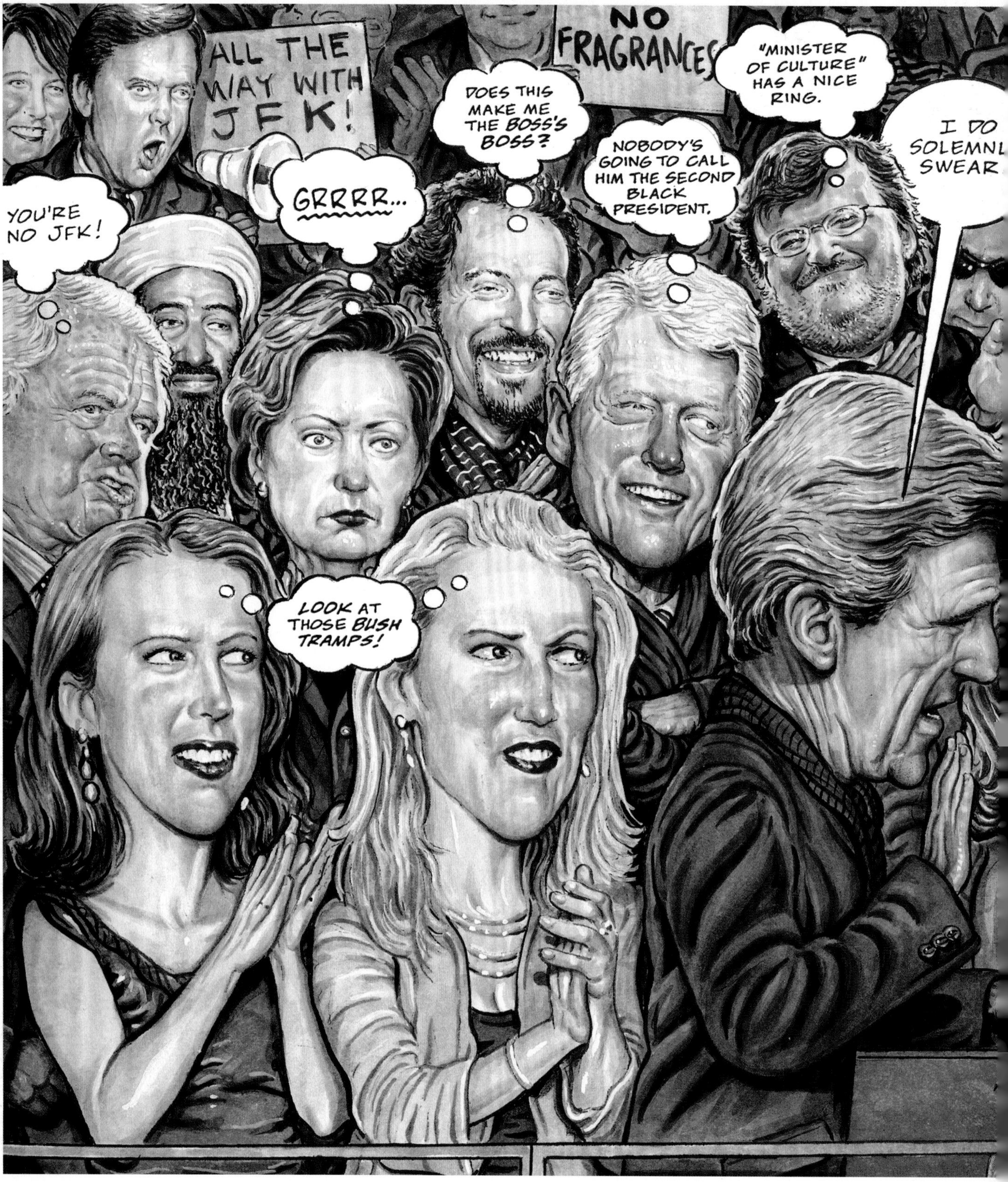
ALL THE WAY WITH JFK!
NO FRAGRANCES
"MINISTER OF CULTURE" HAS A NICE RING.
DOES THIS MAKE ME THE BOSS'S BOSS?
I DO SOLEMNL SWEAR
NOBODY'S GOING TO CALL HIM THE SECOND BLACK PRESIDENT.
GRRRR...
YOU'RE NO JFK!
LOOK AT THOSE BUSH TRAMPS!

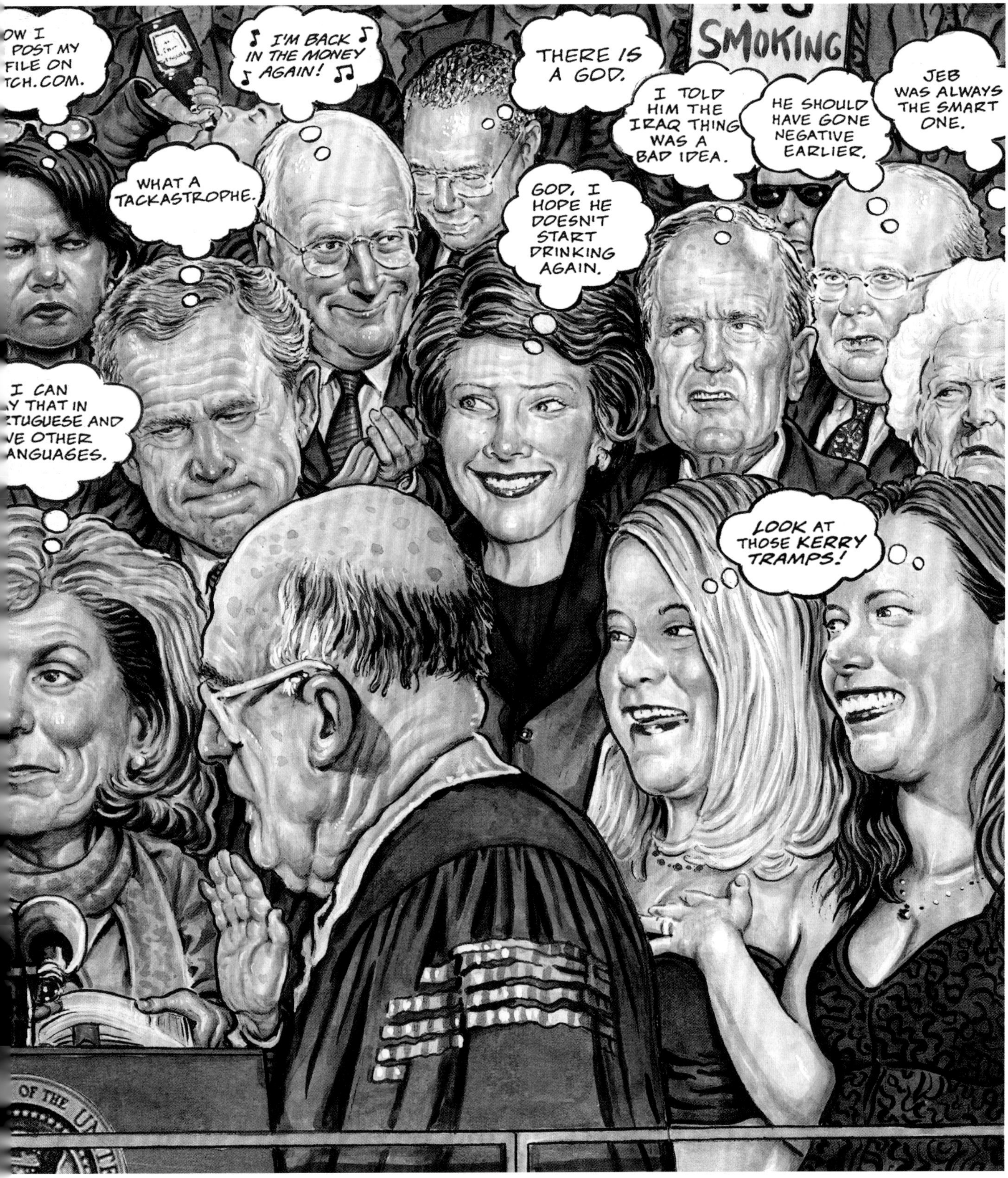
OW I POST MY FILE ON TCH.COM.
I'M BACK IN THE MONEY AGAIN!
THERE IS A GOD.
SMOKING
I TOLD HIM THE IRAQ THING WAS A BAD IDEA.
HE SHOULD HAVE GONE NEGATIVE EARLIER.
JEB WAS ALWAYS THE SMART ONE.
WHAT A TACKASTROPHE.
GOD, I HOPE HE DOESN'T START DRINKING AGAIN.
I CAN Y THAT IN TUGUESE AND VE OTHER ANGUAGES.
LOOK AT THOSE KERRY TRAMPS!

WEEKLY STANDARD

In some cases, I had no idea who
I was being asked to draw for *WS*.
No matter.

JACQUES CHIRAC

JEB BUSH

JOSCHKA FISCHER

BIL LANN LEE

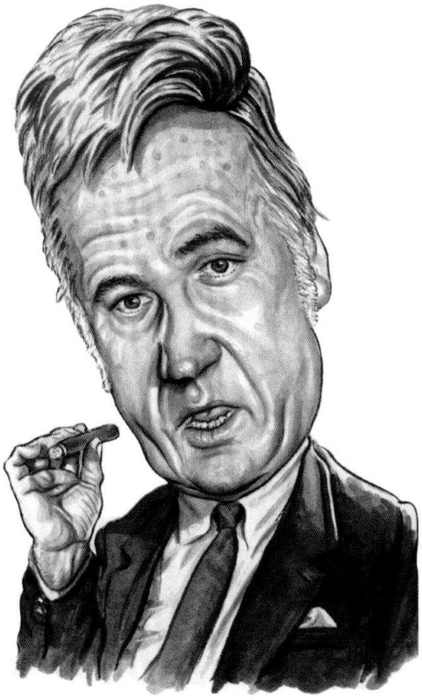

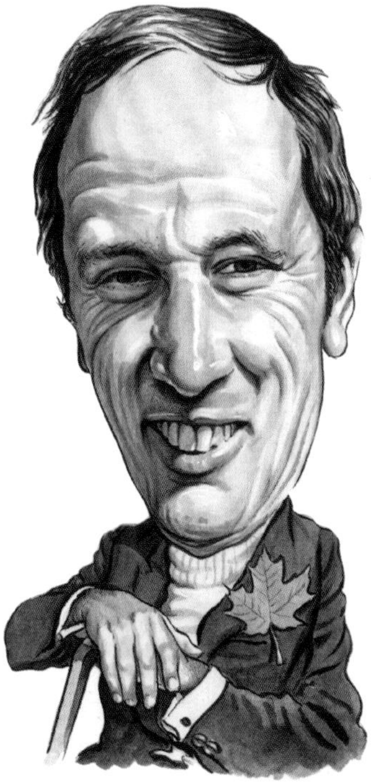

JOHN TRAFICANT

PIERRE TRUDEAU

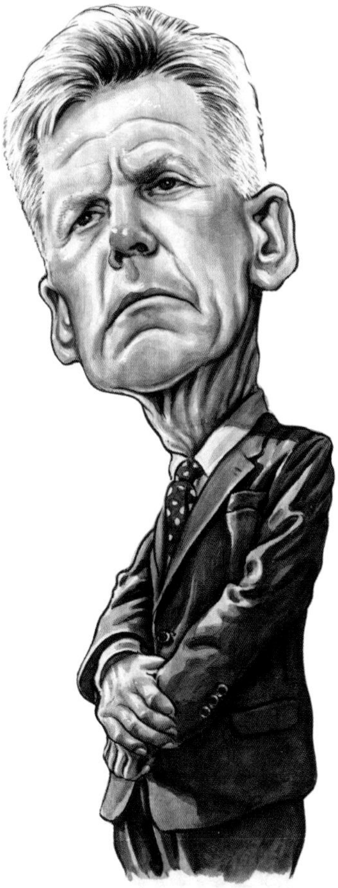

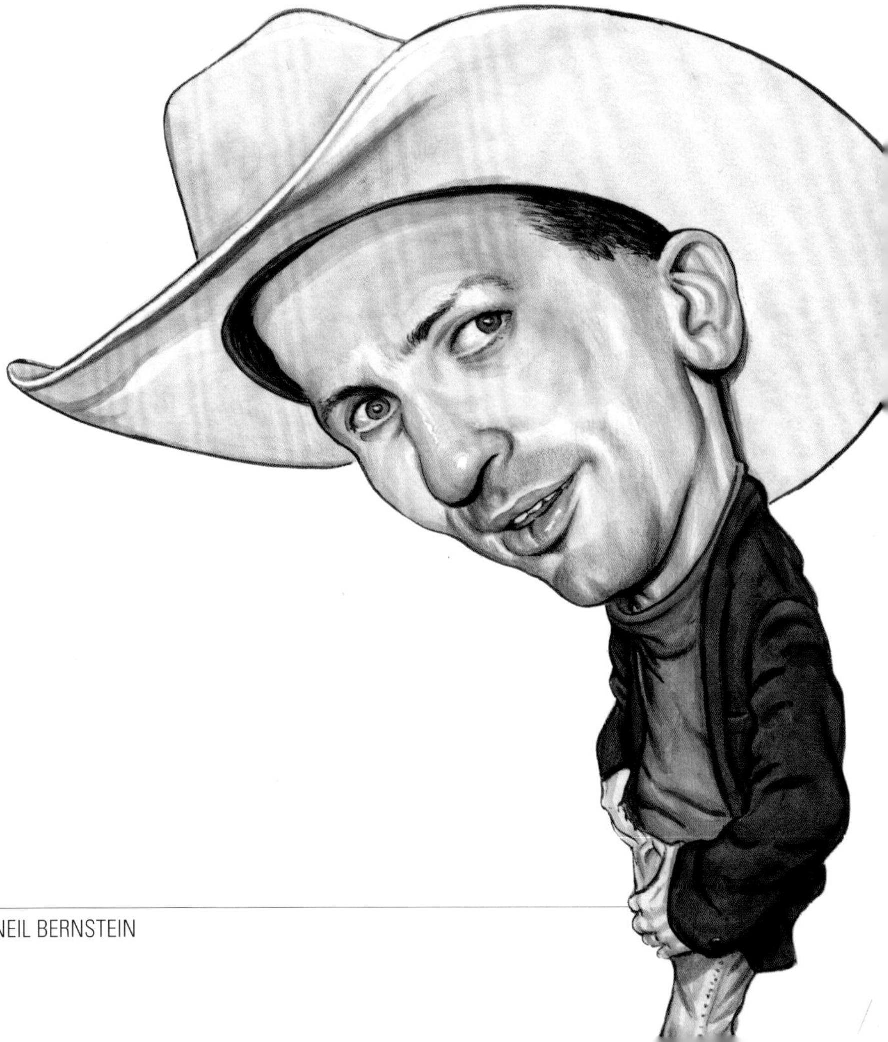

GARY CONDIT

NEIL BERNSTEIN

"FED CHAIRMAN BEN BERNANKE—*ROCK STAR.*"

BUSINESS WEEK

"HANK PAULSON—BIRDWATCHER."

BLOOMBERG NEWS

Treasury Secretary **Hank Paulson**.

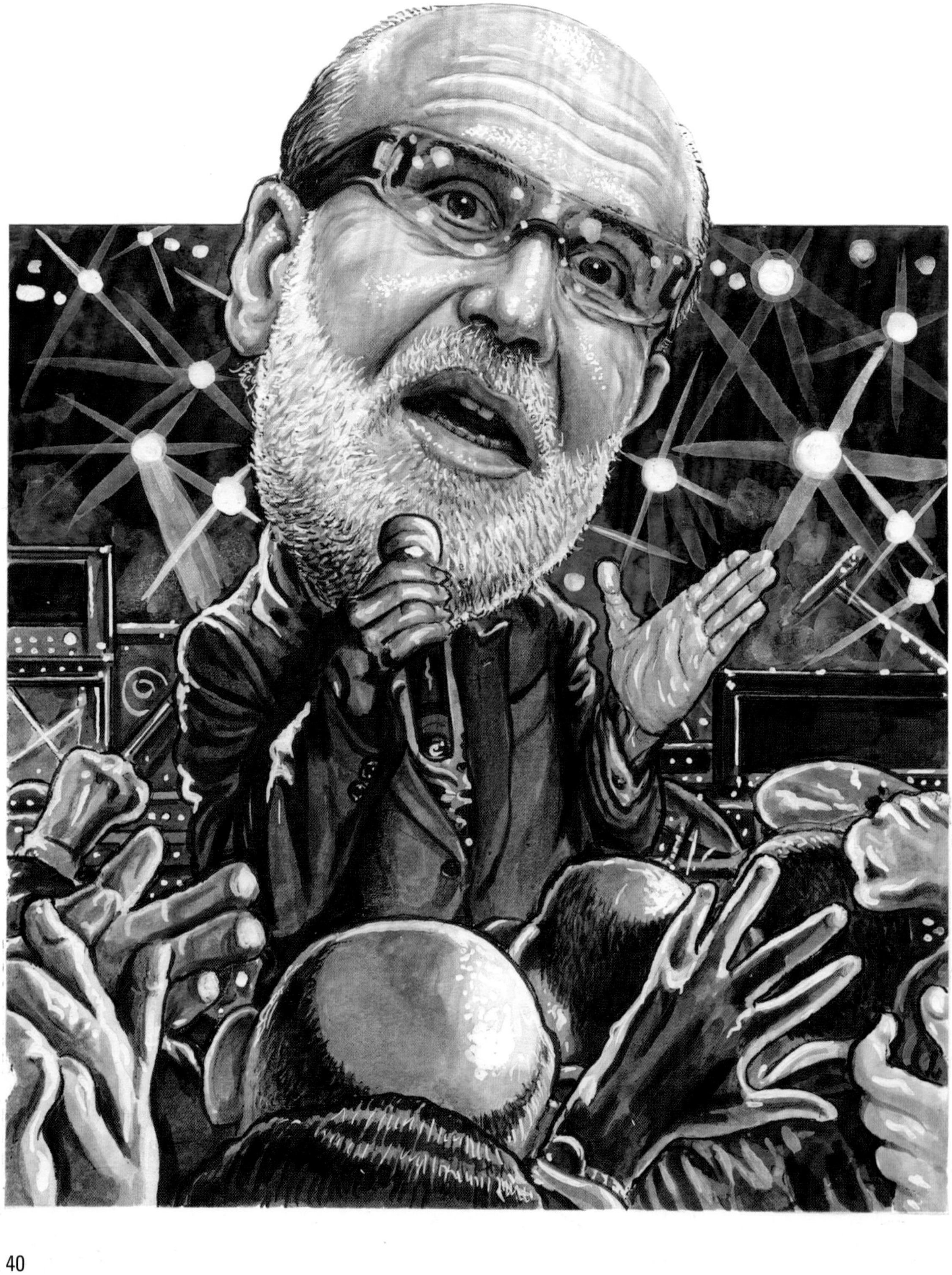

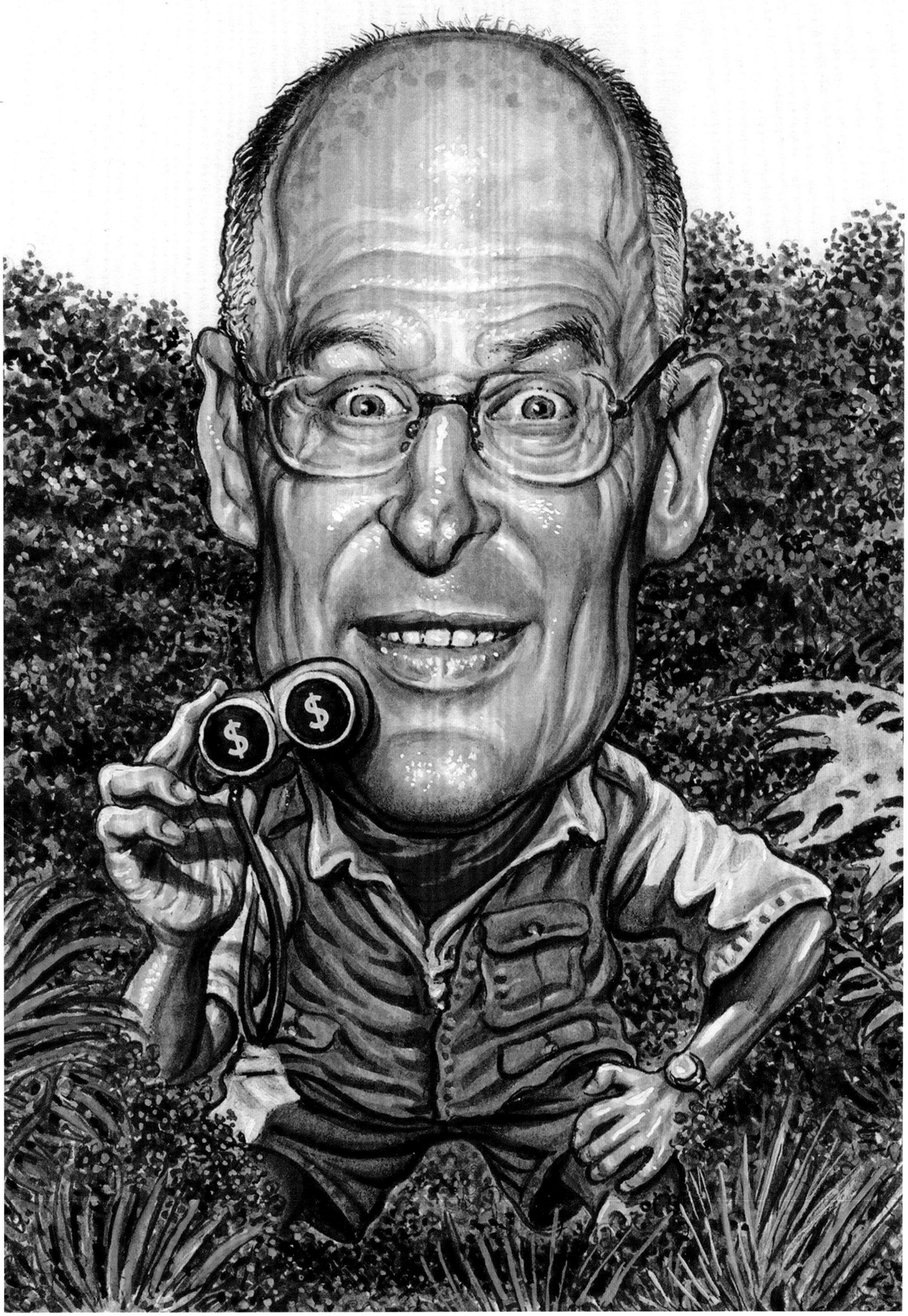

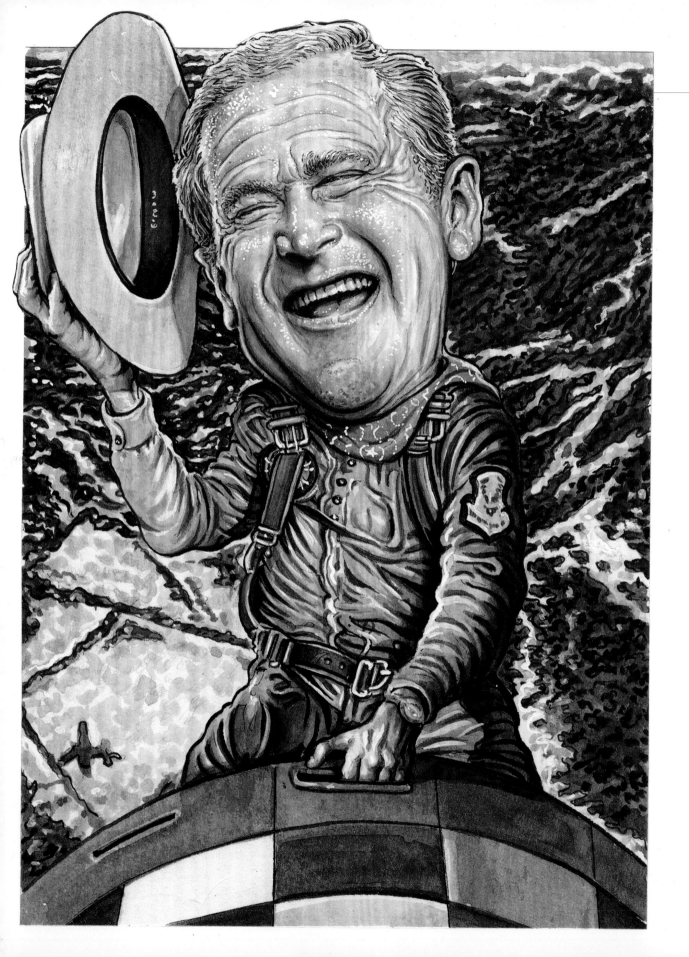

"YEEE-HAW!!"

TEXAS MONTHLY

George W. Bush channels Major Kong from *Dr. Strangelove.*

"DANCING WITH THE DICK."

THE NEW REPUBLIC

To try to redeem his declining reputation, **Dick Cheney** takes to *Dancing With the Stars.*

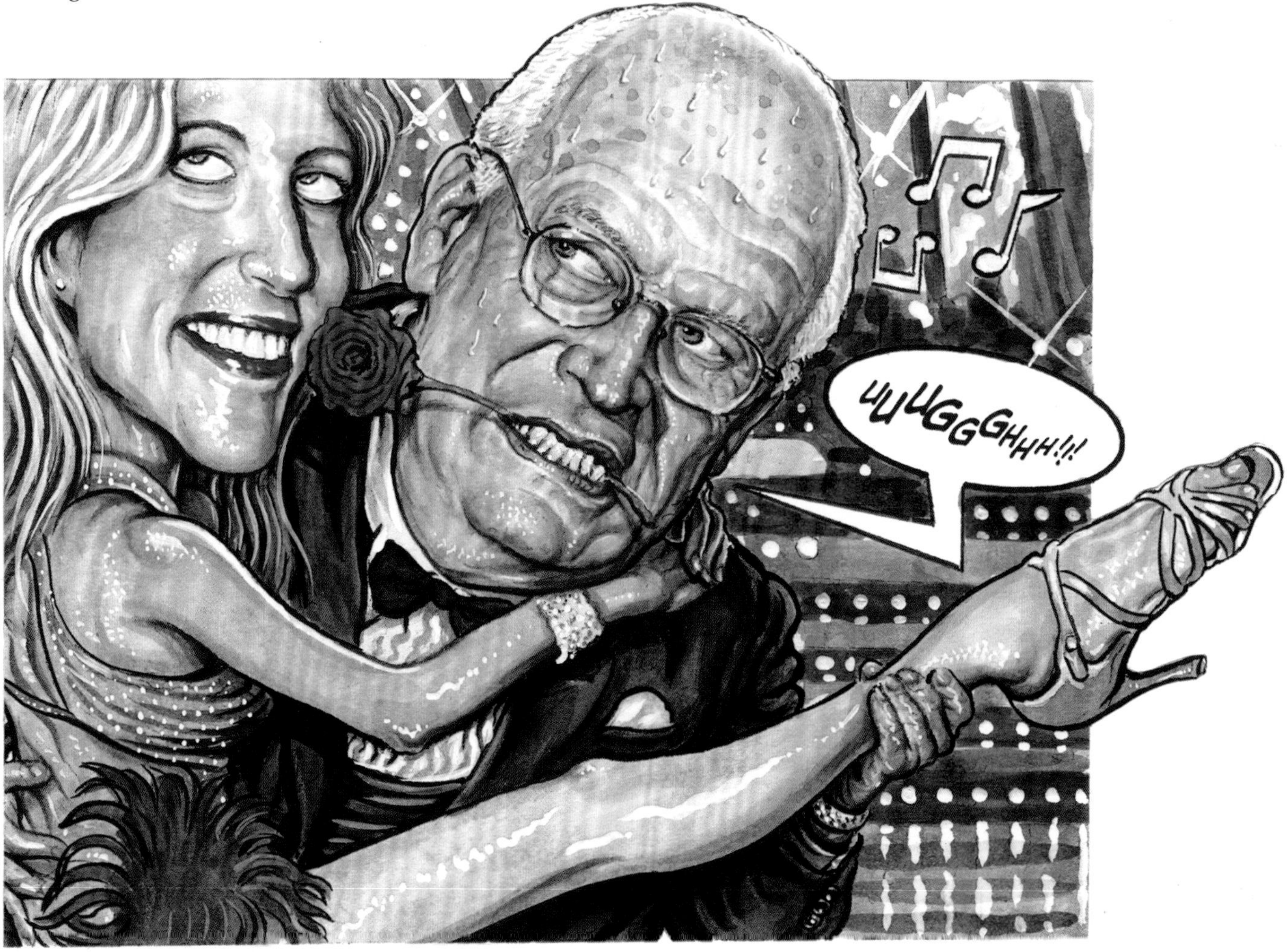
UUUGGGHHH!!!

"A RESTLESS RUMMY."

THE NEW REPUBLIC

Donald Rumsfeld in forced retirement.

"A BOY LOSES HIS BALLOON."

THE WEEK (cover)

George W. Bush says fare-thee-well to his beloved **Karl Rove**.

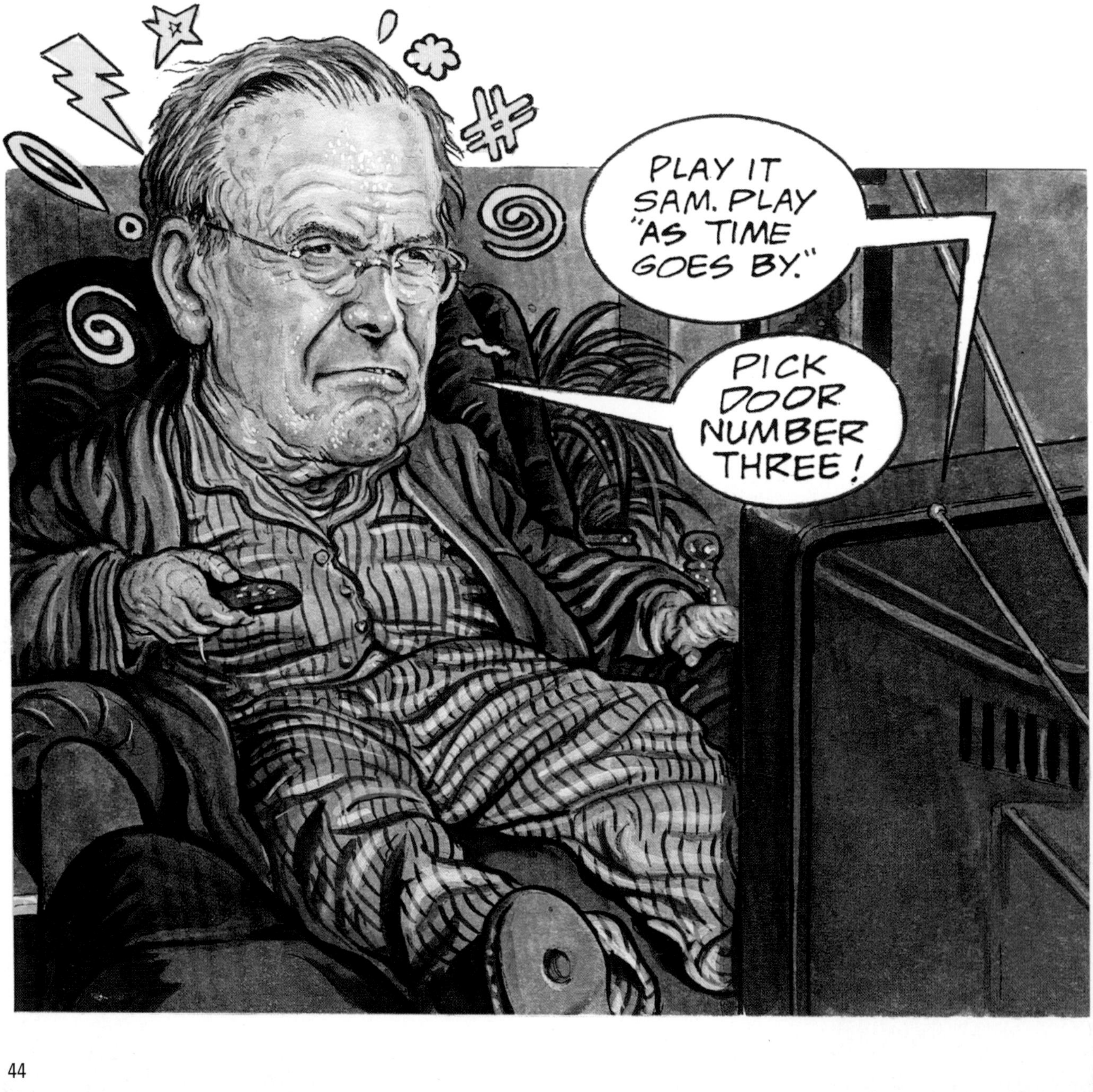
PLAY IT SAM. PLAY "AS TIME GOES BY."
PICK DOOR NUMBER THREE!

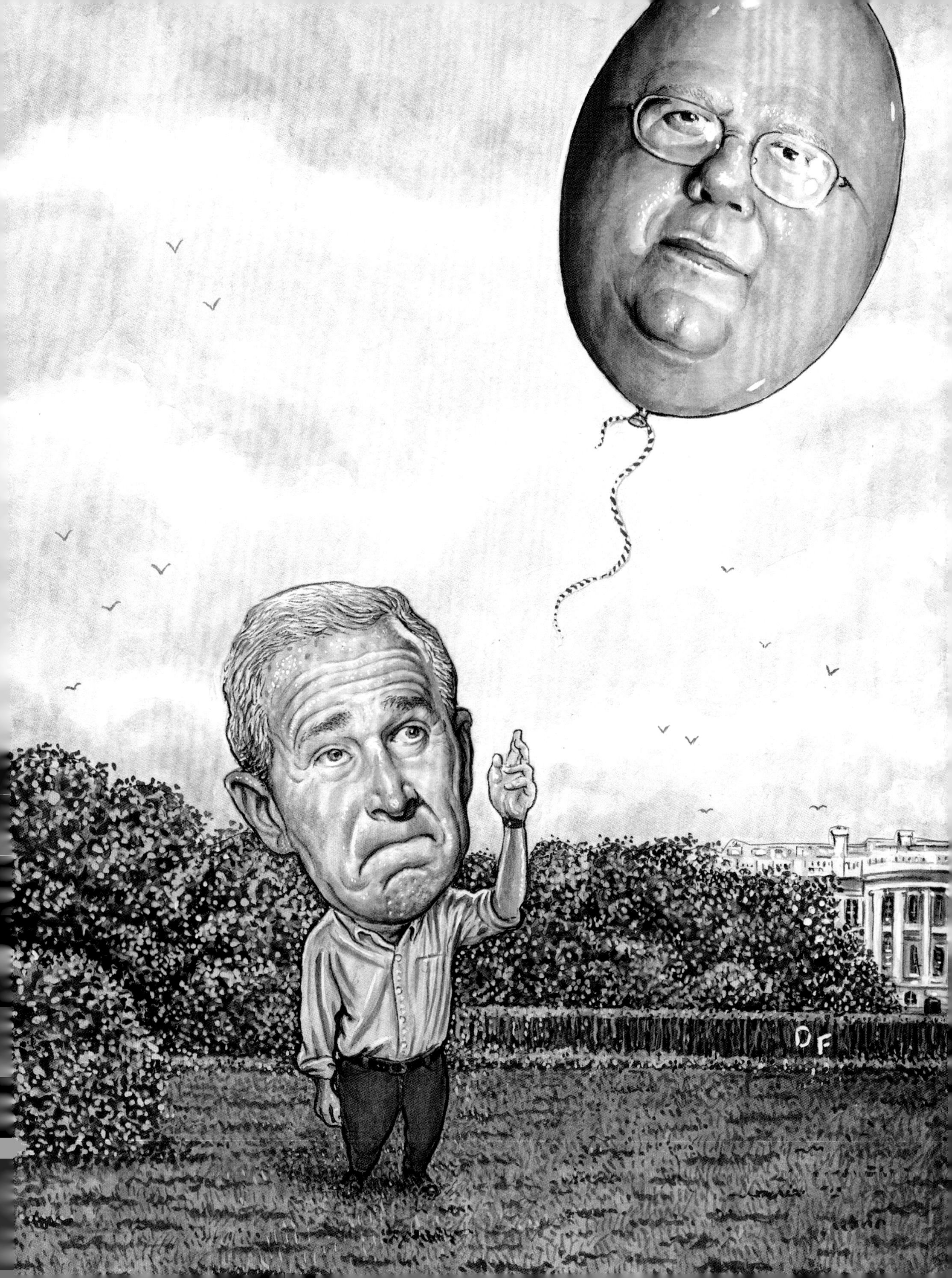
DF

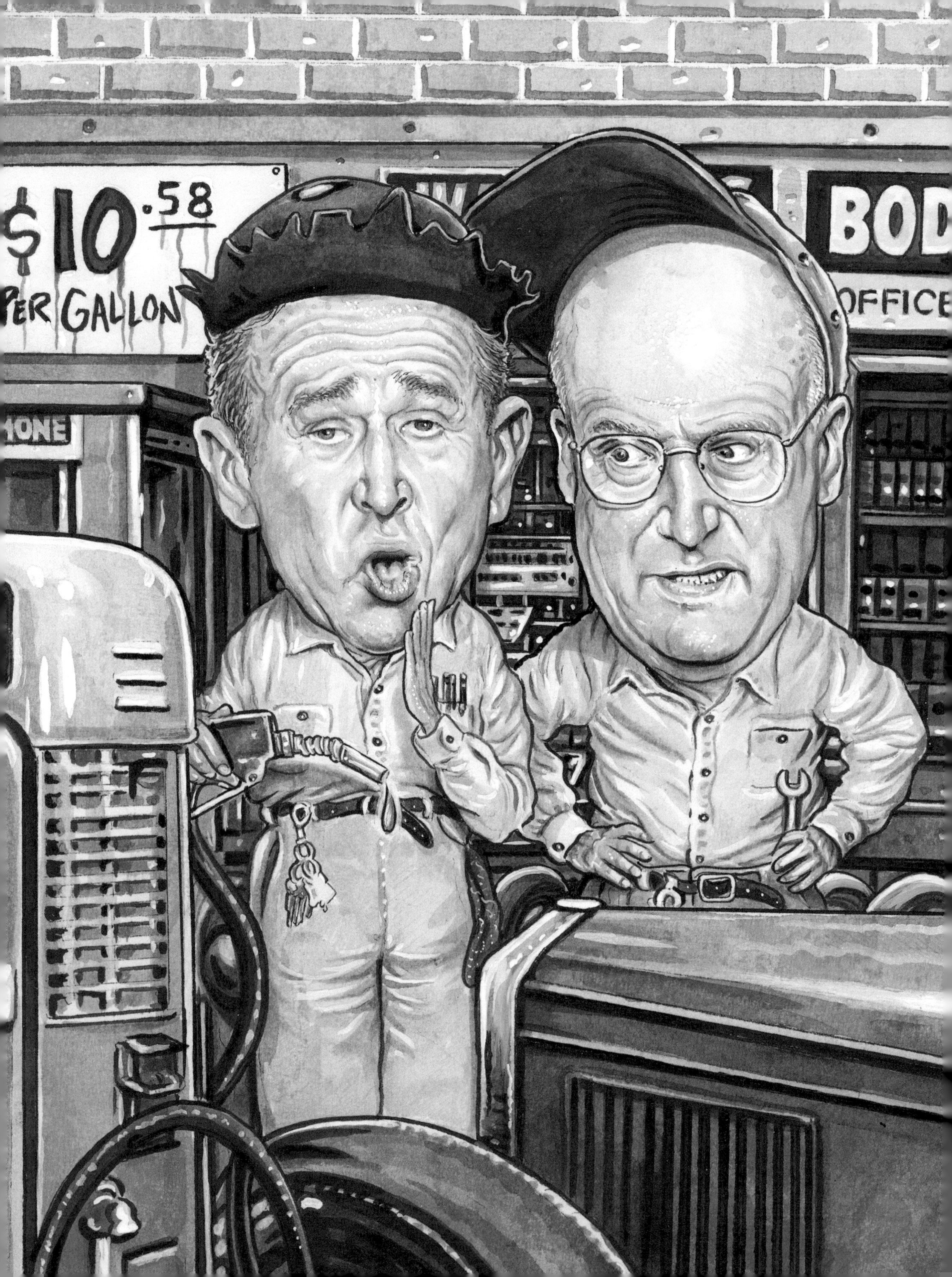
$10.58
PER GALLON
BOD
OFFICE
HONE

"THE G.O.P.'S GOOBER & GOMER."

THE NEW REPUBLIC (cover)

George and **Dick** in Mayberry.

"DICK CHENEY RESUMES HIS HUNTING HOBBY."

THE NEW REPUBLIC

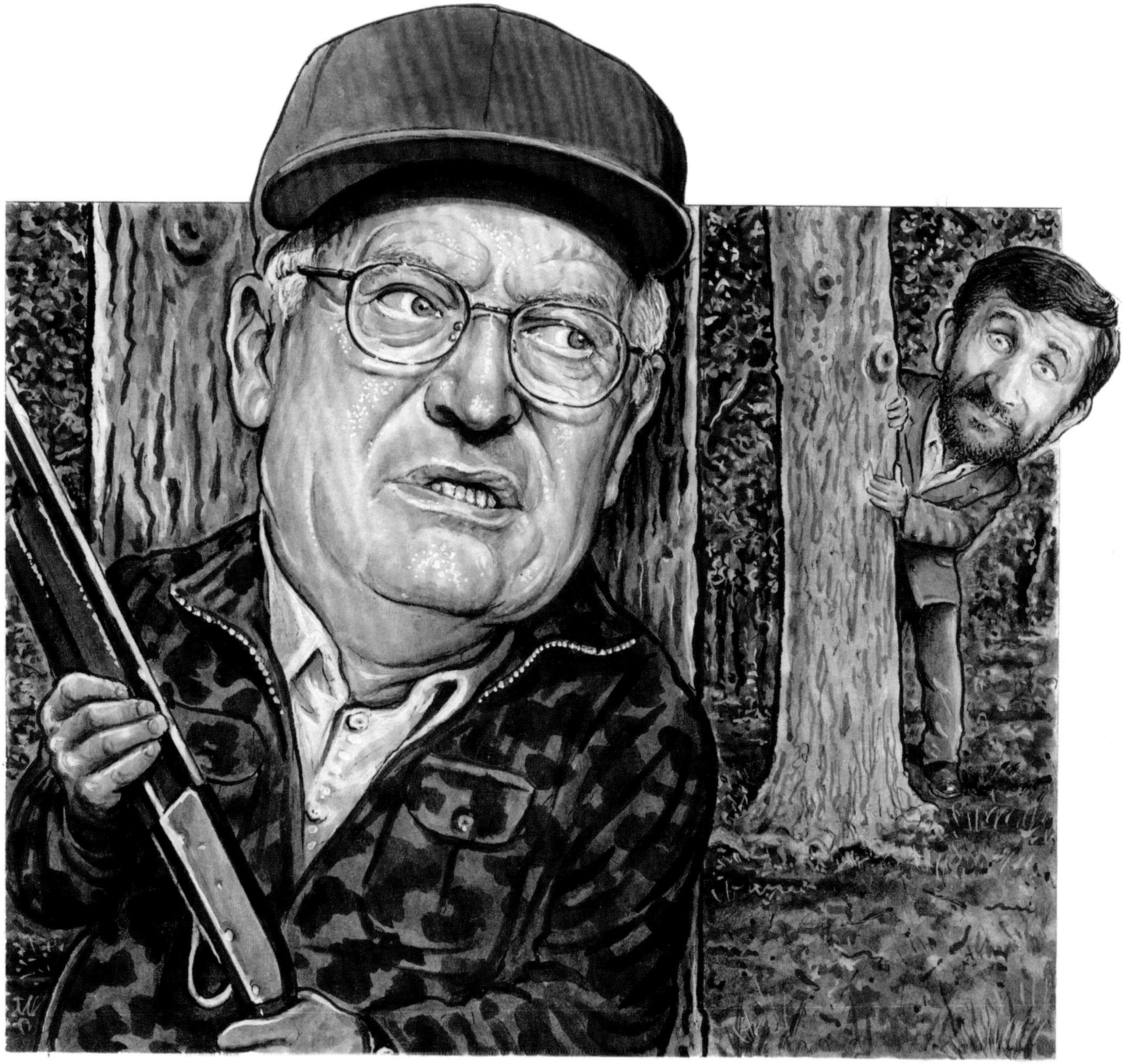

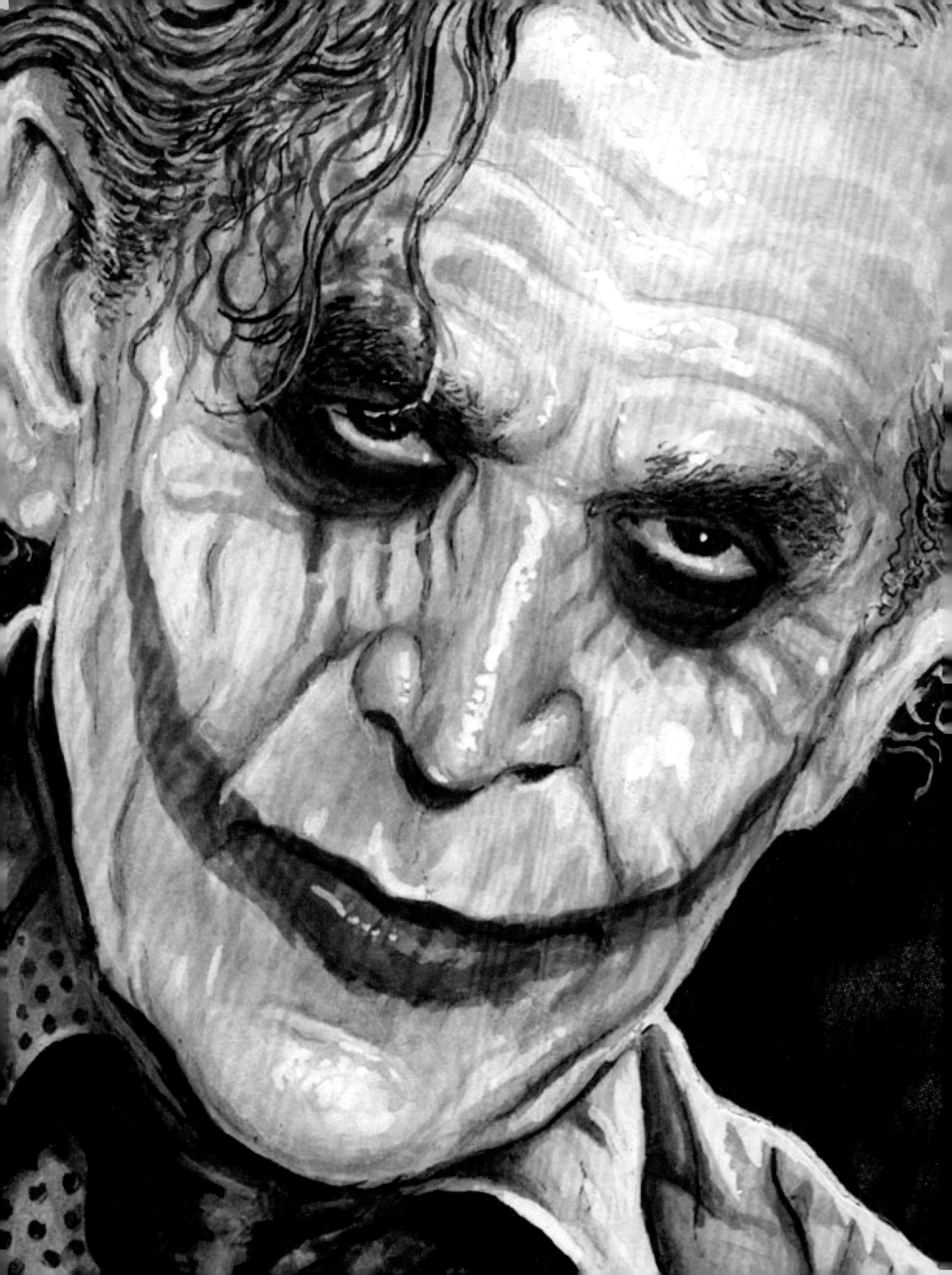

"NO JOKE."

VANITY FAIR ONLINE

I created this image of Bush as The Joker, an agent of chaos, destruction and death, all the while seemingly laughing through it all, when the ***Batman: The Dark Knight*** movie came out and at the height of the war in Iraq. More than a year later, posters of new president-elect Obama began popping up all over LA depicting him as The Joker with the line "SOCIAL-ISM" underneath. I was asked to respond and dismissed it with the "Imitation is the sincerest form of flattery" line, but later expanded my comments to say I didn't think the Obama/Joker analogy worked at all, as satire or social commentary. Aside from being a clearly provocative image, what does being a supposed Sociaiist have to do with The Joker? (And wouldn't Socialism be the ***opposite*** of The Joker's nihilistic anarchism?) It just didn't make sense.

"SAY GOODNIGHT, DICK."

THE NEW REPUBLIC

Nearing the end of the Bush presidency, **Dick Cheney** prepares for bed.

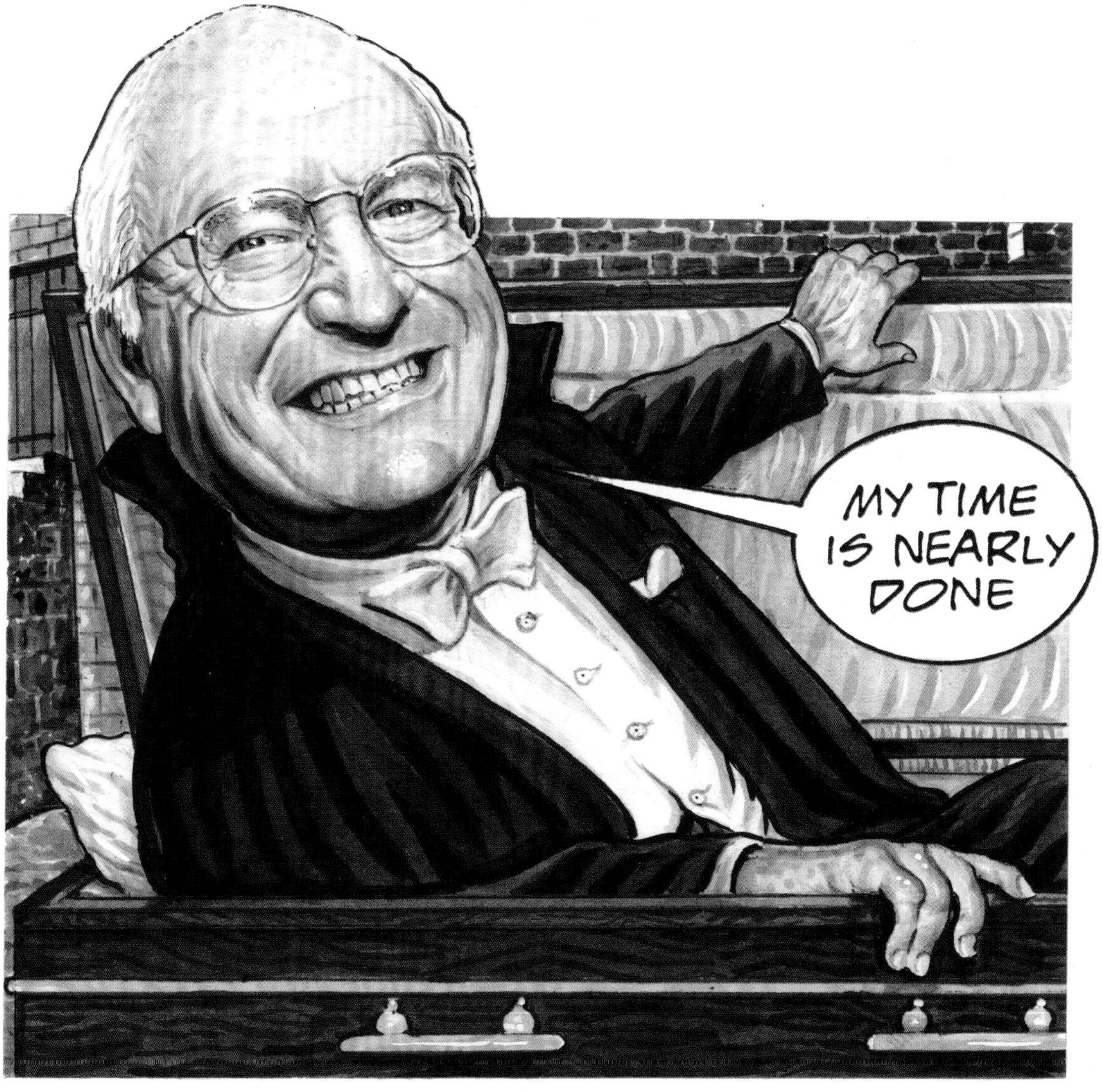
MY TIME IS NEARLY DONE

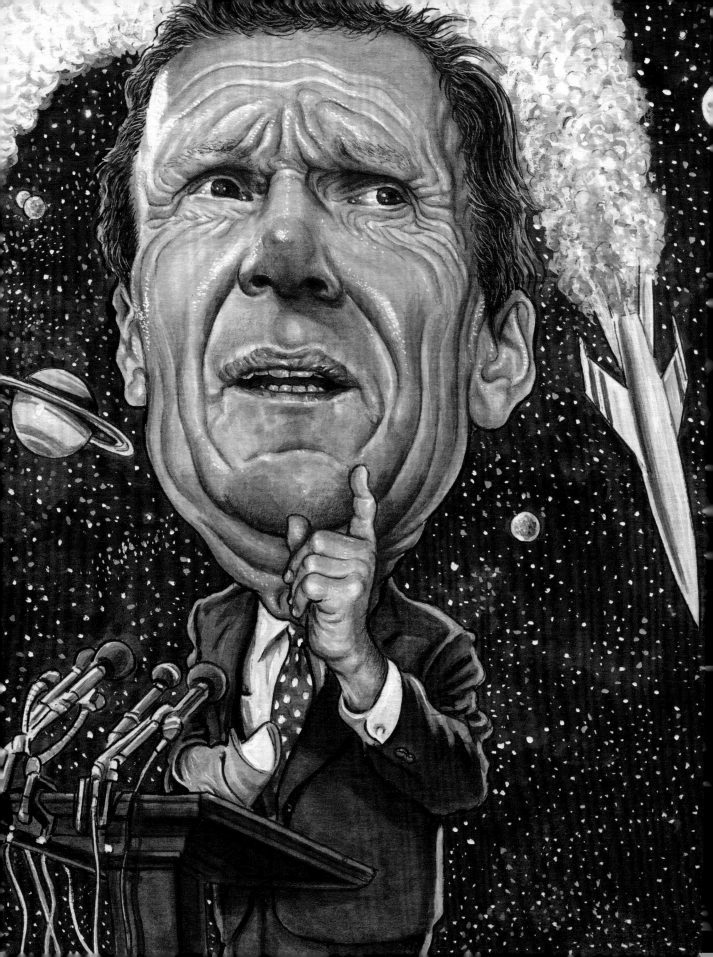

"AND THE DAN QUAYLE AWARD GOES TO…"

MOTHER JONES

Senator **Tom Daschle**, who denounced spending billions on Bush's space-based missile-defense system, saying, "This isn't rocket science here."

"THE FOUR HORSEMEN OF THE—WTF?"

PLAYBOY (Sweden)

I have absolutely no memory of why I was hired to depict **Tom Cruise**, **James Dean**, Soccer star **David Beckham** and **George W. Bush** as the Four Horsemen of the Apocalypse, but apparently it made sense to the editors of Swedish *Playboy*. And finally receiving a copy proved to be of no help, as it was all of course in Swedish.

Due the next day.

PAT TOOMEY

MICHAEL STEELE

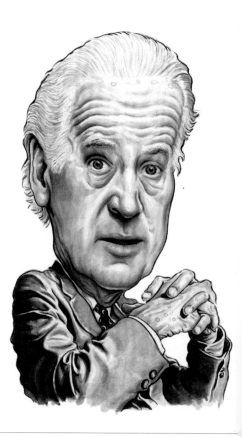

JOE BIDEN

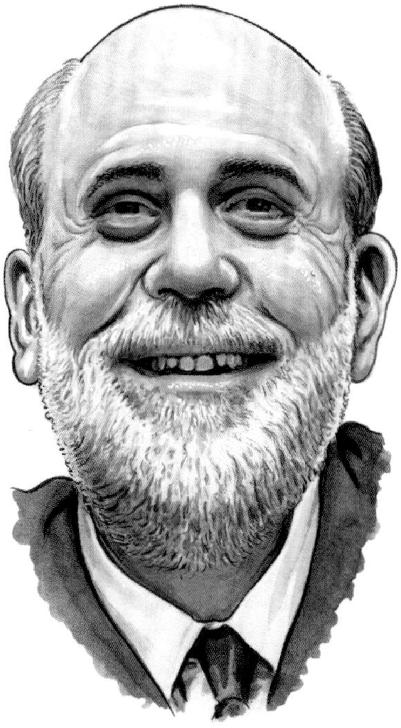

BEN BERNANKE

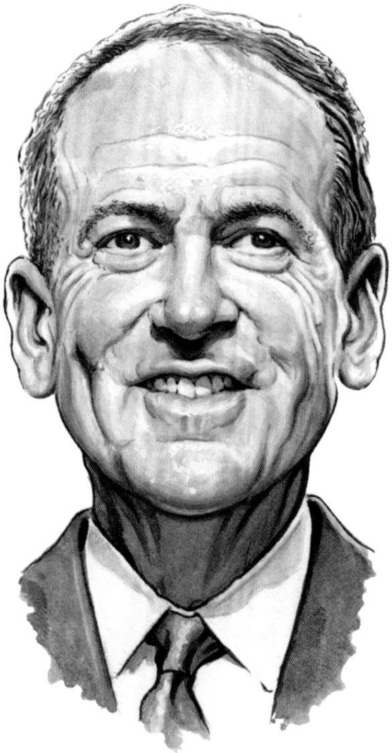

MIKE HUCKABEE

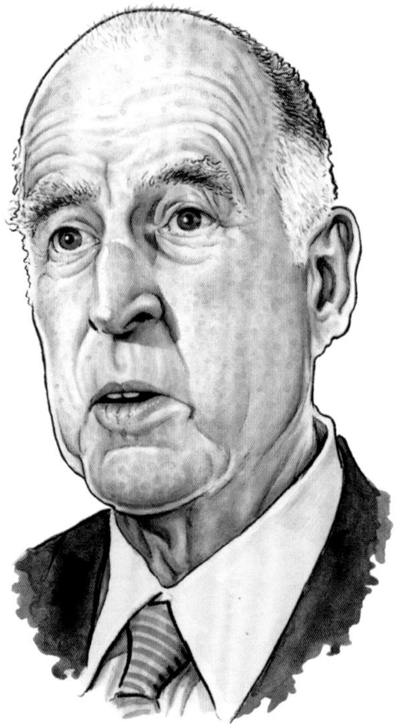

JERRY BROWN

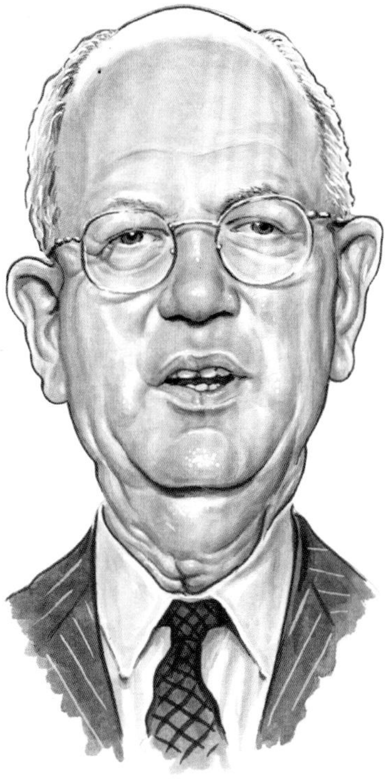

MARTIN FROST

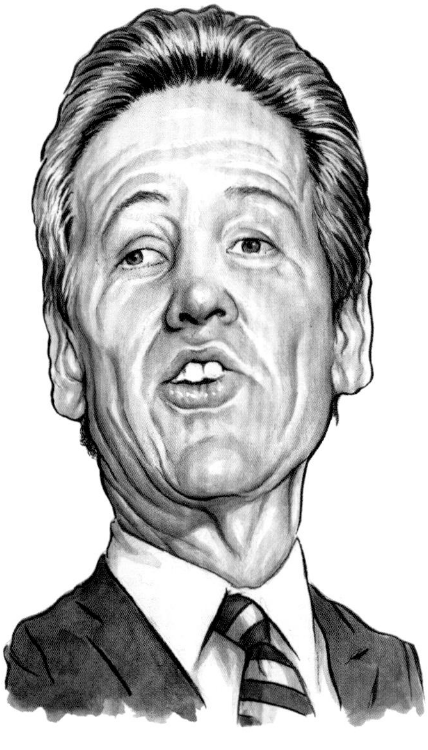

NORM COLEMAN

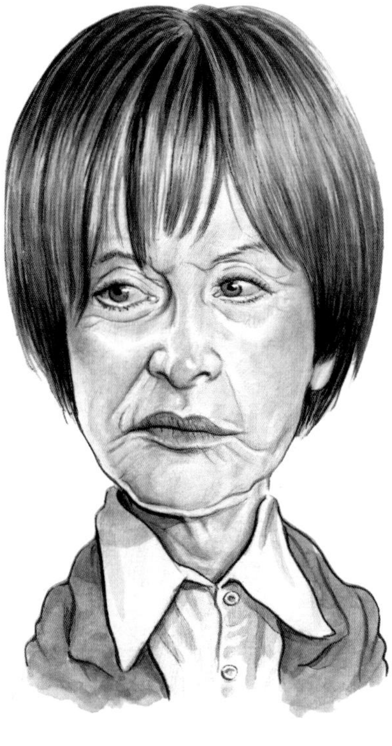

CHARLOTTE BEERS

"THE 911 EXPRESS."

THE NEW REPUBLIC

Rudy Giuliani takes his presidential campaign to the Heartland.

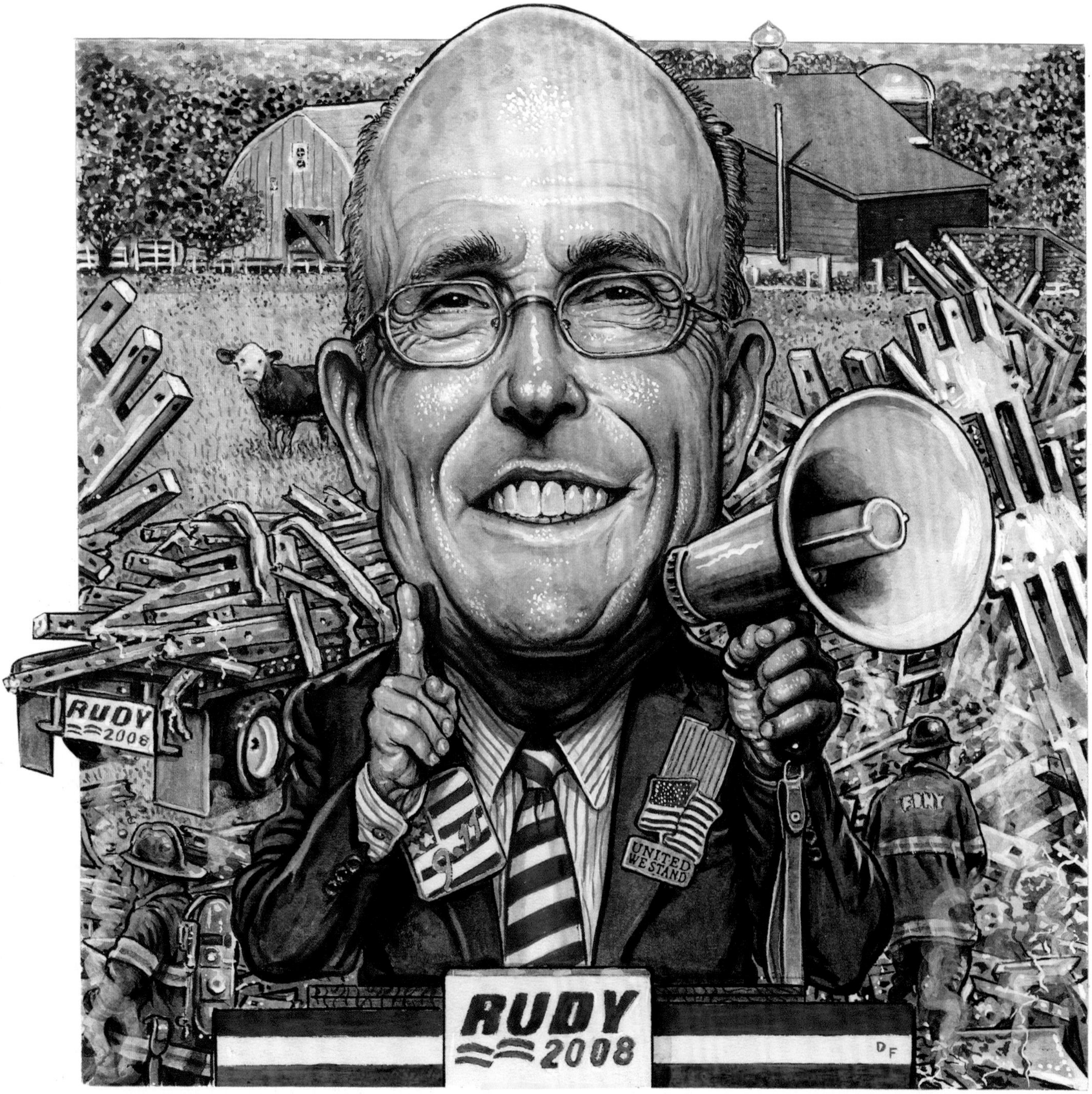
RUDY
2008
UNITED WE STAND
FDNY
RUDY
2008
DF

"G.O.P. GUNSLINGERS."

THE NEW REPUBLIC

GOP Candidates **Fred Thompson**, **John McCain**, and **Rudy Giuliani**, pandering to the NRA.

BAM
POW
BRATTA
POW
KAPOW

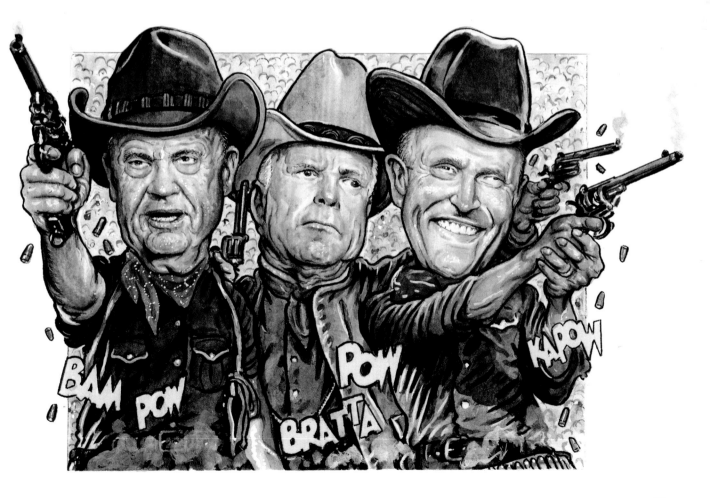

"RUDY LOVES THE JEWS."

THE NEW REPUBLIC

Rudy Giuliani stakes his campaign on South Florida.

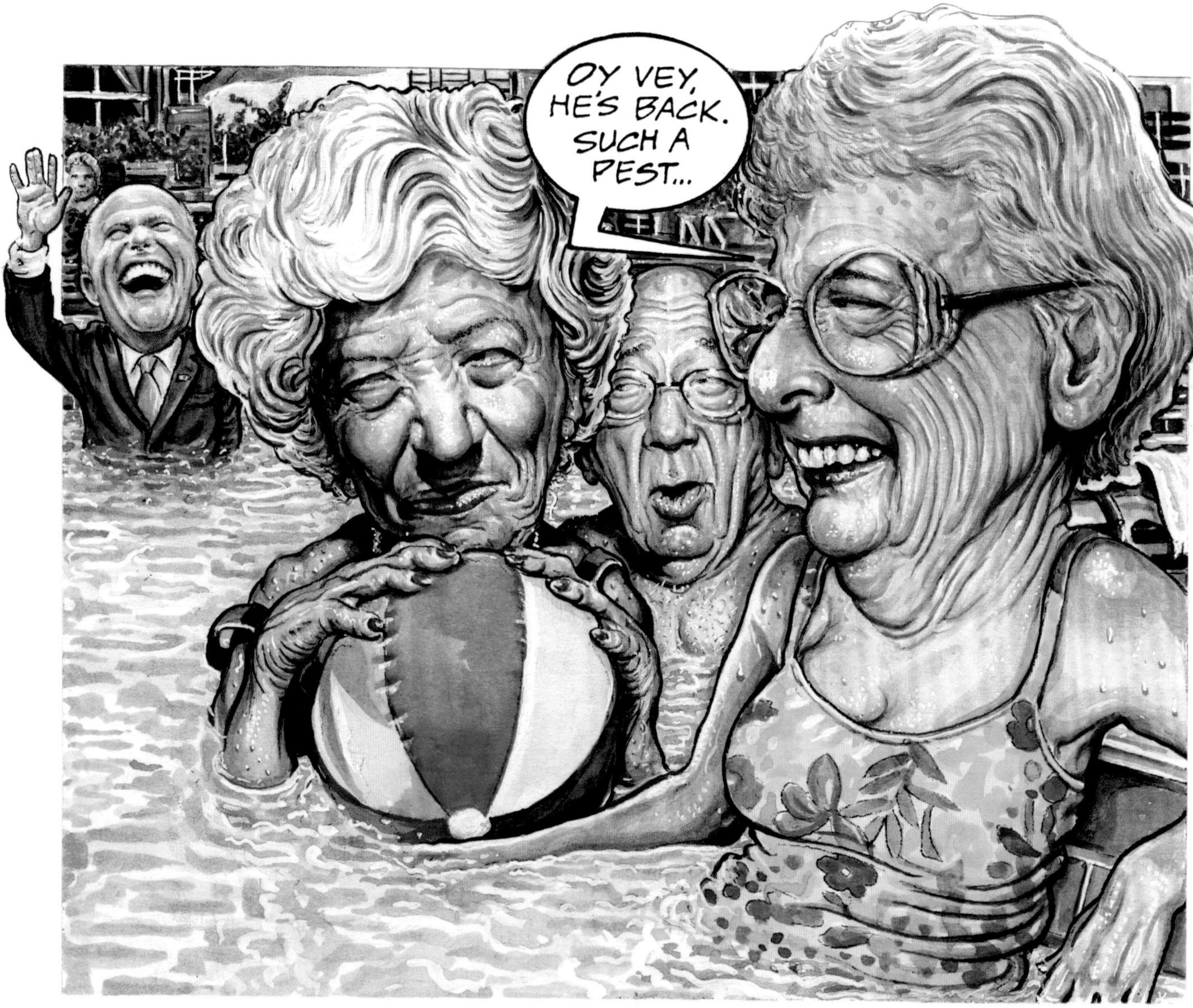
OY VEY, HE'S BACK. SUCH A PEST...

"NOW, AIM FOR THE HEAD."

THE NEW REPUBLIC

Under the tutelage of **Chuck Norris**, **Mike Huckabee** trains for Iowa.

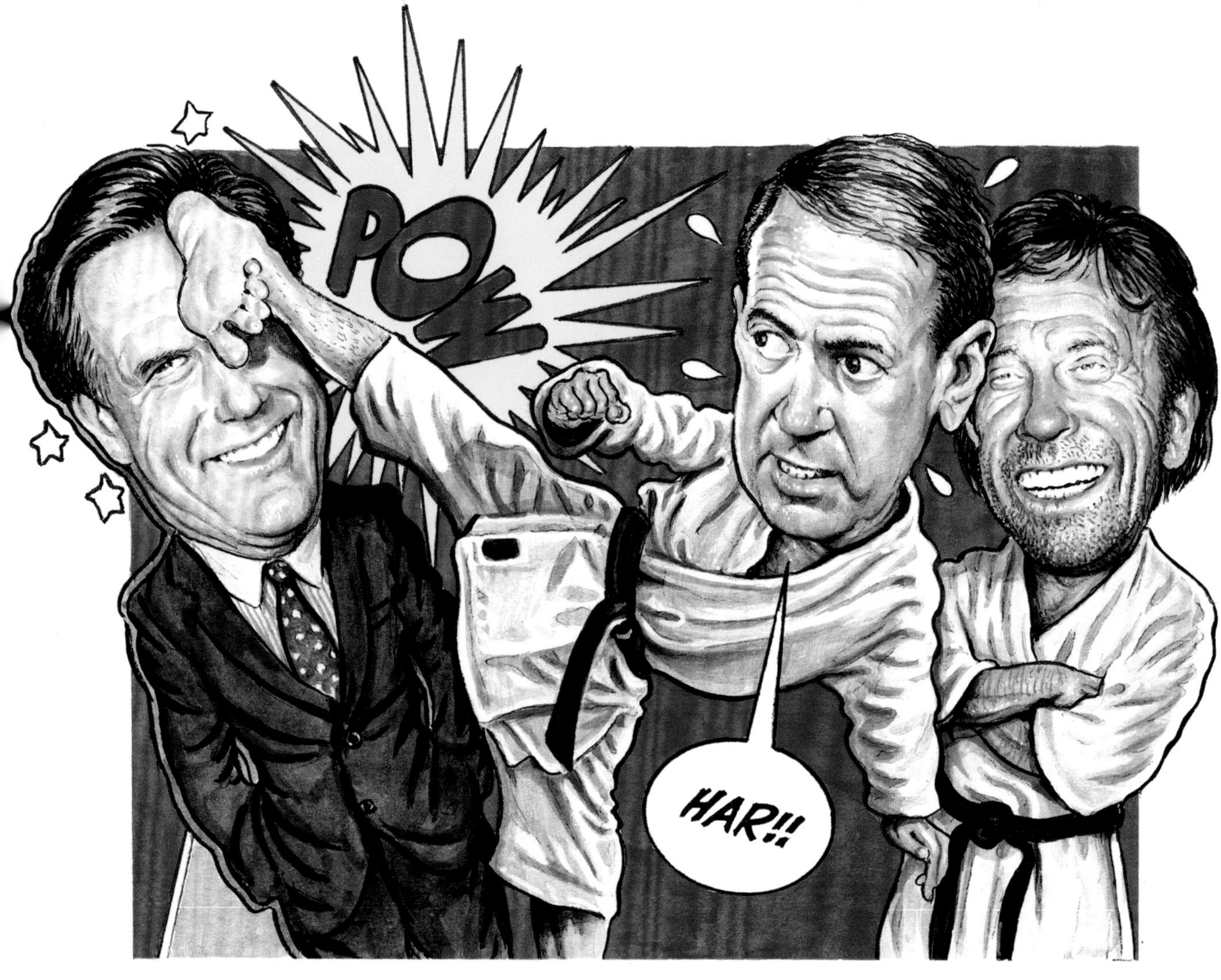

POW
HAR!!

"LIMBAUGH IN LOVE."

THE NEW REPUBLIC

Realizing that there might be worse things than a female president, **Rush Limbaugh** discovers his true feelings for Hillary Clinton.

"CYBER CAFÉ CANDIDATES."

DIRECT (cover)

The candidates take their campaigns to the internets.

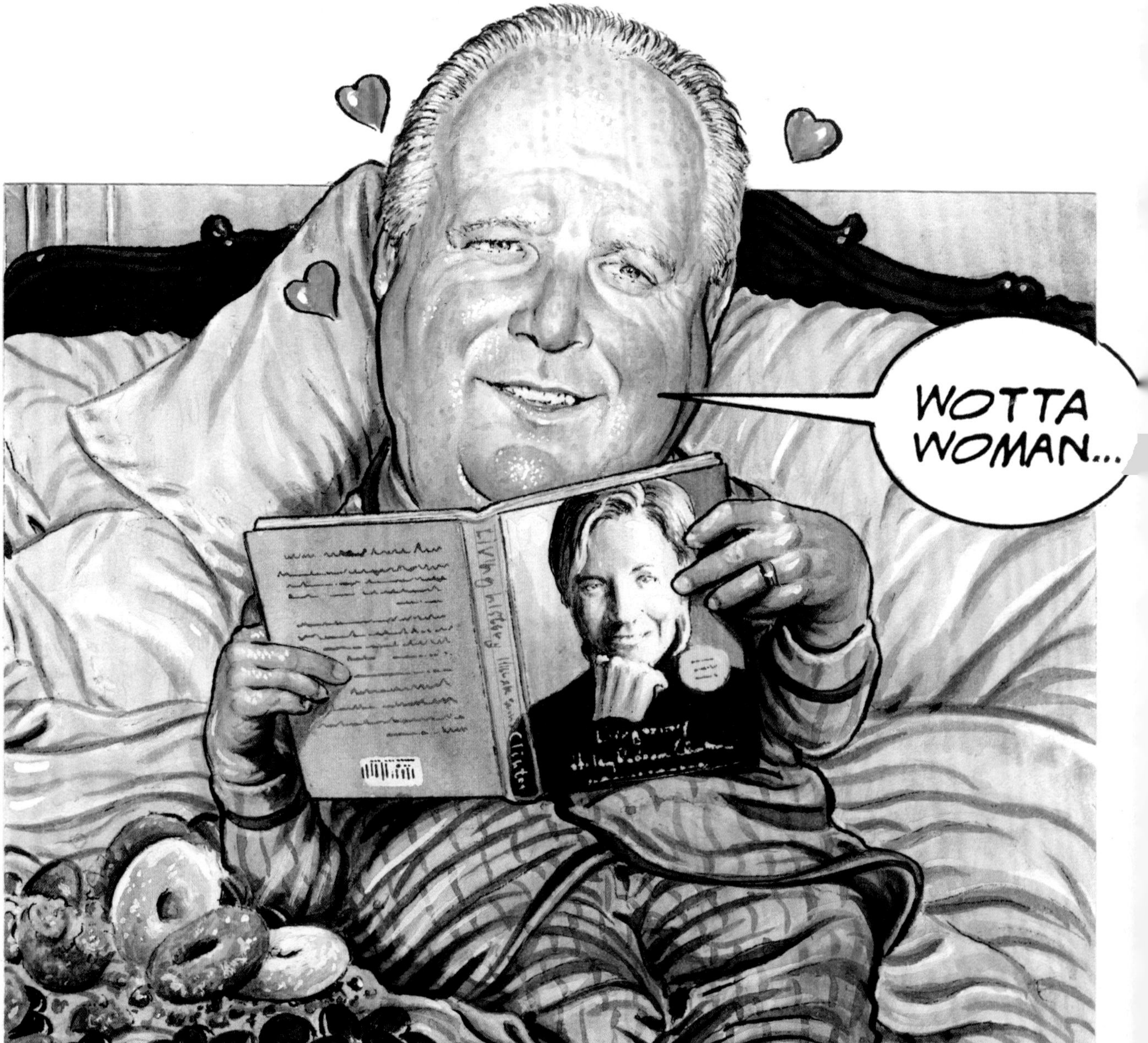
WOTTA WOMAN...

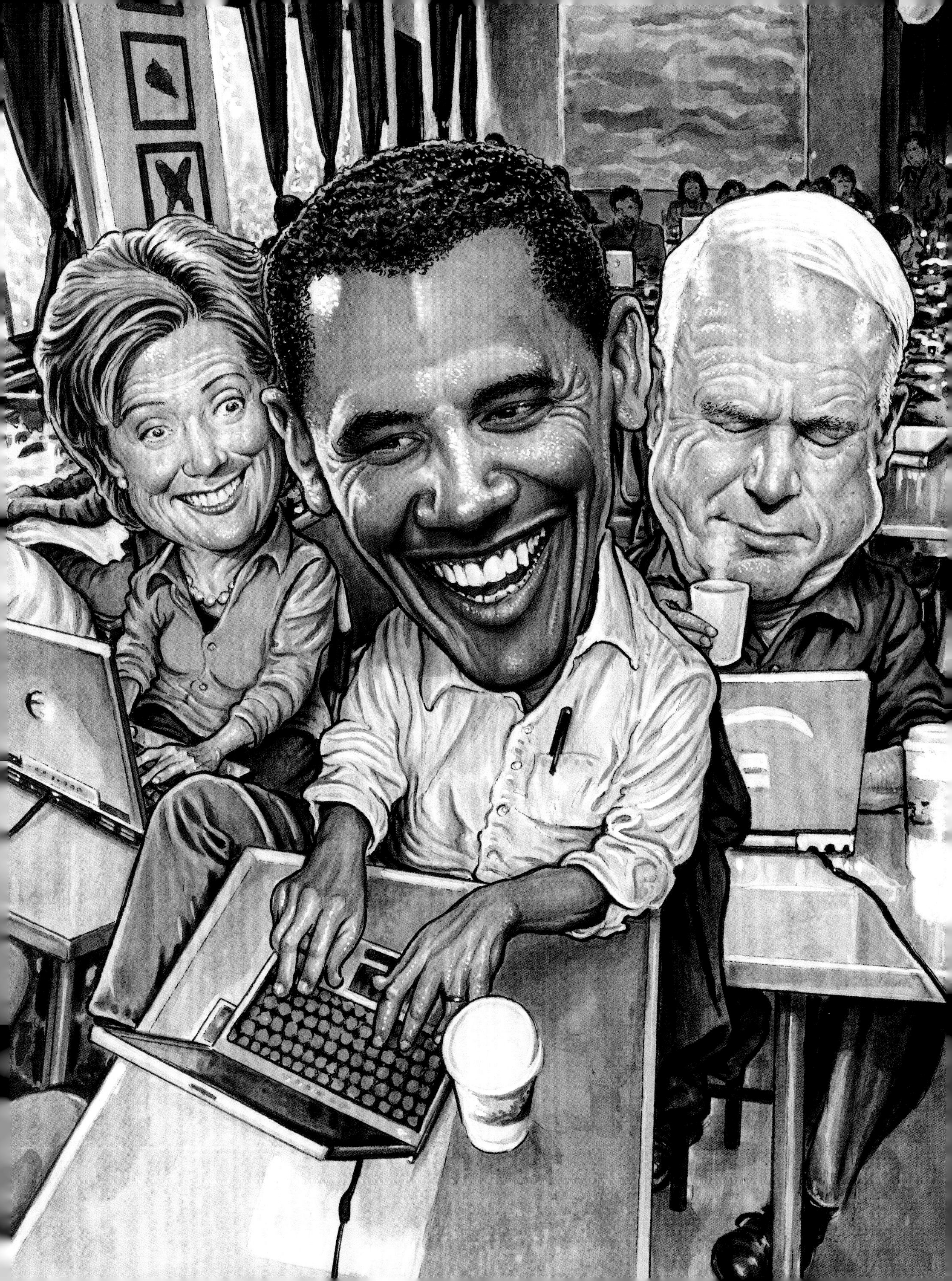

"CYBER STUMPING"

PROMO (cover)

The Presidential candidates are forced to enter the digital age, seeking votes and cash. Only **Barack Obama** seems to be enjoying himself.

"PRESS WHORES"

THE NATION (cover)

Journalists **Fareed Zakaria** (*Newsweek*), **Chris Matthews** (MSNBC), **Mika Brzezinski** (MSNBC), and **Nicholas Kristof** (*NY Times*), completely smitten with GOP Presidential candidate **John McCain**, cosy up with him in bed.

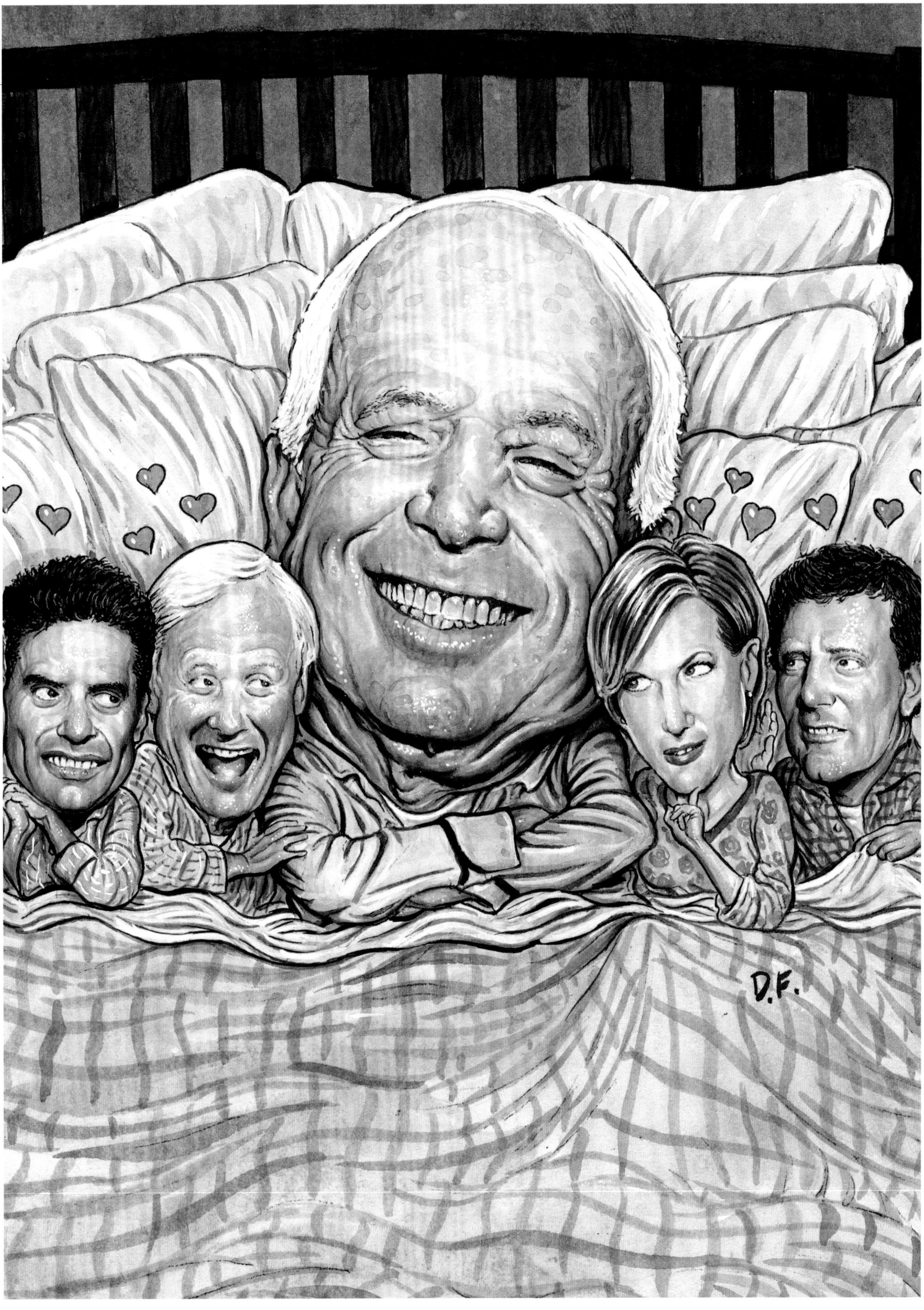
D.F.

"CLINTON'S COOKIES."

THE NEW REPUBLIC

Bill Clinton demonstrates his cookie-baking prowess as the future "First Man."

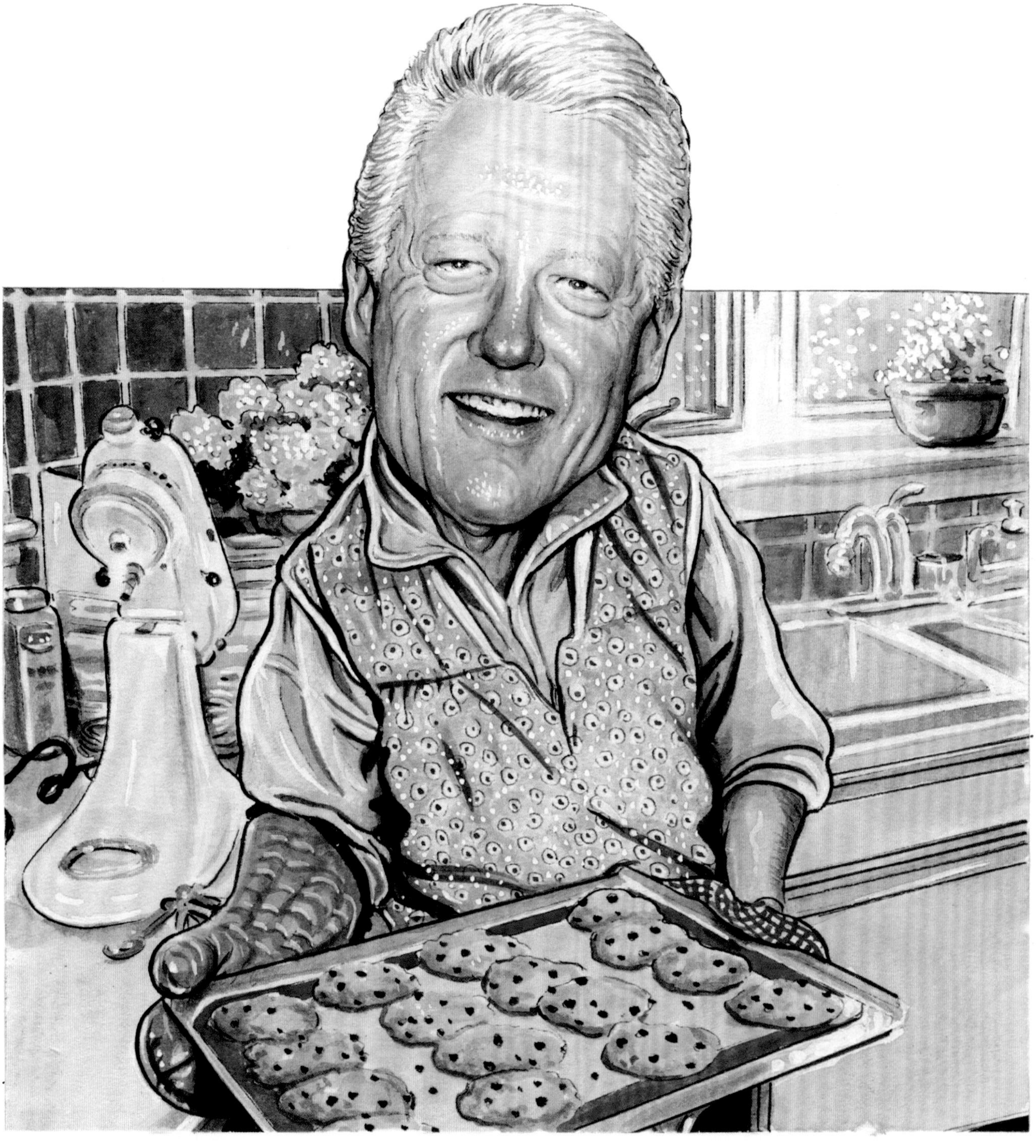

"AHEM, LET ME DO THE TALKING, JOE."

THE NEW REPUBLIC

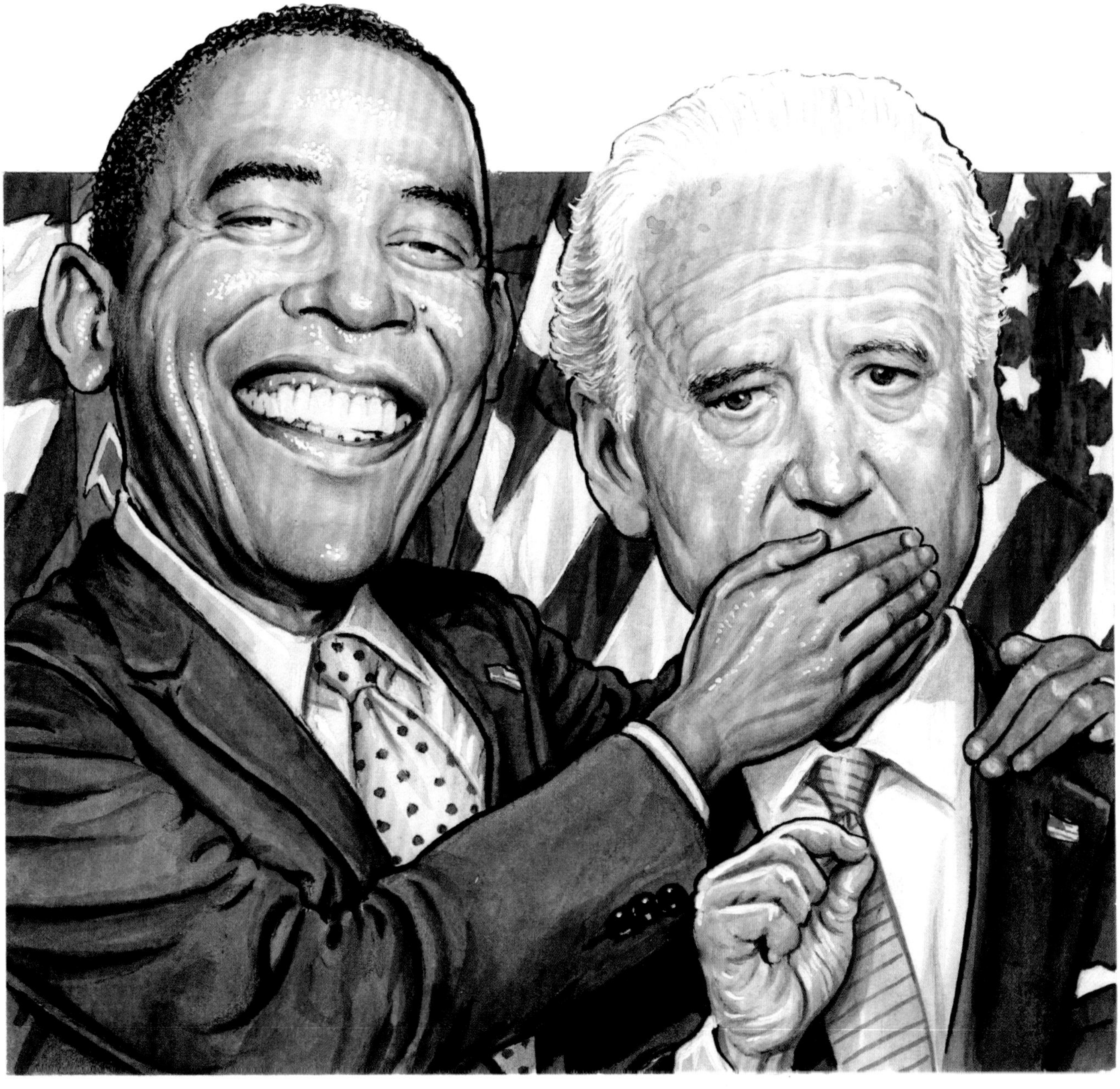

"READY TO RUMBLE."

THE NEW REPUBLIC

"Wild" **Cindy McCain** vs. "Nasty" **Michelle Obama**.

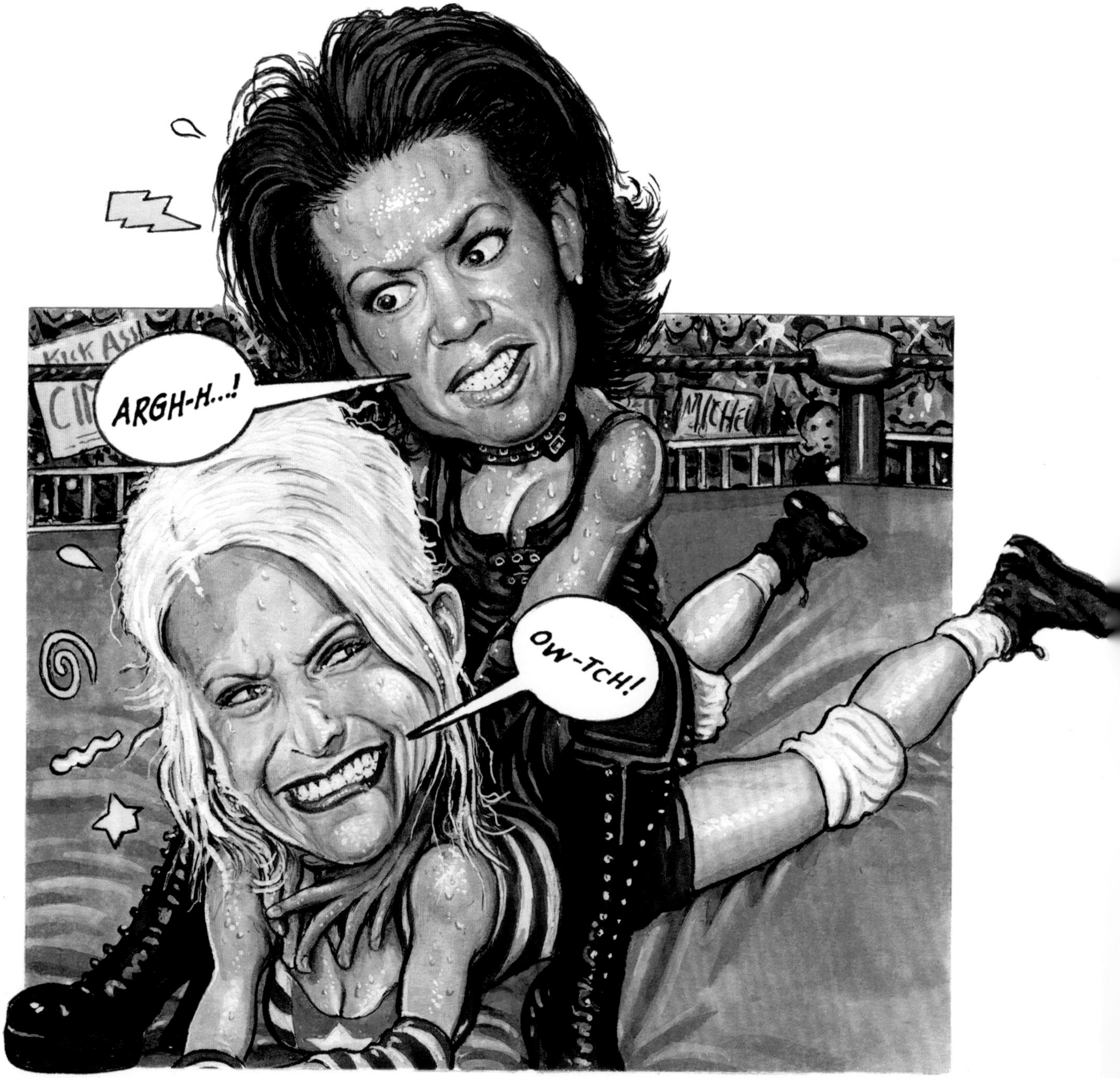
ARGH-H...!
OW-TCH!

"BEDTIME WITH JOHN & CINDY."

THE NEW REPUBLIC

Cindy and **John McCain** enjoy an intimate moment.

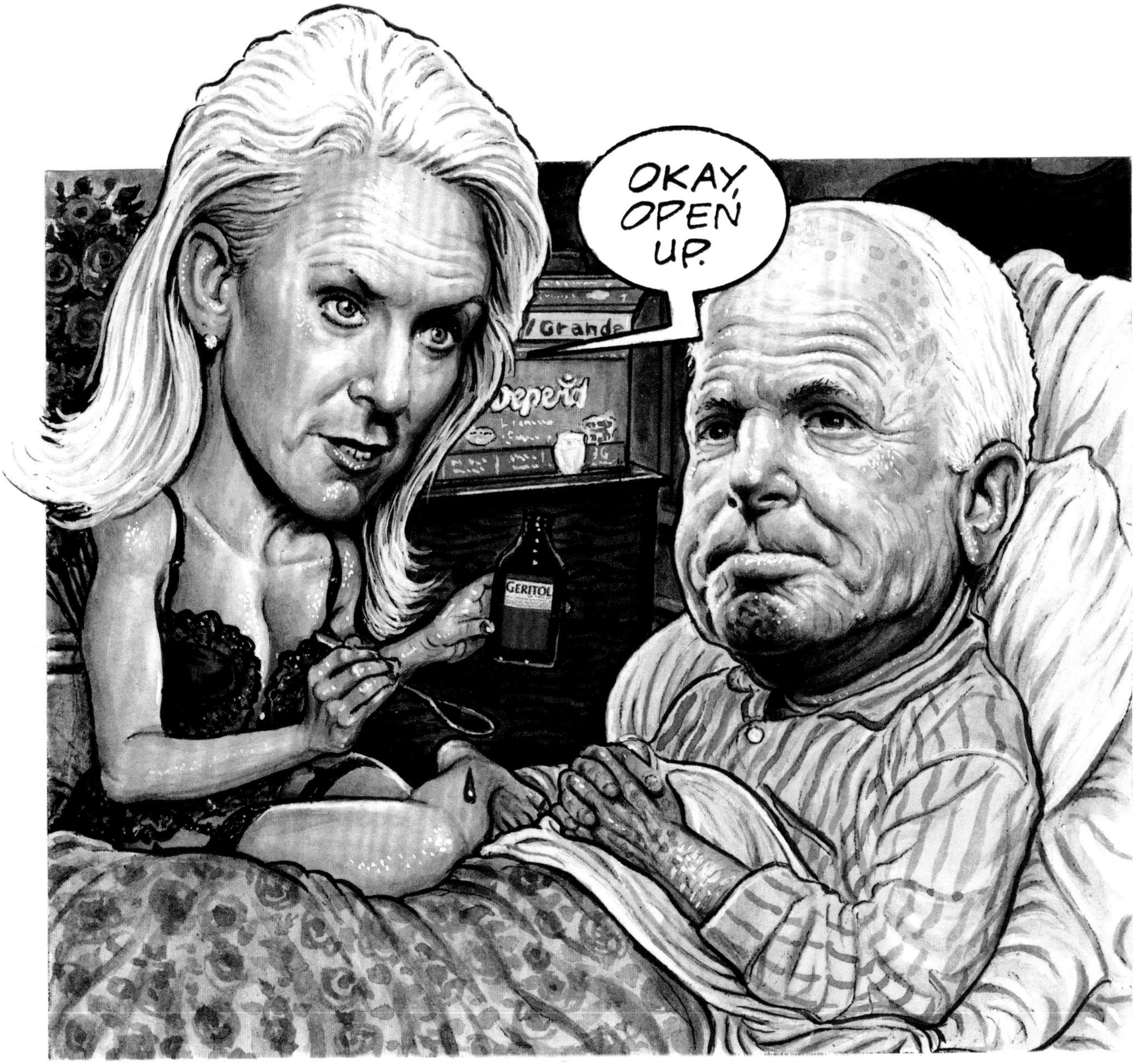
OKAY, OPEN UP.
Grande
GERITOL

"BARACK OBAMA,
***SUPERSTAR.*"**

TIME

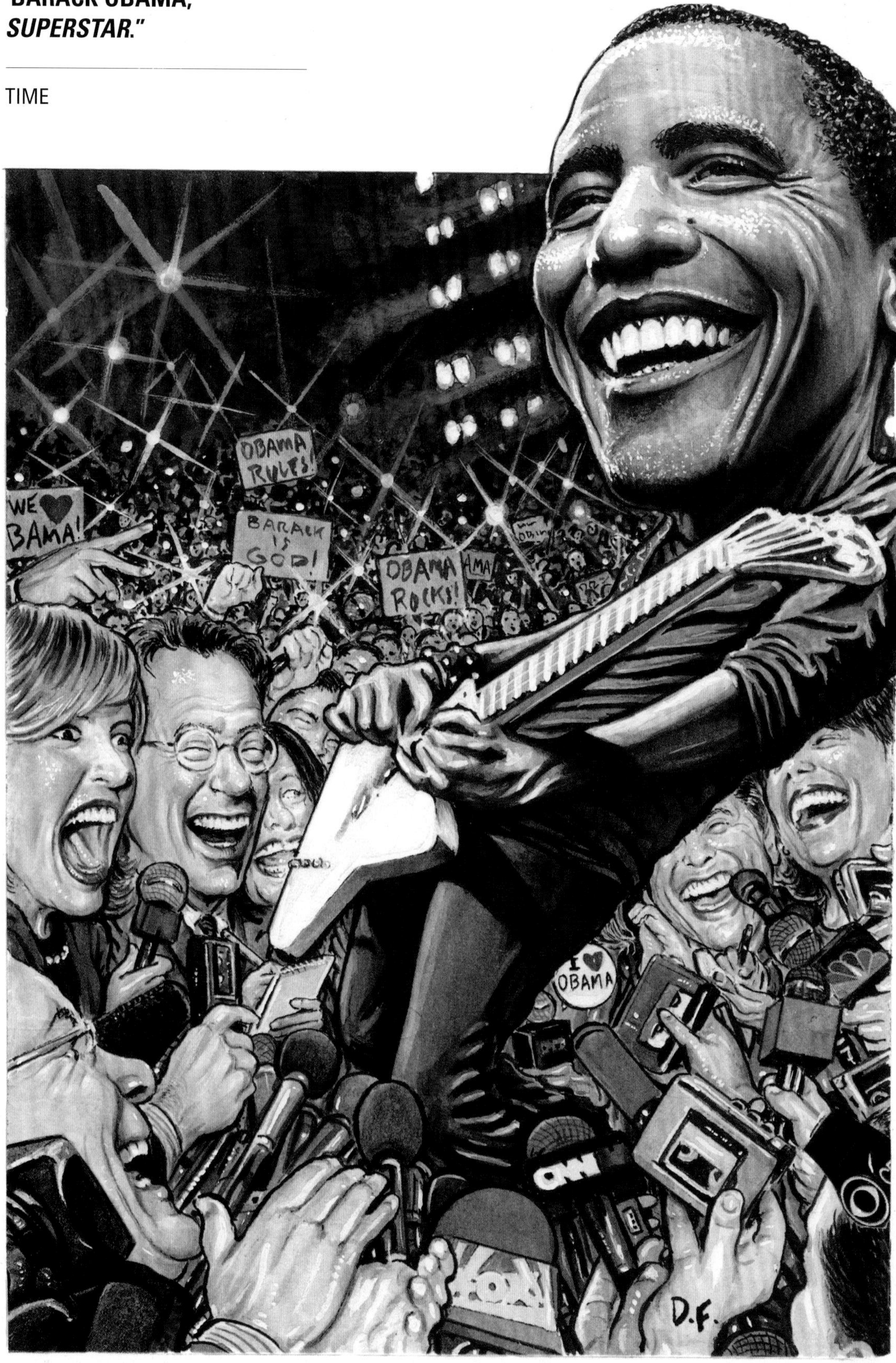
OBAMA RULES!
WE ♥ OBAMA!
BARACK IS GOD!
OBAMA ROCKS!
I ♥ OBAMA
CNN
FOX
D.F.

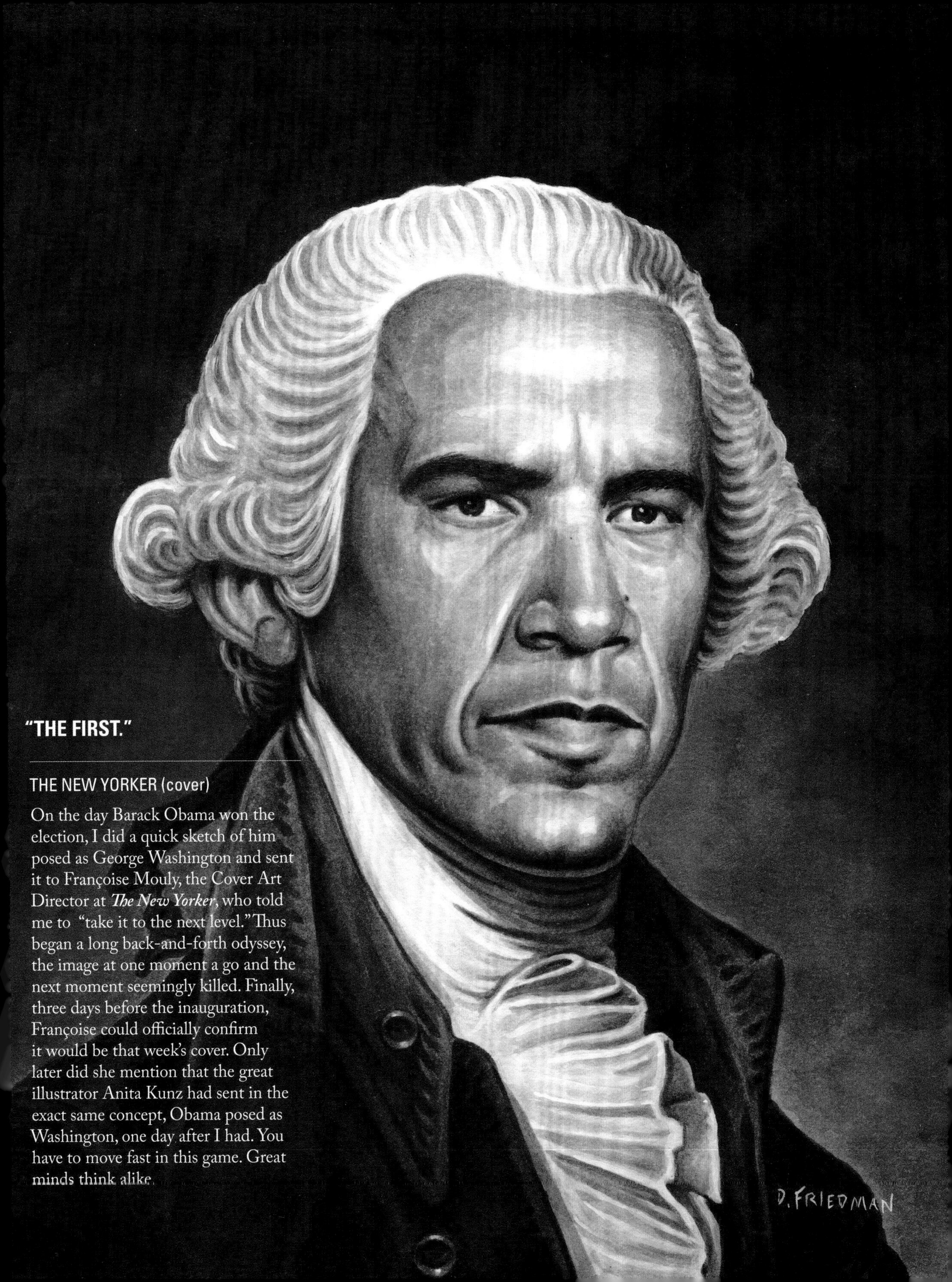
D. FRIEDMAN

"THE FIRST."

THE NEW YORKER (cover)

On the day Barack Obama won the election, I did a quick sketch of him posed as George Washington and sent it to Françoise Mouly, the Cover Art Director at *The New Yorker*, who told me to "take it to the next level." Thus began a long back-and-forth odyssey, the image at one moment a go and the next moment seemingly killed. Finally, three days before the inauguration, Françoise could officially confirm it would be that week's cover. Only later did she mention that the great illustrator Anita Kunz had sent in the exact same concept, Obama posed as Washington, one day after I had. You have to move fast in this game. Great minds think alike.

"THE QUITTER & THE BULLSHITTER."

THE NEW REPUBLIC

Sarah Palin and **Joe the Plumber** rehearse for 2012.

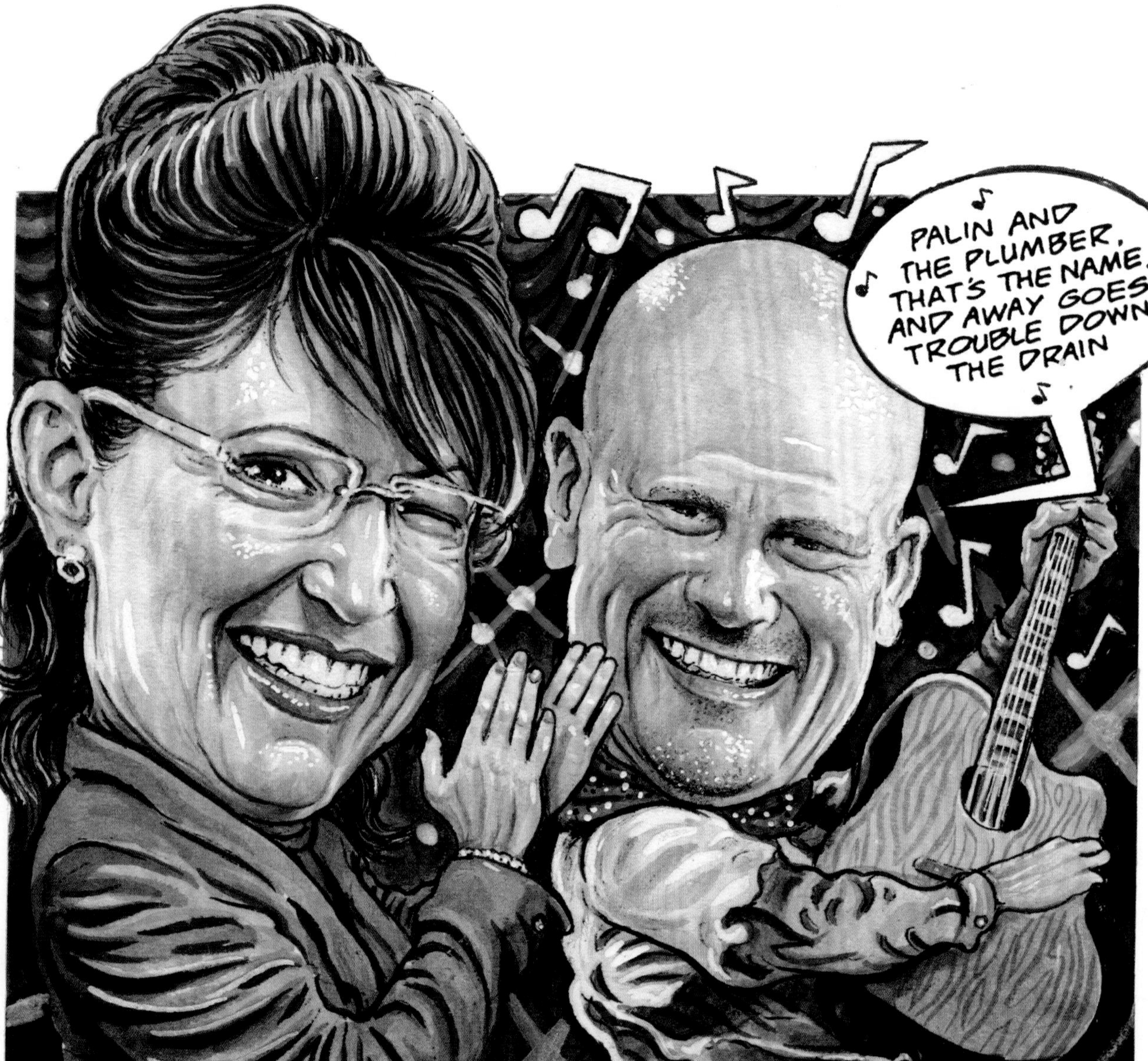
PALIN AND THE PLUMBER, THAT'S THE NAME. AND AWAY GOES TROUBLE DOWN THE DRAIN

"OBAMA SEASON."

THE NEW REPUBLIC

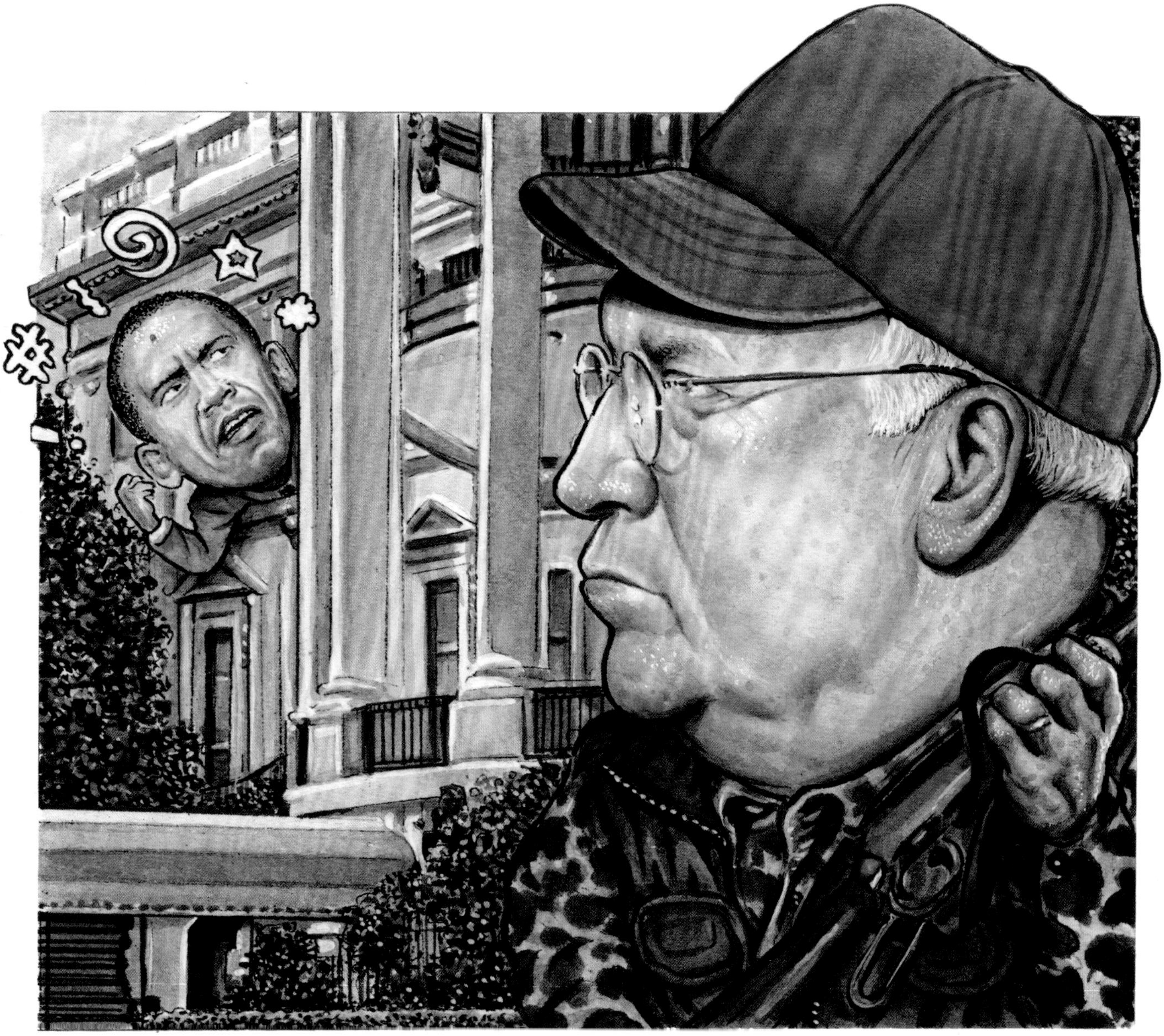

"KEITH & SEAN."

THE NEW REPUBLIC

Keith Olbermann and **Sean Hannity** discuss the issues.

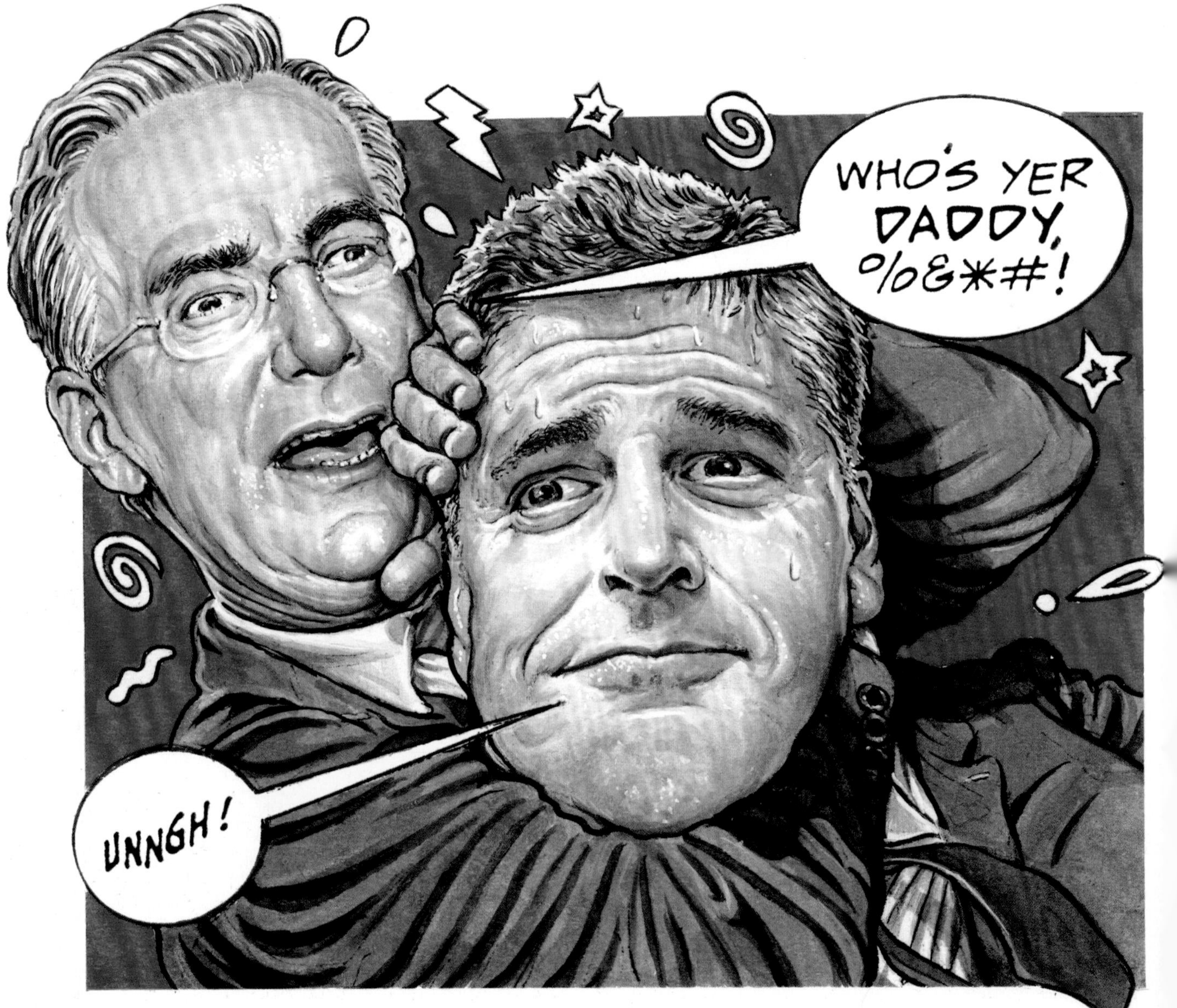
WHO'S YER DADDY, %&*#!
UNNGH!

"THE NEW GODFATHER."

THE NEW REPUBLIC

GOP Party Chairman **Michael Steele** pays respects to his *padrone*.

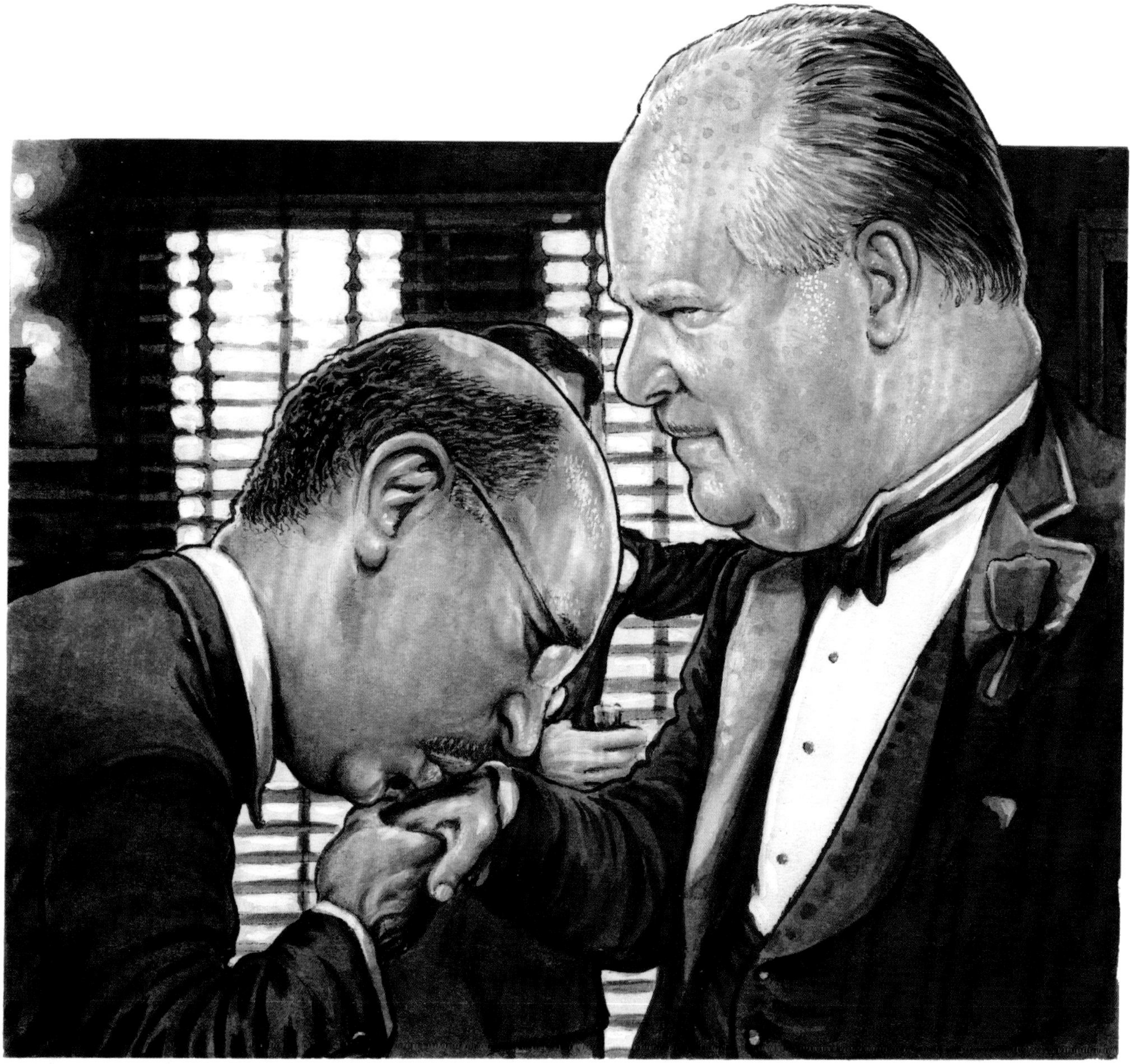

"CIGARETTE BREAK."

THE NEW REPUBLIC

The new President steals time for a smoke.

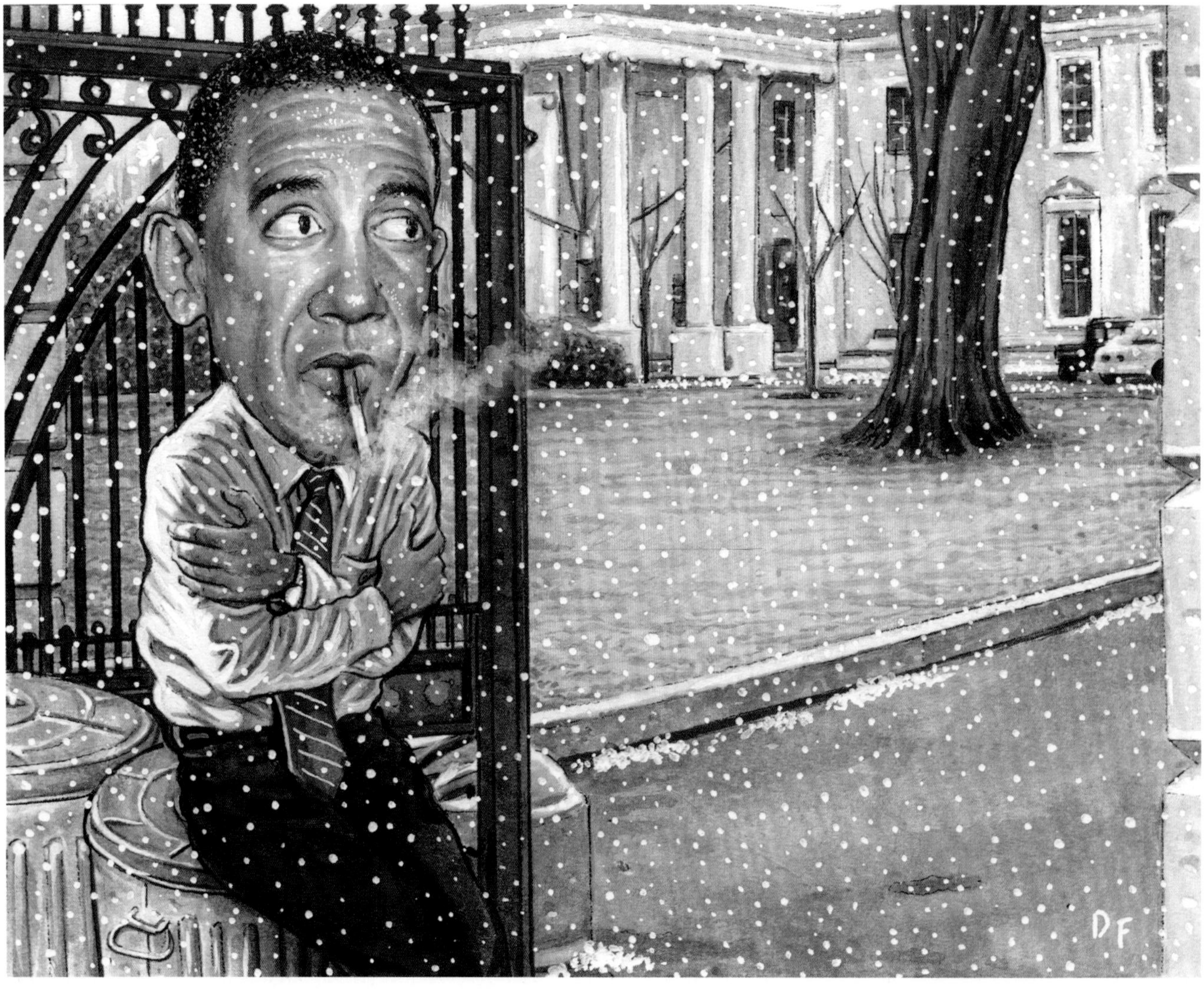
DF

"YOU CAN'T WIN, TIMOTHY GEITHNER."

THE NEW REPUBLIC

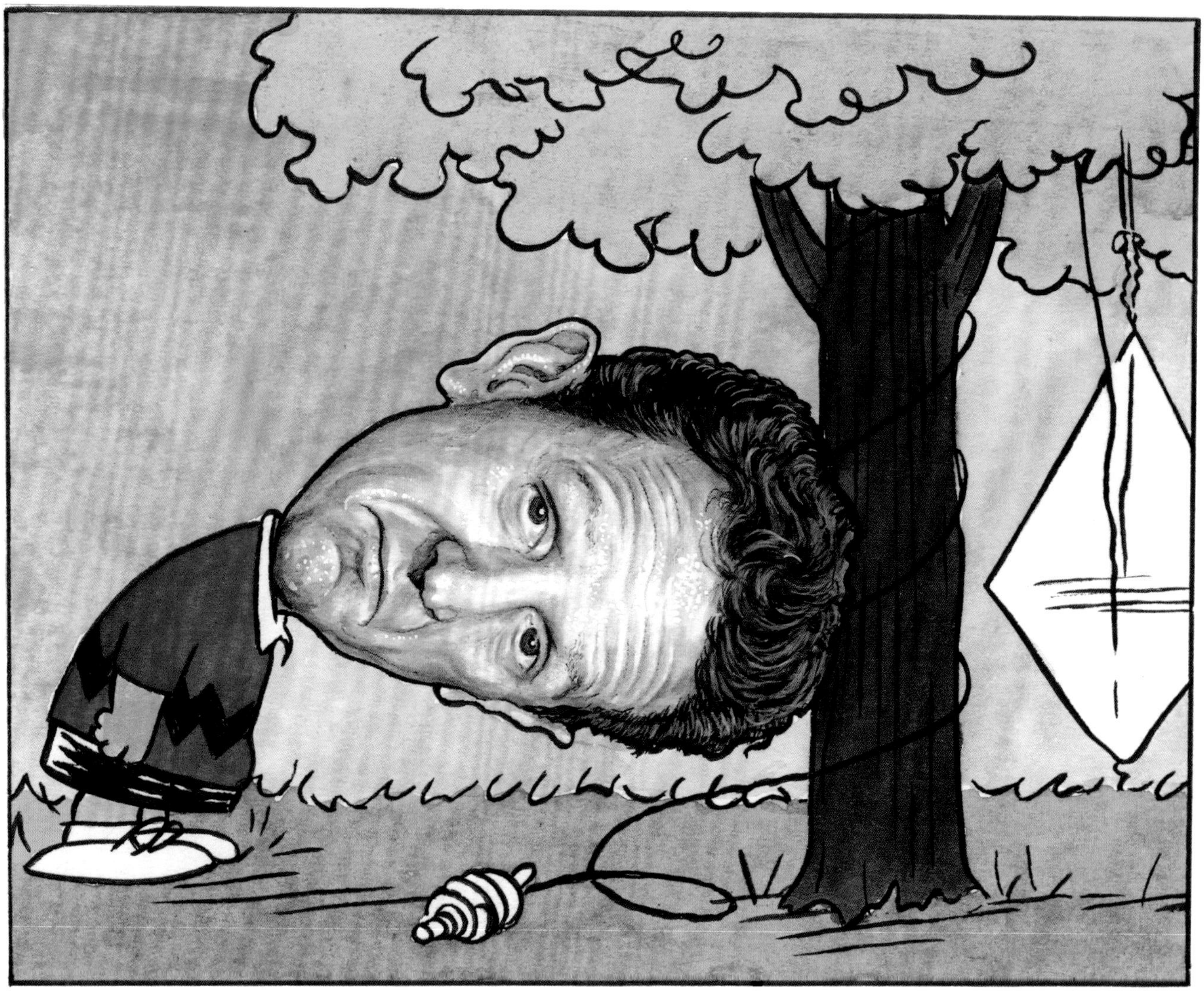

"THE NEW KID IN TOWN."

THE NEW REPUBLIC

Pennsylvania's newest Democratic Junior Senator, **Arlen Specter**.

"BLOOMBERG, ROUND THREE."

THE NEW YORK OBSERVER (unpublished)

Mike Bloomberg takes the oath as NY Mayor for the third time. This piece was "killed" for a "Mike as *Avatar*" image.

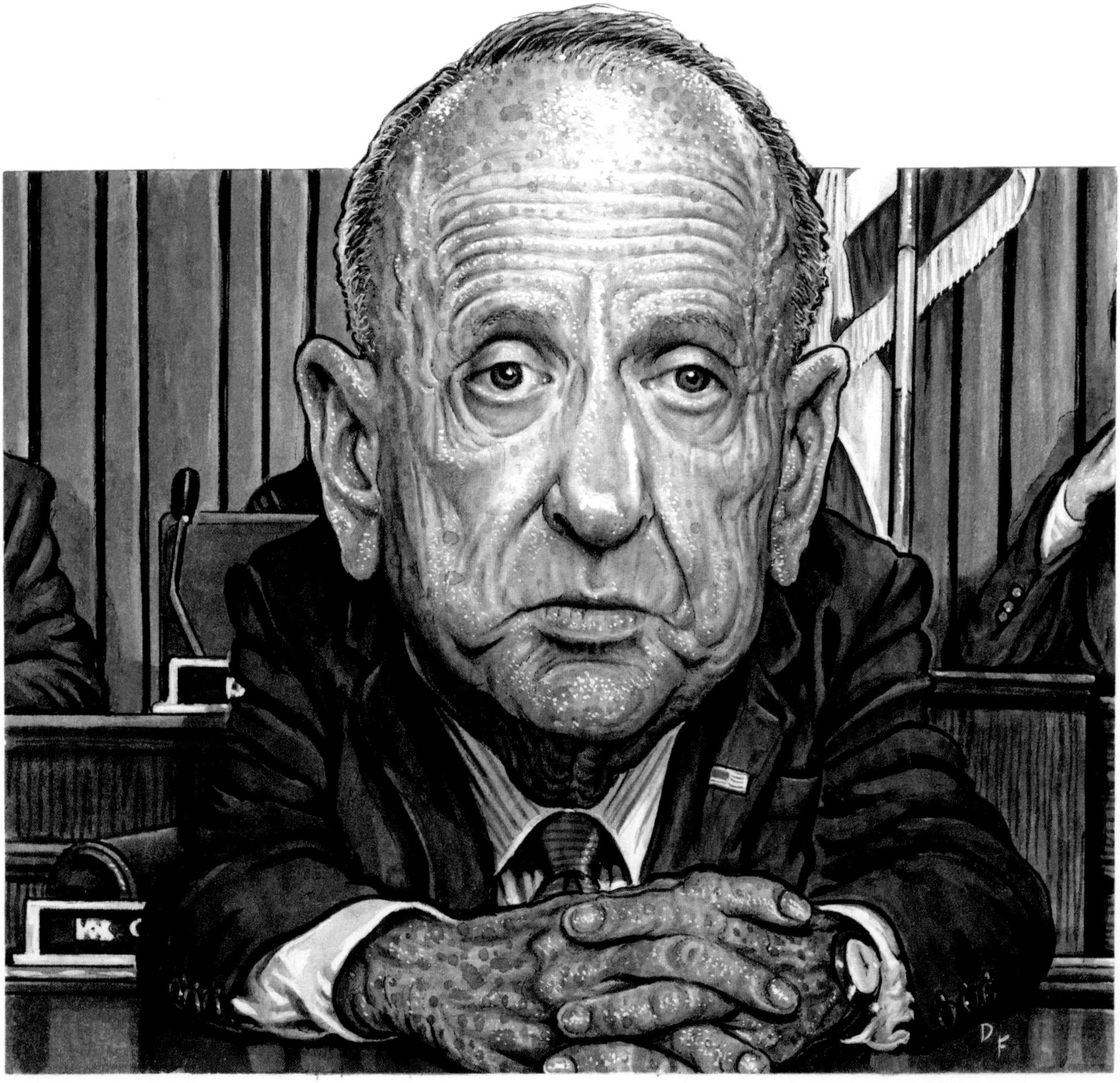
DF

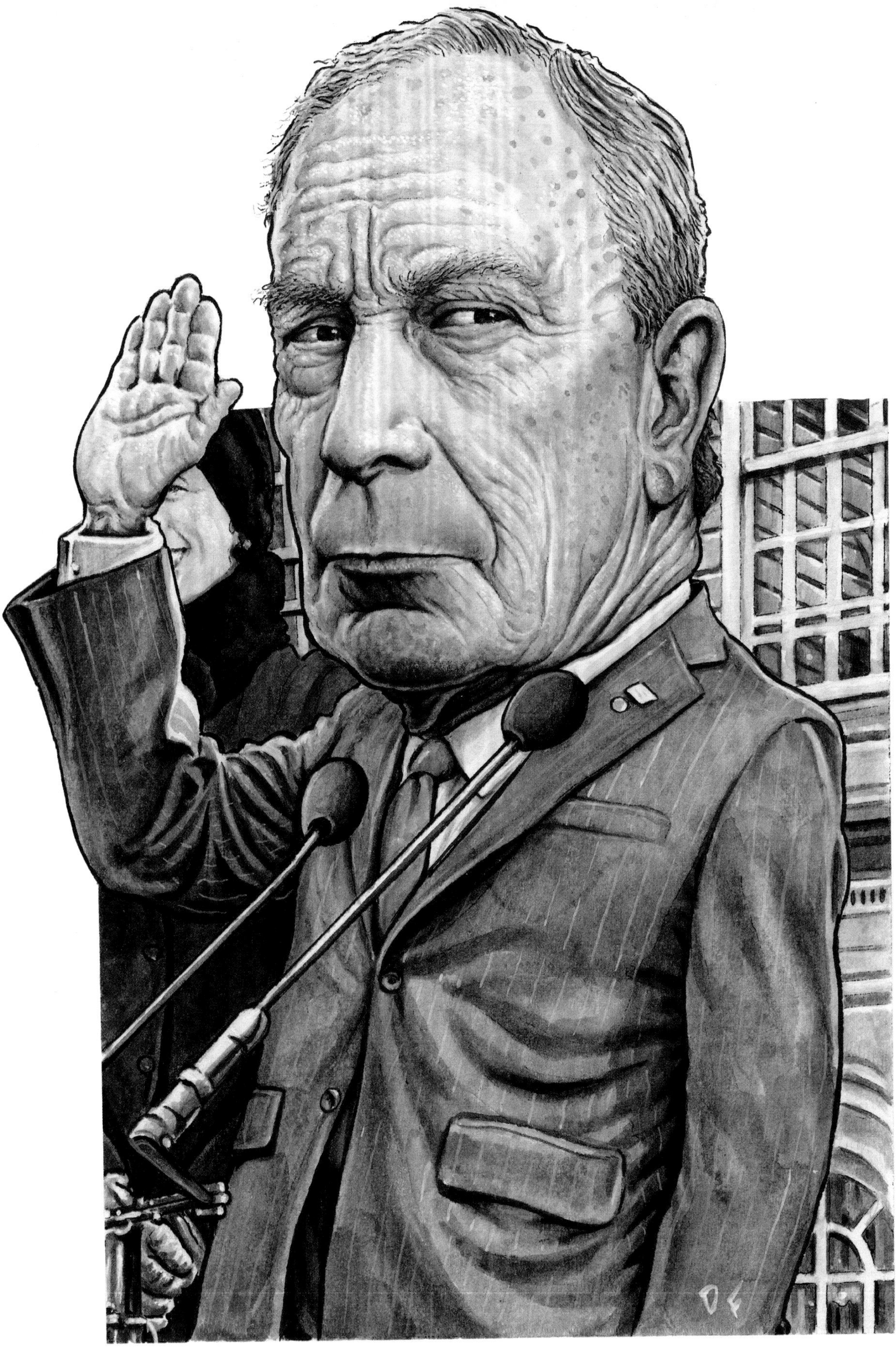

"SARAH'S BIG GAME."

THE NEW REPUBLIC

Sarah Palin savors Levi Johnston's pictorial in the new *Playgirl*.

Concept by K. Bidus, who awakened me at 3 A.M. to relate it to me.

"SWINE FLU."

THE WEEK (cover)

A sick pig.

Get it?

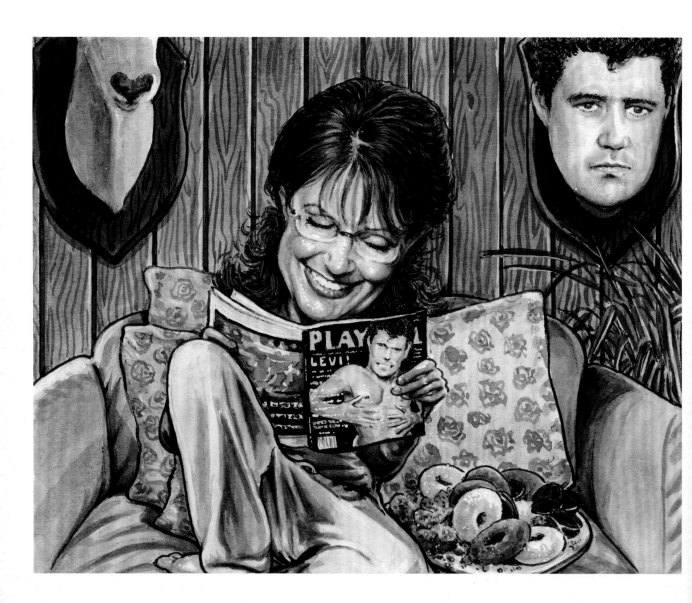

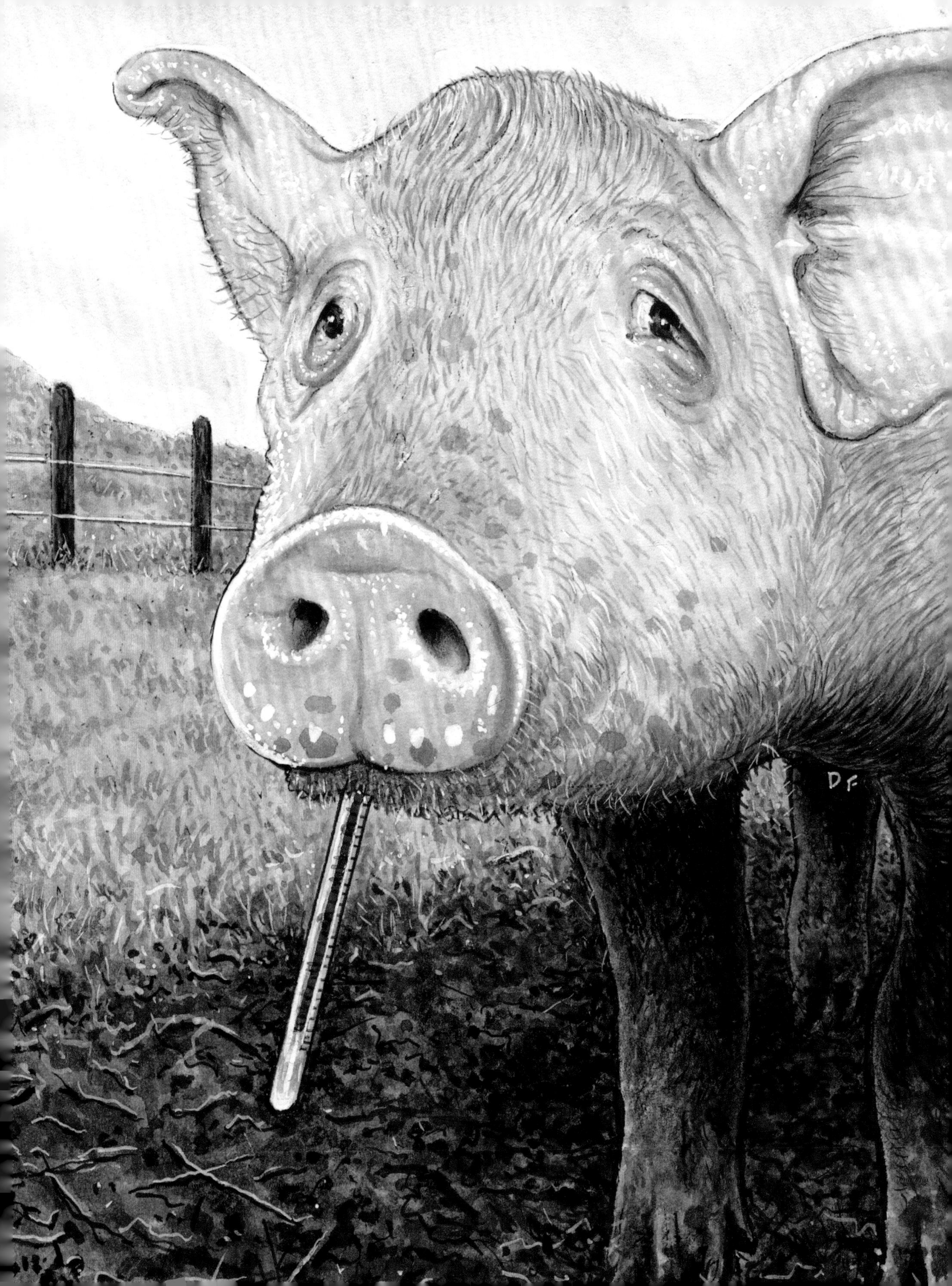

"THE CAMPAIGN THAT WILL NEVER END."

THE NEW REPUBLIC

In the Fall of 2035, the **Coleman-Franken** contest remains still unsettled.

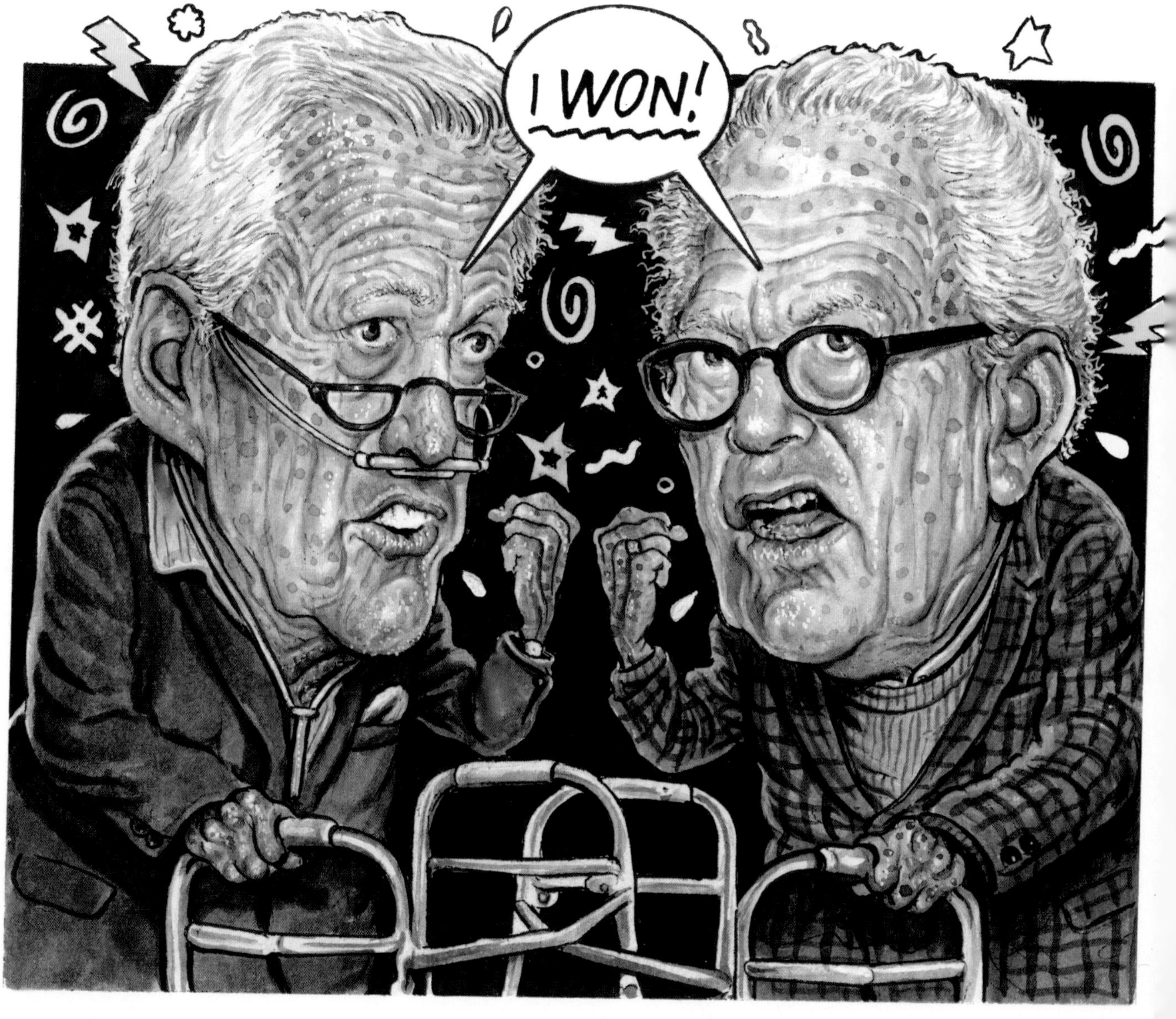
I WON!

"BOBBY JINDAL LOOKS BACK."

THE NEW REPUBLIC

Little **Bobby Jindal** begins writing his memoirs.

"ALICE IN WACKOLAND."

FOLLOWING SPREAD

THE NATION

Wingnuts **Glenn Beck** as The Mad Hatter, **Sarah Palin** as The Queen of Hearts, and **Rush Limbaugh** as The Cheshire Cat. This image was "flipped" when it appeared on the cover because the editors felt the mailing label would obscure poor, innocent Alice. They were also pushing me to make Beck look more "evil," which I tried to do, but as I pointed out, he's basically a pudgy-faced, nondescript guy, a former "comic" who looks like every other guy performing at "Chuckles" or "Wacky's" on any given night. And besides that, The Mad Hatter wasn't an evil character, just "mad," so the analogy might get lost down the looking glass.

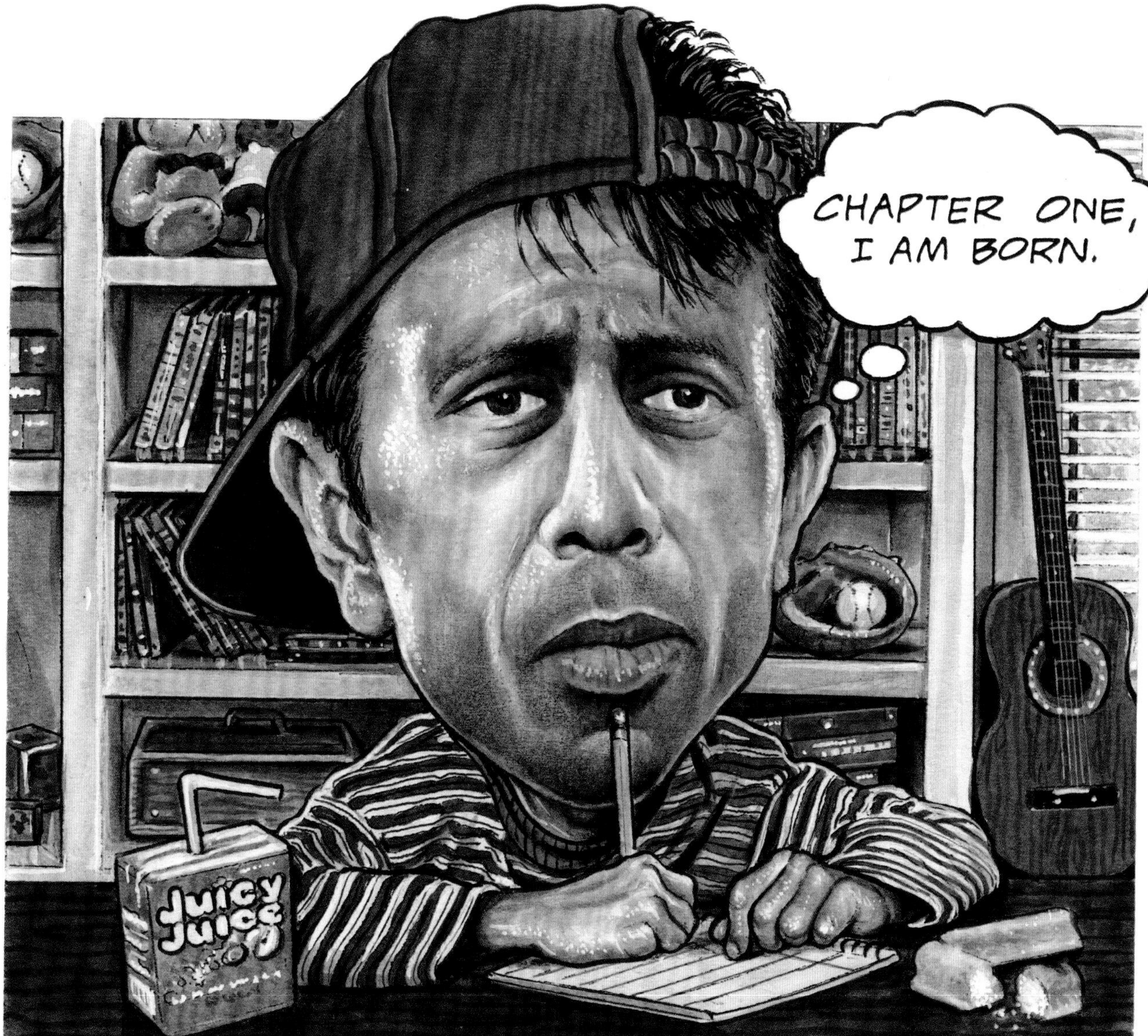
CHAPTER ONE, I AM BORN.
Juicy Juice

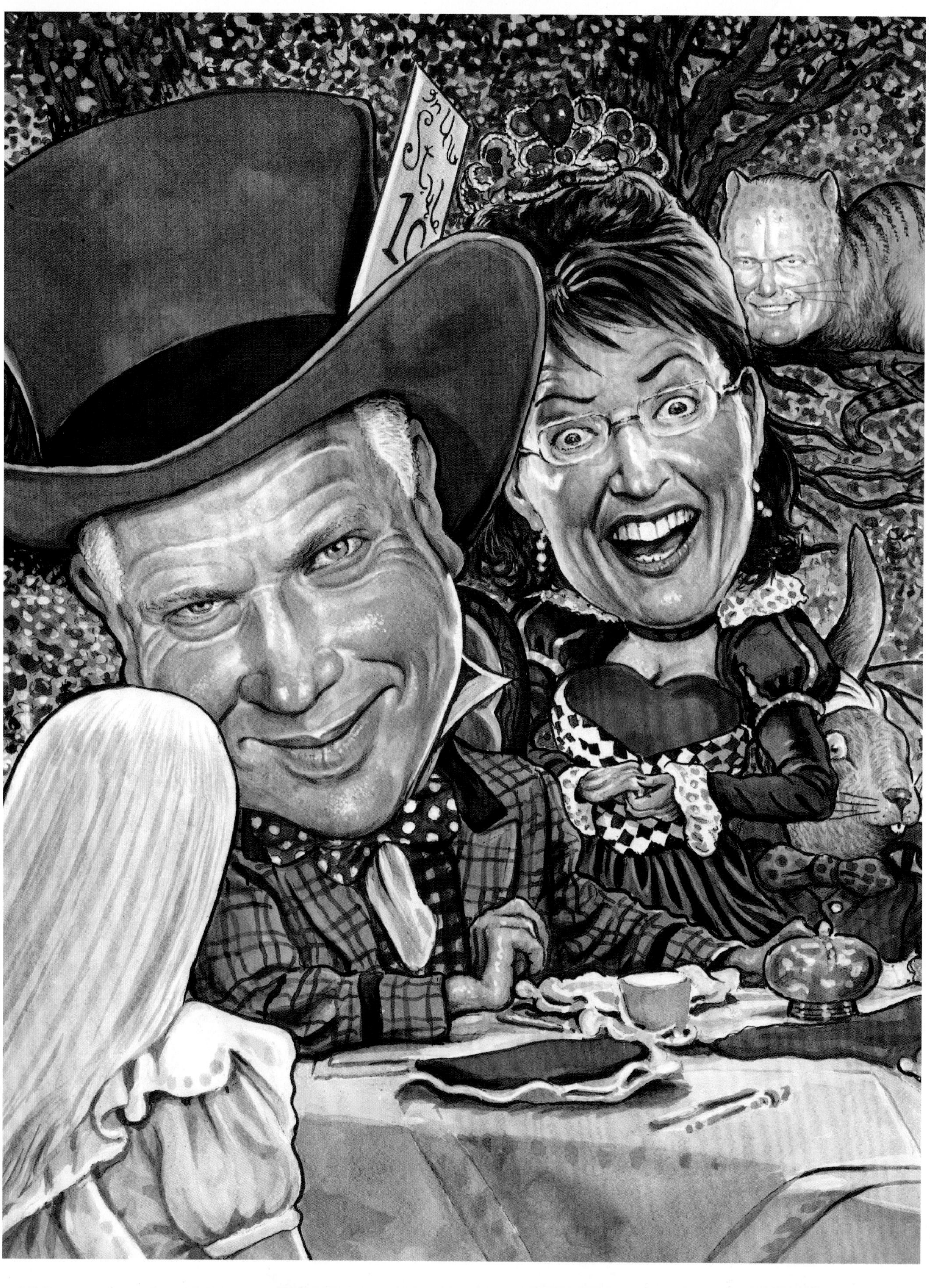
Style
10

SHOWBIZ

"There's no damn business like show business. You have to keep smiling to keep from throwing up."
— Billie Holiday

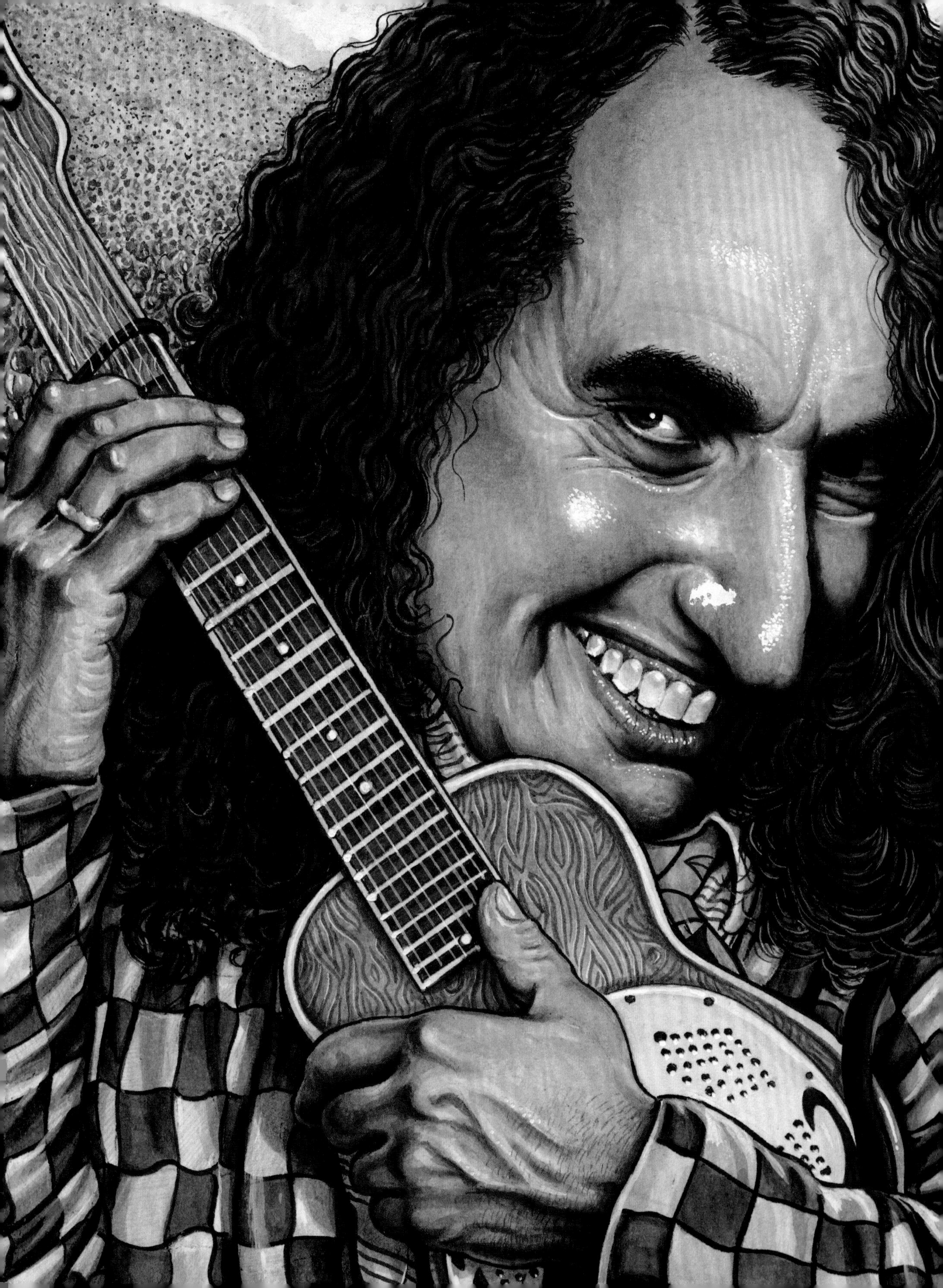

"TINY TIM."

Herbert Khaury a.k.a. Tiny Tim. Posed in the tulip-field.

"RAYMOND SCOTT."

The "Maestro of the Machine Age." Commissioned to celebrate the legendary composer's centennial in 2008.

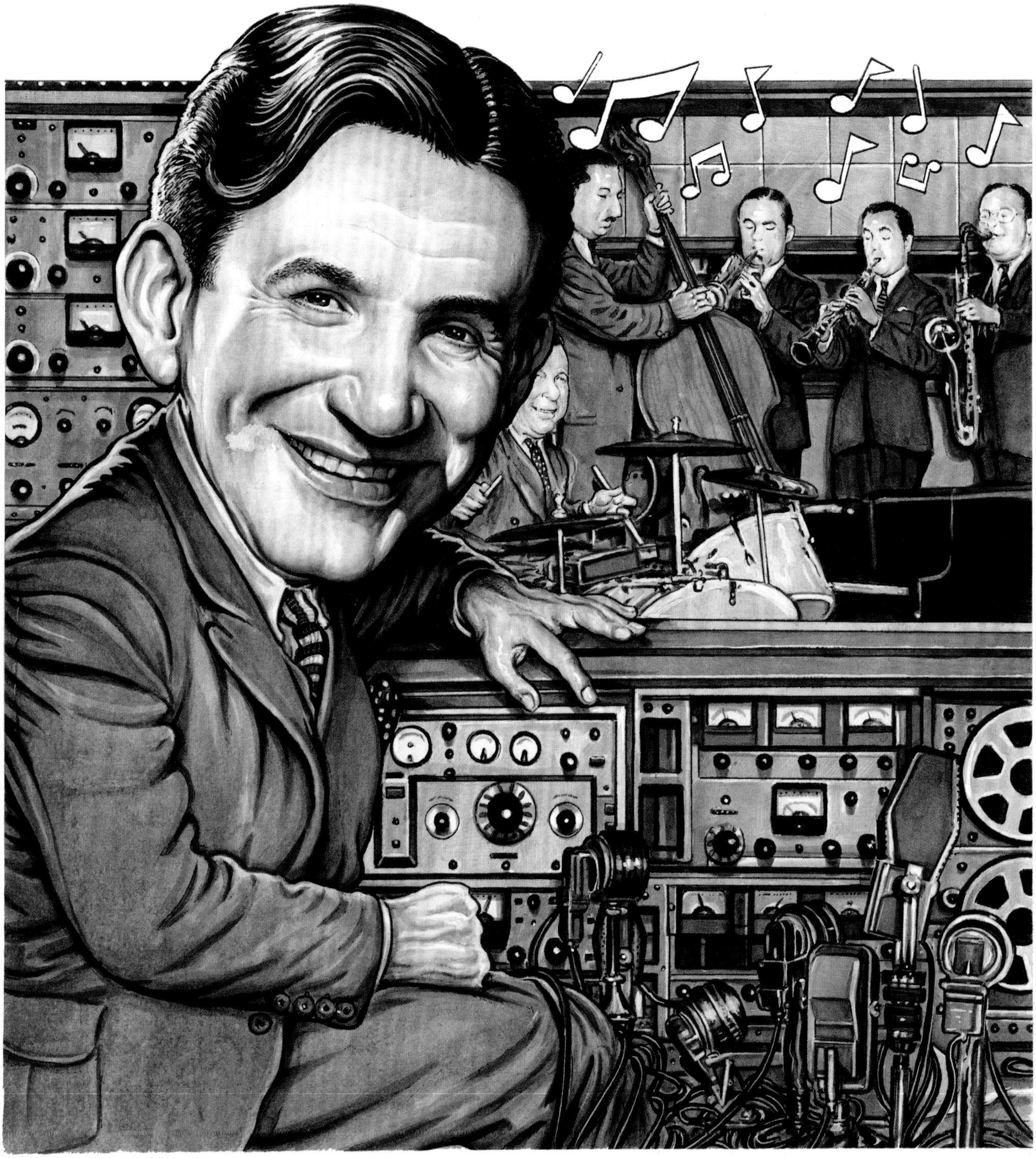

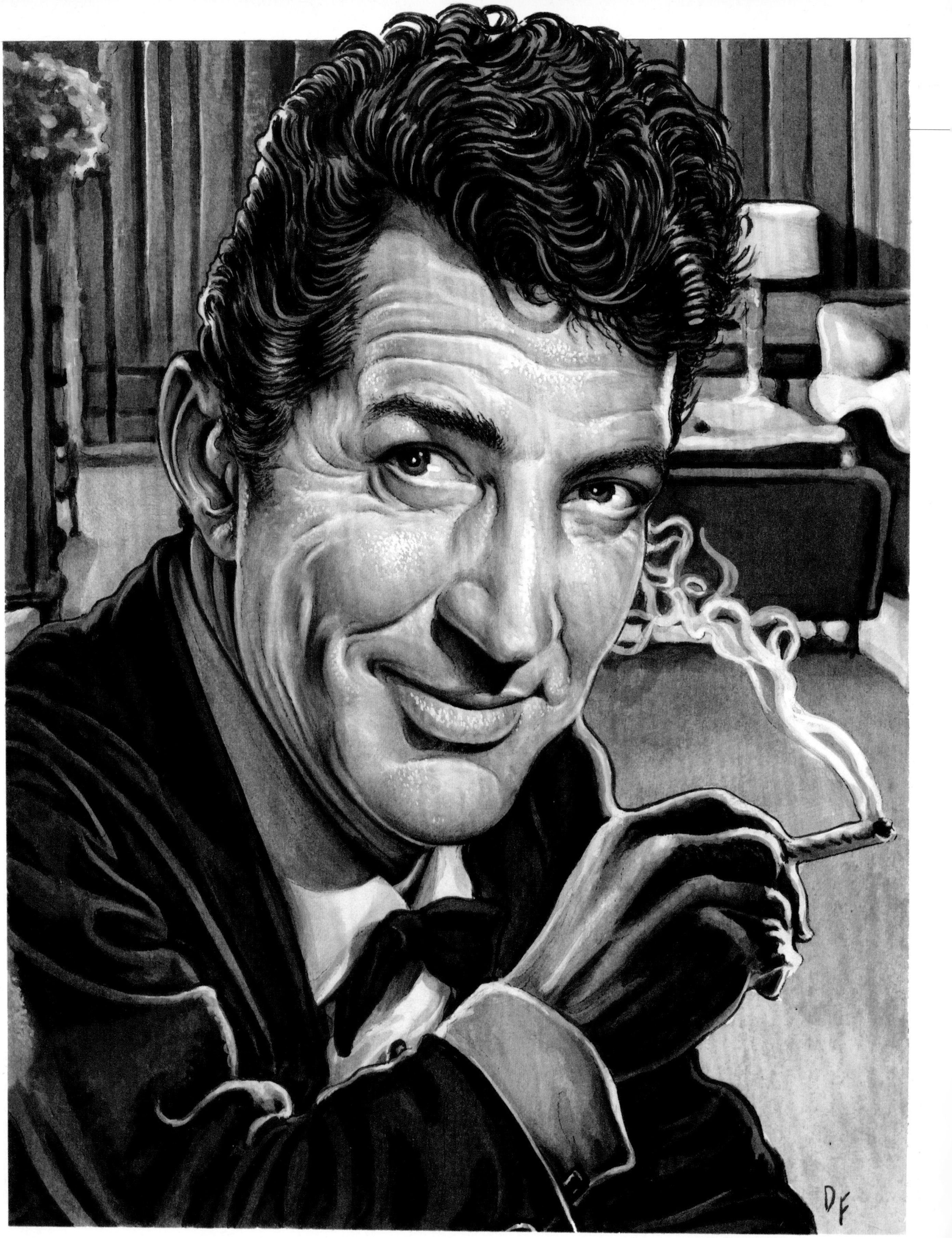
DF

"DINO."

Debonair, seductive crooner, laconic actor, Vegas/Hollywood Rat Pack immortal, the one and only **Dean Martin**.

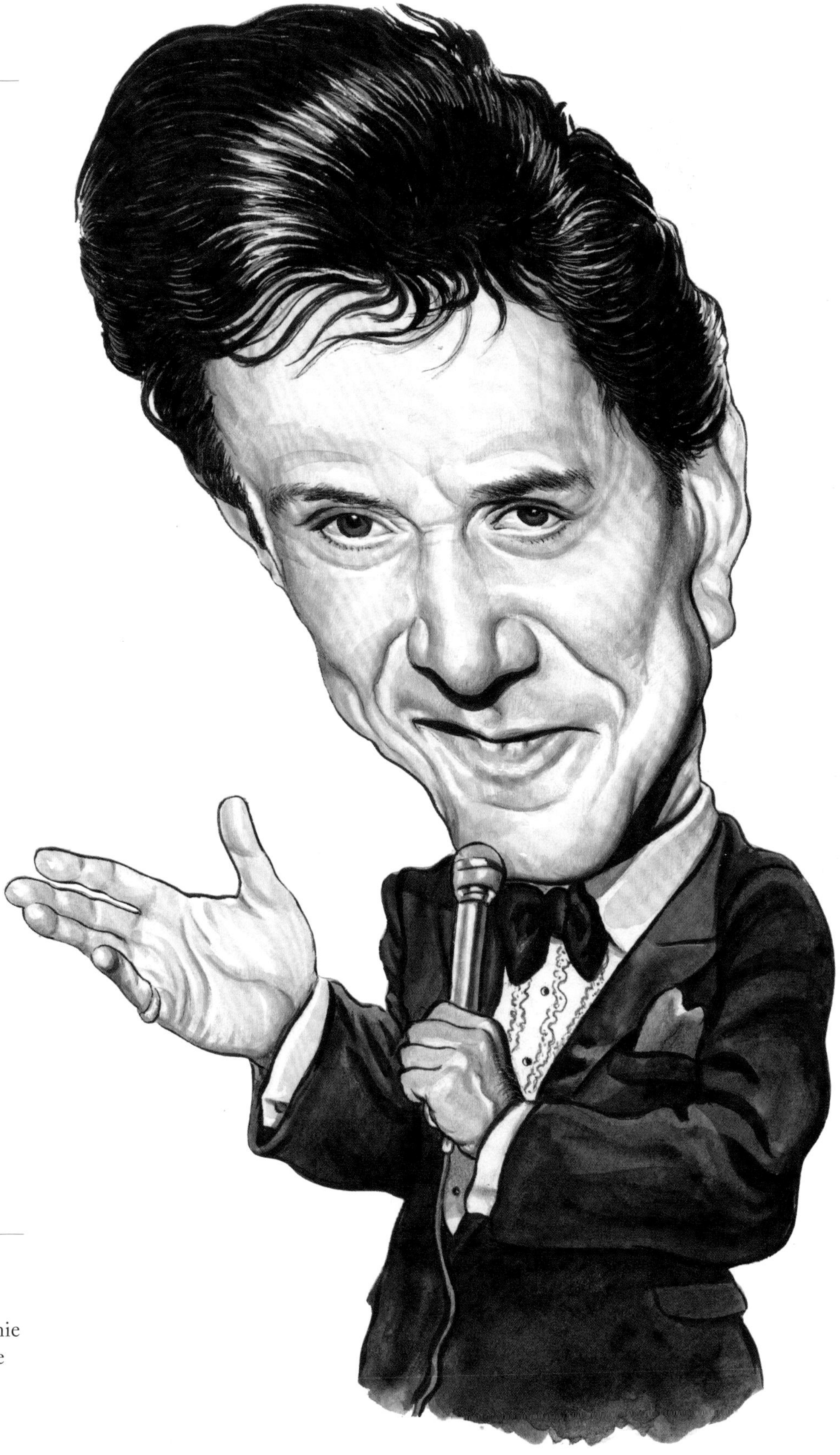

"EDDIE FISHER."

THE WALL STREET JOURNAL

Sometime husband (Debbie Reynolds, Elizabeth Taylor, Connie Stevens), sometime father (Carrie Fisher), sometime singer **Eddie Fisher**.

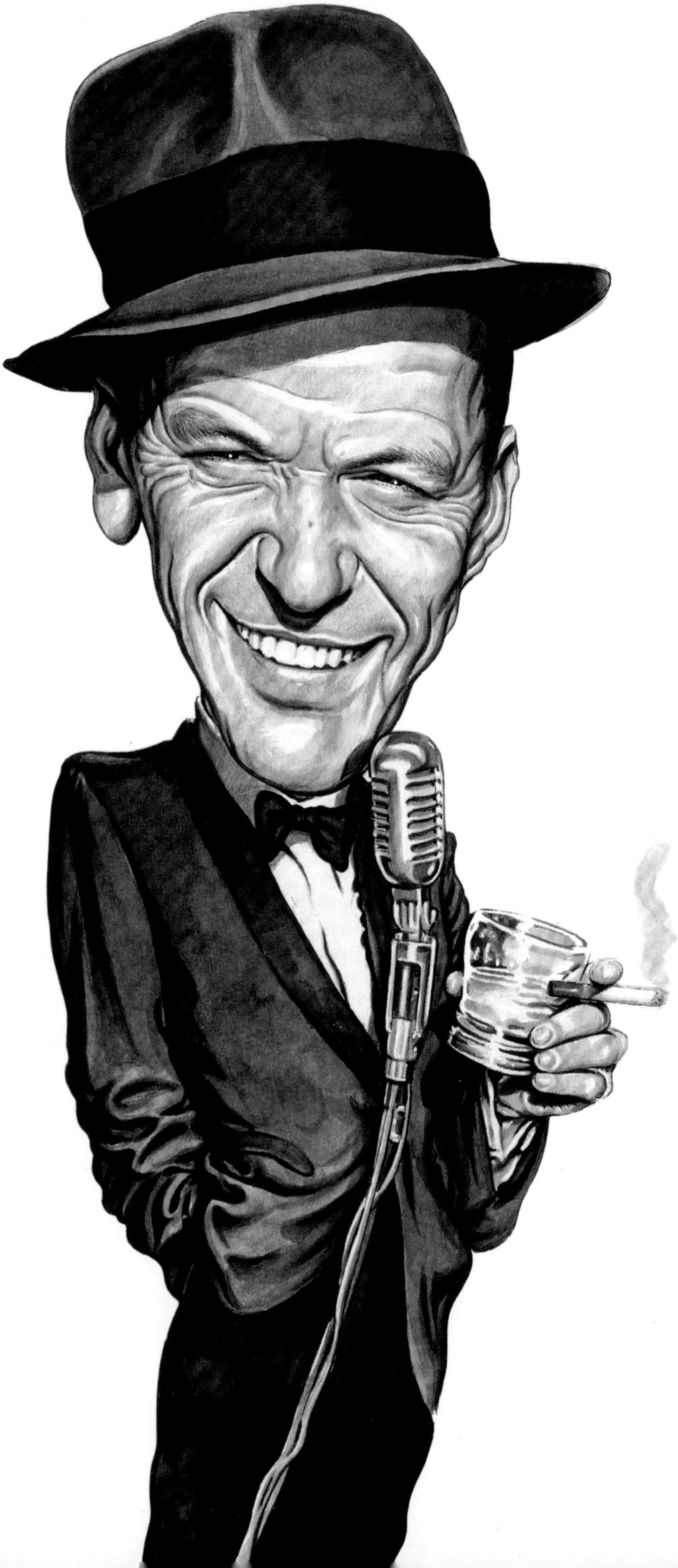

"I'LL BE AROUND."

THE NEW YORK OBSERVER

A portrait of the "Chairman of the Board," **Frank Sinatra,** drawn the weekend he died, for a tribute by director Peter Bogdanovich.

"THEIR WAY."

NEW YORK DAILY NEWS

The three interpretations of the Paul Anka lyriced tune "My Way."

Sex Pistol **Sid Vicious**, tuxedo-clad **Frank Sinatra**, Vegas-era **Elvis Presley**.

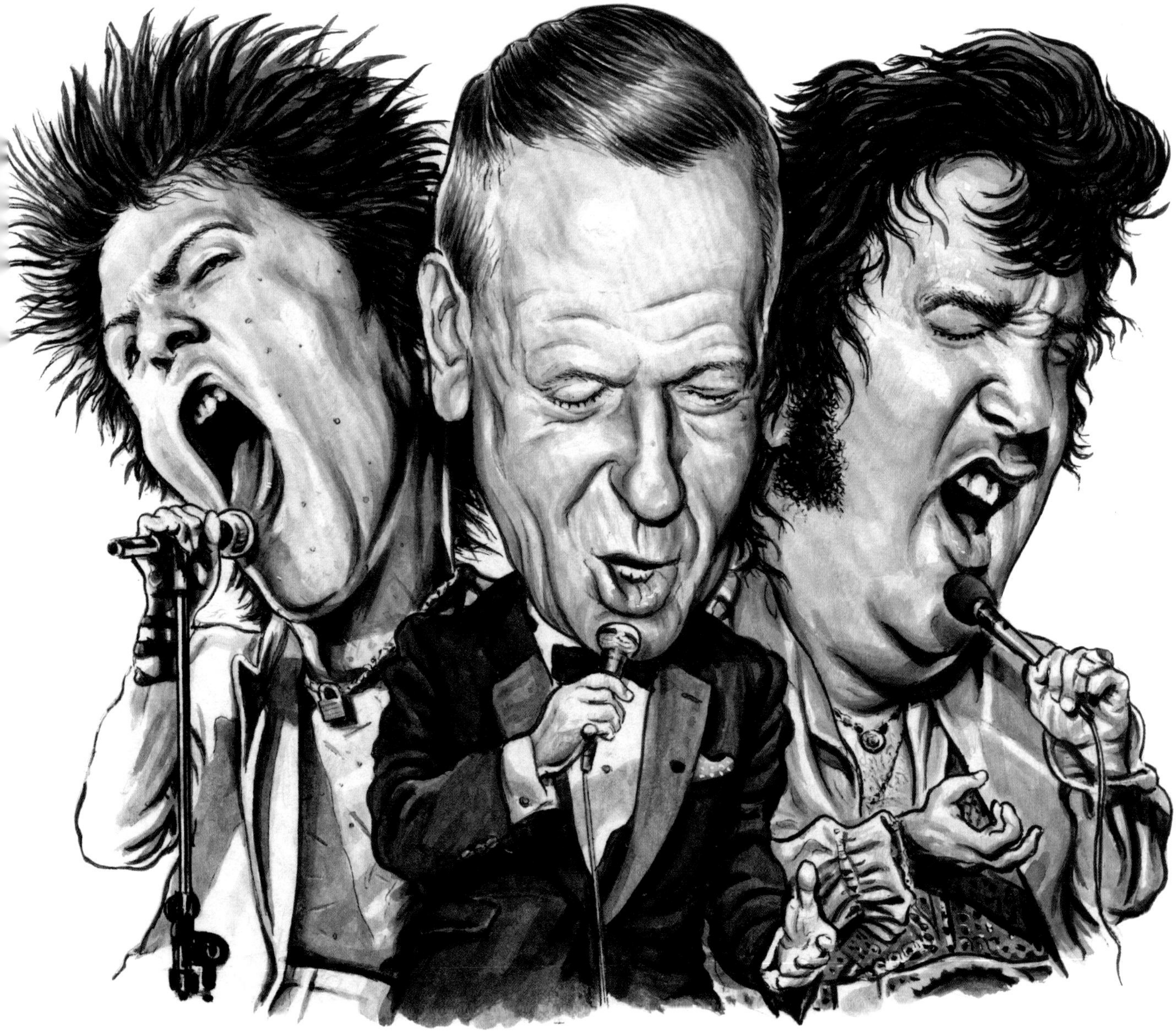

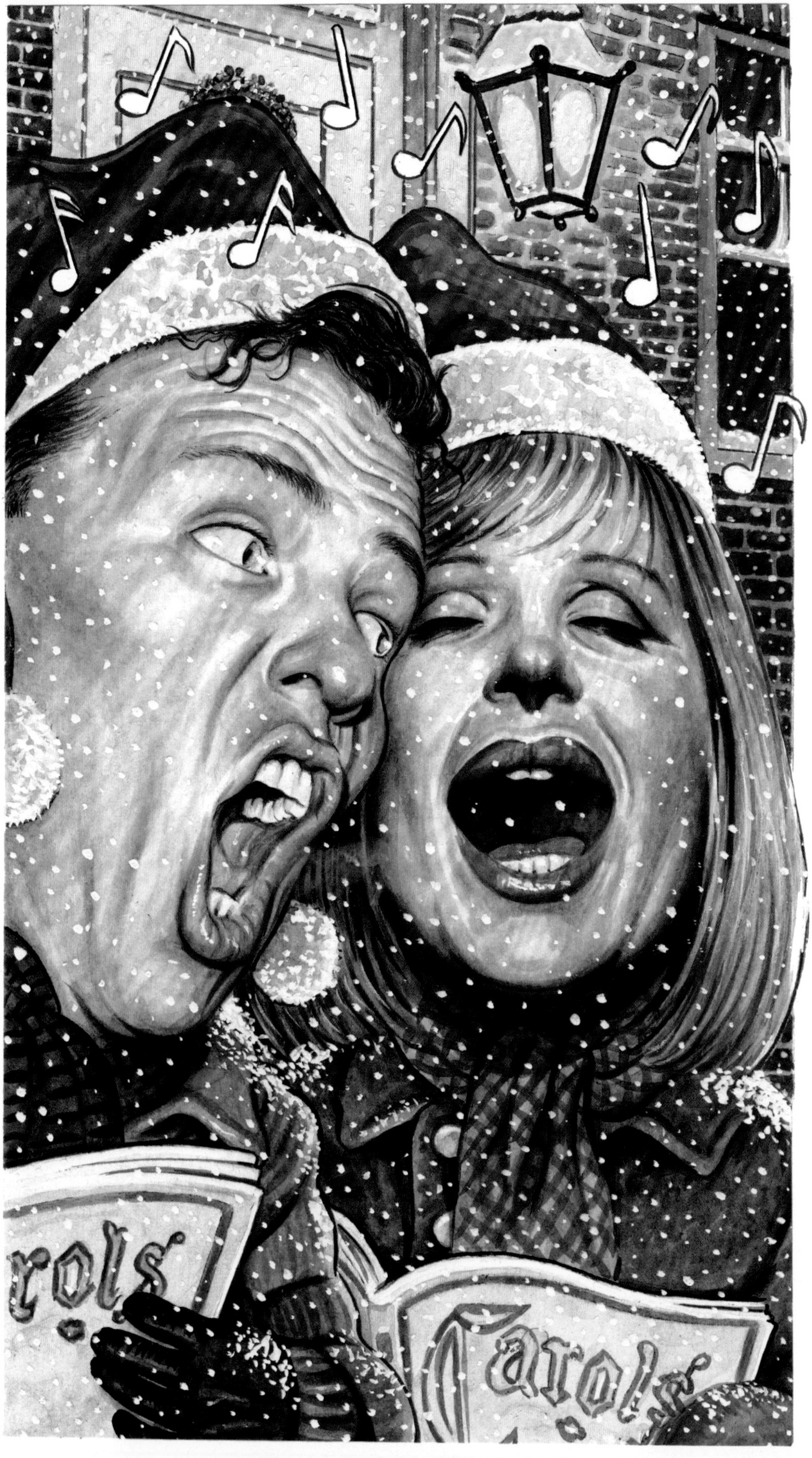
rols
Carols

"CLAUS ENCOUNTERS."

ENTERTAINMENT WEEKLY

New CD compilations by **Frank Sinatra** and **Barbra Streisand** singing Christmas tunes.

"*HANG 'EM HIGH* UPON THE HIGHEST BOUGH."

ENTERTAINMENT WEEKLY

New holiday DVD collections of **Clint Eastwood** and **Judy Garland** films.

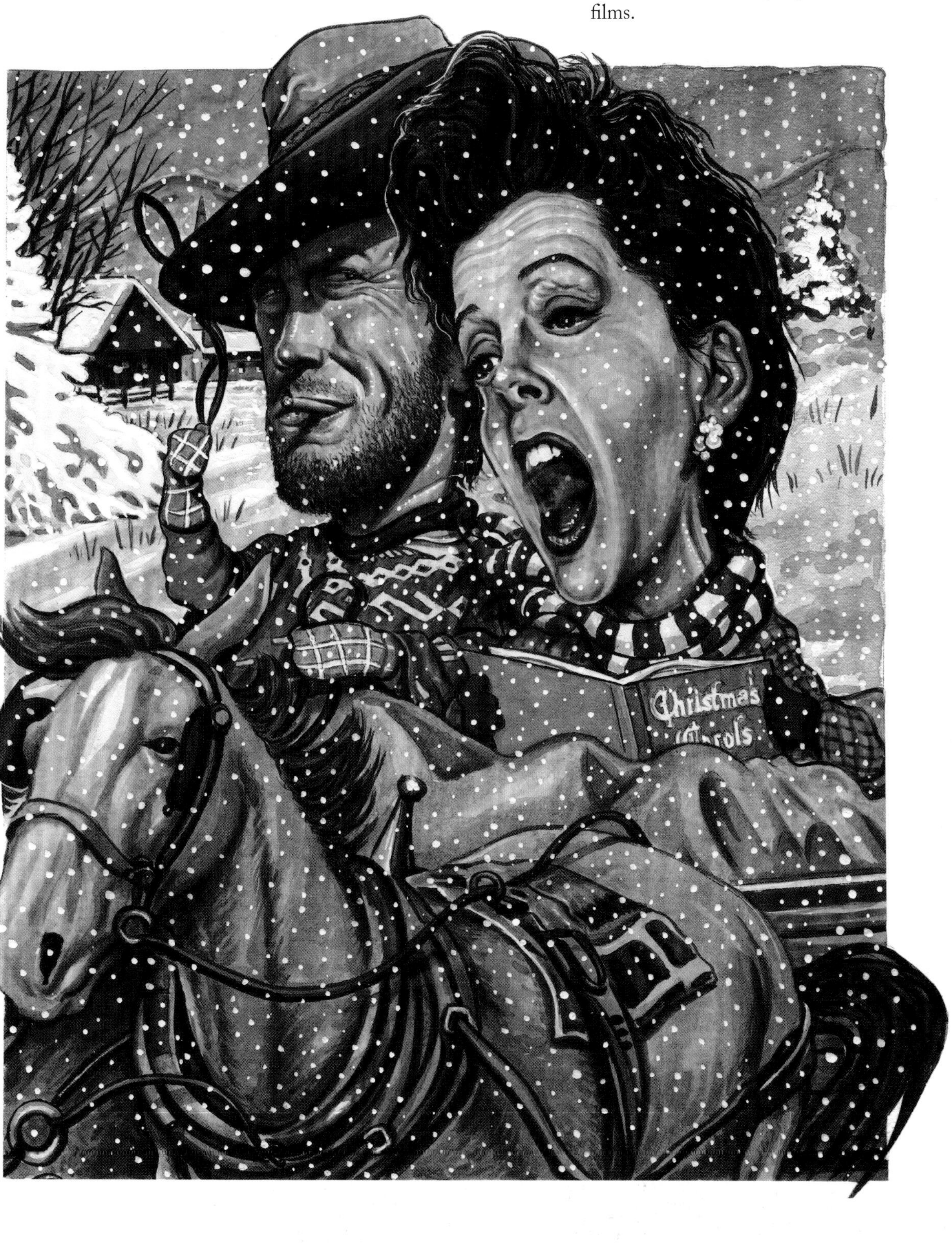
Christmas
Carols

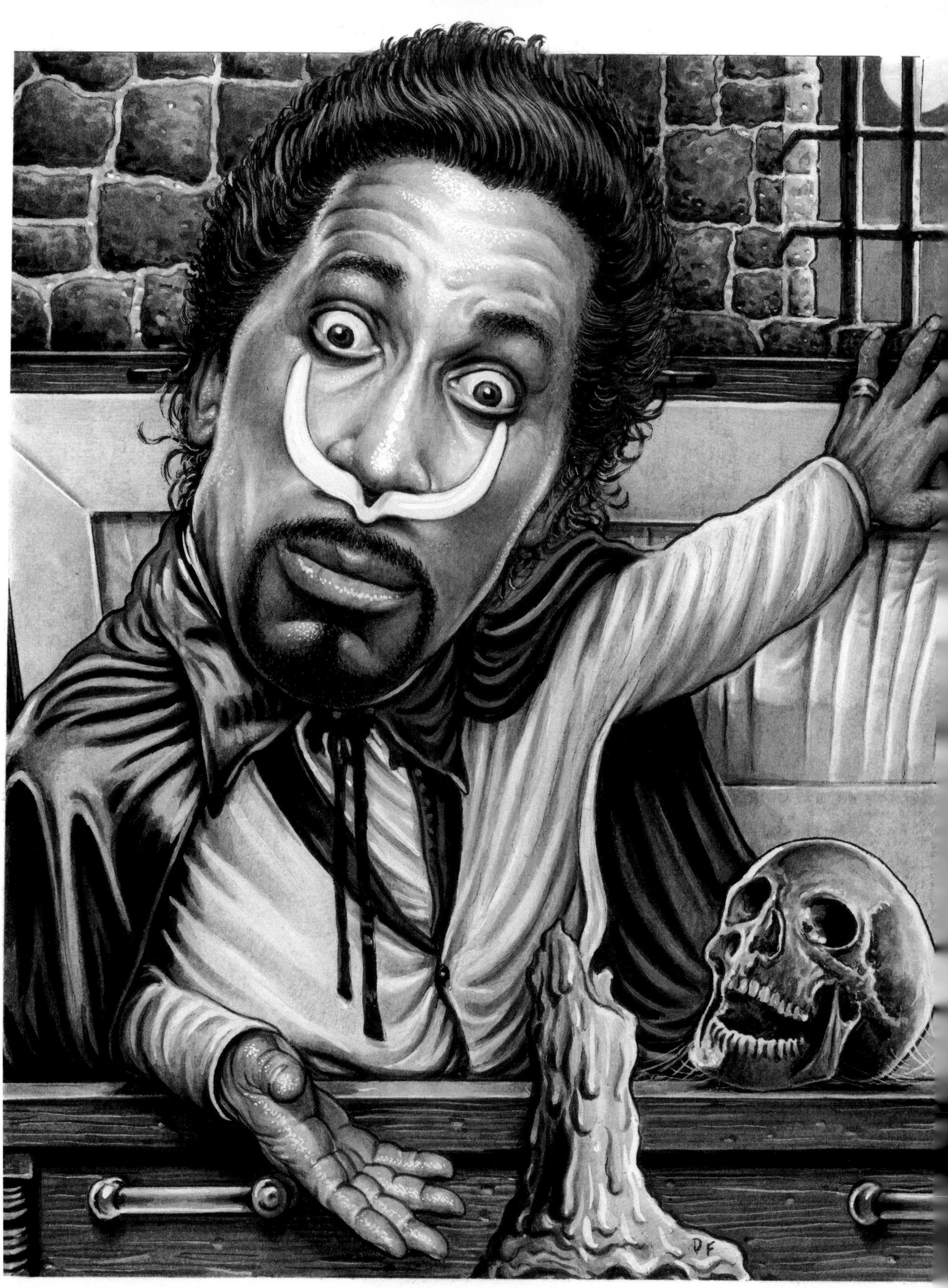

"I PUT A SPELL ON YOU."

Jalacy Hawkins, a.k.a. "Screamin' Jay Hawkins," the original "Shock Rocker," and father of 57 children.

"MR. EXCITEMENT."

BLAB!

Jack Leroy ("Jackie") **Wilson**, "Mr. Excitement," greets his adoring fans outside the Apollo Theatre in Harlem.

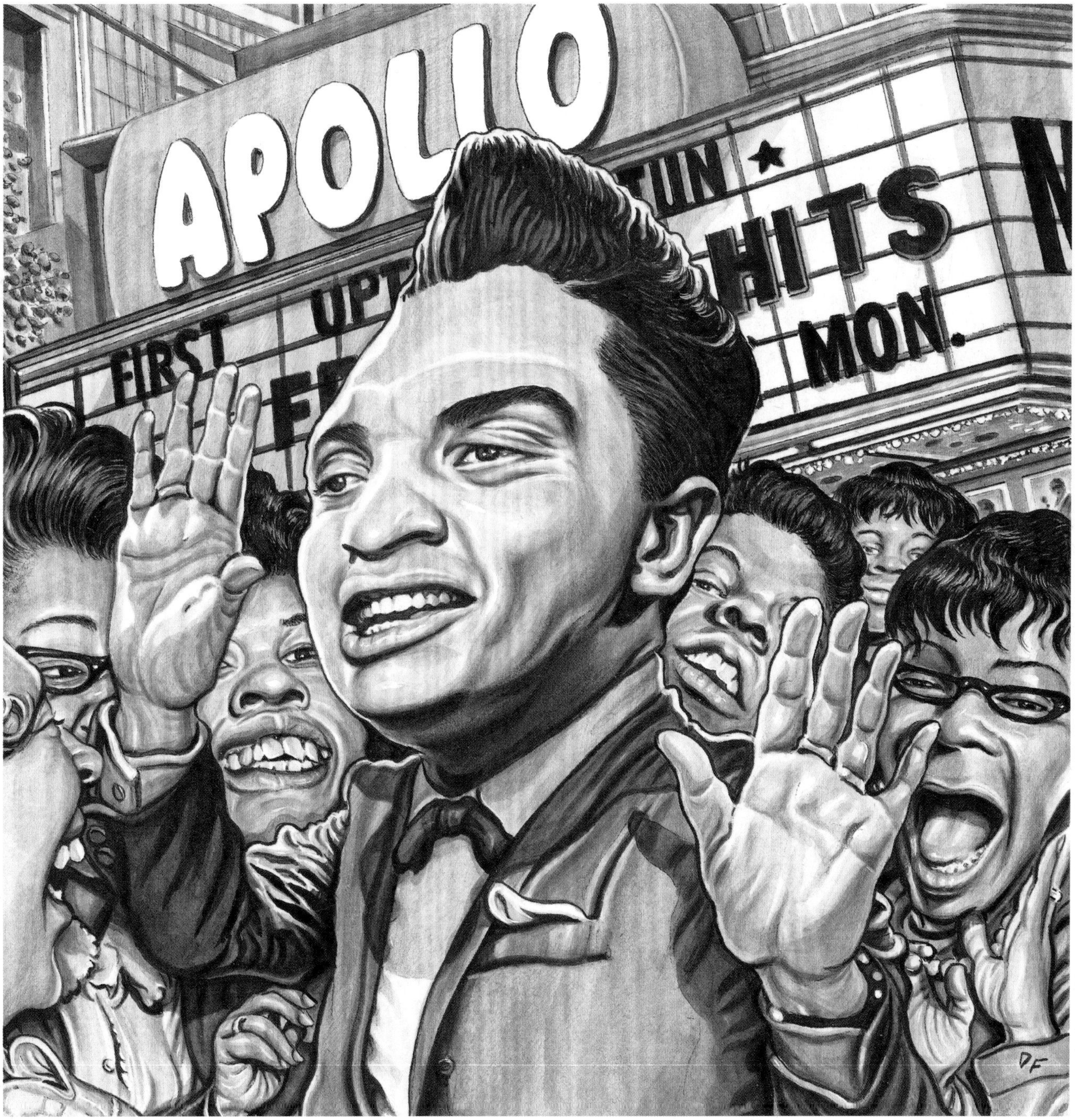
APOLLO
FIRST
MON.
HITS
DF

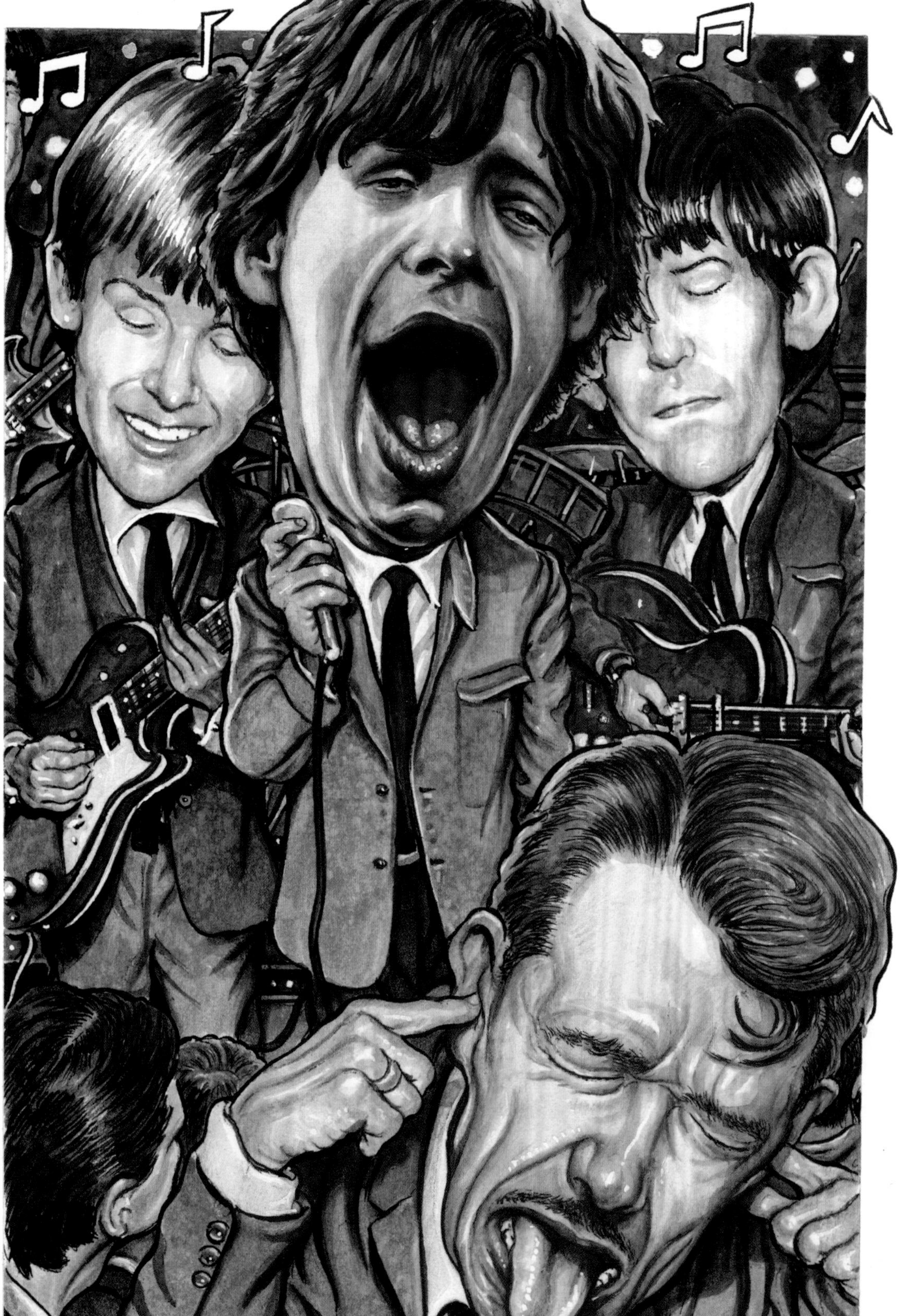

"THE SINGER WILL HAVE TO GO."

MEN'S HEALTH

Eric Easton, new manager of the Rolling Stones, commenting on **Mick Jagger** in 1963. One of the "16 Most Wrongheaded Judgements of All Time."

"CHEAP THRILLS."

1968: **Robert Crumb** presents his *Cheap Thrills* cover art to **Janis Joplin** and members of her band backstage at the Filmore West in SF.

An imagined meeting.

Commissioned by the owner of the original *Cheap Thrills* art as a companion piece.

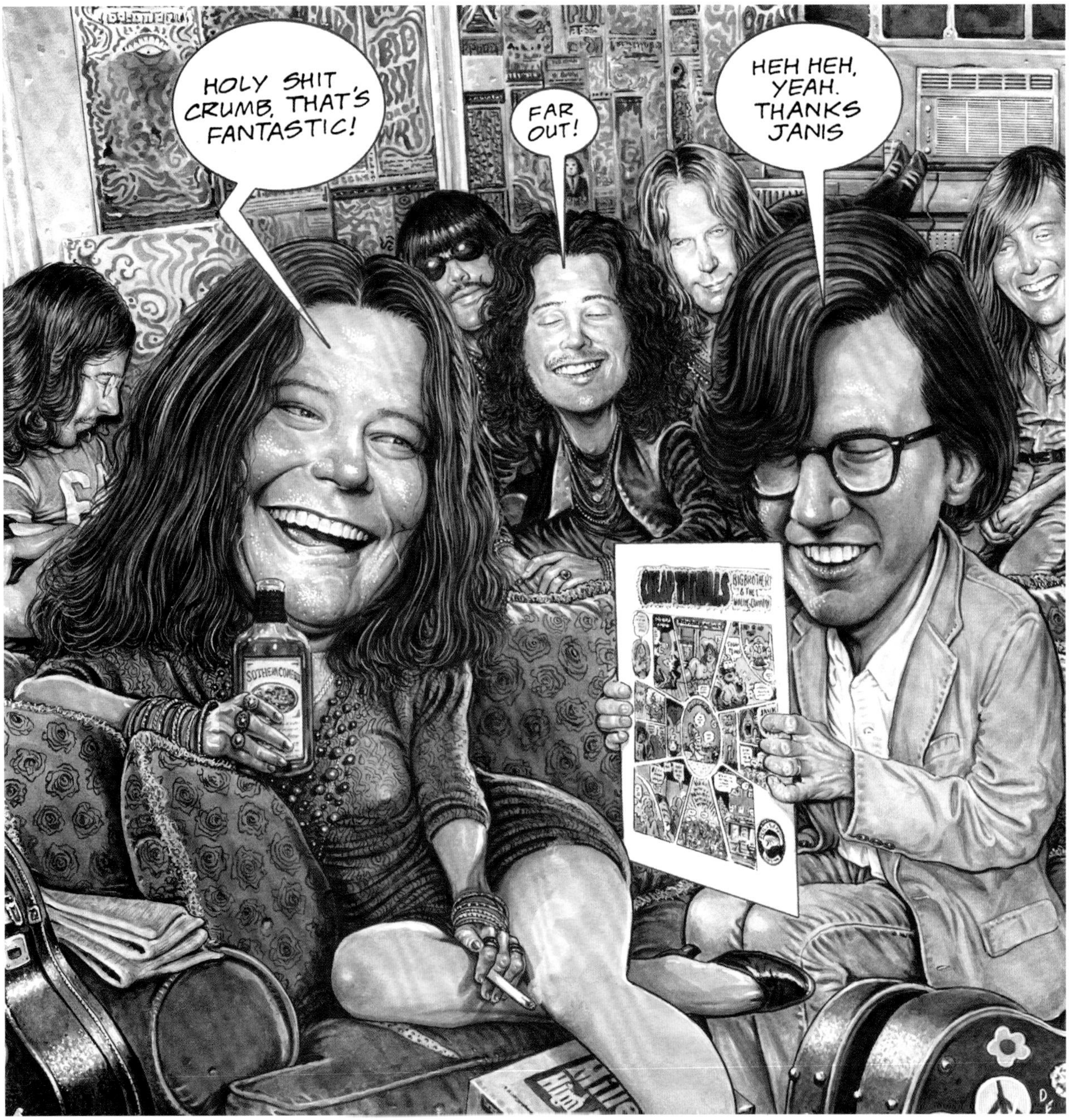
HOLY SHIT CRUMB, THAT'S FANTASTIC!
FAR OUT!
HEH HEH, YEAH. THANKS JANIS
CHEAP THRILLS

VARIOUS PORTRAITS OF MUSICIANS

JOAN JETT

NEIL YOUNG embracing LUCINDA WILLIAMS

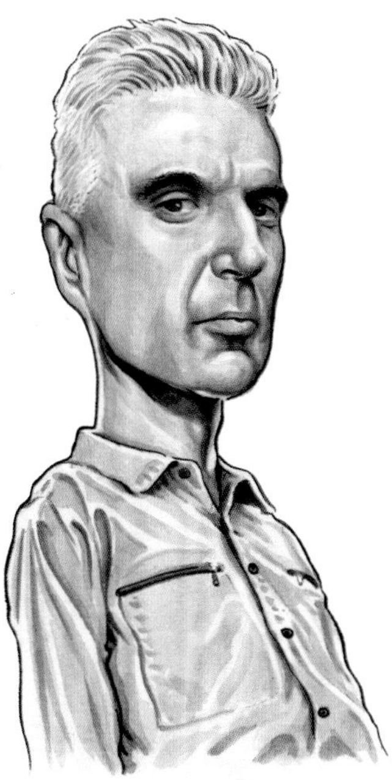

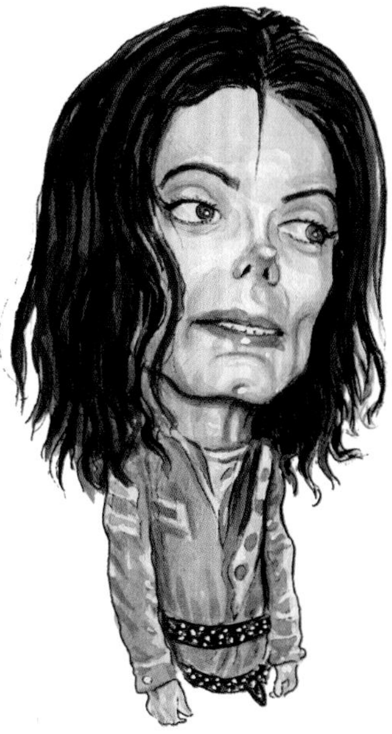

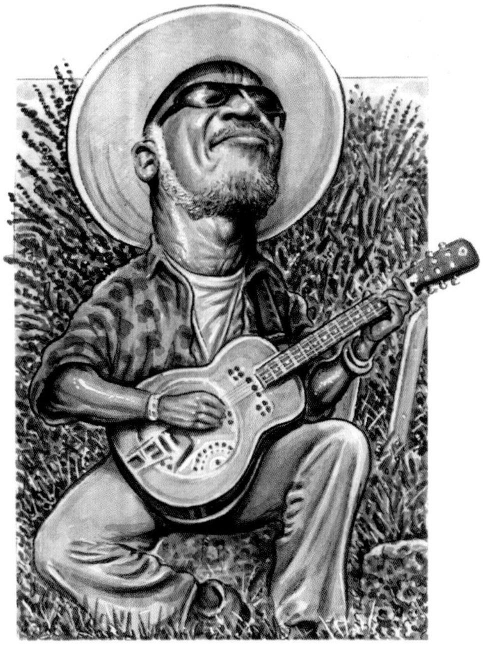

DAVID BYRNE

MICHAEL JACKSON

TAJ MAHAL

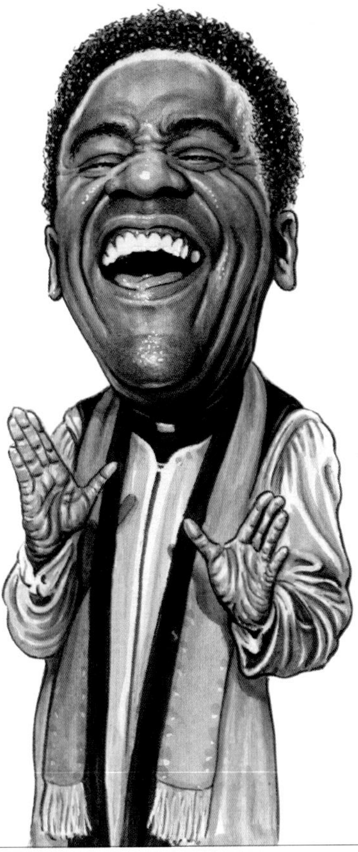

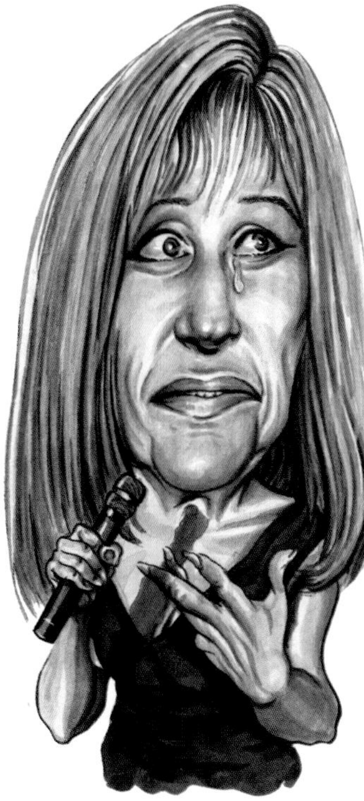

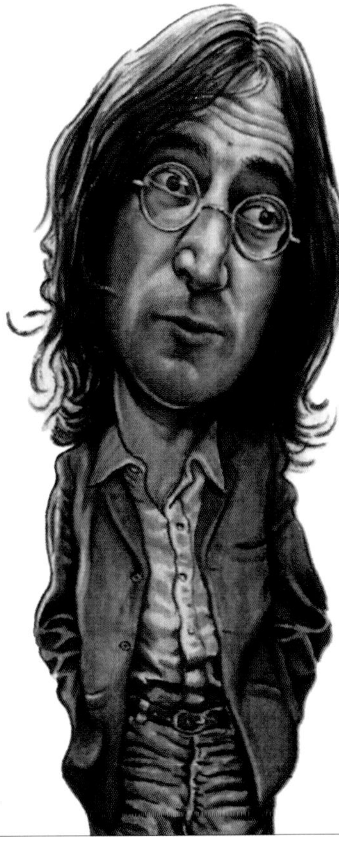

The REVEREND AL GREEN

A compassionate
BARBRA STREISAND

For a *Time* Magazine tribute by
Sir Paul McCartney—JOHN LENNON

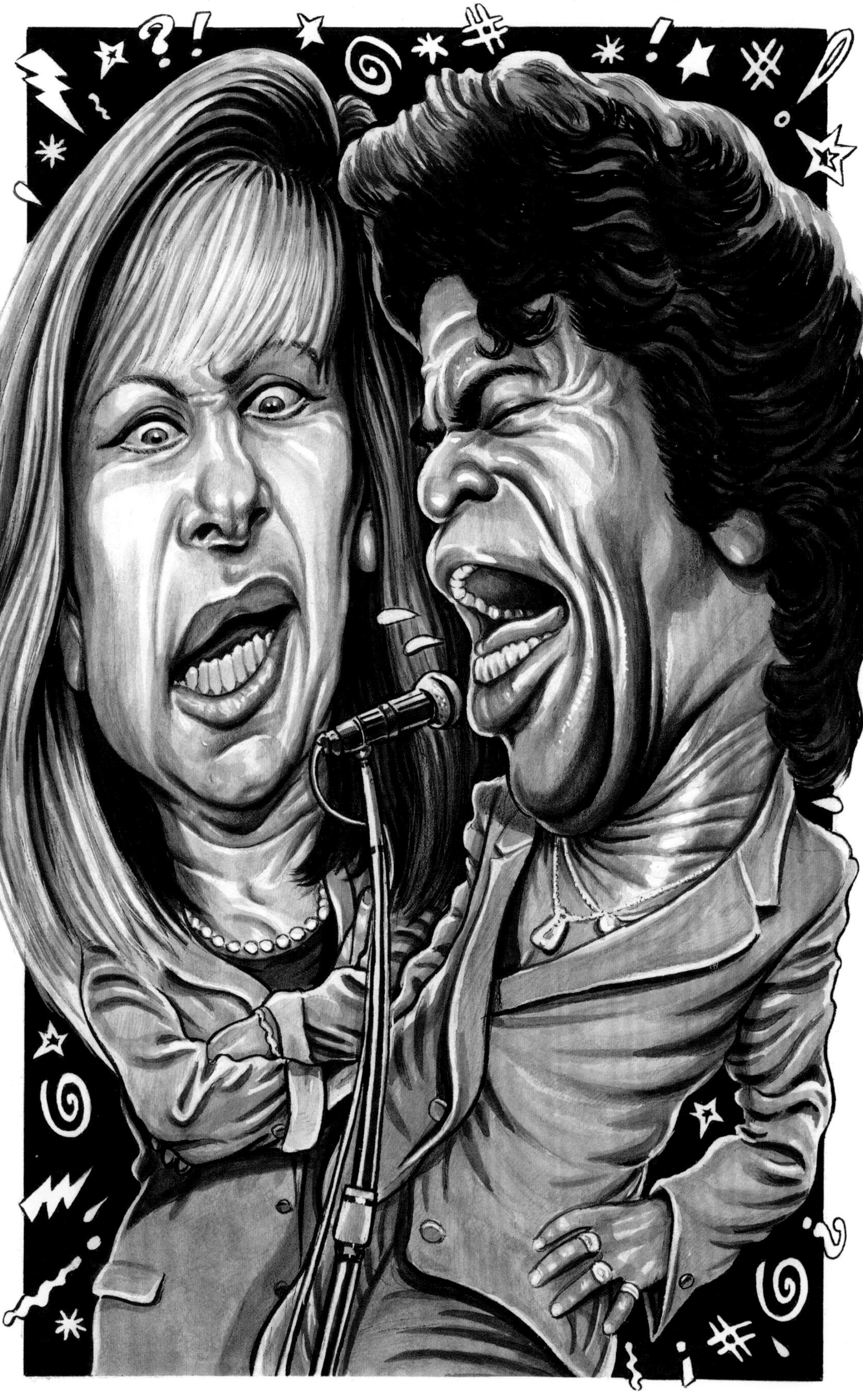

"INDECENT EXPOSURE."

ENTERTAINMENT WEEKLY

Celebrities... At Their Worst! Volume 2

Catching the rich and famous in the act of making fools of themselves. **Barbra Streisand** and **James Brown**.

"THE 'AGELESS' DONNY OSMOND."

THE WALL STREET JOURNAL

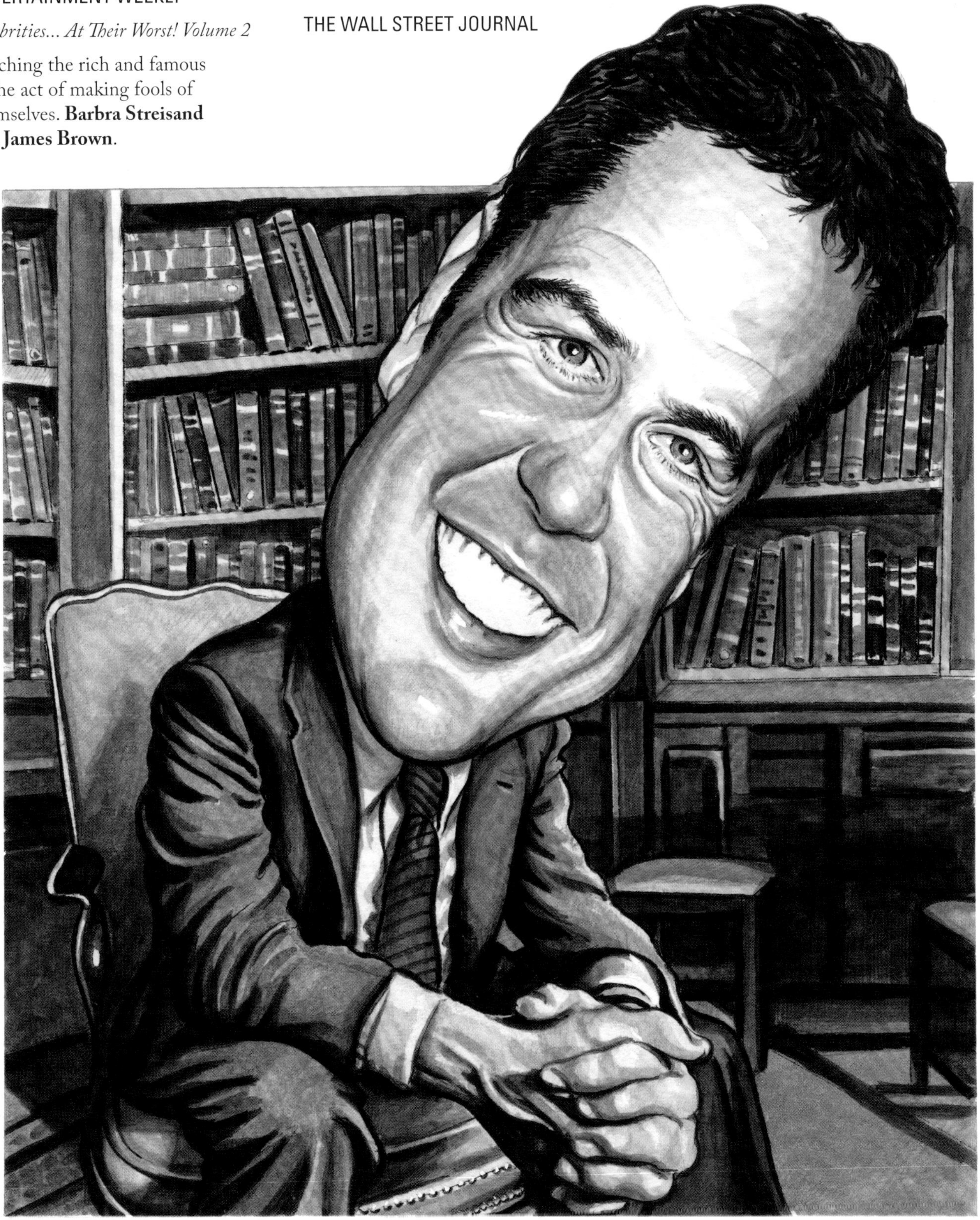

"IT'S NOT UNUSUAL."

THE WALL STREET JOURNAL

What celebrities charge to make a personal appearance at your home. For just $50,000, you can have **Tom Jones** swing and sway at your next lawn party.

"BOB DYLAN'S *MODERN TIMES*."

MOJO

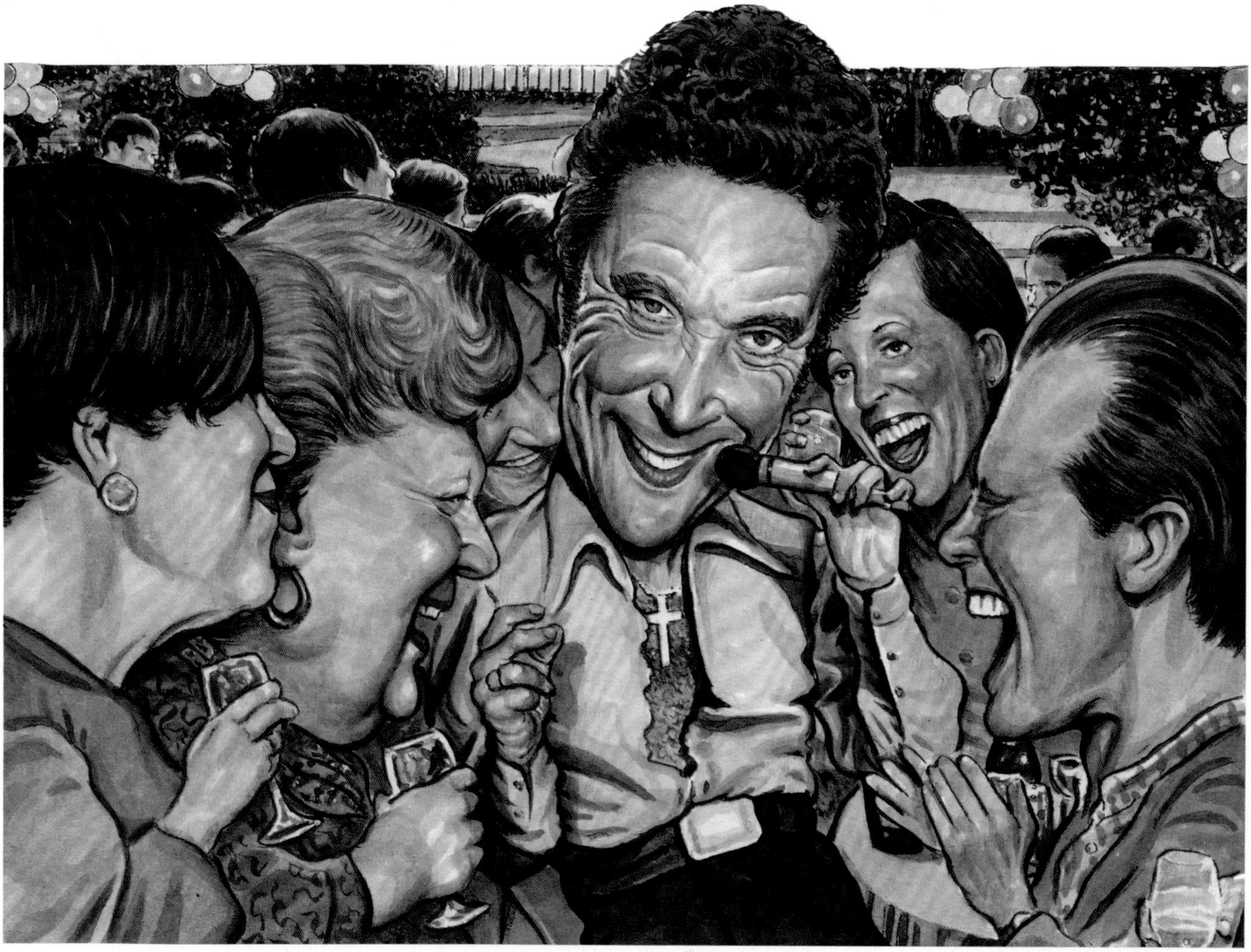

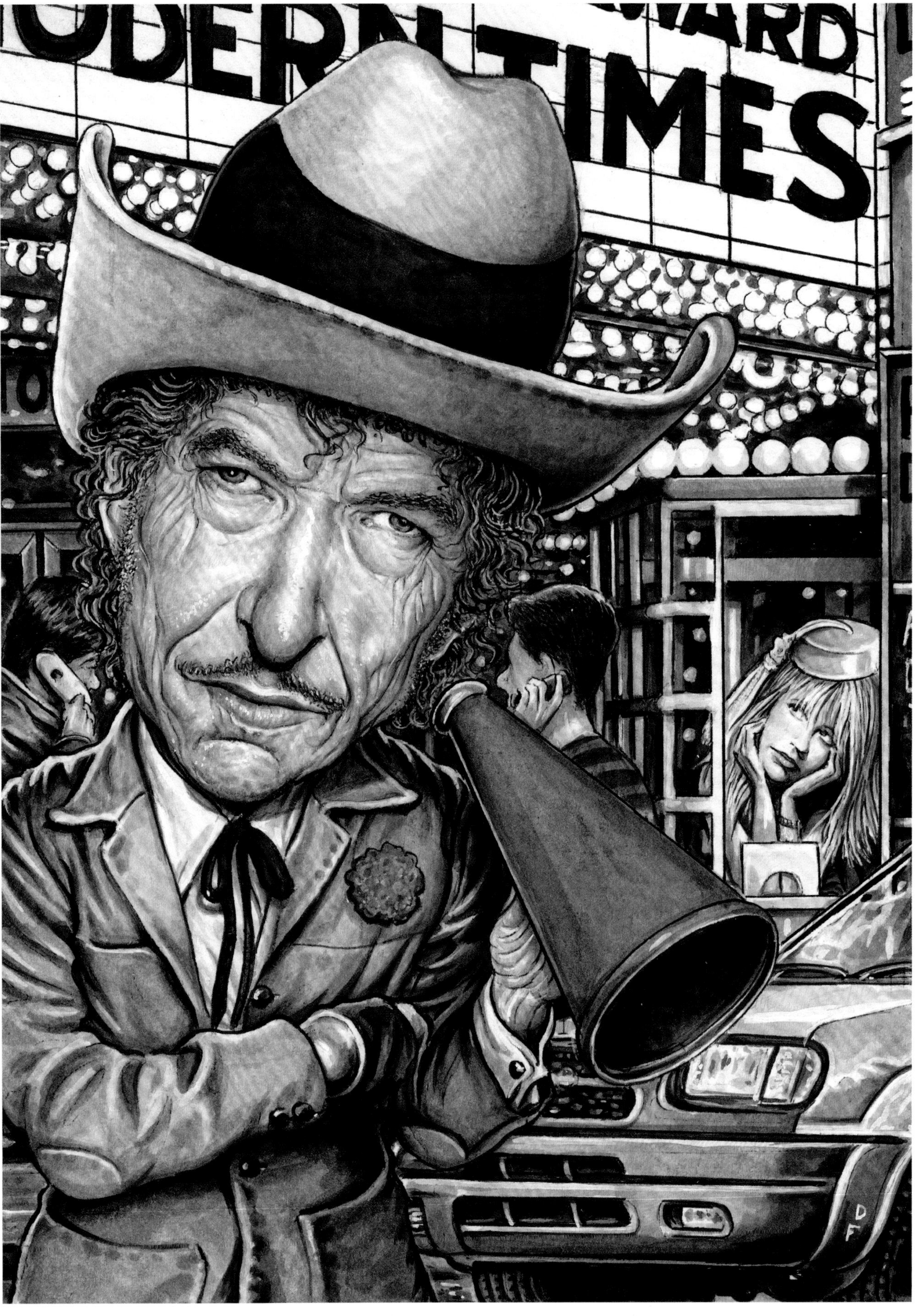
TIMES

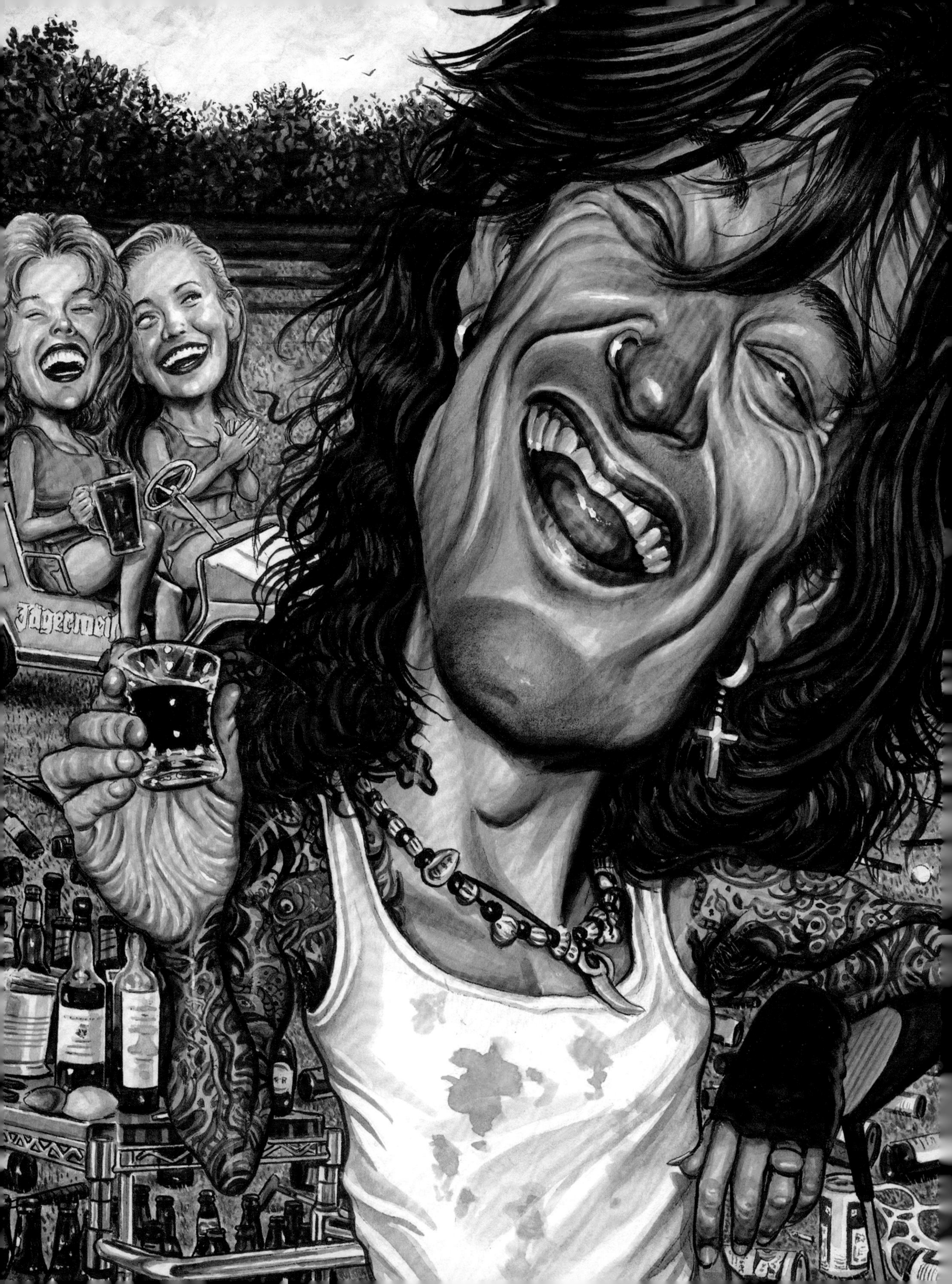

"TEE OFF WITH LEE."

MAXIMUM GOLF

Although I've never been at all interested in playing golf (miniature golf was more my game) I was hired by this "hip" golf magazine to illustrate various celebrities' golf experiences. First up, Mötley Crüe drummer and former Pamela Anderson squeeze **Tommy Lee**.

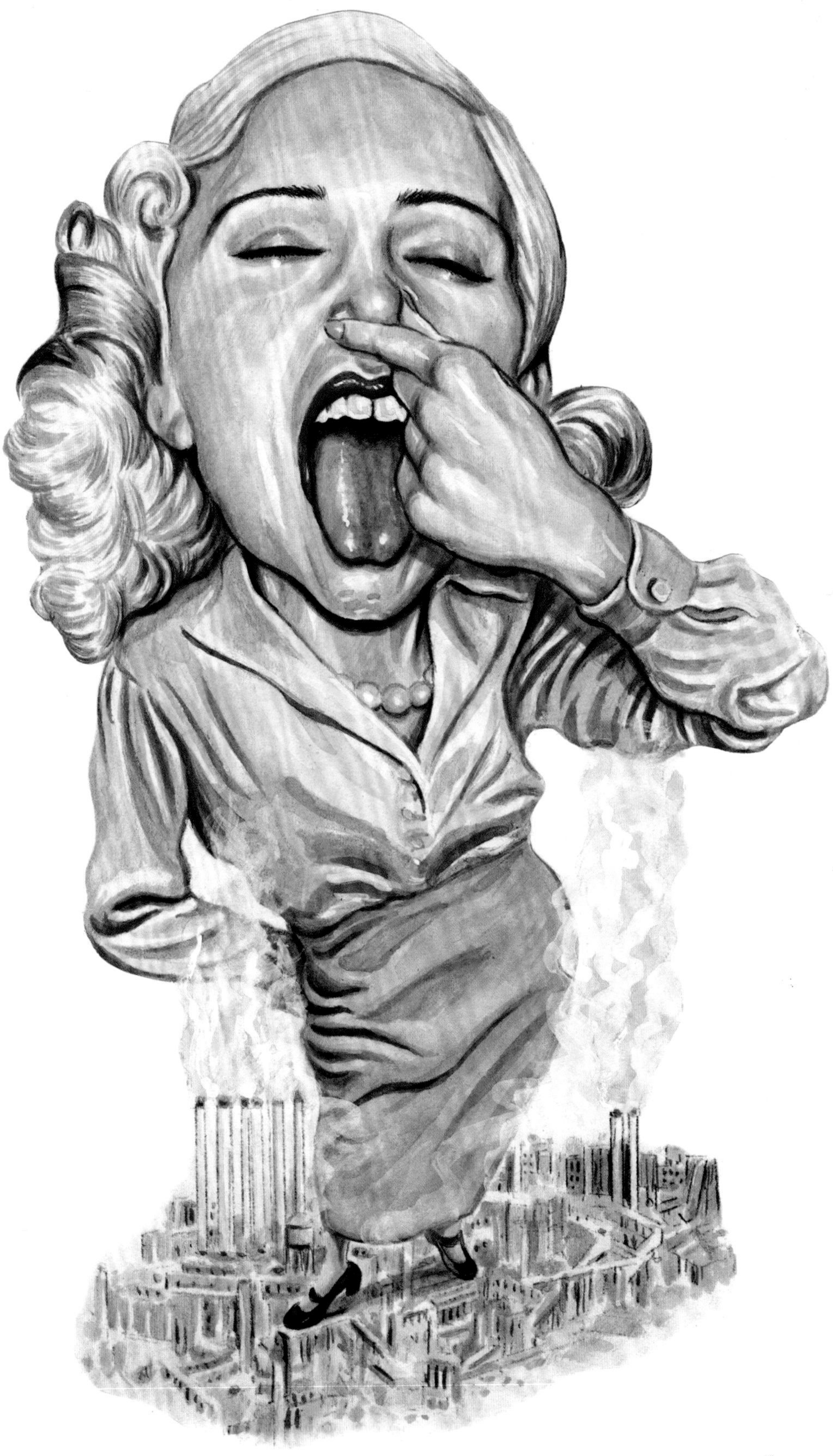

"*PEE-YOU*, THIS TOWN STINKS!"

PREMIERE

When the Mayor of Bay City, Michigan was asked if he would consider giving former resident **Madonna** the key to the city, he replied, "No way, she referred to the Bay City as 'a smelly little town.'"

MORE MUSICIAN PORTRAITS

ENTERTAINMENT WEEKLY

PERRY FARRELL, addicted to his
boom-box.

"Bon bon" shaker RICKY MARTIN,
as a "muchacho."

SIR PAUL McCARTNEY — working on his
kid's book, which stars a squirrel and frog.

MOBY holds his new book, *Teany*.

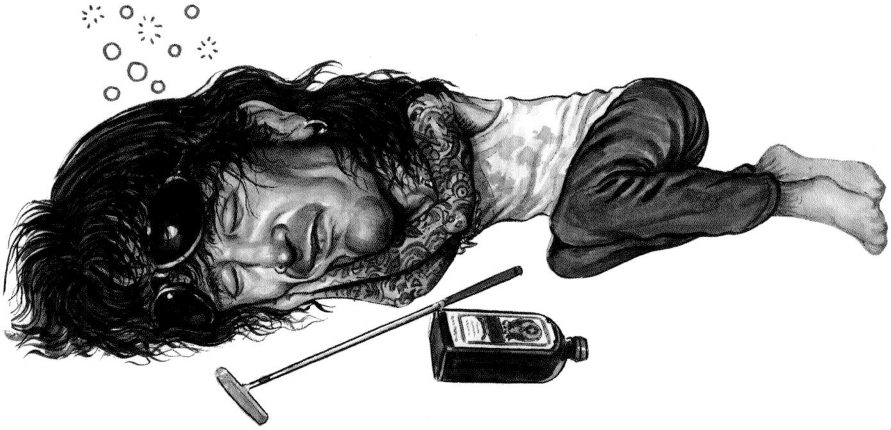

TOMMY LEE takes a snooze.

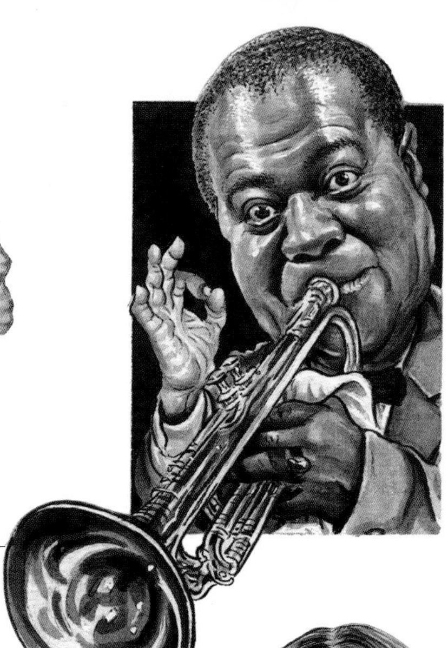

SATCHMO is A-OK.

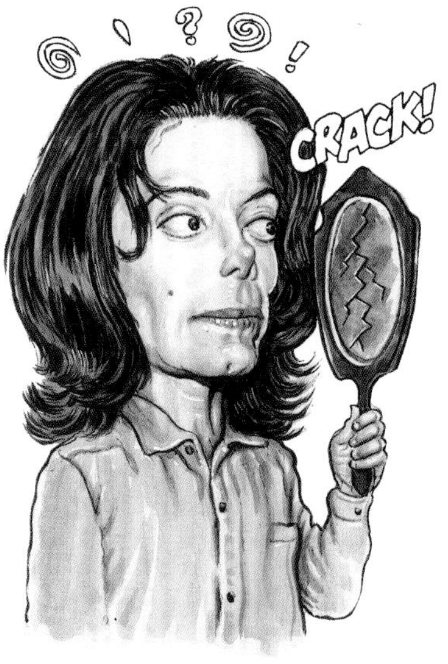
CRACK!

The mirror never lies.

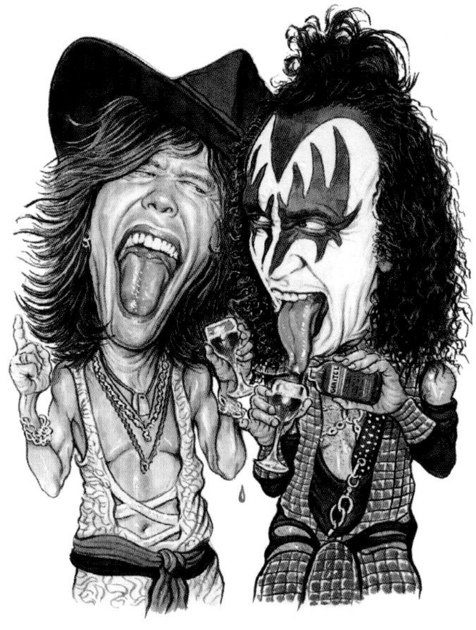

Aging rock and roll bad-boys STEVEN TYLER and GENE SIMMONS.

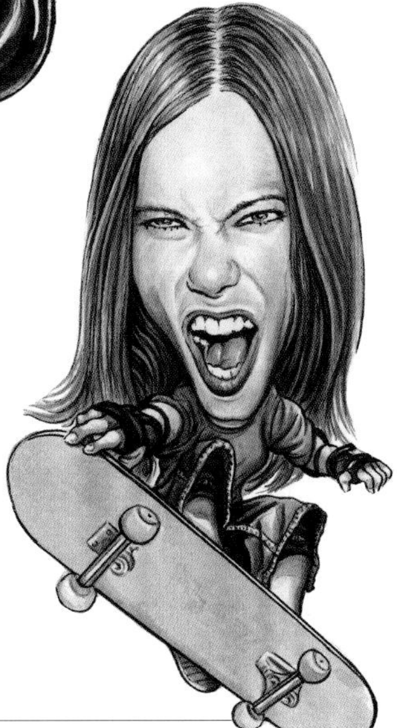

AVRIL LAVIGNE, skateboarder.

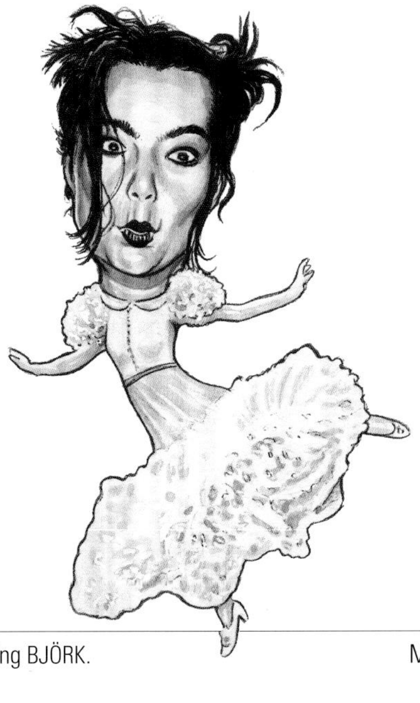

A pirouetting BJÖRK.

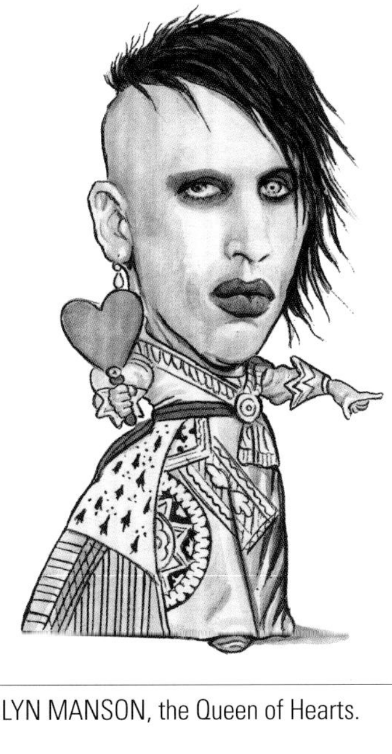

MARILYN MANSON, the Queen of Hearts.

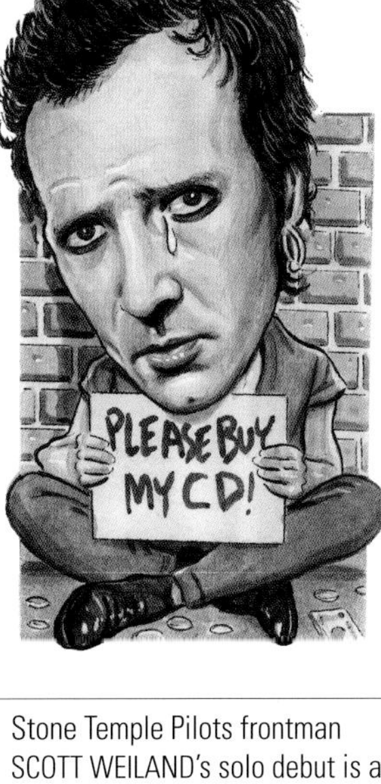
PLEASE BUY MY CD!

Stone Temple Pilots frontman SCOTT WEILAND's solo debut is a dud.

"HOLLYWOOD LEGENDS."

COVER IMAGE for the book,
"THE WICKED WIT OF THE WEST"

This was a phrase coined by Groucho Marx about his friend, the legendary comedy screenwriter **Irving Brecher**.

George Burns, **Jack Benny**, **Milton Berle**, **Harpo Marx**.

Groucho Marx, **Judy Garland**, **Jackie Gleason**, all of whom worked with and were friends of Irv's.

Irv wrote two Marx Bros. films, dialog for *The Wizard of Oz*, the screenplay for *Meet Me in St. Louis* and created *The Life of Riley*.

My wife and I had the pleasure of meeting him shortly before he died at age 94, and he was still as funny and cutting as ever.

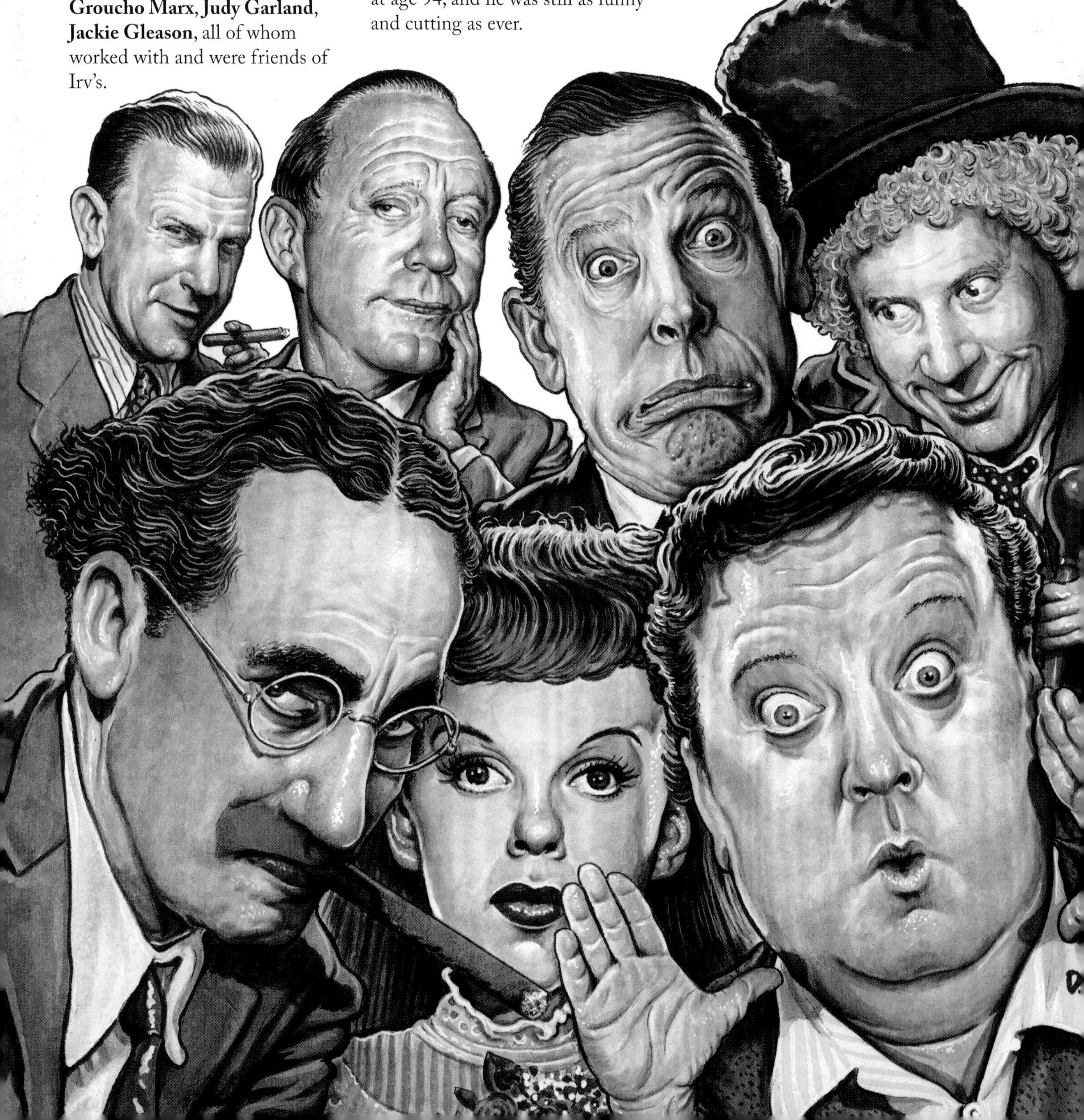

"DOROTHY & THE CORONER."

Created for MEMORIES OF A MUNCHKIN by MEINHARDT RAABE

Raabe played "The Munchkin Coroner" in *The Wizard of Oz*. Artists were asked to place him in various scenes and situations to do with the film.

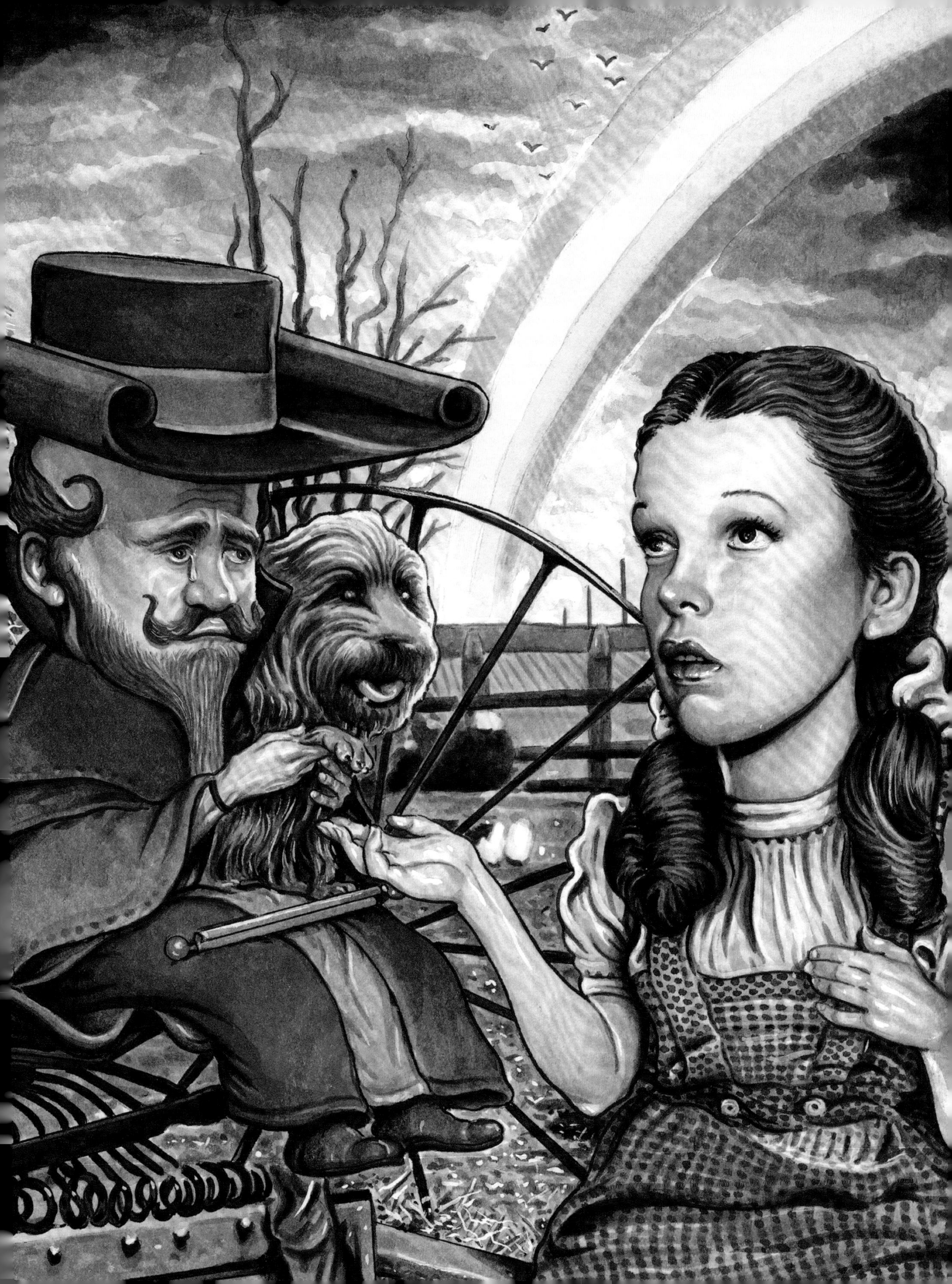

"GETTING HIGH MARX."

ENTERTAINMENT WEEKLY

Reimagining the "Stateroom Scene" from *A Night at the Opera.* **Robin Williams** as Groucho, **Chris Rock** as Chico, **Ellen DeGeneres** as Harpo. This was done in charcoal.

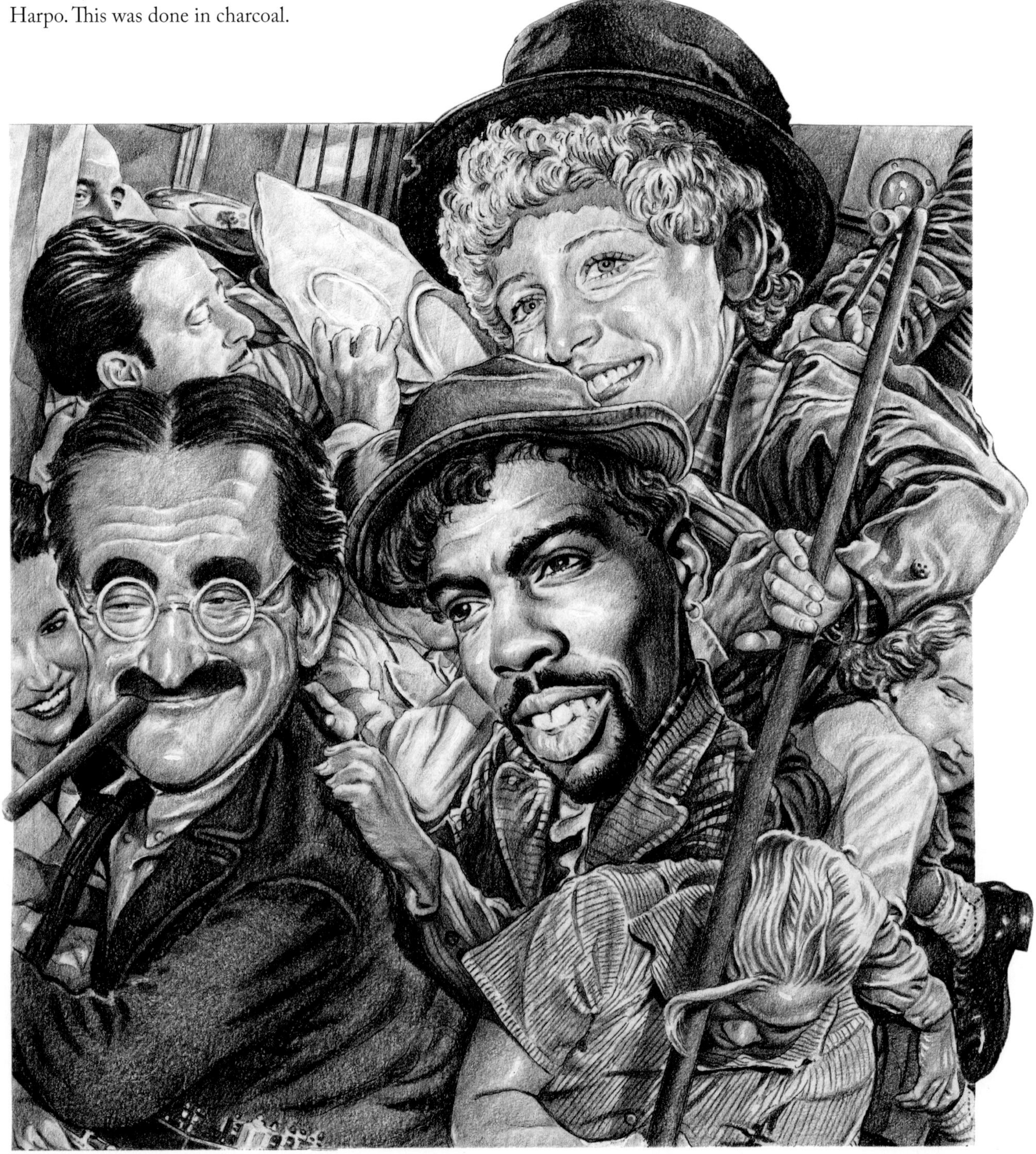

"THE THREE STOOGES & VERNON DENT."

Shemp, **Larry**, **Moe**, circa mid-'40s, posed with their long-time comic foil, **Vernon Dent**.

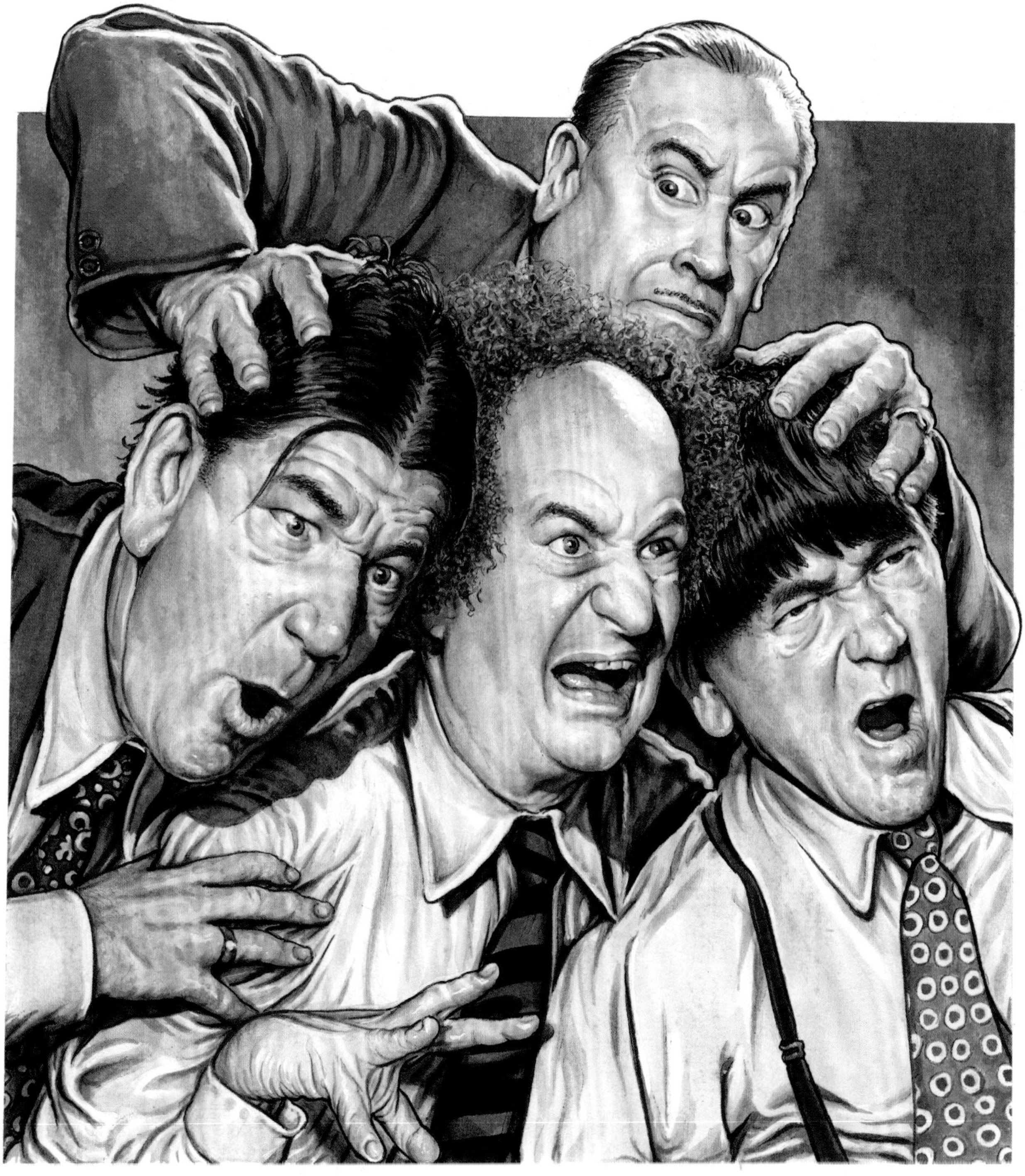

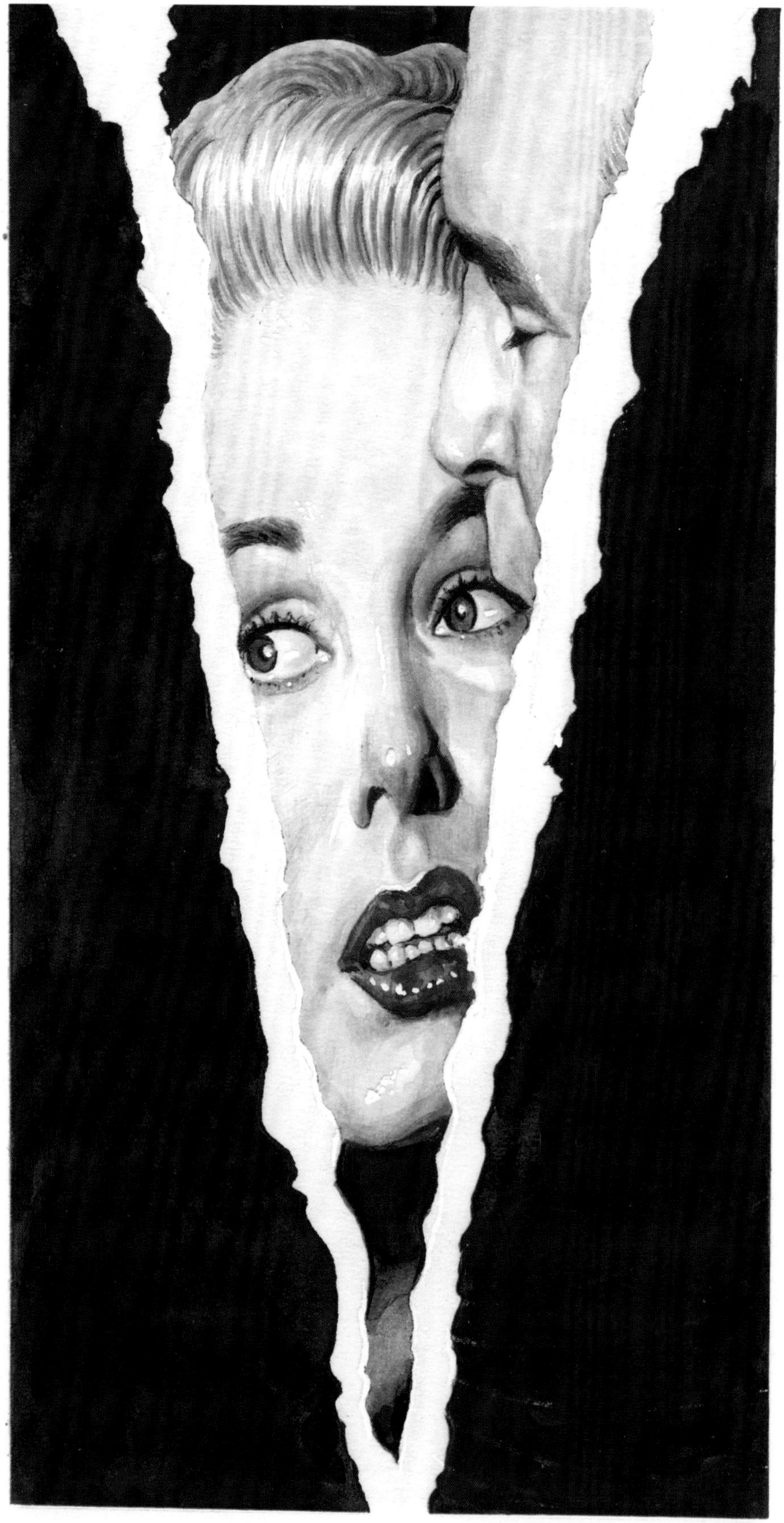

"ALFRED HITCHCOCK'S *VERTIGO*."

LOS ANGELES MAG

Kim Novak, James Stewart.

"THE PRINCES OF HOLLYWOOD."

NEWSWEEK

Former movie star glamor boys **George Hamilton**, **Robert Wagner** and **Tony Curtis** had new autobiographies out. Here they are in their glory, lounging poolside at the Beverly Hills Hotel.

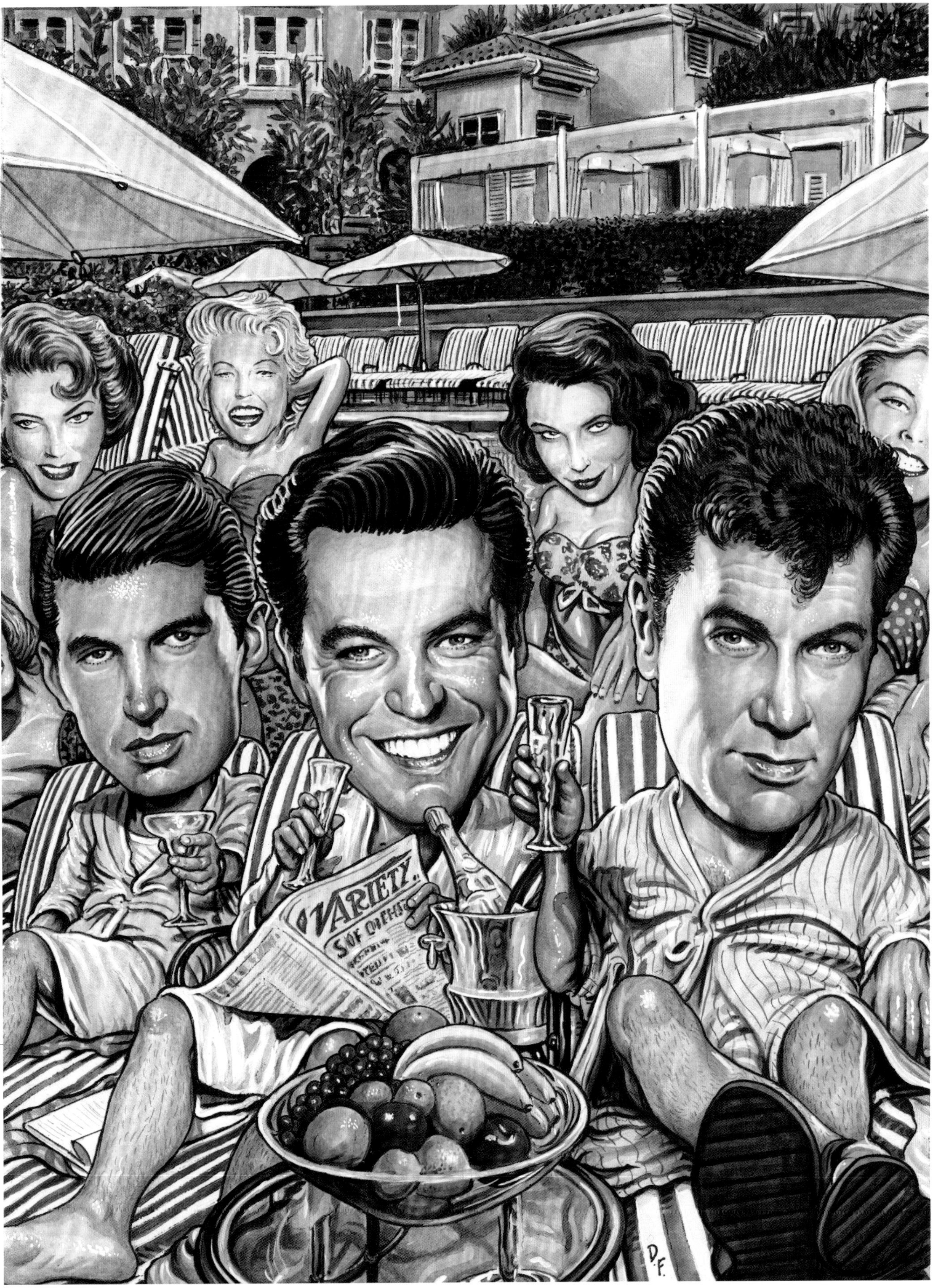
VARIETY
D.F.

"FLYING WITH FLUBBER."

ENTERTAINMENT WEEKLY

Fred MacMurray as "The Absent-Minded Professor."

"SUDDENLY, *NEXT* SUMMER."

NEWSWEEK

A 1998 preview for the following year's summer films. At the time, the long-awaited return of the *Star Wars* franchise was a wildly anticipated event (thus, everyone posed in the original *Star Wars* cantina). Alas, it was *A Dubious Hit* (think "Jar-Jar Binks").

Rosie O'Donnell (as a gorilla) in an animated *Tarzan*, **Tom Hanks** in *The Green Mile*, **Yoda** and **R2-D2**, **Liam Neeson** as a Jedi knight, **Julia Roberts** in *Runaway Bride*, **Mike Myers** in *Austin Powers 2*, **Will Smith** in *Wild Wild West*.

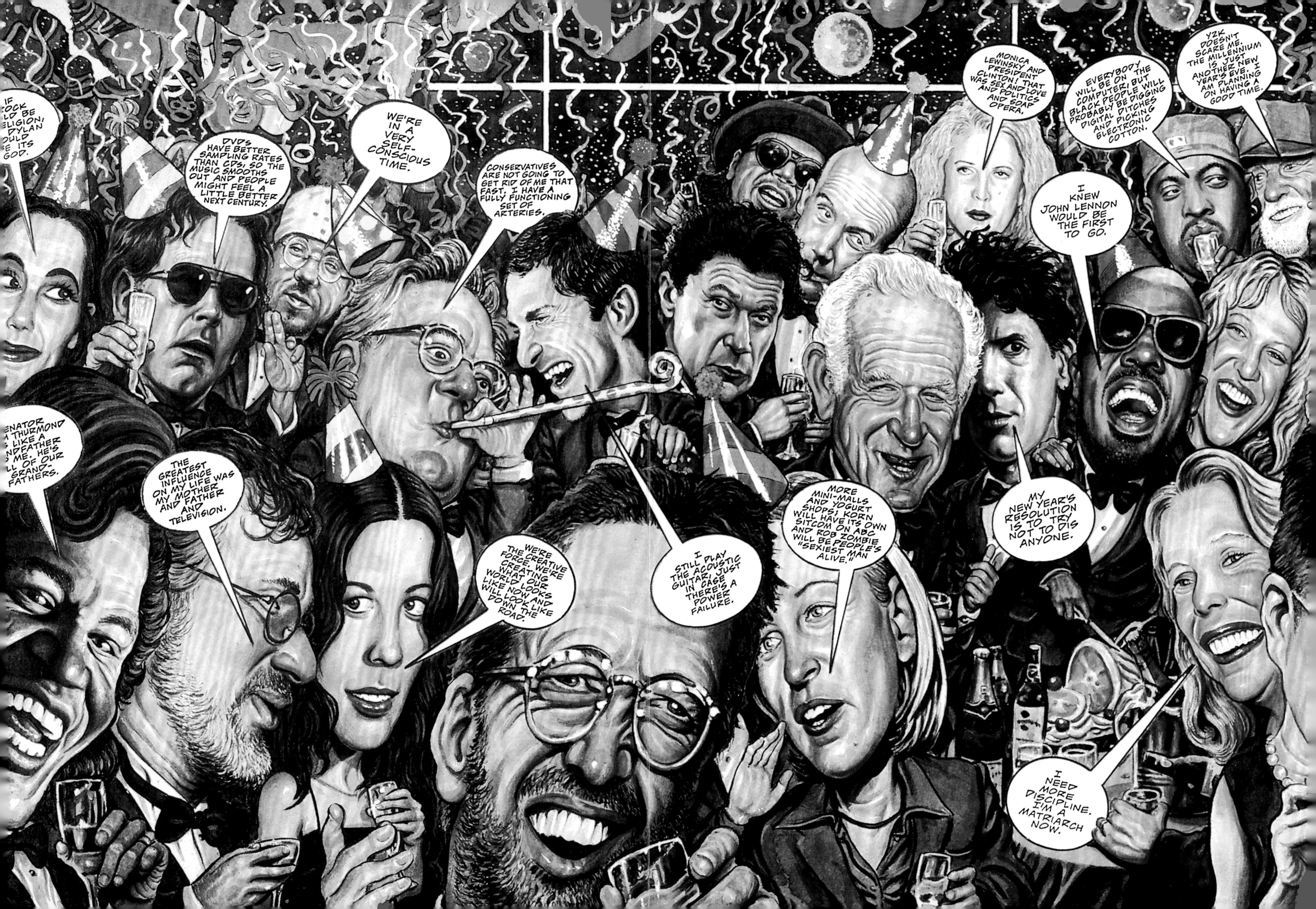
IF ROCK ULD BE ELIGION, DYLAN OULD E ITS GOD.
DVDS HAVE BETTER SAMPLING RATES THAN CDS, SO THE MUSIC SMOOTHS OUT AND PEOPLE MIGHT FEEL A LITTLE BETTER NEXT CENTURY.
WE'RE IN A VERY SELF-CONSCIOUS TIME.
CONSERVATIVES ARE NOT GOING TO GET RID OF ME THAT FAST. I HAVE A FULLY FUNCTIONING SET OF ARTERIES.
MONICA LEWINSKY AND PRESIDENT CLINTON! THAT WAS SEX AND LOVE AND POLITICS AND SOAP OPERA.
EVERYBODY WILL BE ON THE COMPUTER, BUT BLACK PEOPLE WILL PROBABLY BE DIGGING DIGITAL DITCHES AND PICKING ELECTRONIC COTTON.
Y2K DOESN'T SCARE ME. THE MILLENNIUM IS JUST ANOTHER NEW YEAR'S EVE. I AM PLANNING ON HAVING A GOOD TIME.
I KNEW JOHN LENNON WOULD BE THE FIRST TO GO.
ENATOR M THURMOND S LIKE A NDFATHER O ME. HE'S LL OF OUR GRAND-FATHERS.
THE GREATEST INFLUENCE ON MY LIFE WAS MY MOTHER AND FATHER AND TELEVISION.
WE'RE THE CREATIVE FORCE. WE'RE CREATING WHAT OUR WORLD LOOKS LIKE NOW AND WILL LOOK LIKE DOWN THE ROAD.
I STILL PLAY THE ACOUSTIC GUITAR, JUST IN CASE THERE'S A POWER FAILURE.
MORE MINI-MALLS AND YOGURT SHOPS; KORN WILL HAVE ITS OWN SITCOM ON ABC AND ROB ZOMBIE WILL BE PEOPLE'S "SEXIEST MAN ALIVE."
MY NEW YEAR'S RESOLUTION IS TO TRY NOT TO DIS ANYONE.
I NEED MORE DISCIPLINE. I'M A MATRIARCH NOW.

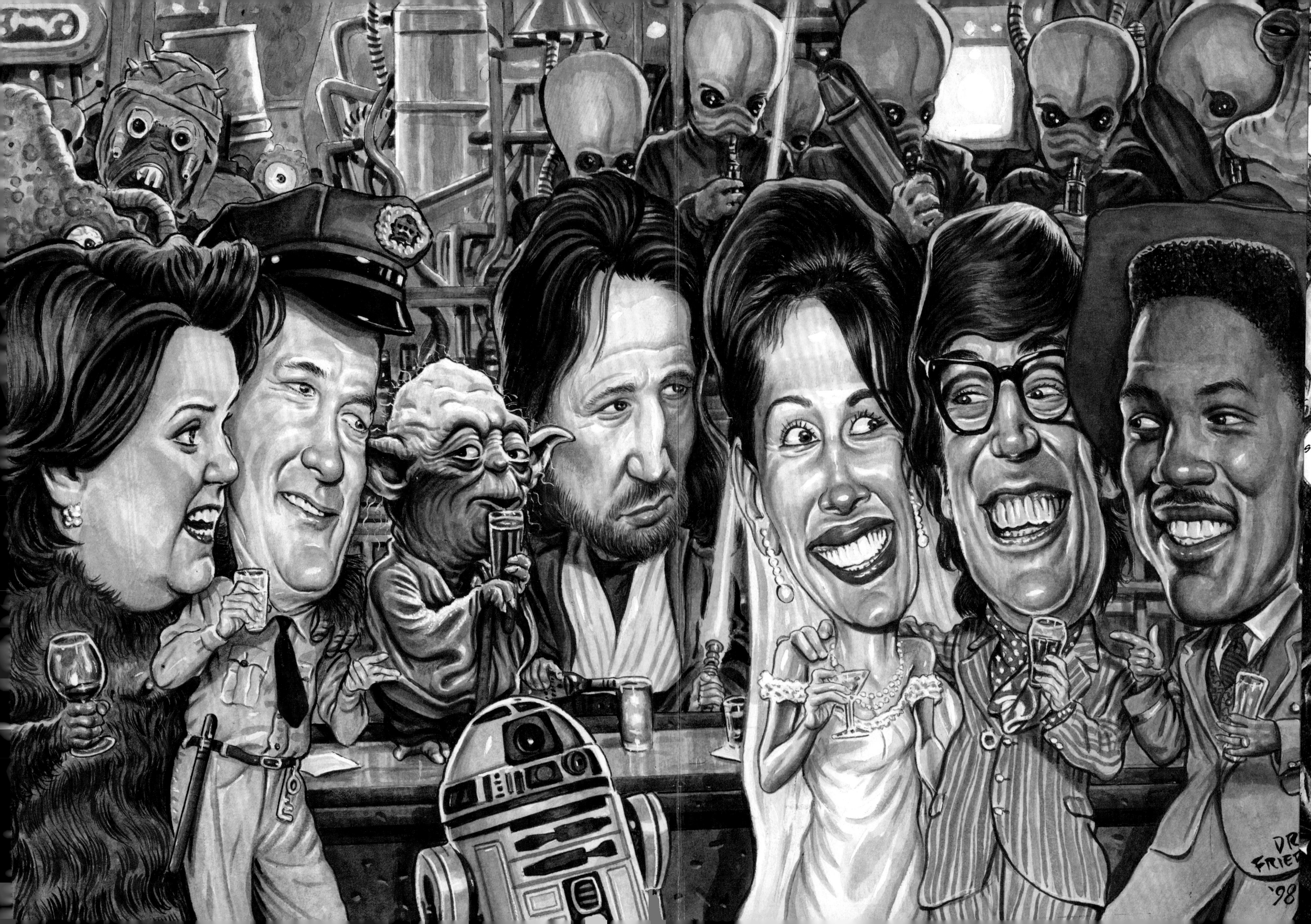

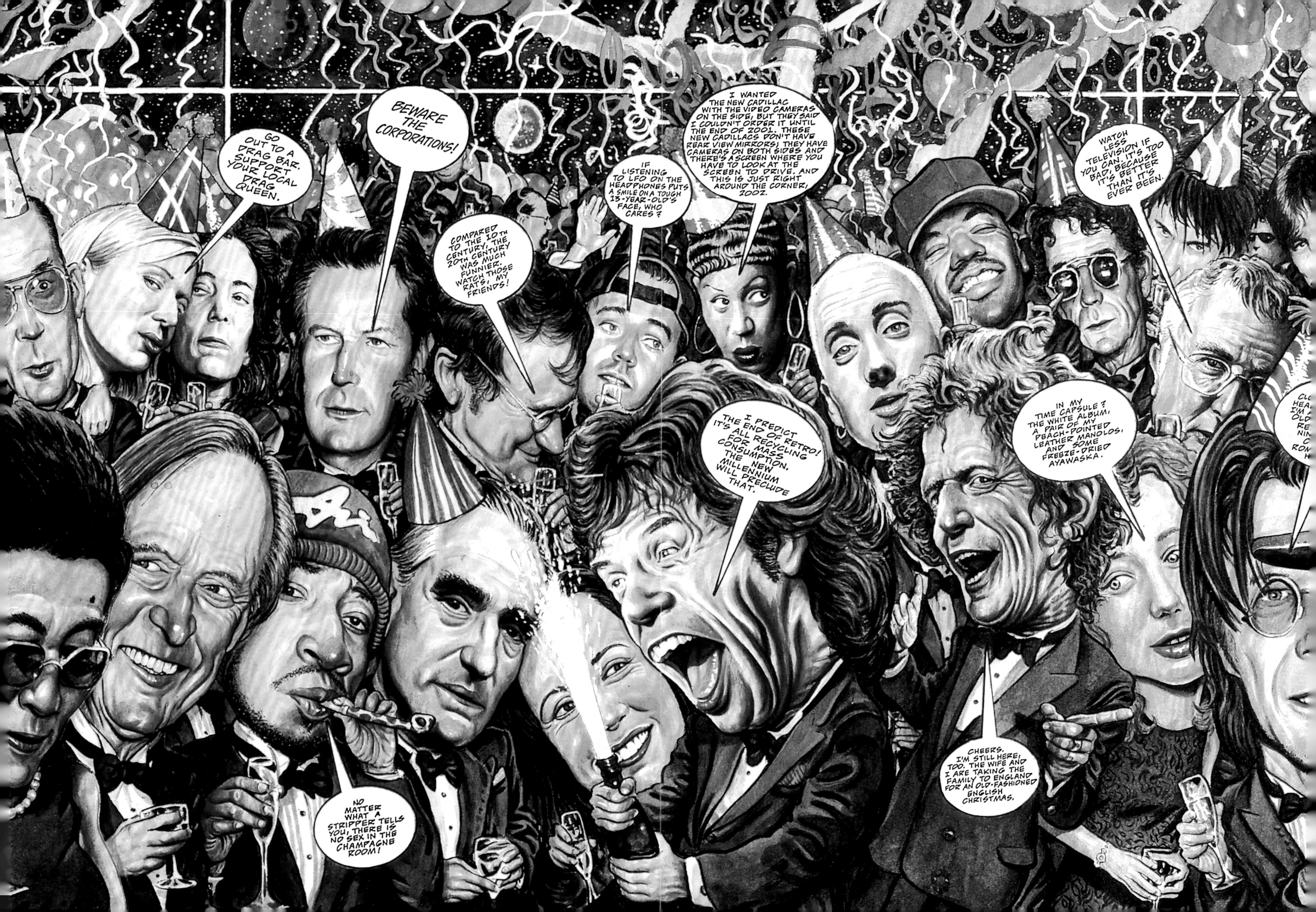
GO OUT TO A DRAG BAR. SUPPORT YOUR LOCAL DRAG QUEEN.
BEWARE THE CORPORATIONS!
COMPARED TO THE 20TH CENTURY, THE 20TH CENTURY WAS MUCH FUNNIER. WATCH THOSE RATS, MY FRIENDS!
IF LISTENING TO LFO ON THE HEADPHONES PUTS A SMILE ON A TOUGH 13-YEAR-OLD'S FACE, WHO CARES?
I WANTED THE NEW CADILLAC WITH THE VIDEO CAMERAS ON THE SIDE, BUT THEY SAID I COULDN'T ORDER IT UNTIL THE END OF 2001. THESE NEW CADILLACS DON'T HAVE REAR VIEW MIRRORS; THEY HAVE CAMERAS ON BOTH SIDES AND THERE'S A SCREEN WHERE YOU HAVE TO LOOK AT THE SCREEN TO DRIVE. AND THIS IS JUST RIGHT AROUND THE CORNER, 2002.
WATCH LESS TELEVISION IF YOU CAN. IT'S TOO BAD, BECAUSE IT'S BETTER THAN IT'S EVER BEEN.
I PREDICT THE END OF RETRO! IT'S ALL RECYCLING FOR MASS CONSUMPTION. THE NEW MILLENNIUM WILL PRECLUDE THAT.
IN MY TIME CAPSULE? THE WHITE ALBUM, A PAIR OF MY PEACH-POINTED LEATHER MANOLOS, AND SOME FREEZE-DRIED AYAWASKA.
NO MATTER WHAT A STRIPPER TELLS YOU, THERE IS NO SEX IN THE CHAMPAGNE ROOM!
CHEERS. I'M STILL HERE, TOO. THE WIFE AND I ARE TAKING THE FAMILY TO ENGLAND FOR AN OLD-FASHIONED ENGLISH CHRISTMAS.

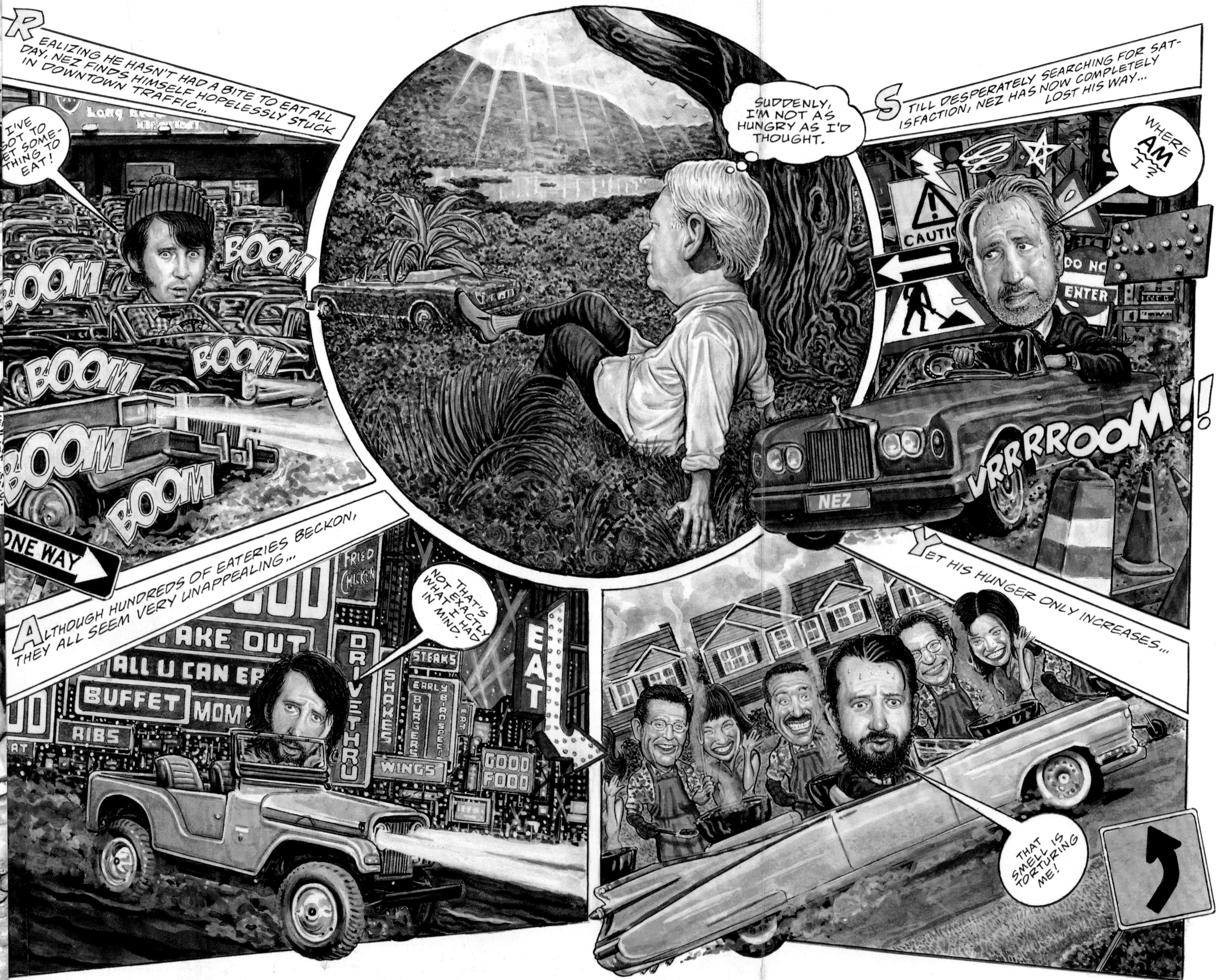
REALIZING HE HASN'T HAD A BITE TO EAT ALL DAY, NEZ FINDS HIMSELF HOPELESSLY STUCK IN DOWNTOWN TRAFFIC...
I'VE GOT TO GET SOME-THING TO EAT!
BOOM
BOOM
BOOM
BOOM
BOOM
BOOM
ONE WAY
SUDDENLY, I'M NOT AS HUNGRY AS I'D THOUGHT.
STILL DESPERATELY SEARCHING FOR SATISFACTION, NEZ HAS NOW COMPLETELY LOST HIS WAY...
WHERE AM I?
CAUTIO
DO NO
ENTER
NEZ
VRRRROOM!!!
ALTHOUGH HUNDREDS OF EATERIES BECKON, THEY ALL SEEM VERY UNAPPEALING...
THAT'S NOT EXACTLY WHAT I HAD IN MIND.
FRIED CHICKEN
TAKE OUT
ALL U CAN EA
BUFFET
MOM'
RIBS
DRIVE THRU
STEAKS
SHAKES
EARLY BURGERS
WINGS
EAT
GOOD FOOD
YET HIS HUNGER ONLY INCREASES...
THAT SMELL IS TORTURING ME!

Cover art for **Michael Nesmith's** CD *Rays*.

Co-written with K. Bidus

(Lettering by Phil Felix)

"THE PARTY."

PREVIOUS SPREAD

TOP ROW, L to R

P.J. Harvey, Bob Weir, David Foster Wallace, Barney Frank, Perry Farrell, Robbie Robertson, Carlos Santana, Moby, Norman Mailer, Stevie Nicks, Mike D., Stevie Wonder, Chuck D, Courtney Love, Willie Nelson, Hunter S. Thompson, Jewel, Patti Smith, Don Henley, Robin Williams, Carson Daly, Missy Elliot, Eminem, Dr. Dre, Lou Reed, Trent Reznor, Randy Newman, Cameron Crowe, Steven Tyler

BOTTOM ROW, L to R

James Brown, Steven Spielberg, Alanis Morissette, Eric Clapton, Ellen DeGeneres, Joni Mitchell, Yoko Ono, Tom Wolfe, Prince Paul, Martin Scorsese, Janeane Garofalo, Mick Jagger, Keith Richards, Tori Amos, David Bowie, John Lee Hooker

"OSCAR ROBBERIES."

GQ MAGAZINE

"And the winner is...
What the f--k?!"

"Loser" **Orson Welles** (to *Sgt. York*'s Gary Cooper) for *Citizen Kane*, winner **Rex Harrison** for *My Fair Lady*, winner **Marisa Tomei** for *My Cousin Vinny*, winner **Sean Penn** for *Mystic River*, loser **Peter Sellers** (to Harrison) for *Dr. Strangelove*.

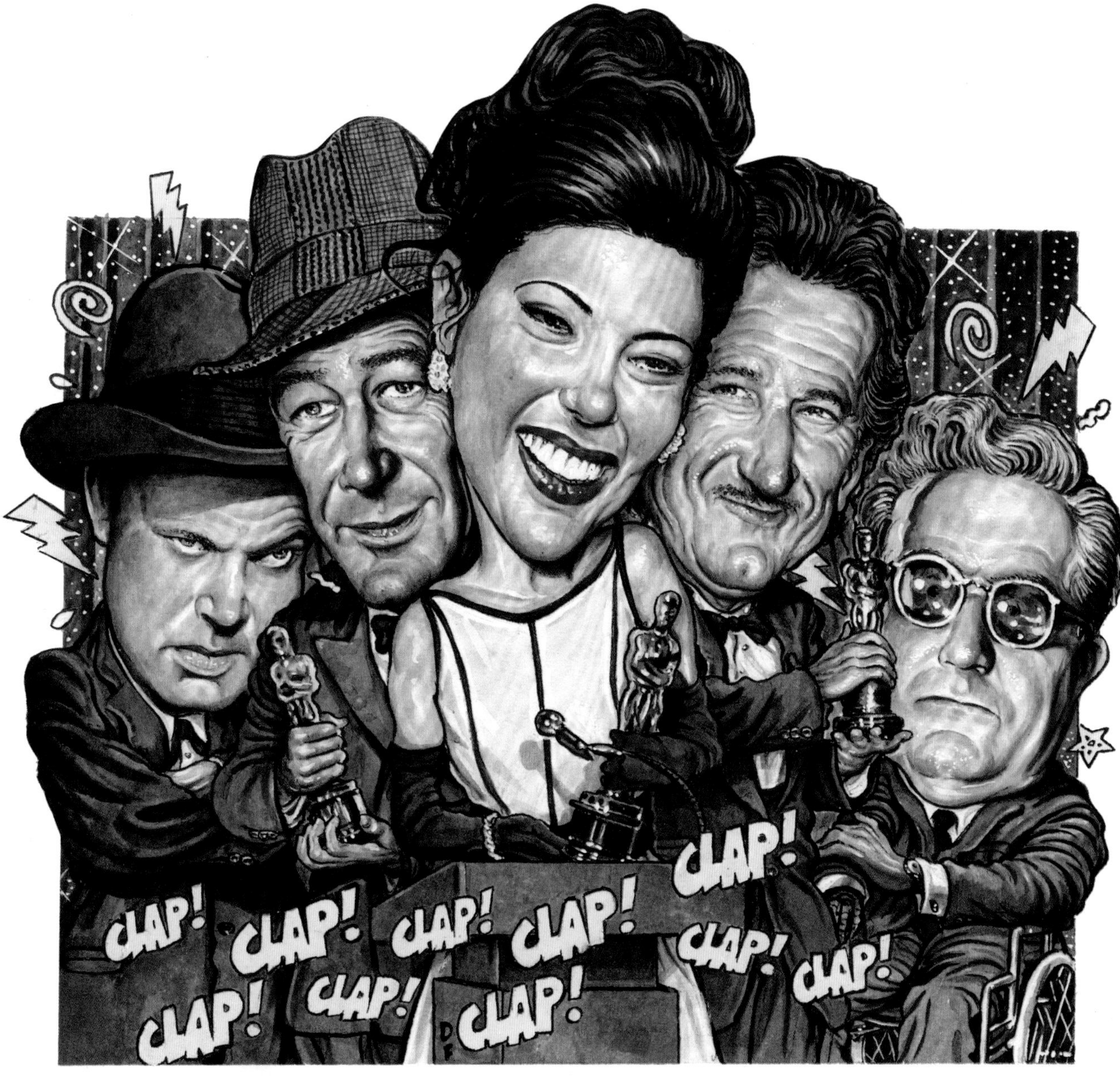
CLAP!
CLAP!
CLAP!
CLAP!
CLAP!
CLAP!
CLAP!
CLAP!
CLAP!
CLAP!

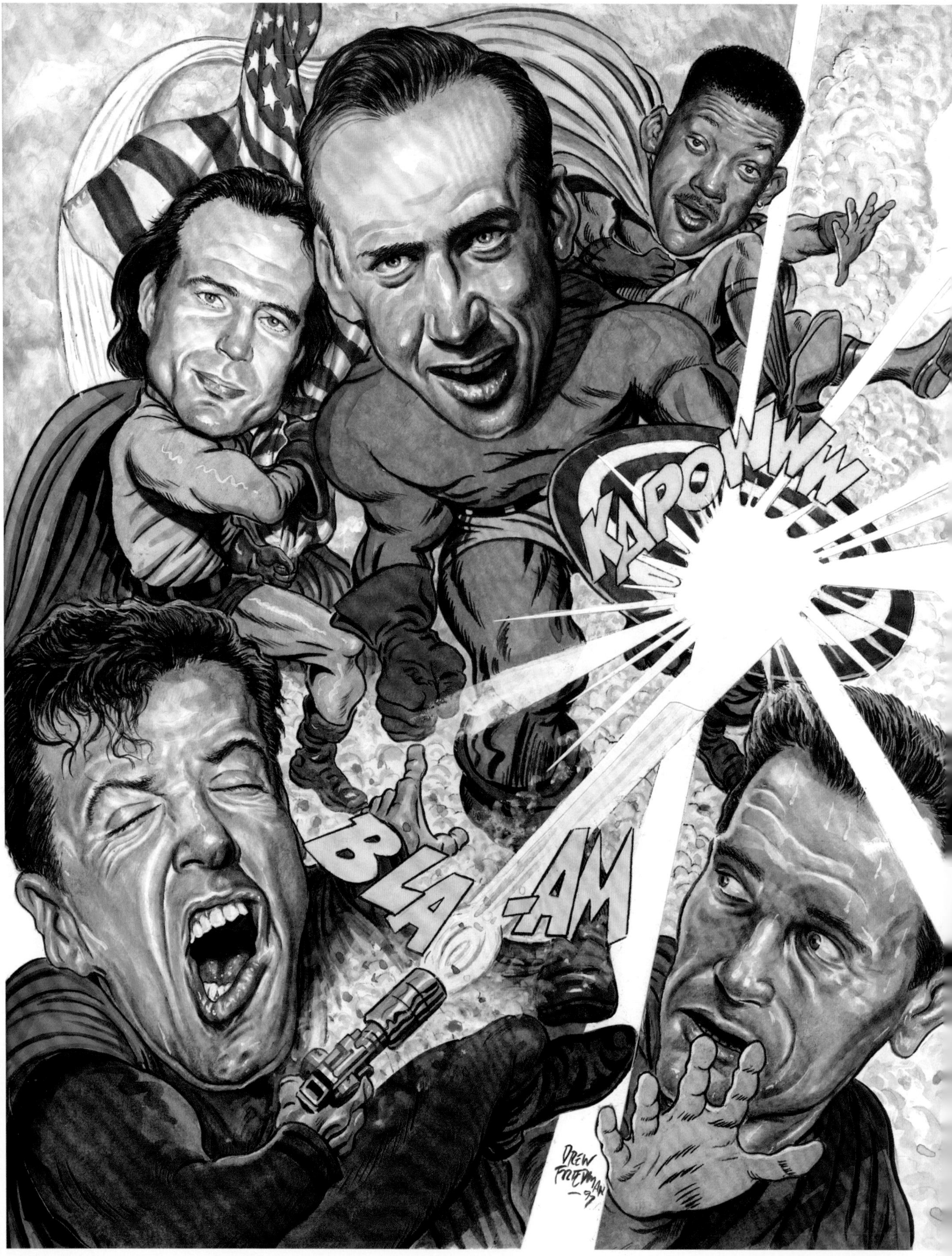
KAPOWWW
BLA-AM
DREW FRIEDMAN -97

"A PIECE OF THE ACTION."

NEWSWEEK

A demolition derby as Hollywood attempts a changing of the action hero guard: **Jason Patric**, **Nicolas Cage** and **Will Smith** battle **Sly** and **Arnold**. (I loved that Stallone face so much, I used it again. See Page 126).

"CHAN OF COMMAND."

ENTERTAINMENT WEEKLY

Chan Kong Sang, a.k.a. **Jackie Chan**.

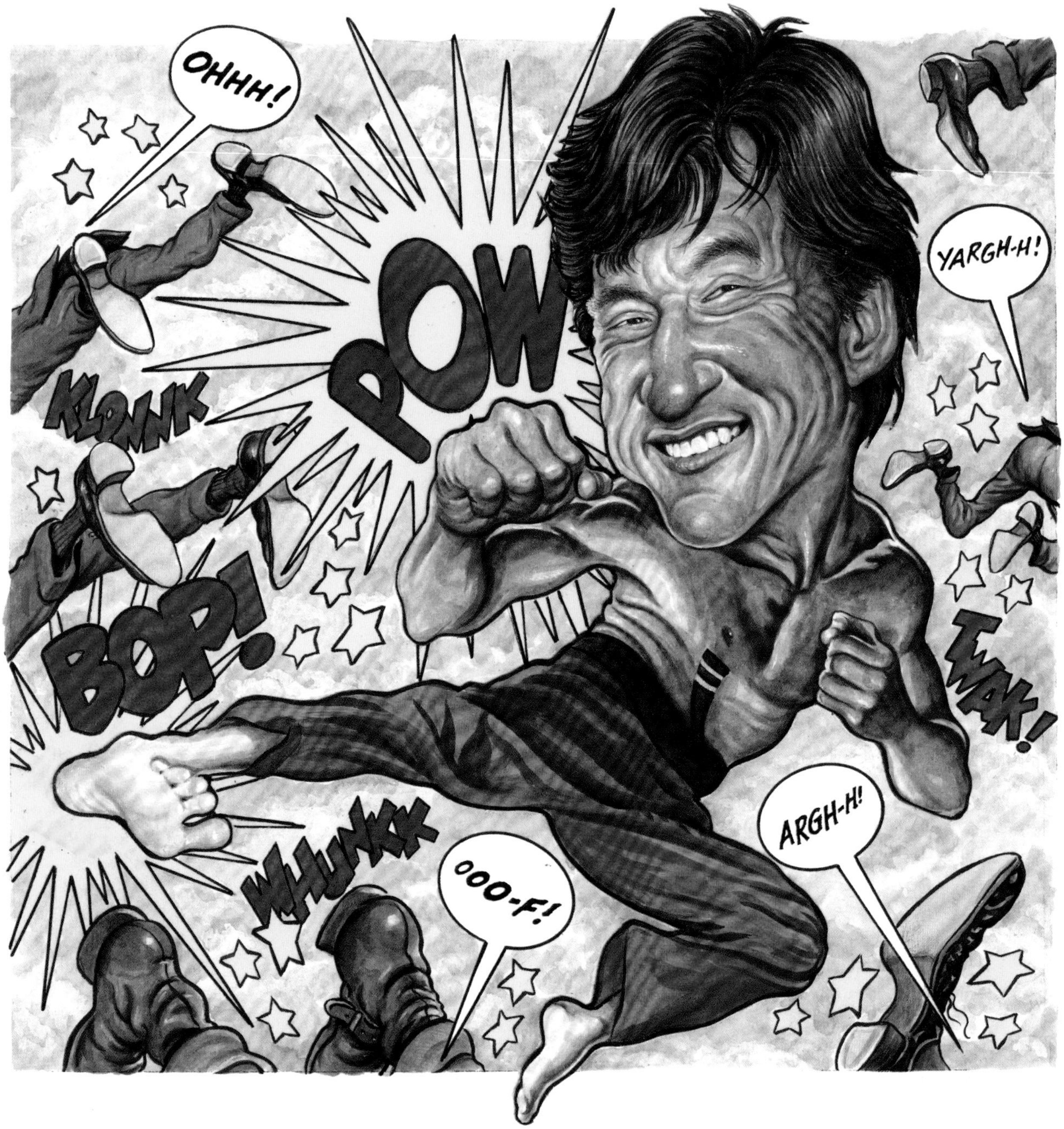
OHHH!
KLONNK
POW
YARGH-H!
BOP!
TWAK!
ARGH-H!
WHUNKK
OOO-F!

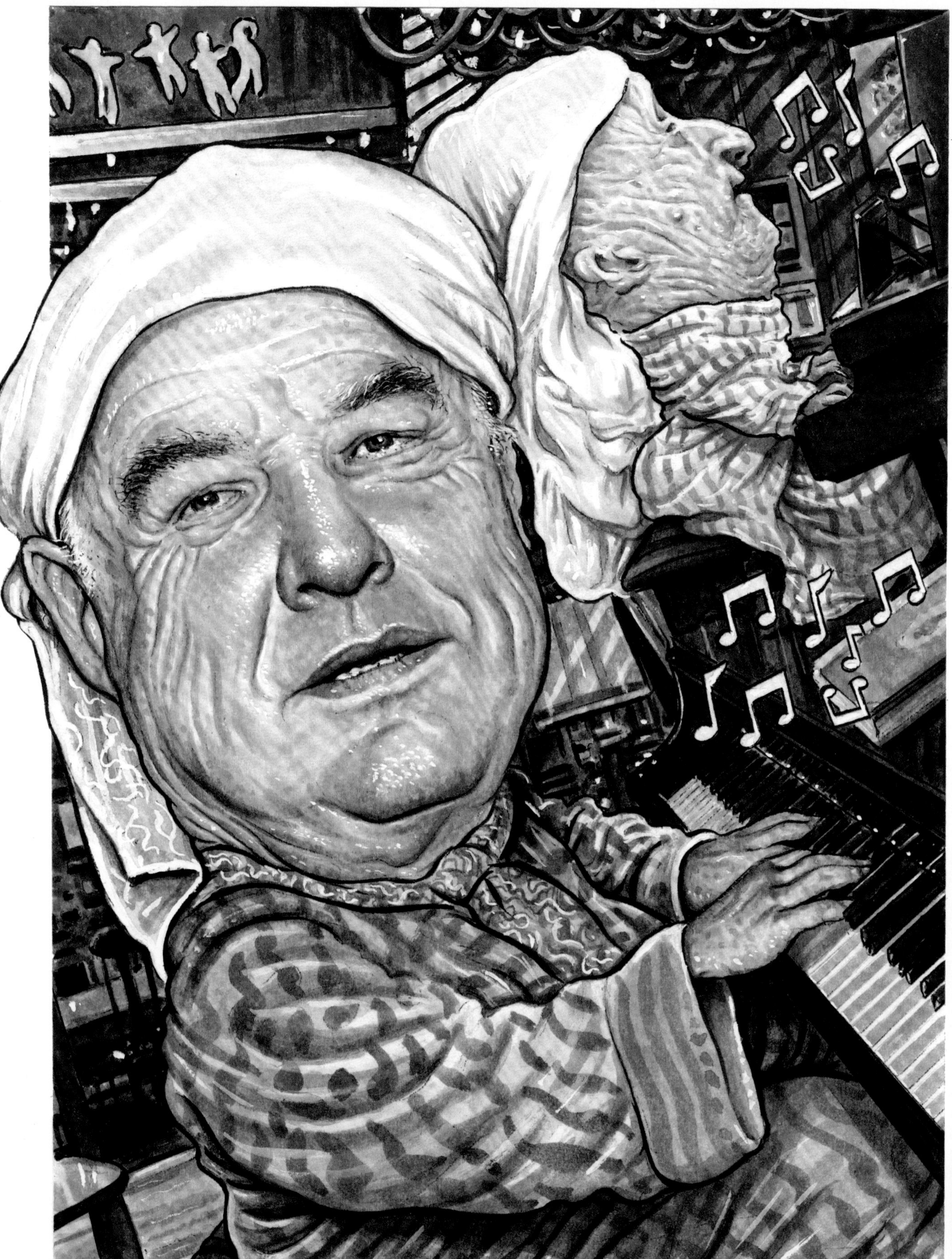

"THE GRUESOME TWOSOME FROM *THE ISLAND OF DR. MOREAU*."

ENTERTAINMENT WEEKLY

Muumuu-clad **Marlon Brando** plays Chopin at the piano as 28-inch tall **Nelson de la Rosa** tinkles away above him.

"BOBBY IN WONDERLAND."

ENTERTAINMENT WEEKLY

Robert De Niro as the Mad Hatter. For this "Power Issue" of *EW*, all the artists were asked to depict the participants in fairy tale settings.

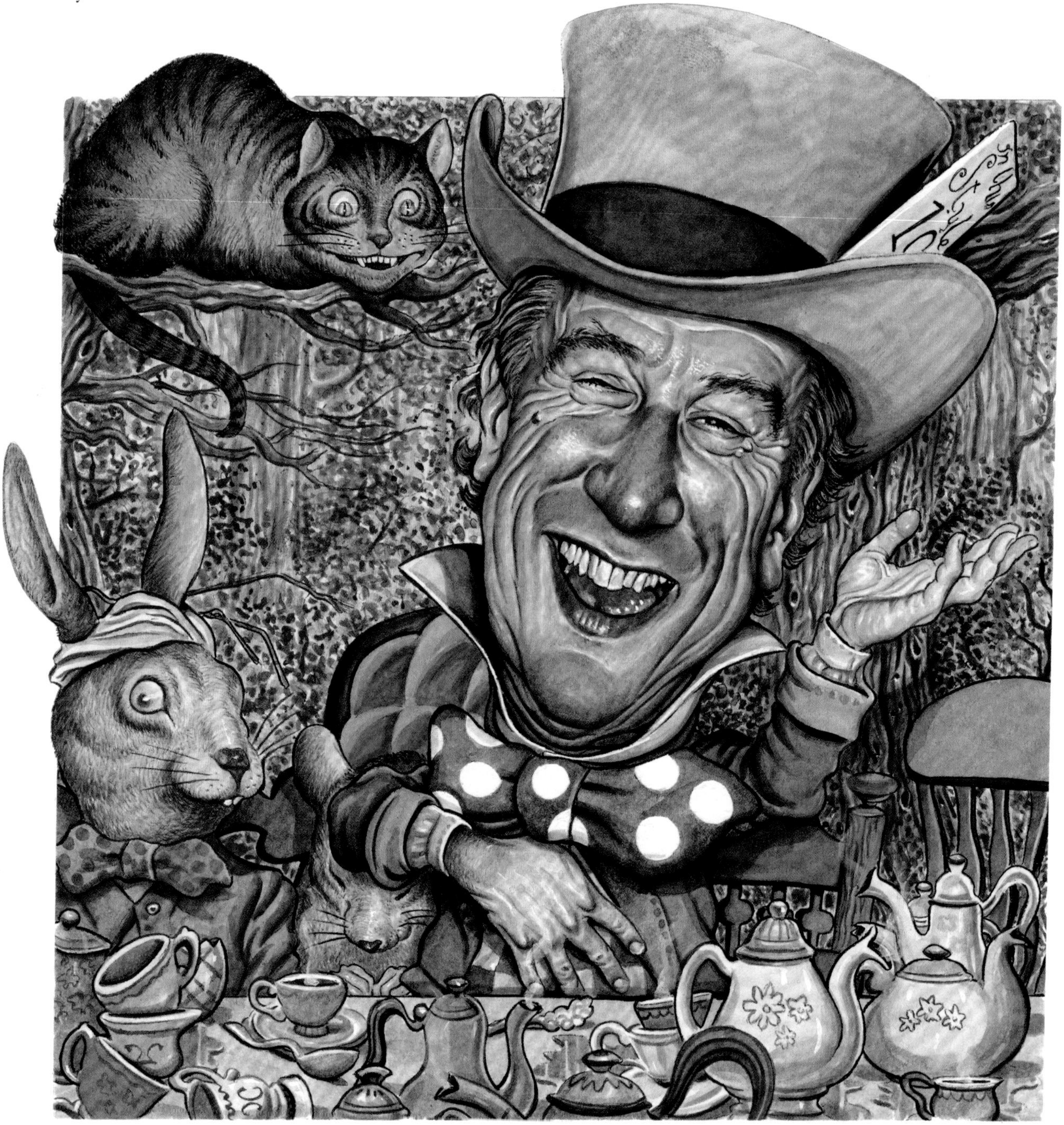

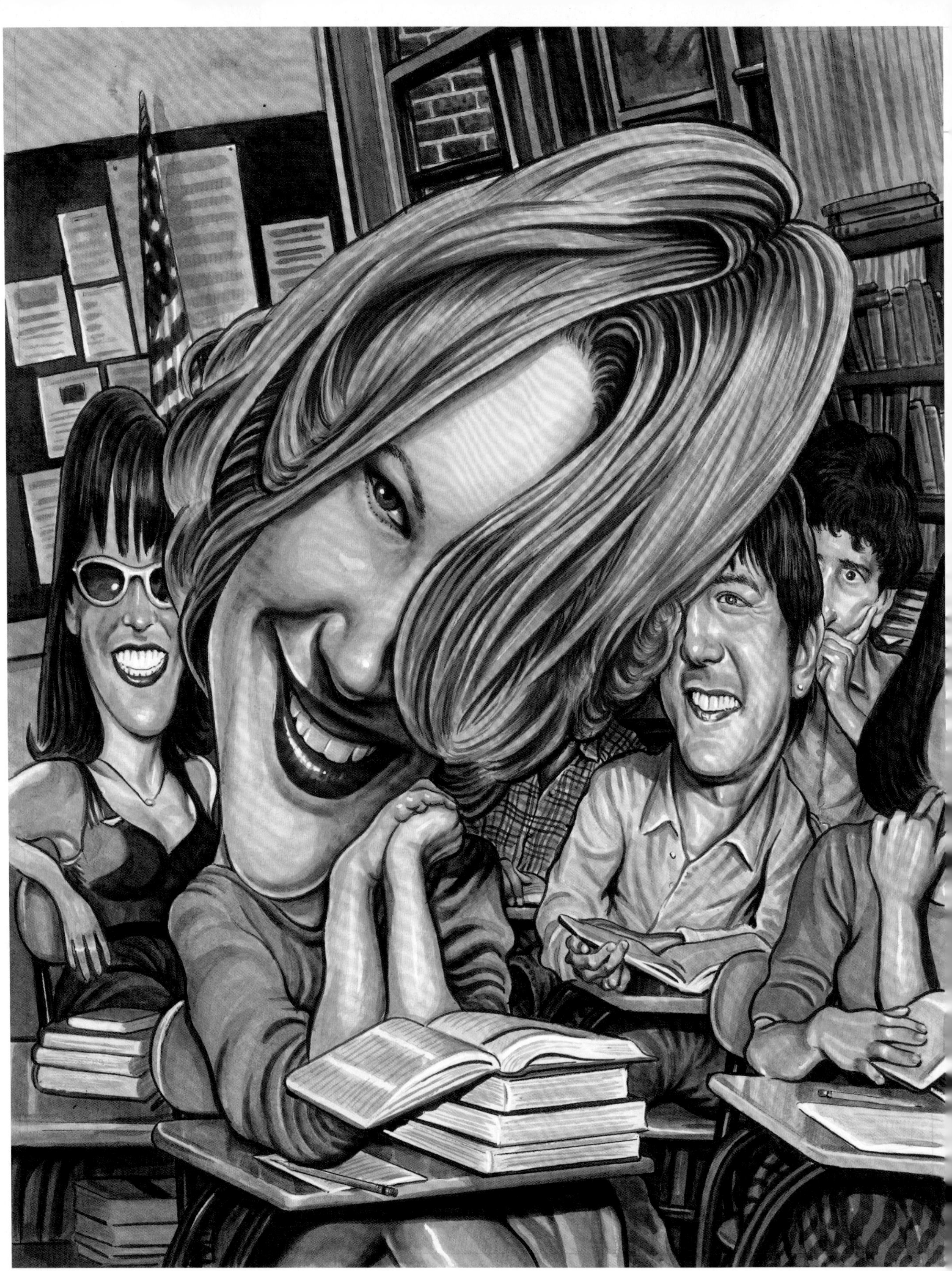

"SOMEBODY, PLEASE KISS ME."

US AIR MAGAZINE

Oh-so-adorable **Drew Barrymore** coyly poses in her film, *Never Been Kissed*, the current "In Flight Film" on US Air.

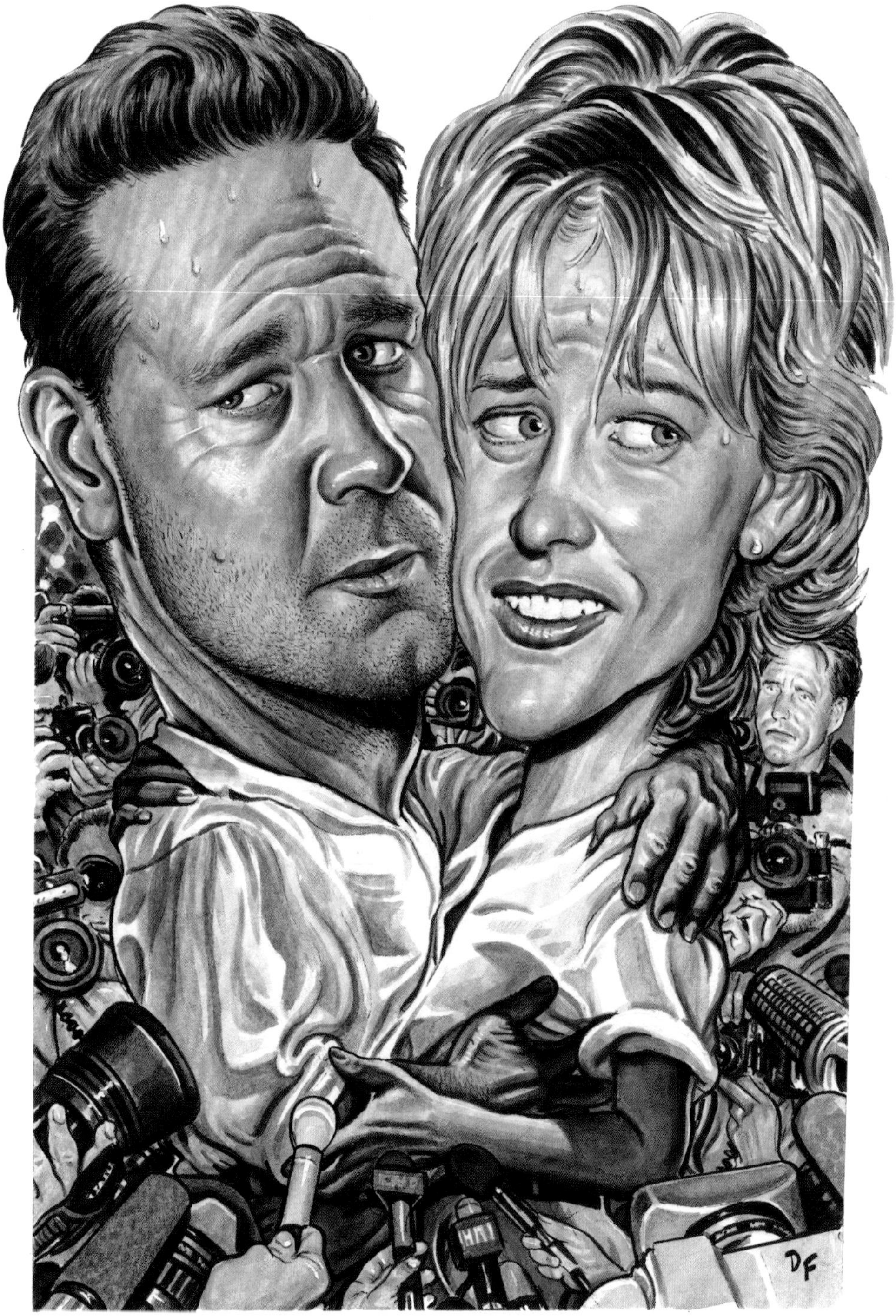
DF

"LOVE IS A BATTLEFIELD."

ENTERTAINMENT WEEKLY

"Look, can't we conduct our highly publicized affair in *private*?"

Russell Crowe and **Meg Ryan's** fling, much to the tabloids' delight.

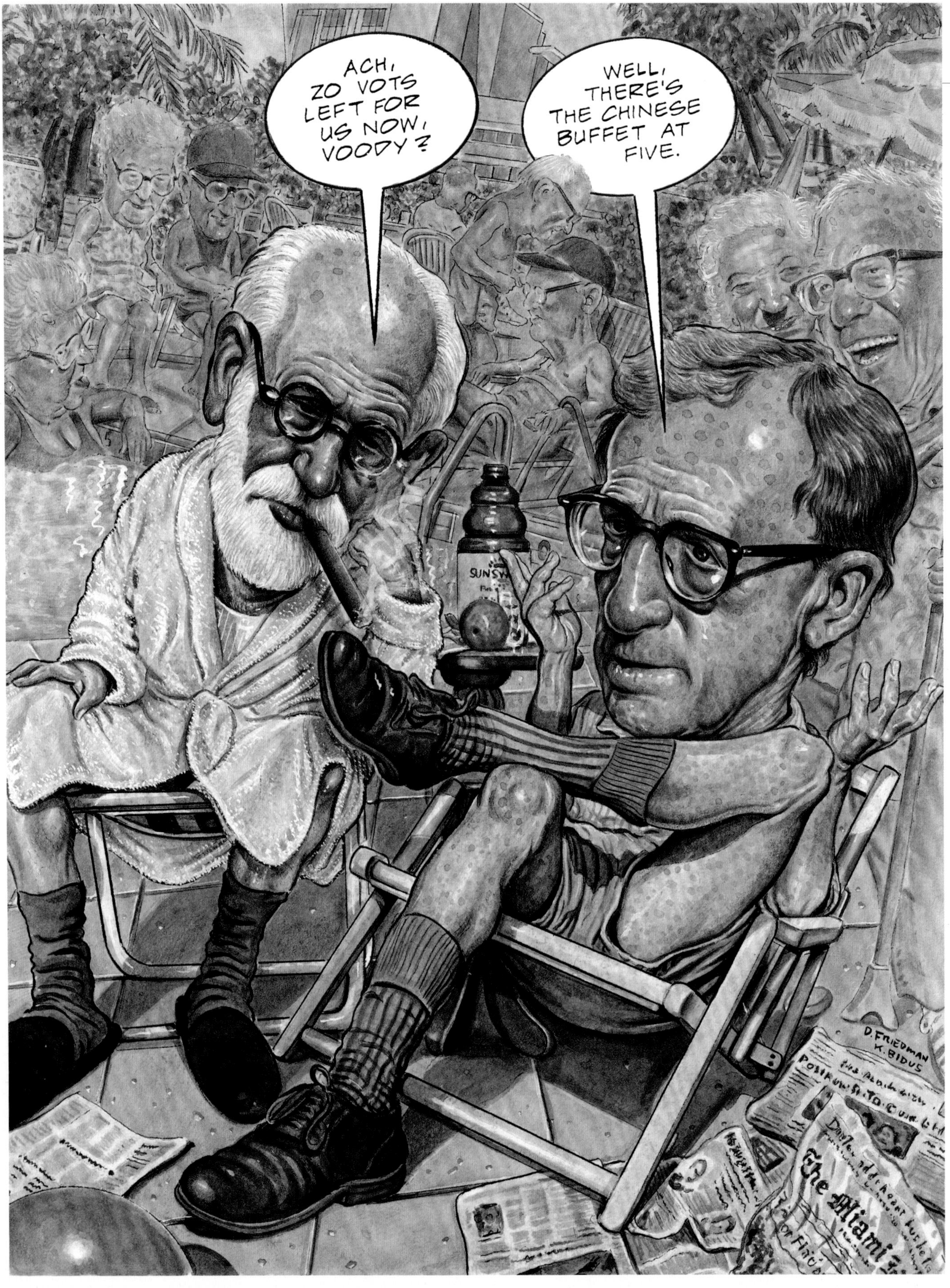
ACH, ZO VOTS LEFT FOR US NOW, VOODY?
WELL, THERE'S THE CHINESE BUFFET AT FIVE.
D. FRIEDMAN K. BIDUS

"SIGMUND & WOODY."

NEW YORK MAGAZINE

Done for a cover story predicting the "End of Psychoanalysis." **Sigmund Freud** and his favorite devotee **Woody Allen**, banished to a Florida retirement community. I always enjoy drawing Woody, although he has not always been thrilled with the results.

"JEAN & WOODY."

NEW YORK MAGAZINE

Woody Allen battles with erstwhile friend and producer **Jean Doumanian**.

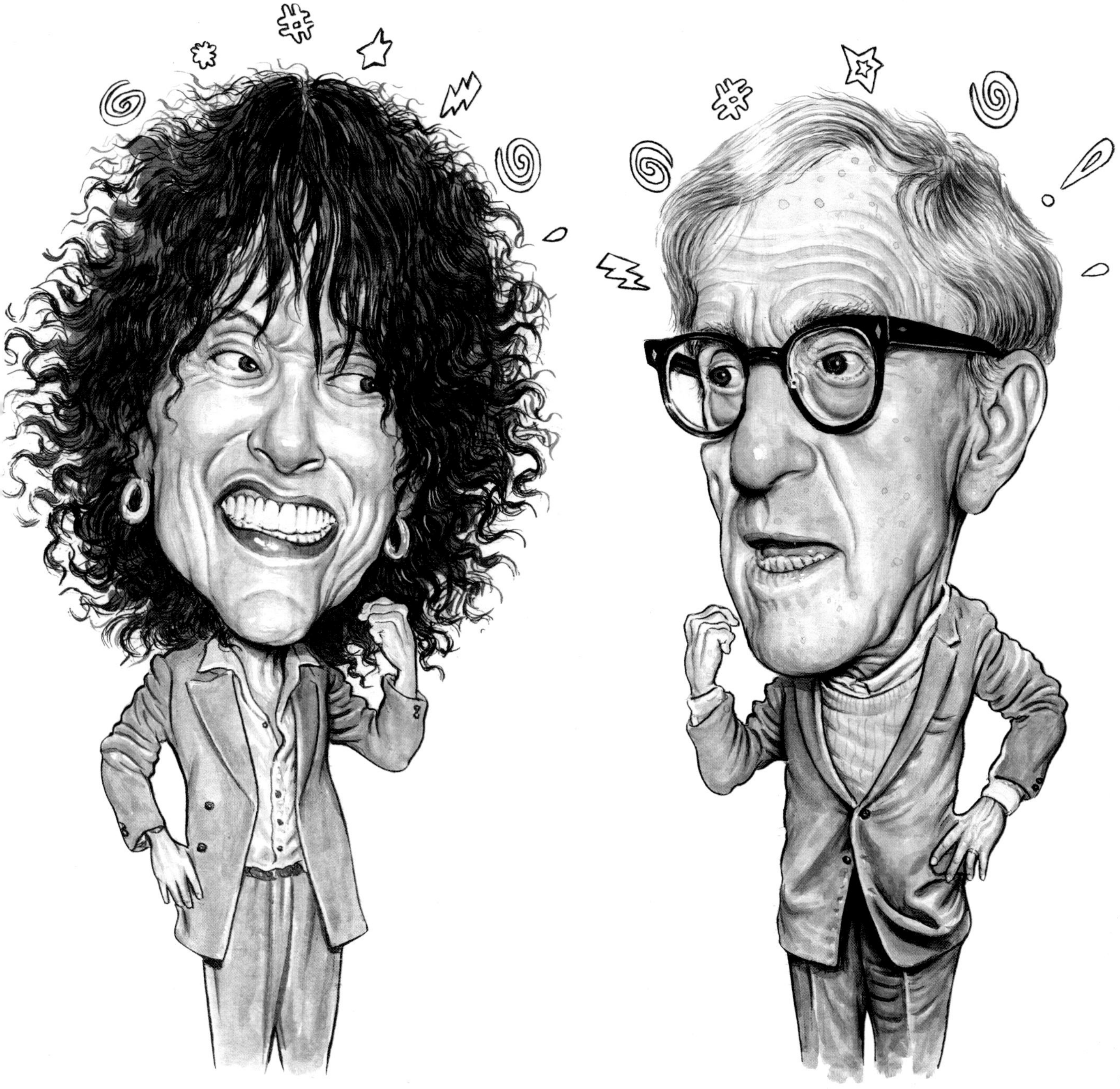

"FIFE."

Portrait of **Don Knotts** as high-strung Mayberry deputy sheriff Barney Fife. A parody of a mid-sixties *LIFE* magazine cover. The date is actually Don Knotts's 40th birthday.

"THE AMAZON CAPTURES HER NEBBISH."

This illustration is based on a rare B&W photo I first saw a few years back in *The R. Crumb Handbook*. The photo was taken backstage, sans props and setting, at the Milton Berle show, where **Arnold Stang** was a regular cast member and **Irish McCalla** was guesting that week as Sheena, Queen of the Jungle (a popular mid-'50s TV series for kids—also very popular with the dads). I instantly saw the potential to someday transform the photo into full color, replete with Arnold adorned with pith helmet and binoculars, an innocent geek-birdwatcher who happened to wander into Sheena's jungle lair. The Queen finds her Prince.

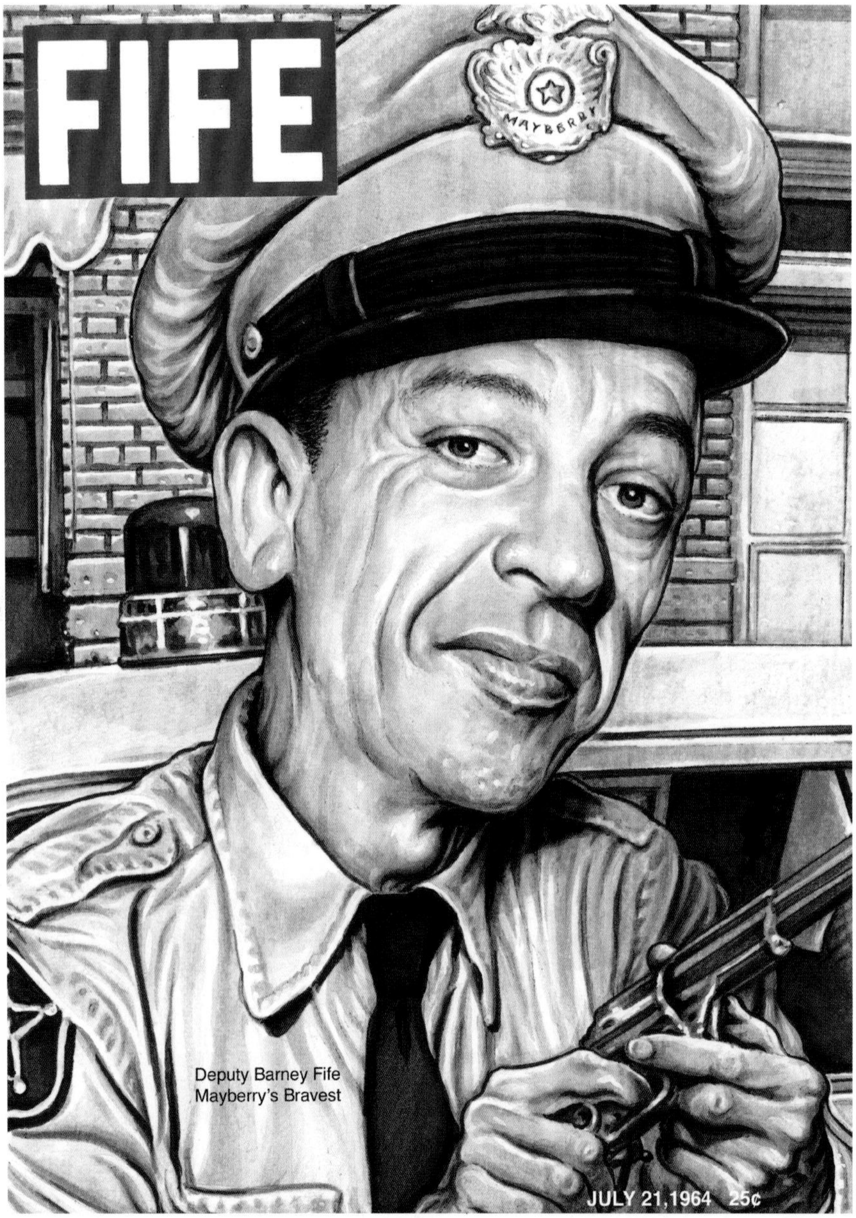
FIFE
MAYBERRY
Deputy Barney Fife
Mayberry's Bravest
JULY 21,1964 25¢

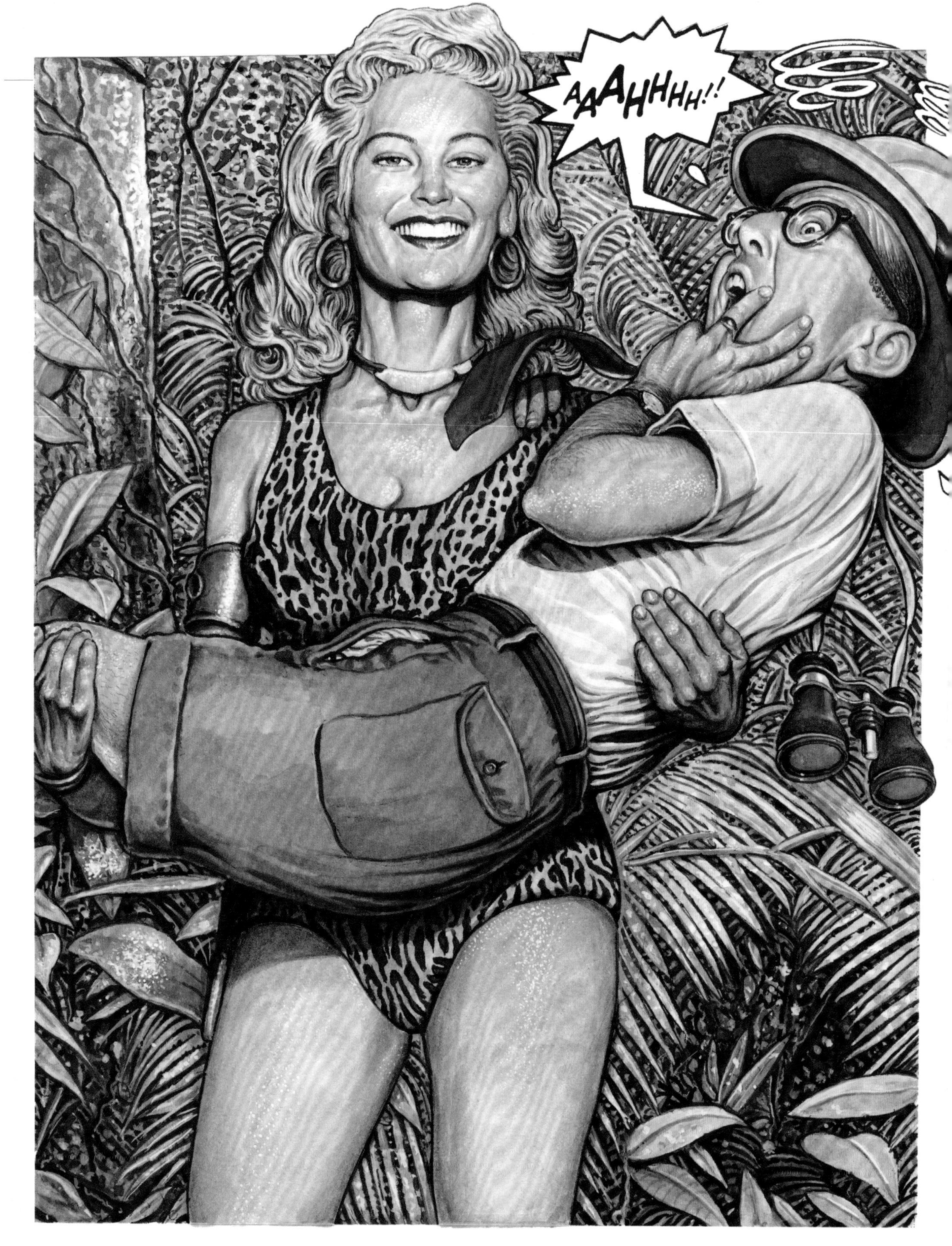
AAAHHHH!!

"SYLVESTER FLIPS HIS BIRDIE."

MAXIMUM GOLF

Two more depictions of celebrities' wacky misadventures on the golf course: Furious **Sly Stallone** throttles his putter, and...

"A WILL TO GOLF."

MAXIMUM GOLF

...**Will Smith's** golf game will not be deterred by inclement weather.

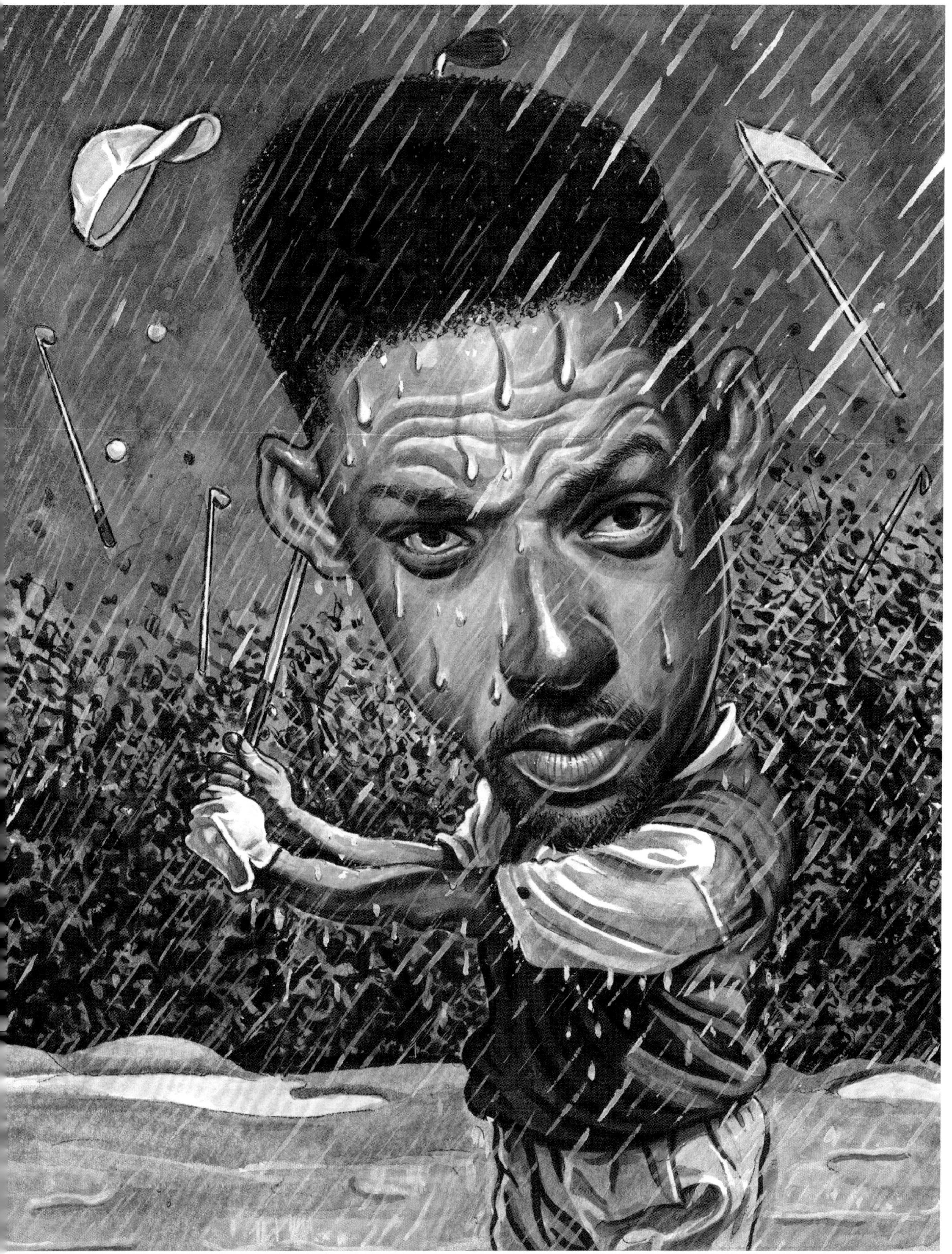

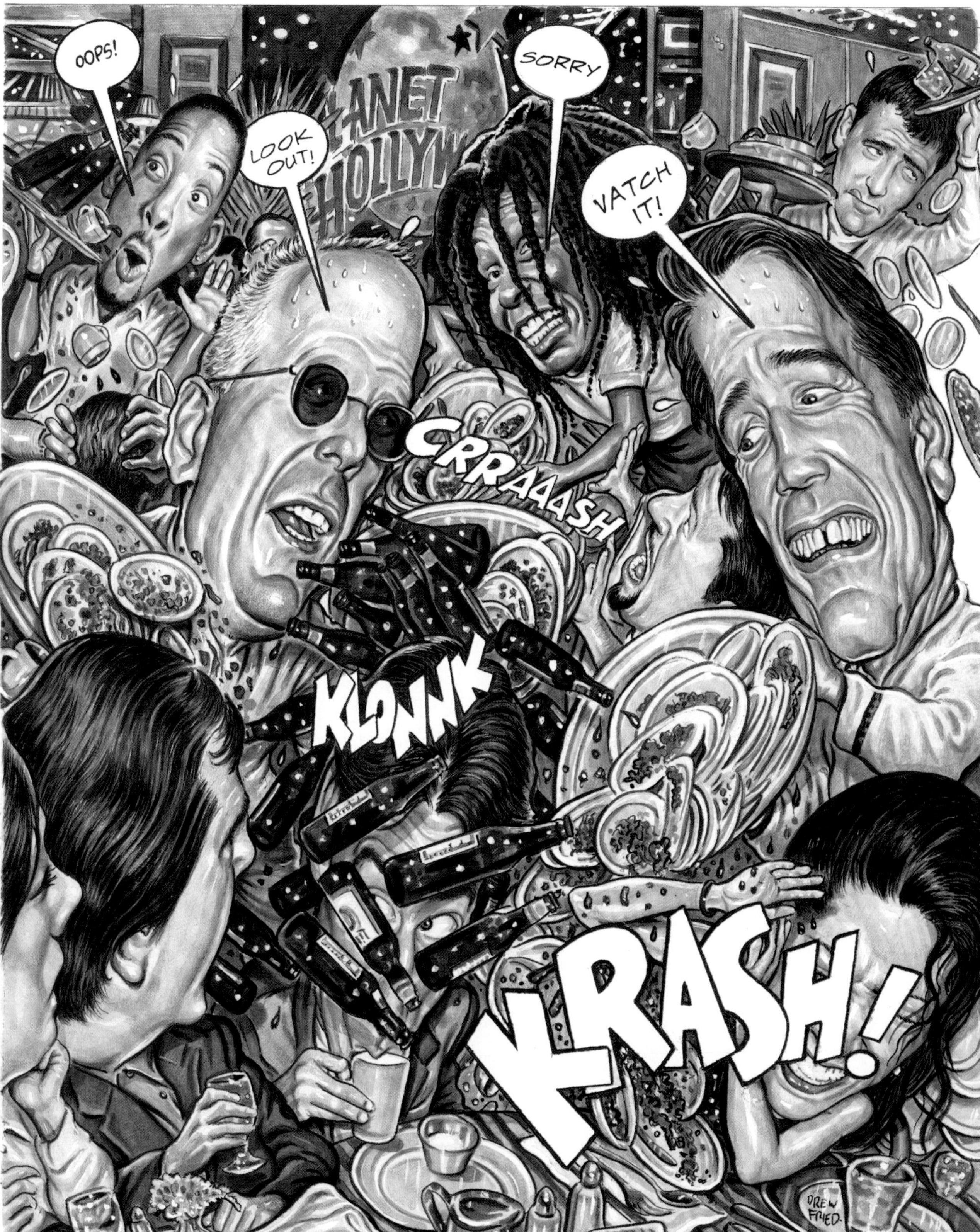
OOPS!
LOOK OUT!
SORRY
VATCH IT!
CRRAAASH
KLONNK
KRASH!
DREW FRIED-MAN

"SAVING THE PLANET."

ENTERTAINMENT WEEKLY

In a Food Fight for its life, Planet Hollywood founders **Arnold Schwarzenegger** and **Bruce Willis** courted younger stars to spice up the franchise's celebrity menu.

Will Smith, B. Willis, **Whoopi Goldberg**, A. Schwarzenegger, **George Clooney**.

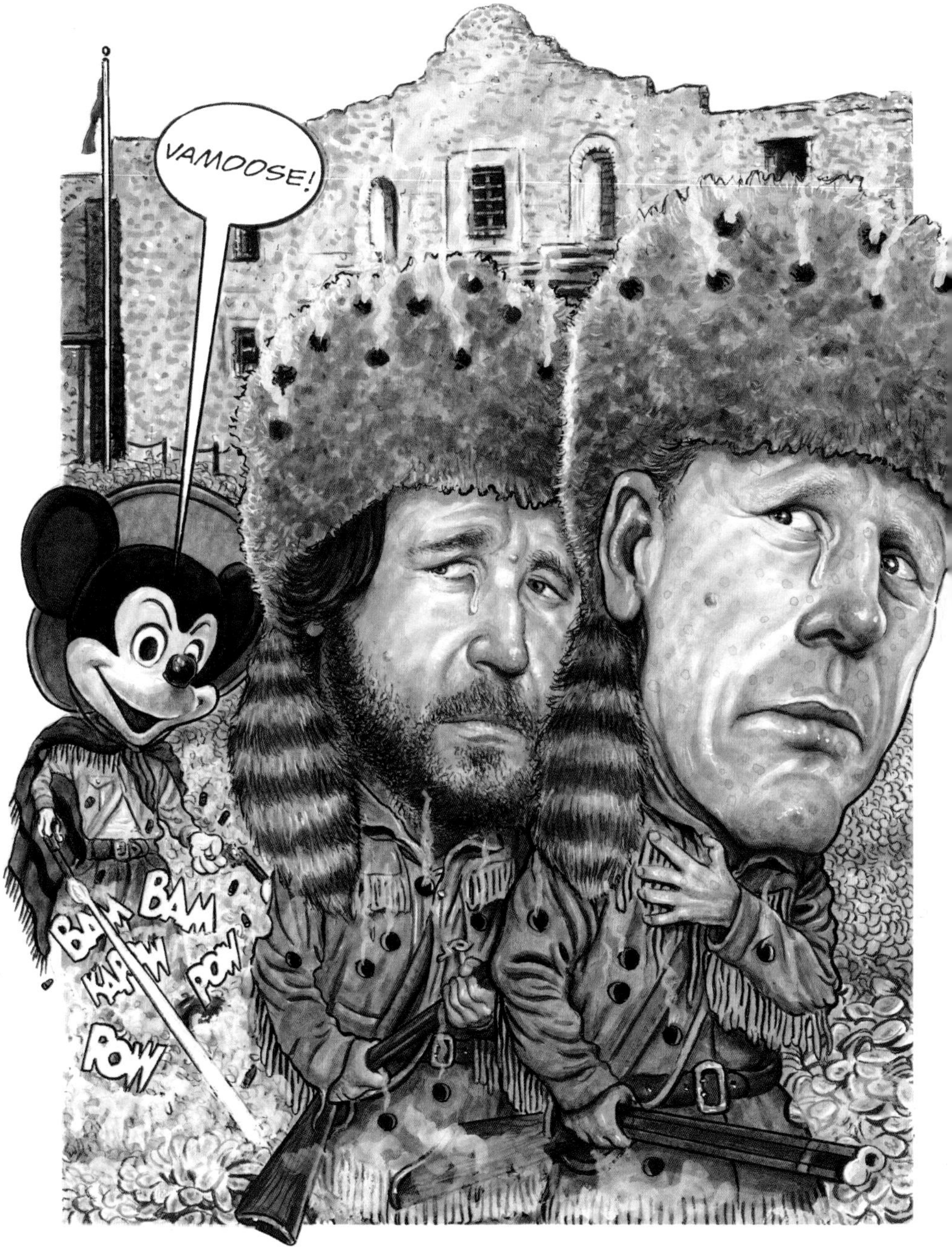
VAMOOSE!
BAM
BAM
KAPOW
POW
POW

"TEXAS TWO-STEP."

ENTERTAINMENT WEEKLY

Why a belt-tightening Disney sent Russell Crowe and Ron Howard packing over *The Alamo*.

Bandito M. Mouse, broken-hearted, buckskin-outfitted **R. Crowe** and **R. Howard**.

VARIOUS FILM FOLK

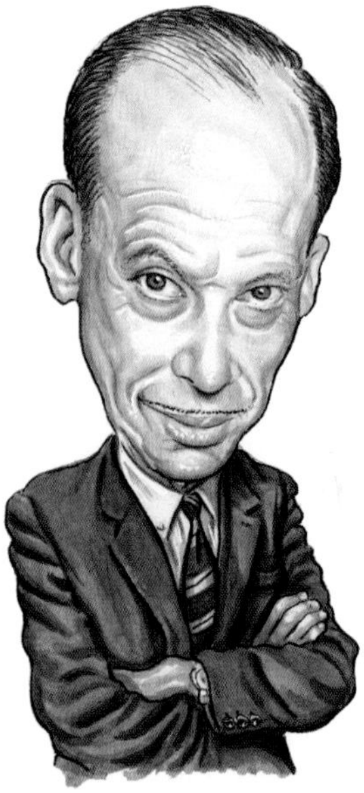

JOHN WATERS, "Naughty Boy of the Week."

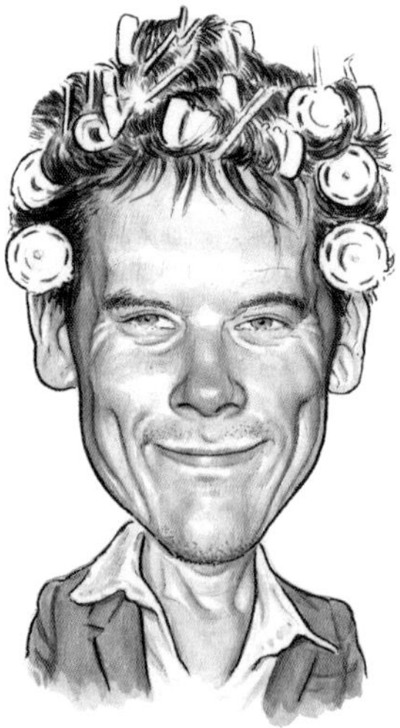

KEVIN BACON, cast as a flamboyant hairdresser in *Beauty Shop*.

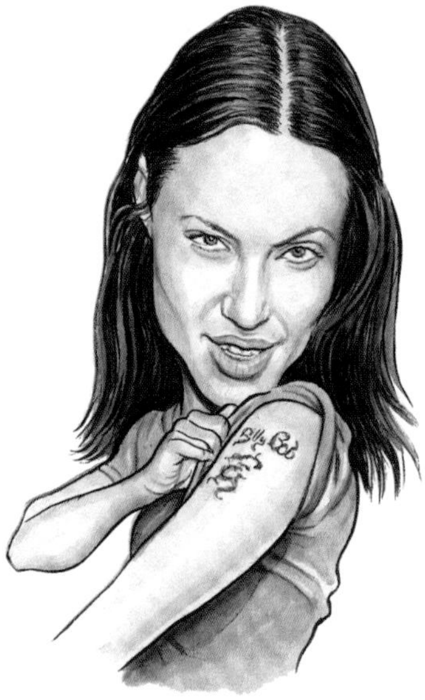

ANGELINA JOLIE displays her everlasting love for Billy Bob Thornton.

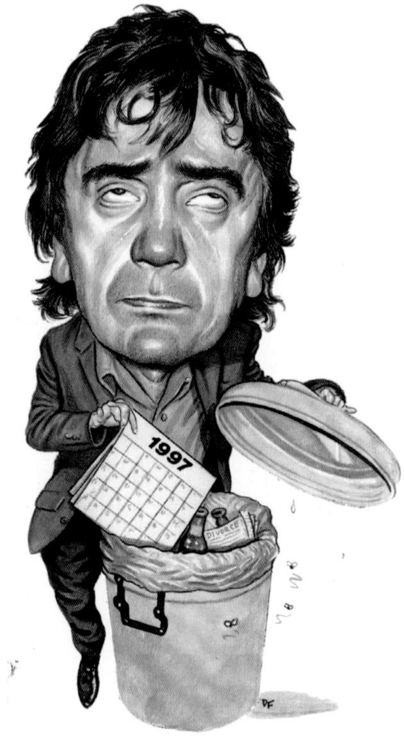
1997
DIVORCE

DUDLEY MOORE says good-bye to his lousy year.

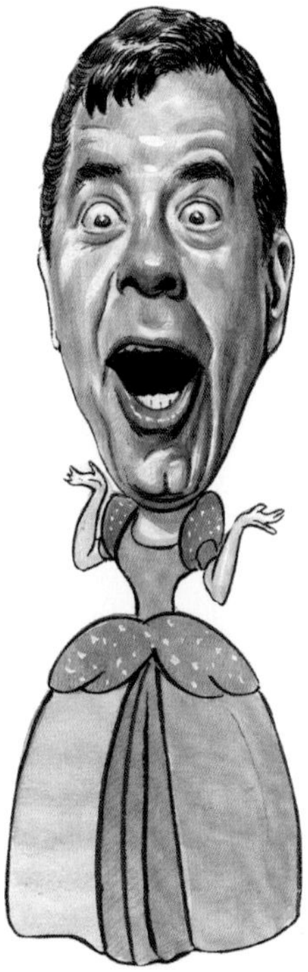

JERRY LEWIS announces a remake of *Cinderfella*.

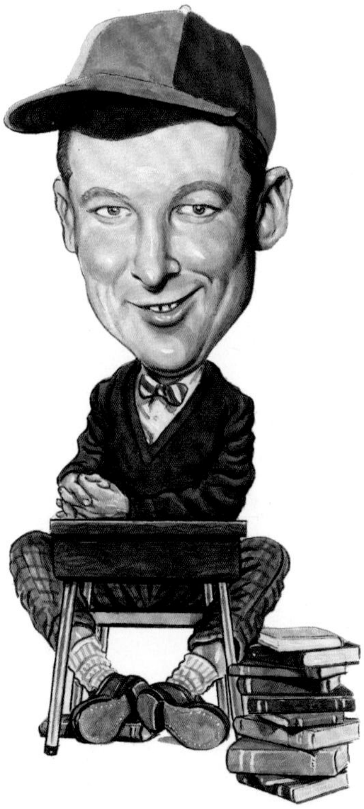

MIKE NICHOLS' classroom memories.

Oh-so-sexy MELANIE GRIFFITH.

BILLY DEE WILLIAMS/Lando Calrissian, penning his further adventures.

RON HOWARD to direct *The Da Vinci Code*.

WOODY ALLEN as the negativity thinker.

KEANU REEVES, in the money.

STANLEY KUBRICK, nervous about the potential reaction to *A Clockwork Orange*.

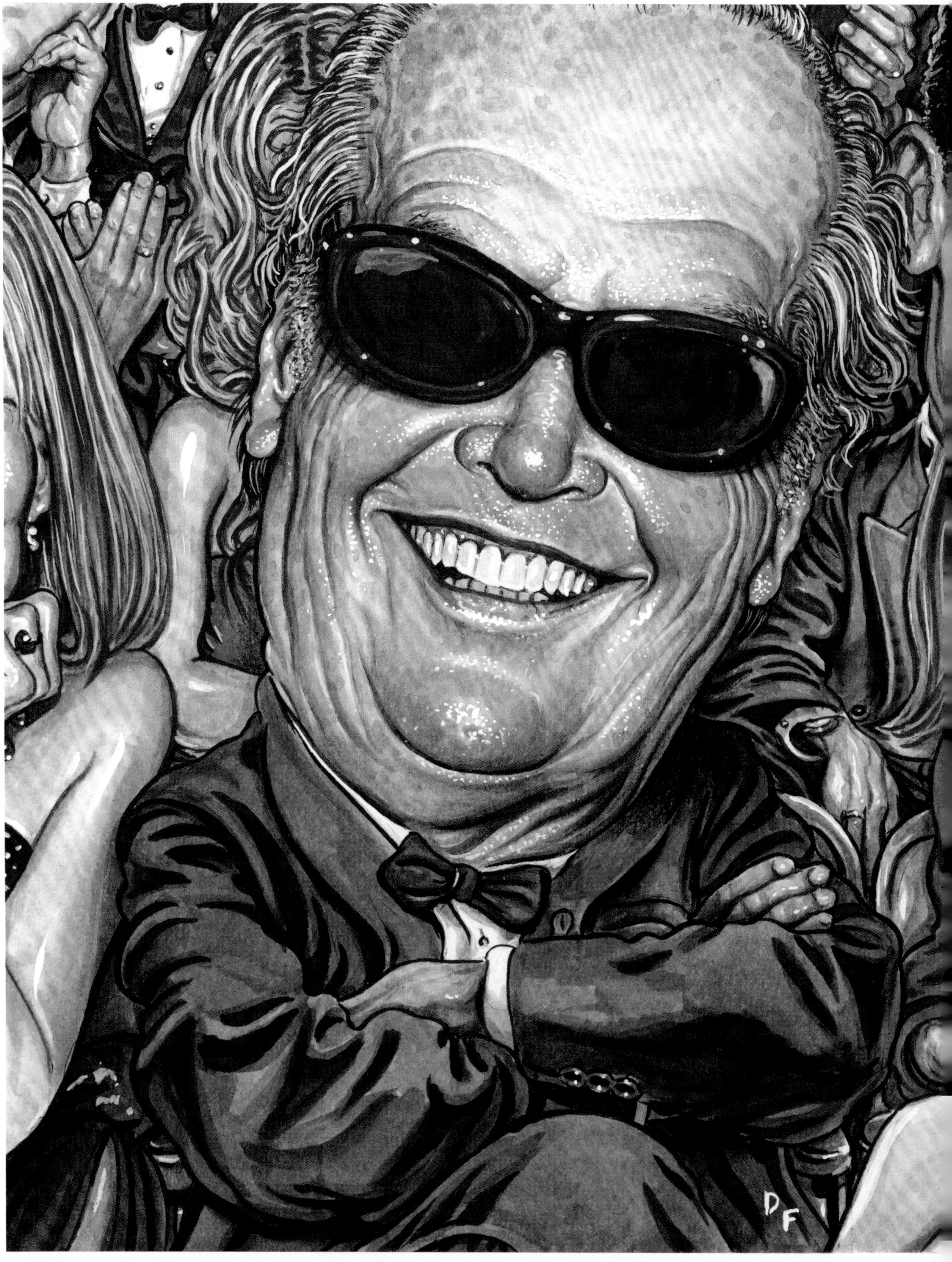
DF

"THE FRESH FACE OF OSCAR NIGHT."

TORONTO STAR

Let's prepare for the big event, *and* its rituals, the long, weepy speeches and... **Jack**—as always, front row, center.

"FALL MOVIE PREVIEW."

ROLLING STONE

Sacha Baron Cohen as *Borat,* **Daniel Craig** as the new James Bond in *Casino Royale*, **Beyoncé Knowles** as one of the *Dream Girls*, **Jack Nicholson** in *The Departed*.

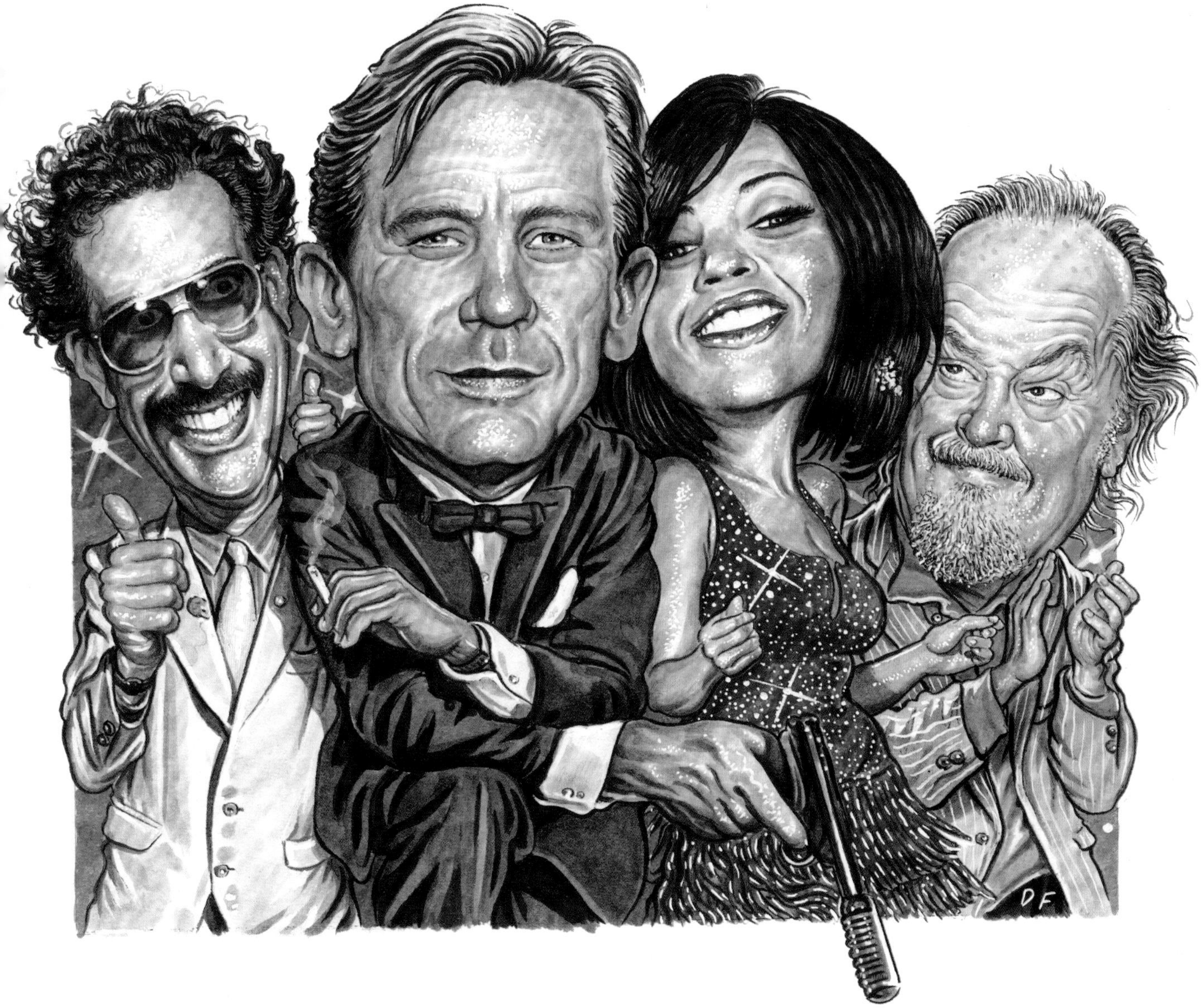
DF

"THE GREATEST DIRTY JOKE YOU'VE NEVER HEARD."

PREMIERE

For the review of the documentary *The Aristocrats*, I was asked to depict the title family in question.

Bottom: **Family Dog**, **Brother**, **Sis**.

Top: **Dad, Mom, Grandma**.

"VEXED PICTURE."

THE WASHINGTON POST

The mayhem surrounding the Oscar season.

Cate Blanchett (*Elizabeth: The Golden Age*), **Daniel Day-Lewis** (*There Will Be Blood*), **Keira Knightley** (*Atonement*), **Ellen Page** (*Juno*), **Johnny Depp** (*Sweeney Todd*), **Cate Blanchett** (*I'm Not There*), **Javier Bardem** (*No Country for Old Men*), **the paparazzi**, and the **lingering writers' strike**.

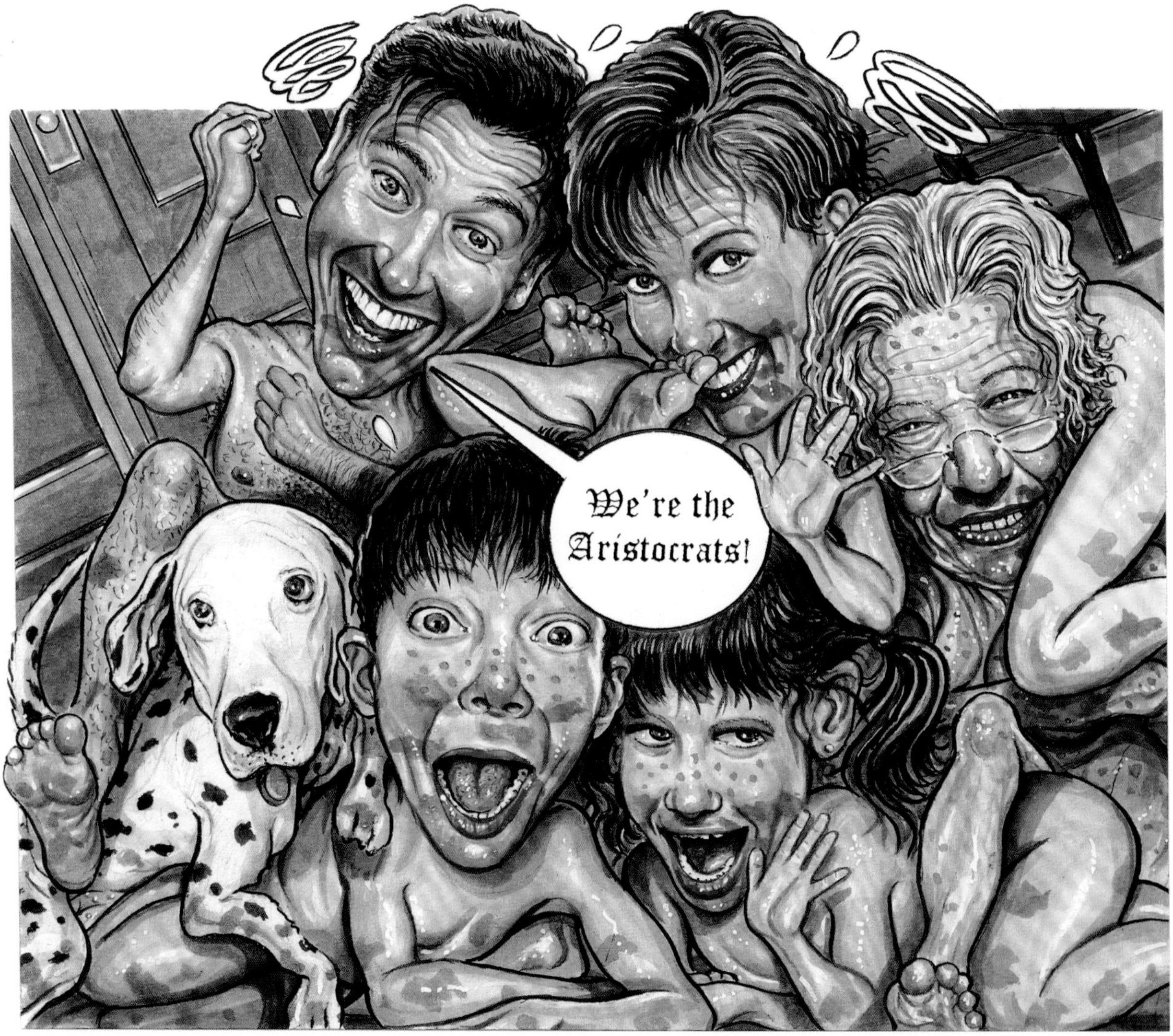
We're the Aristocrats!

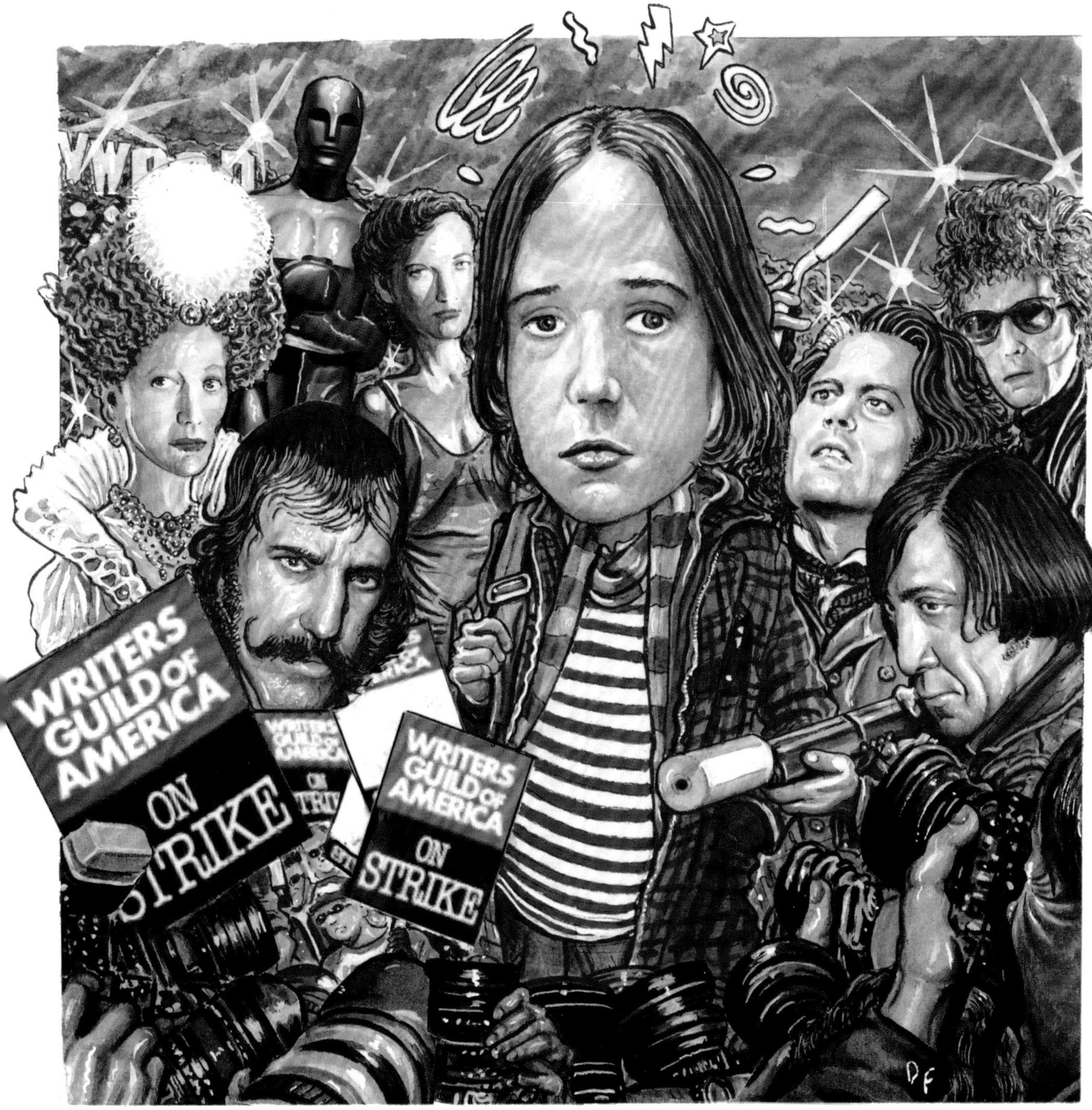
WRITERS GUILD OF AMERICA
ON STRIKE
WRITERS GUILD OF AMERICA
ON STRIKE

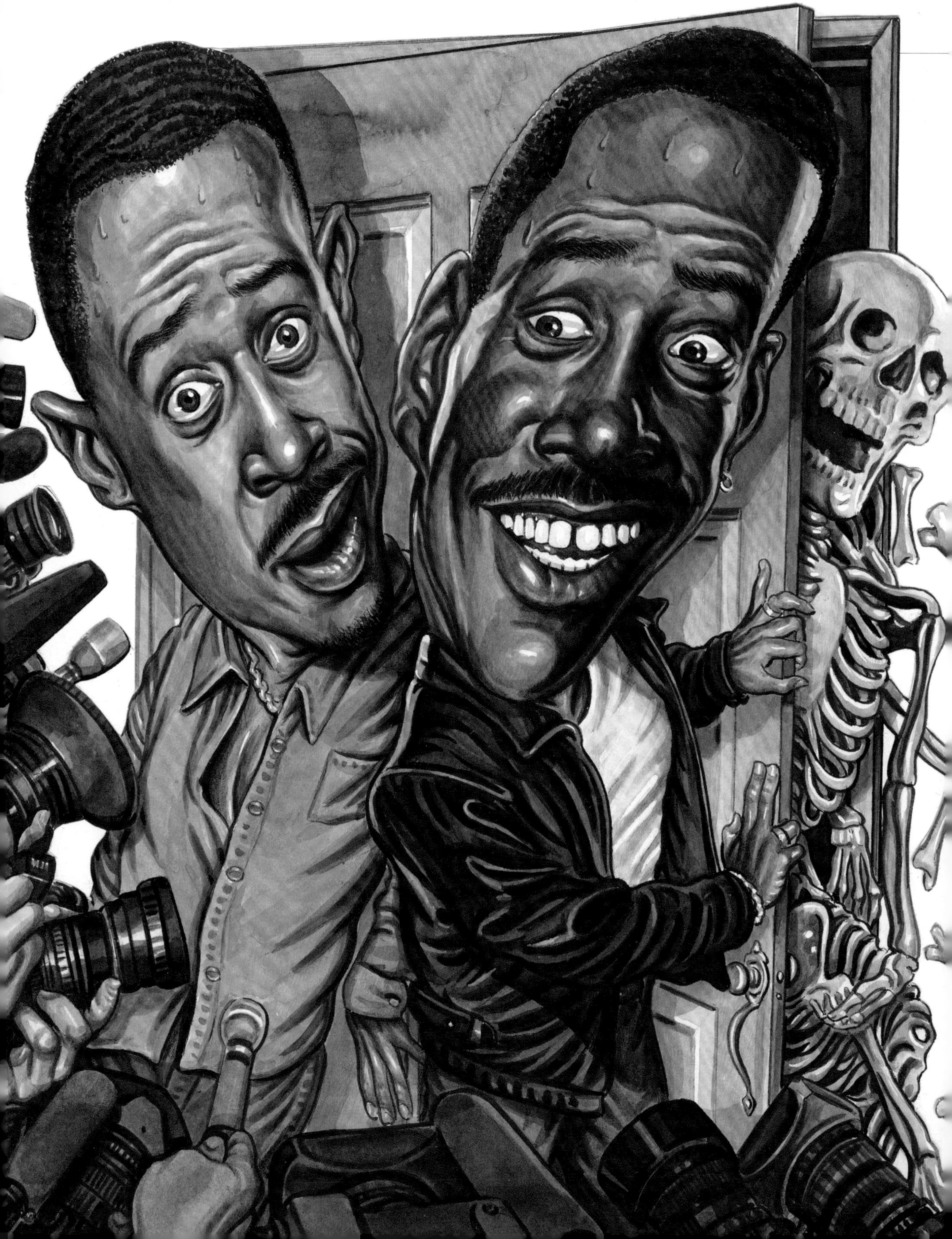

"BAD BOYS, BAD BOYS."

VIBE MAGAZINE

Martin Lawrence and **Eddie Murphy** attempt to keep their skeletons in the closet.

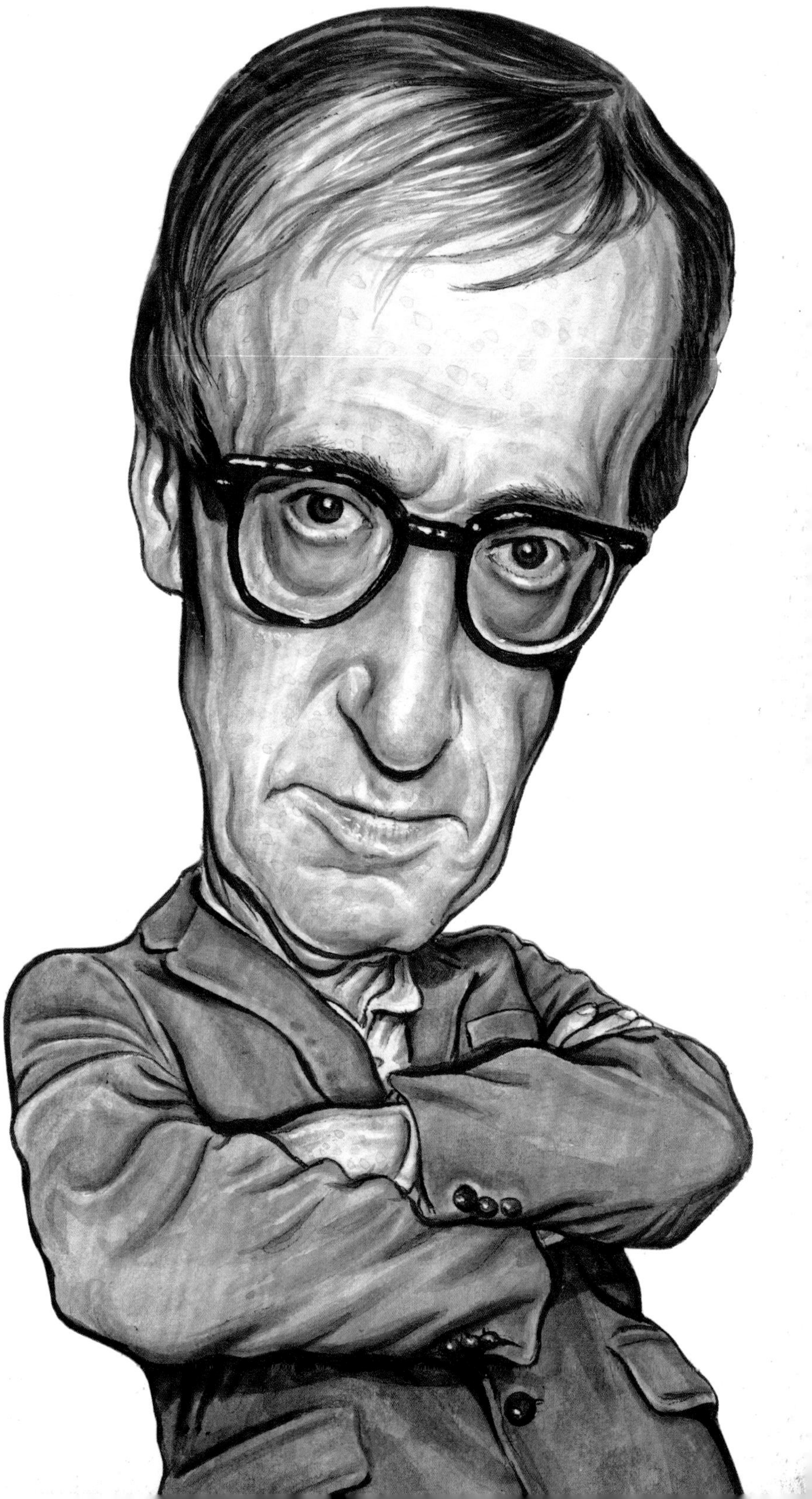

"A DEFIANT WOODY ALLEN."

NEW YORK MAGAZINE

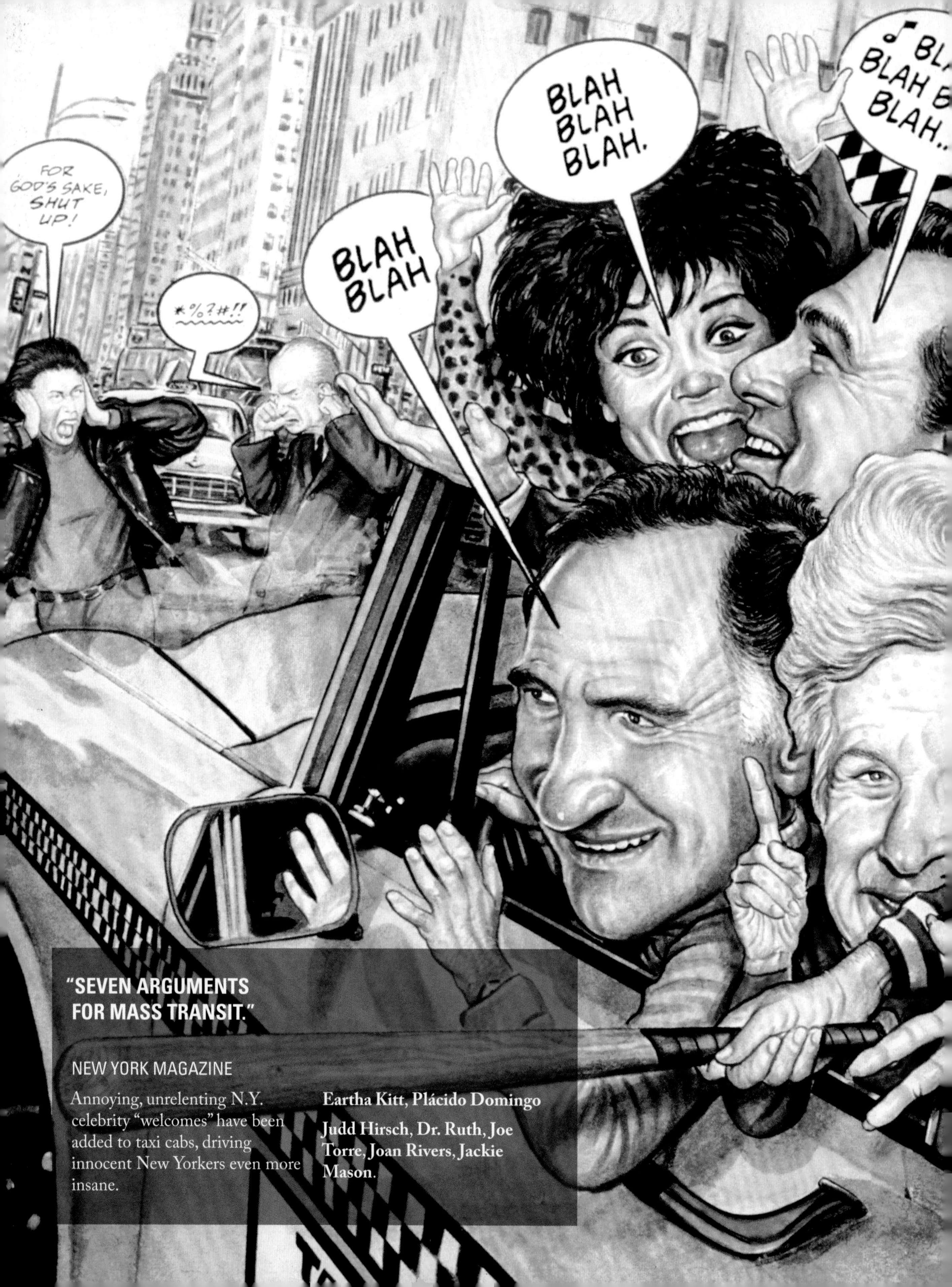
FOR GOD'S SAKE, SHUT UP!
*%?#!!
BLAH BLAH
BLAH BLAH BLAH.
BL BLAH B BLAH..

"SEVEN ARGUMENTS FOR MASS TRANSIT."

NEW YORK MAGAZINE

Annoying, unrelenting N.Y. celebrity "welcomes" have been added to taxi cabs, driving innocent New Yorkers even more insane.

Eartha Kitt, Plácido Domingo

Judd Hirsch, Dr. Ruth, Joe Torre, Joan Rivers, Jackie Mason.

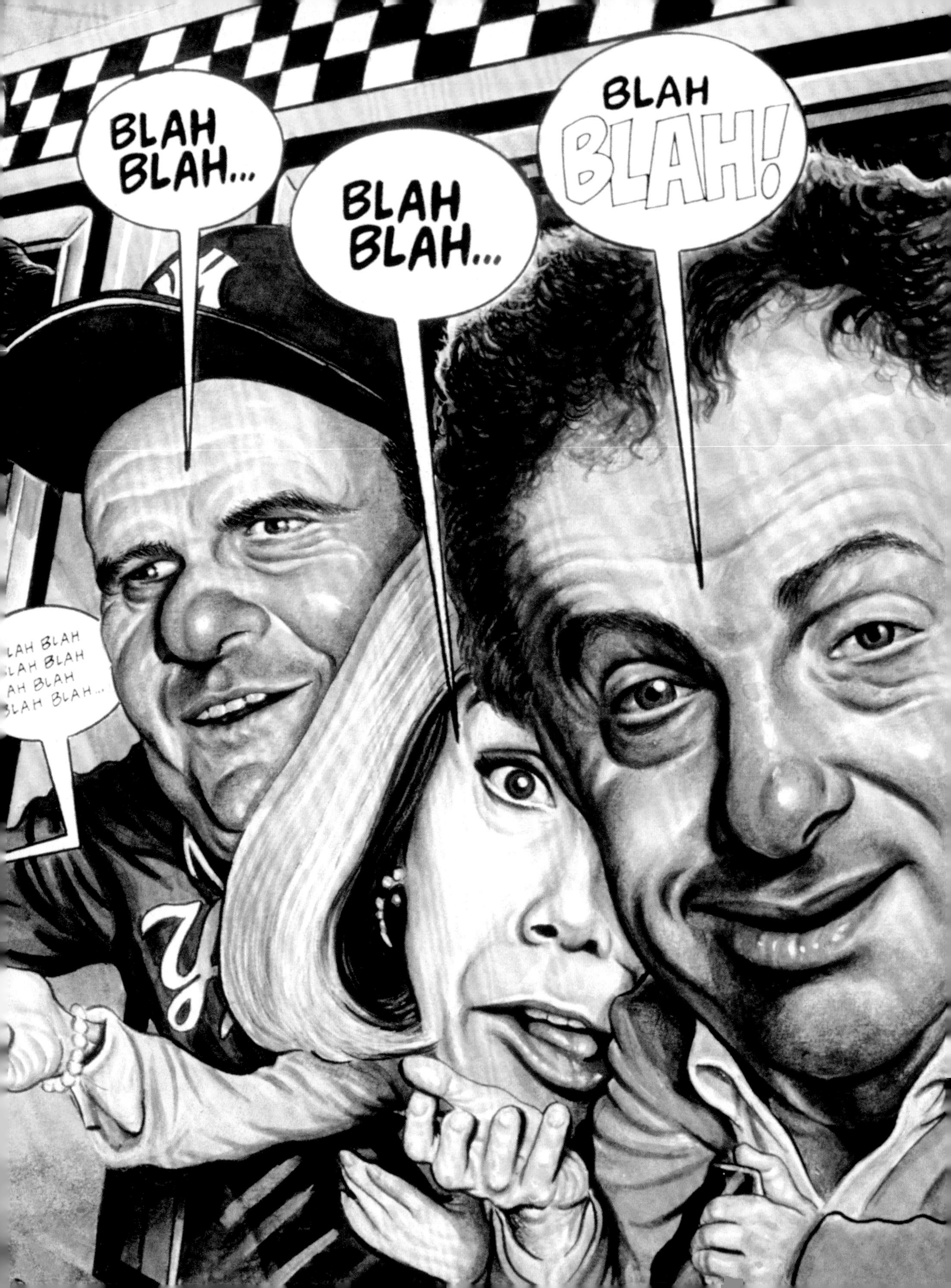
BLAH BLAH...
BLAH BLAH...
BLAH BLAH!
LAH BLAH LAH BLAH AH BLAH BLAH BLAH...

"BEAM ME UP."

PREMIERE

The article explained how **Steven Spielberg** was able to shoot scenes for *The Lost World: Jurassic Park* without actually being on set.

Pete Postlethwaite, in L.A. (below), is directed by Spielberg (right), attending a family function in the Hamptons.

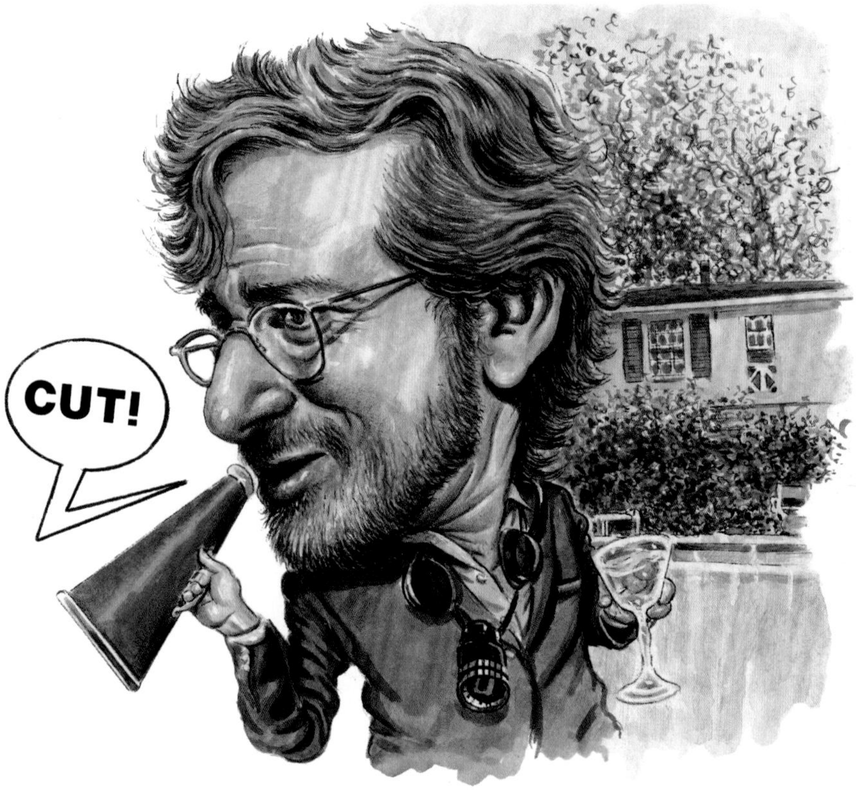
CUT!

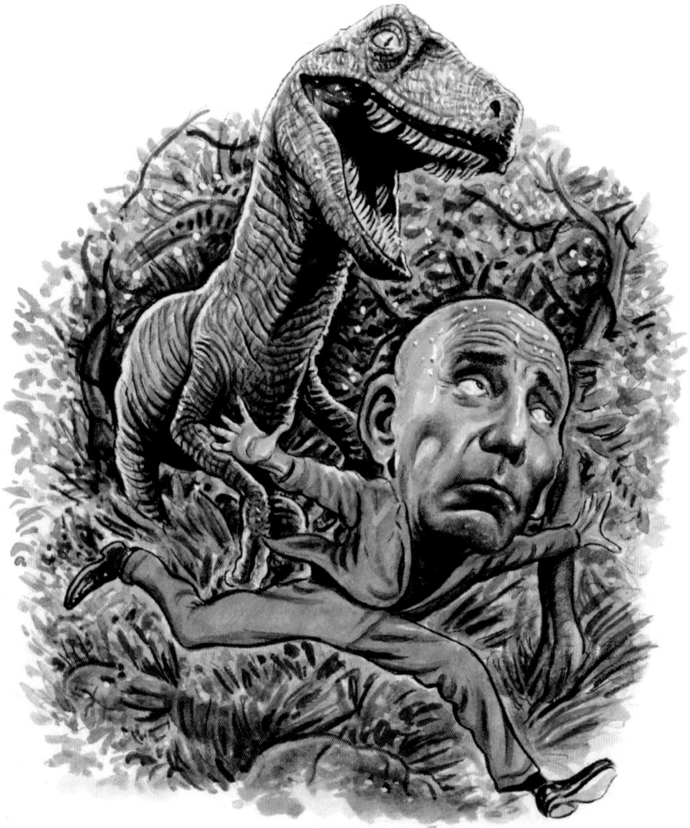

"COVER ME!"

TV GUIDE

"Over the past few months Alyssa Milano, Jessica Biel and Melissa Joan Hart have struck provocative poses on the covers of such so-called laddie magazines as ***Maxim*** and ***Gear***, sometimes drawing the ire of their TV employers in the process. But the recent discovery of classic back issues from these beer-'n'-babes magazines' archives argues that today's starlets are only following in a long-standing TV tradition." (From an article written by Andy Borowitz.)

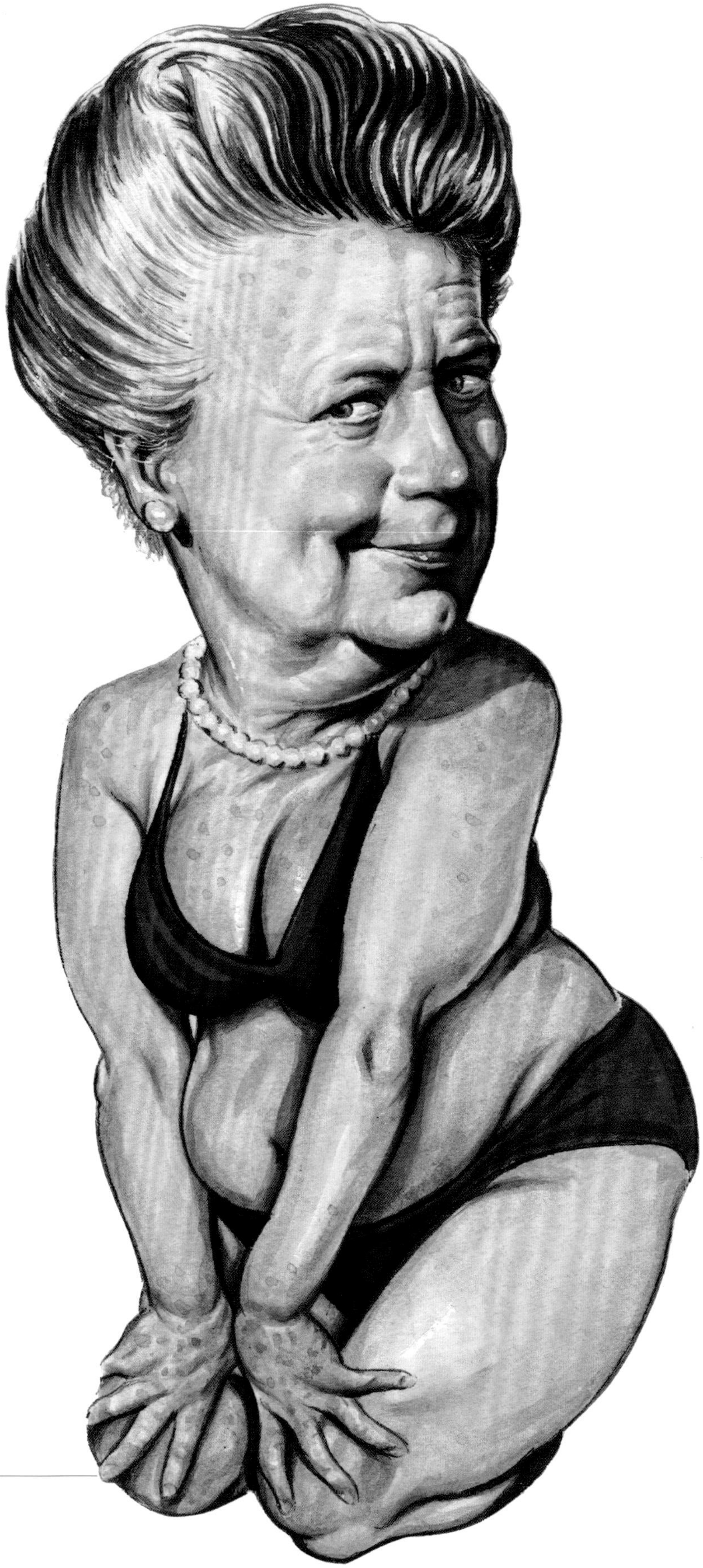

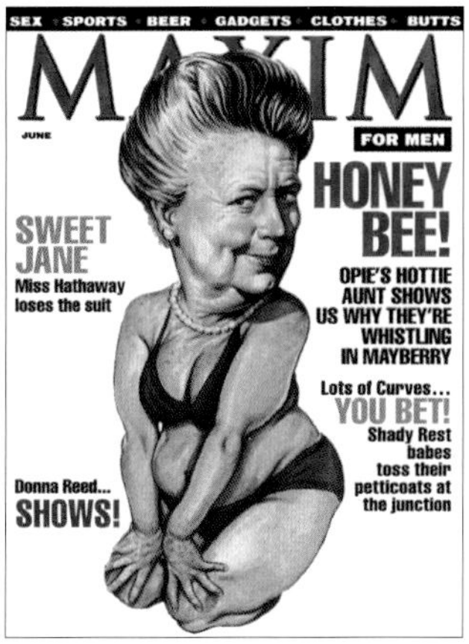
SEX · SPORTS · BEER · GADGETS · CLOTHES · BUTTS
MAXIM
JUNE
FOR MEN
HONEY BEE!
OPIE'S HOTTIE AUNT SHOWS US WHY THEY'RE WHISTLING IN MAYBERRY
SWEET JANE
Miss Hathaway loses the suit
Lots of Curves... YOU BET!
Shady Rest babes toss their petticoats at the junction
Donna Reed... SHOWS!

AUNT BEE

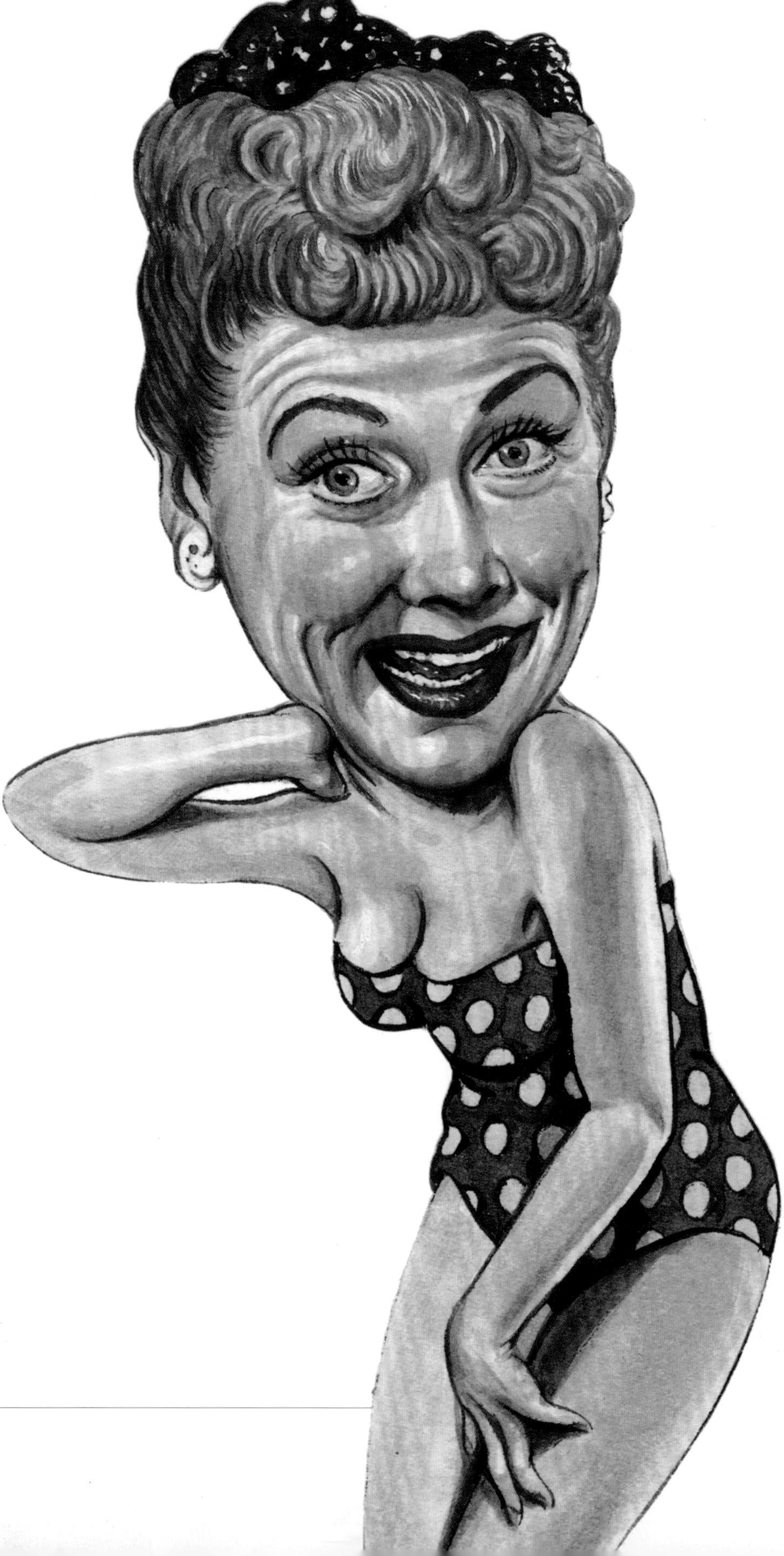

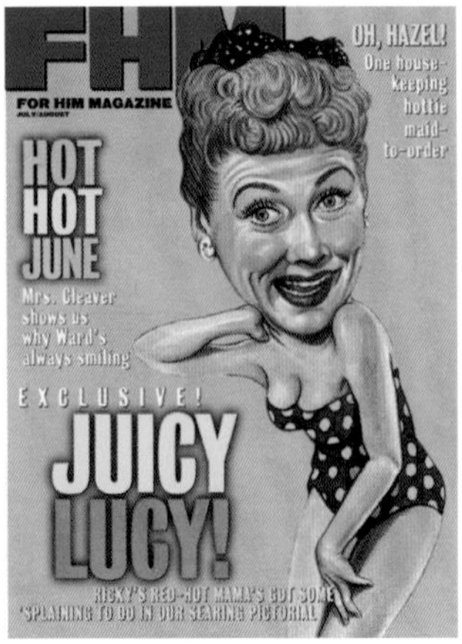
FHM
FOR HIM MAGAZINE
OH, HAZEL!
One house-keeping hottie maid-to-order
HOT HOT JUNE
Mrs. Cleaver shows us why Ward's always smiling
EXCLUSIVE!
JUICY LUCY!
RICKY'S RED-HOT MAMA'S GOT SOME 'SPLAINING TO DO IN OUR SEARING PICTORIAL

LUCY RICARDO

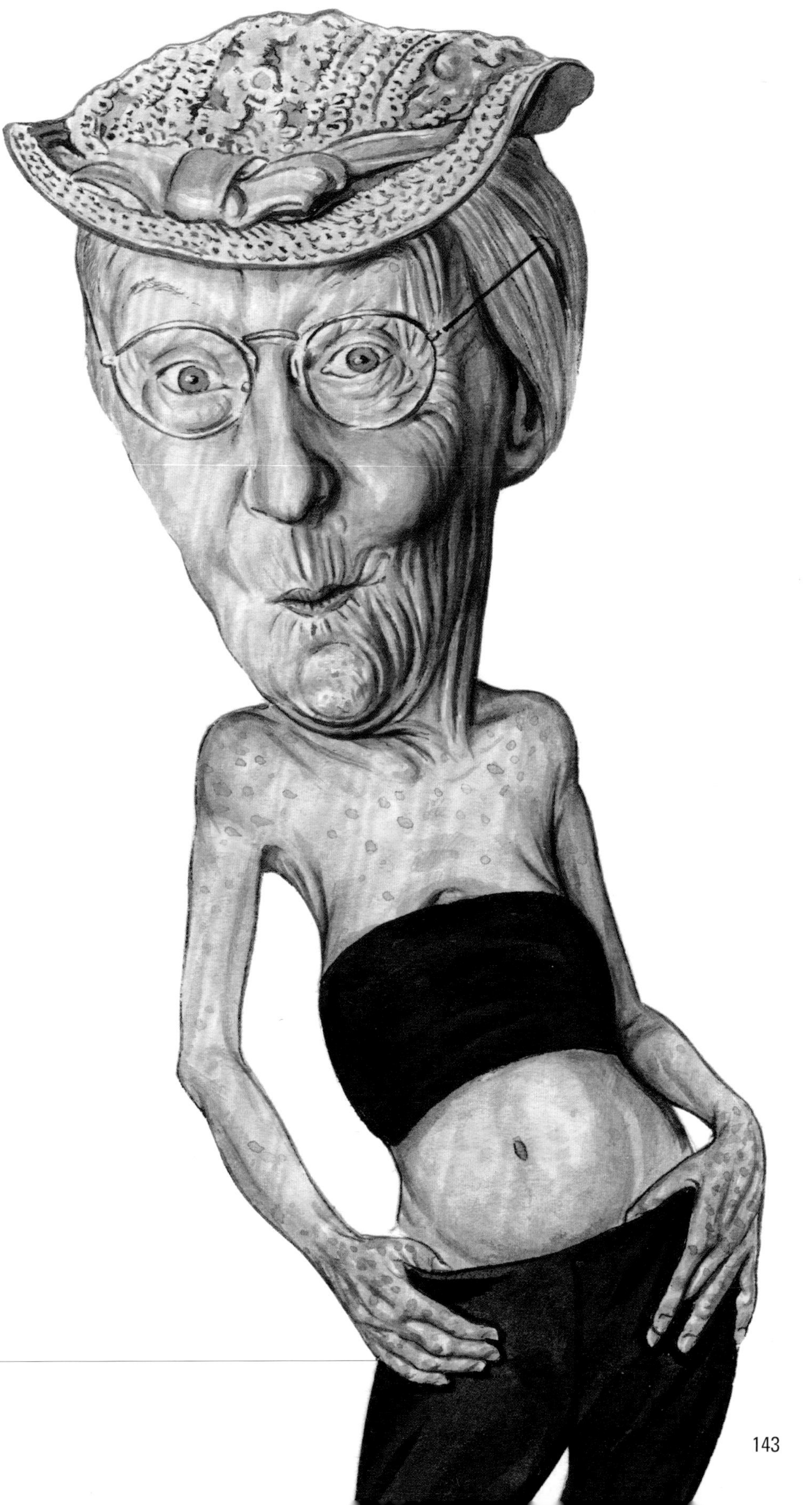

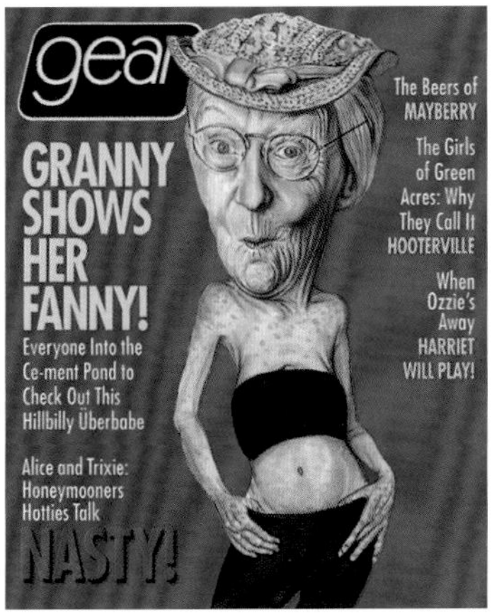
gear
GRANNY SHOWS HER FANNY!
Everyone Into the Ce-ment Pond to Check Out This Hillbilly Überbabe
Alice and Trixie: Honeymooners Hotties Talk NASTY!
The Beers of MAYBERRY
The Girls of Green Acres: Why They Call It HOOTERVILLE
When Ozzie's Away HARRIET WILL PLAY!

GRANNY CLAMPETT

"ALL IN THE BUS."

LIVE & LEARN:

Producer/bus driver **Norman Lear** takes his favorite students on an outing: **Archie Bunker**, **Fred Sanford**, **Mary Hartman**, and **George Jefferson.**

"THE LOSING ZONE."

EMMY MAGAZINE

Sci-Fi TV series never seem to win any Emmys. Clockwise from top, **Leonard Nimoy** (*Star Trek*), **Edward James Olmos** (*Battlestar Galactica*), **Armin Shimerman** (*Star Trek: Deep Space Nine*), **Patrick Stewart** (*Star Trek: The Next Generation*), **Gillian Anderson** (*The X-Files*), **Rod Serling**, and **Sarah Michelle Gellar** (*Buffy the Vampire Slayer*).

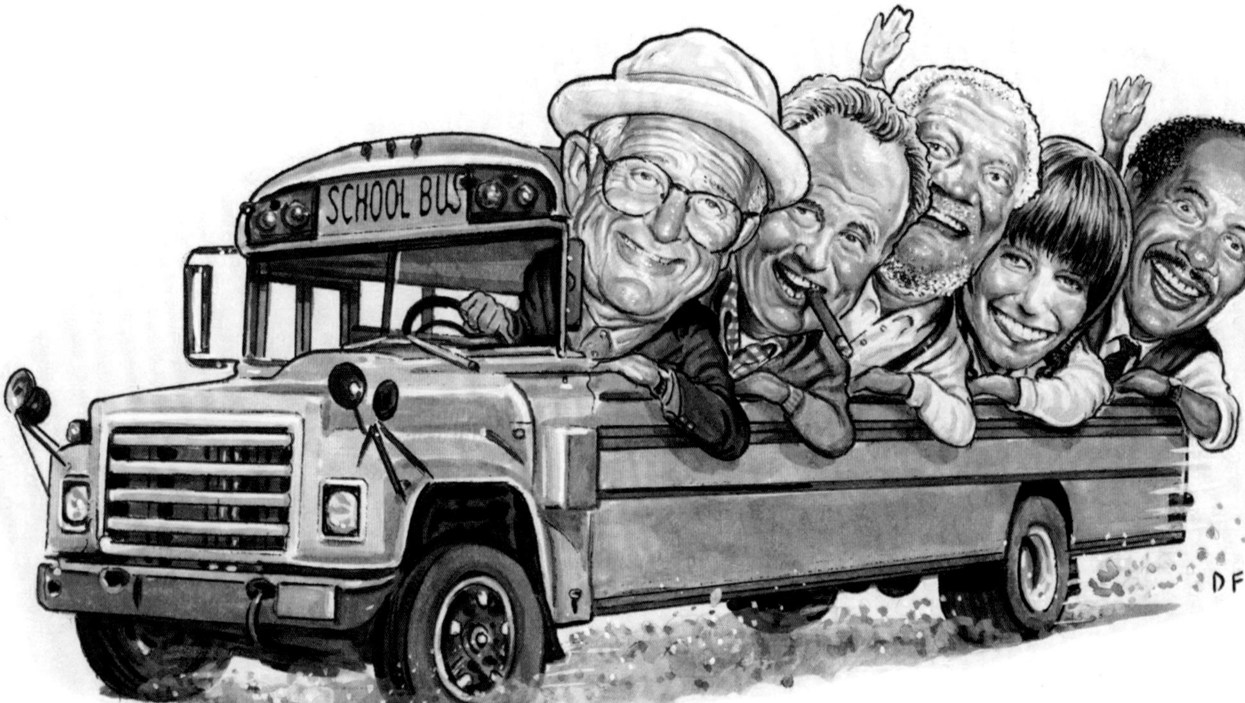
SCHOOL BUS
DF

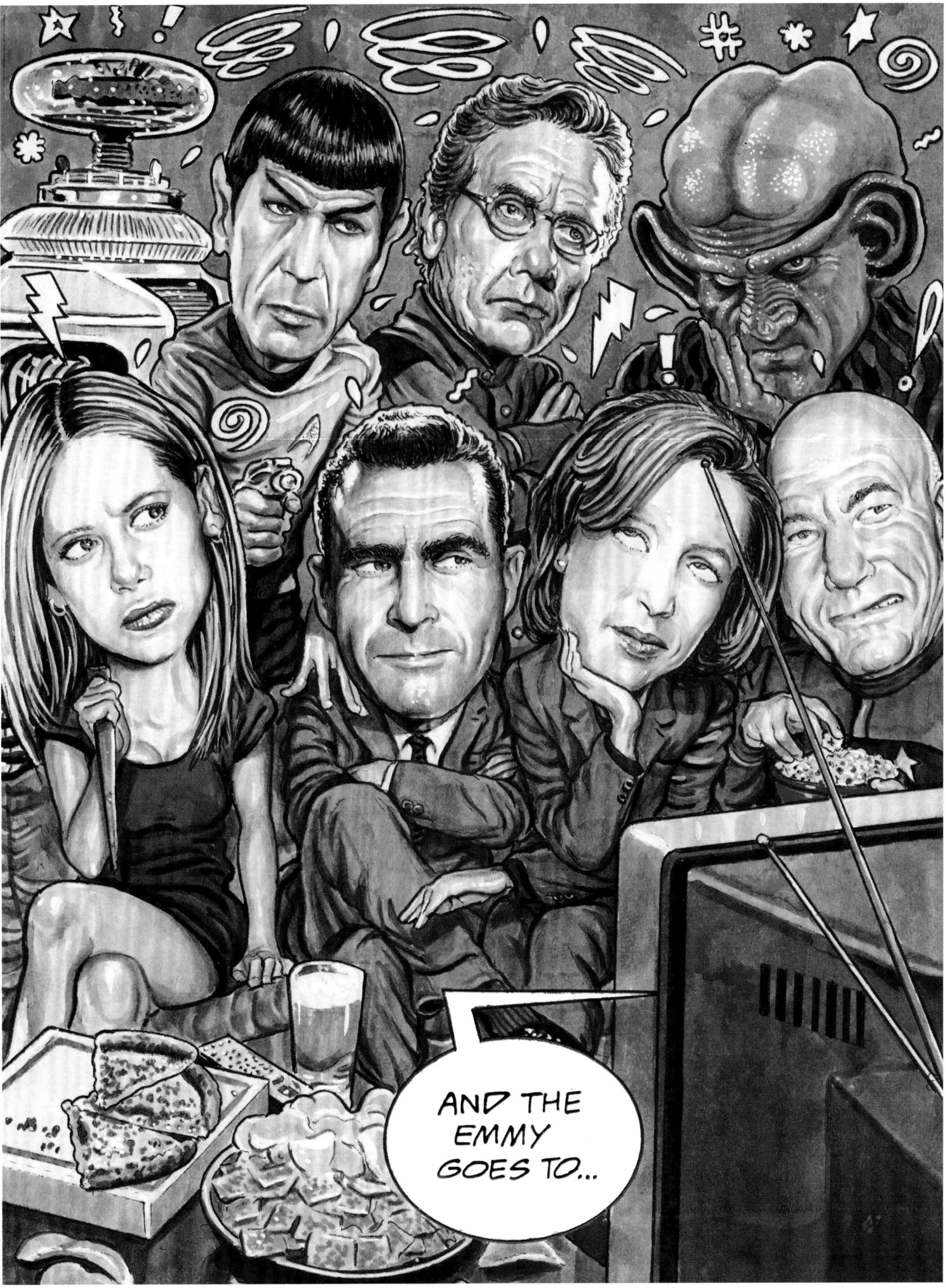
AND THE EMMY GOES TO...

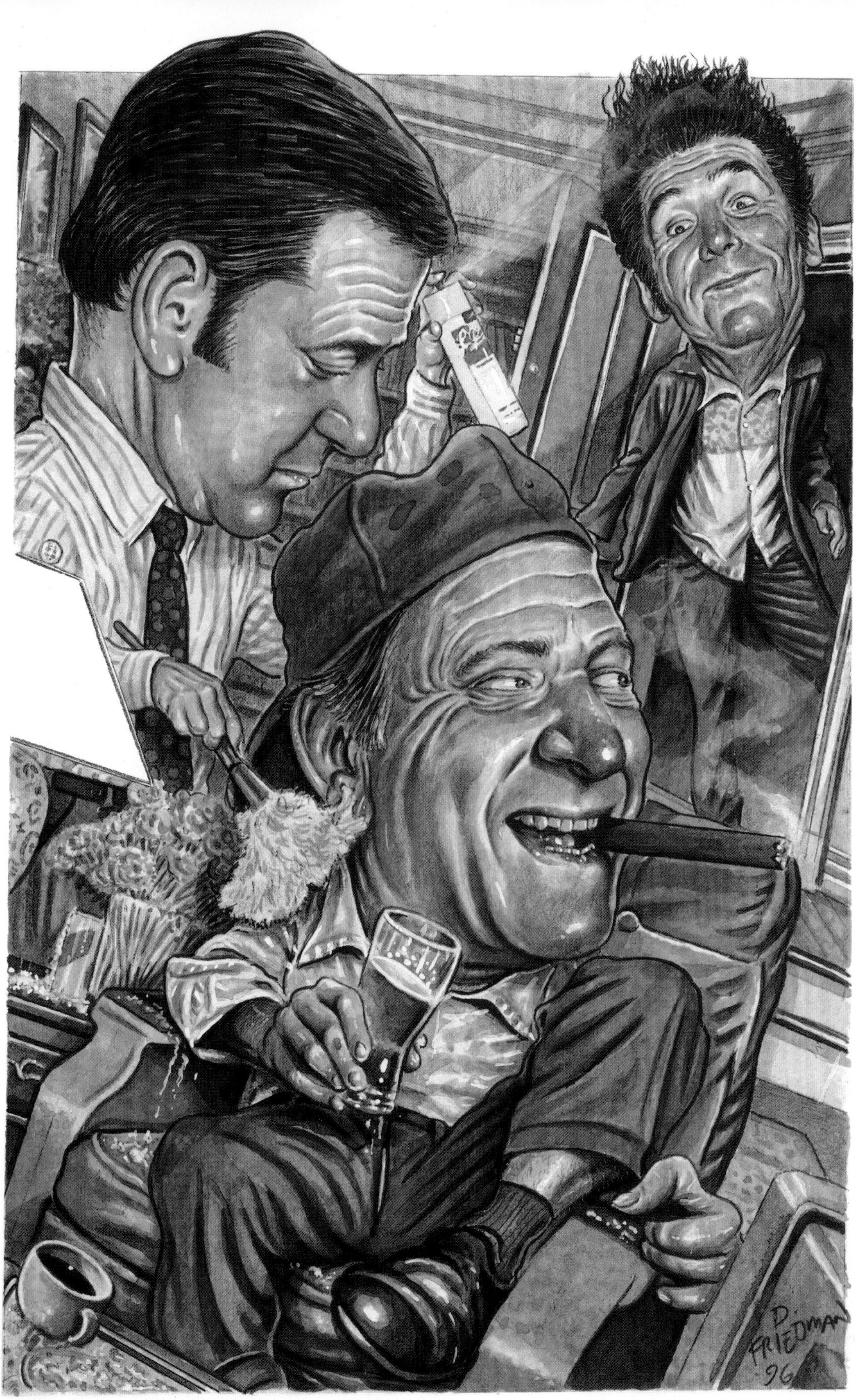
D. FRIEDMAN 96

"THE ODD TRIO."

ENTERTAINMENT WEEKLY

Oops! Kramer enters the wrong apartment.

Tony Randall as Felix Unger, **Jack Klugman** as Oscar Madison, **Michael Richards** as Kramer.

"GAME FACES."

ENTERTAINMENT WEEKLY

"Greats" from *Hollywood Squares*, past and present.

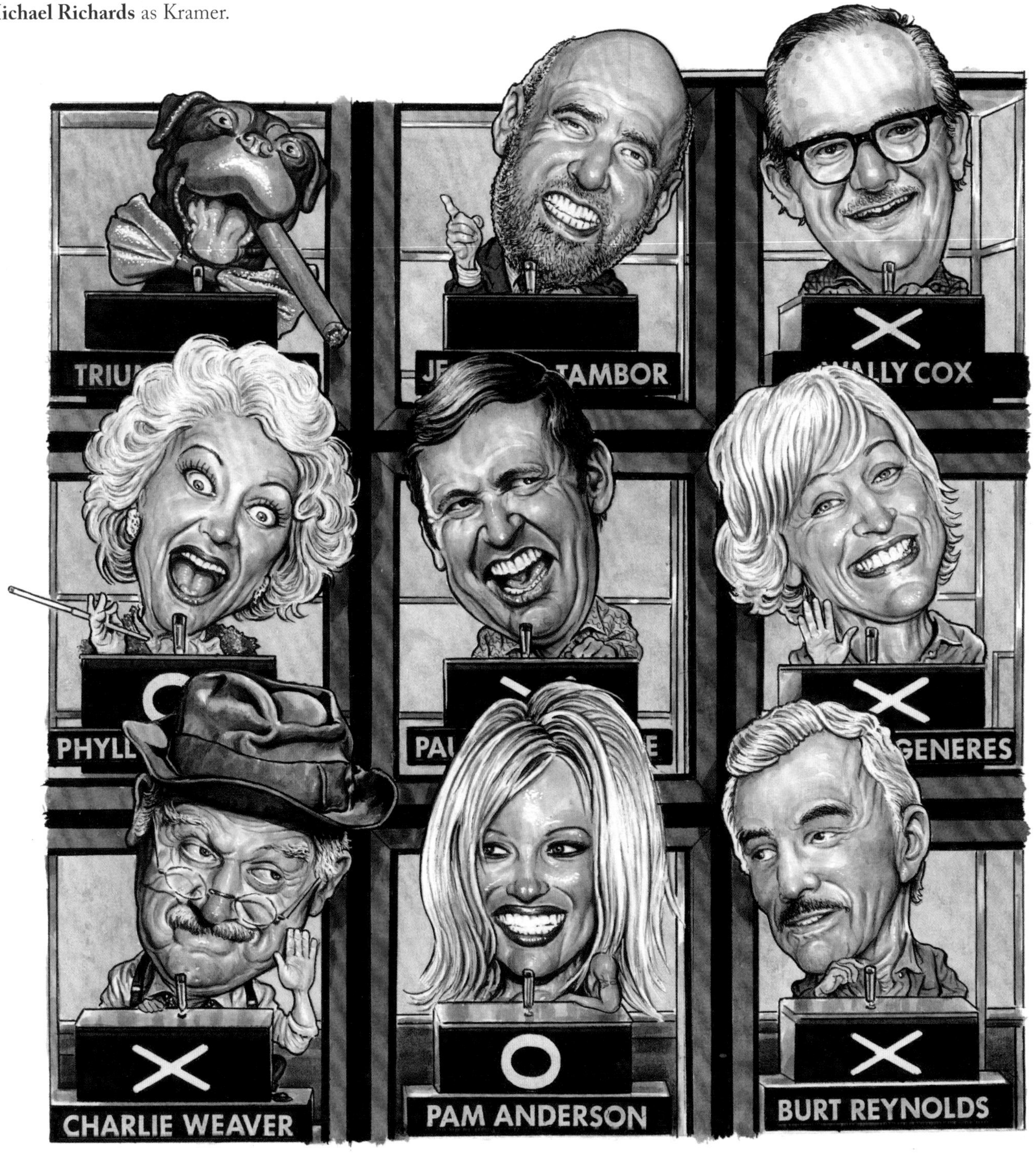
TRIU
JE
TAMBOR
ALLY COX
PHYLL
PAU
GENERES
CHARLIE WEAVER
PAM ANDERSON
BURT REYNOLDS

"MUST SELL, LAST SEASON."

TIME

Apt bldg, all mod convs, many brs, beaut but weird, f—ed up frmr residents. A perfect fixer-upper. Call R. Murdoch @ 1-800-HEATHER.

Rupert Murdoch, **Thomas Calabro** as "Michael," and **Heather Locklear** as "Amanda."

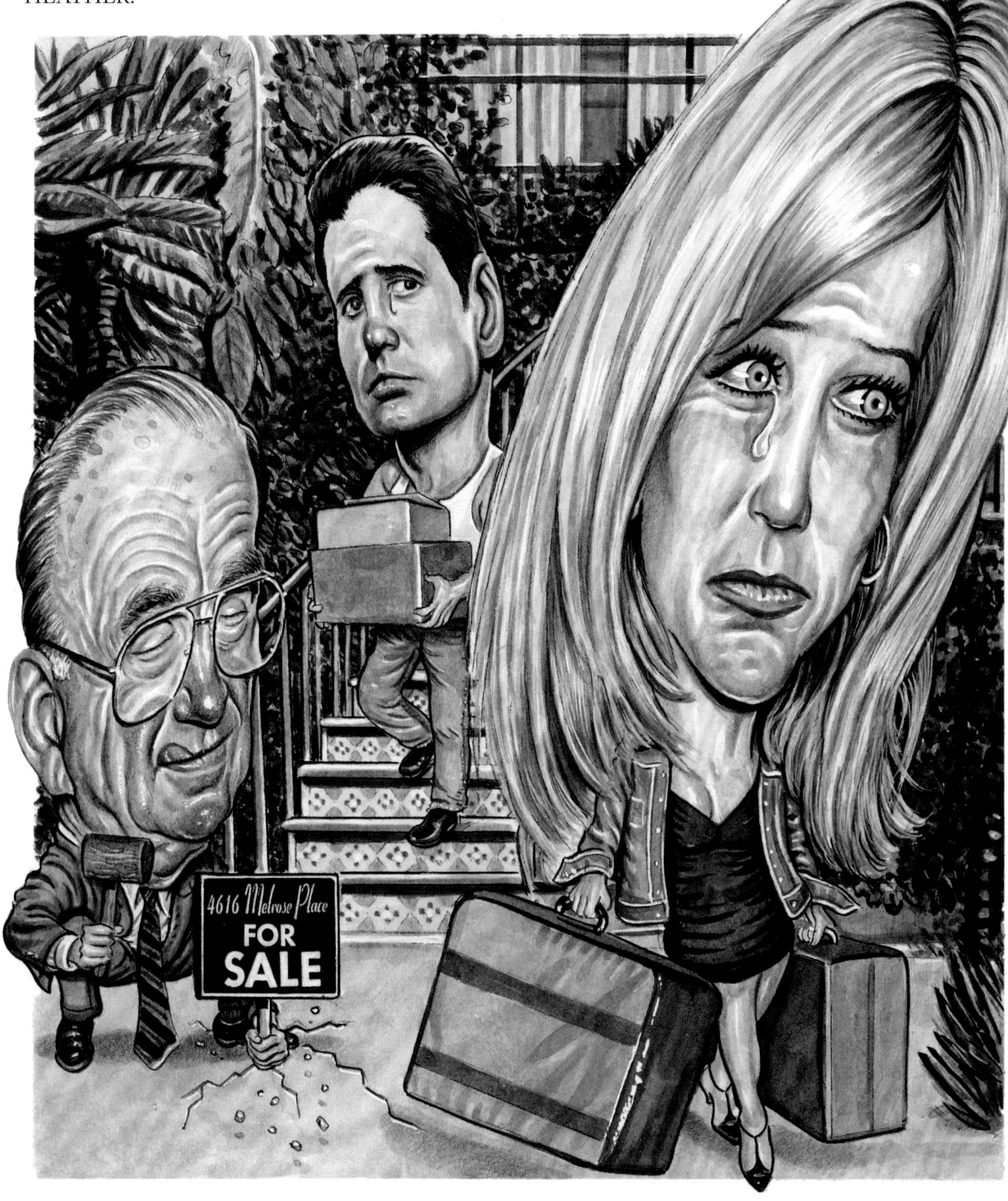
4616 Melrose Place
FOR
SALE

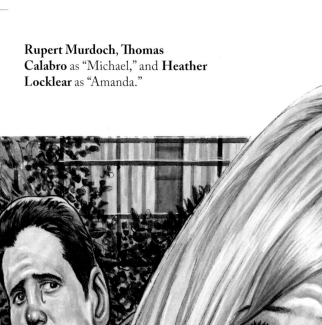

"TV STAR SPOTS."

TV GUIDE

Kelsey Grammer brushes up on his Shakespeare.

Will **Jerry Seinfeld** ever settle down and marry?

ENTERTAINMENT WEEKLY

White socks for **Dave**.

"Name that tune-up." Add **Jim Rockford** to the cast of *Ally McBeal*.

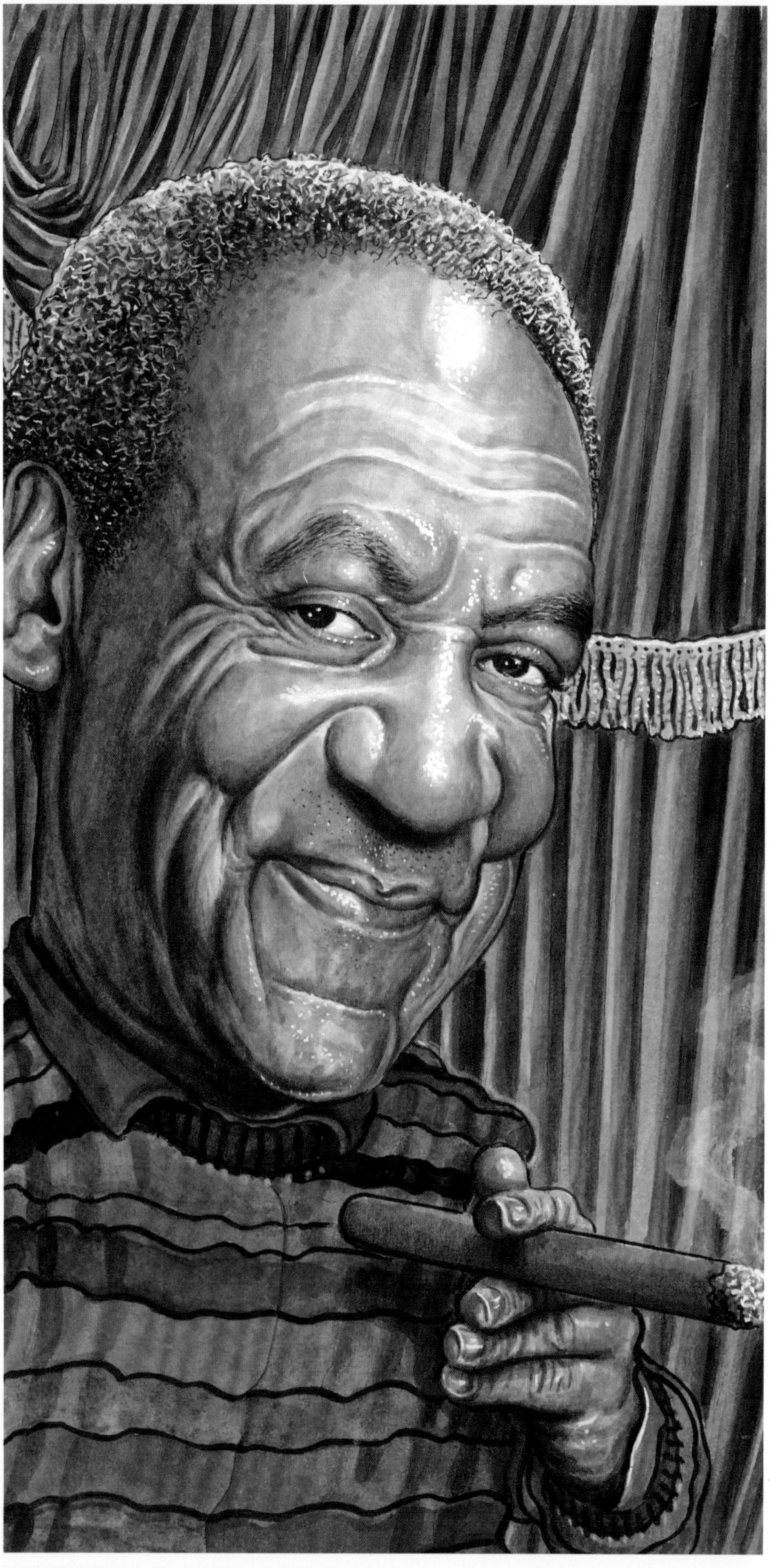

"DR. WILLIAM HENRY 'BILL' COSBY, JR."

ESPREE (cover)

a.k.a. "The Cos."

"TV STARS ON SUMMER BREAK."

TIME

Kelsey Grammer, **Drew Carey**, **Della Reese** (with our beagle Fiona begging off her), **Calista Flockhart**, enjoying the BBQ.

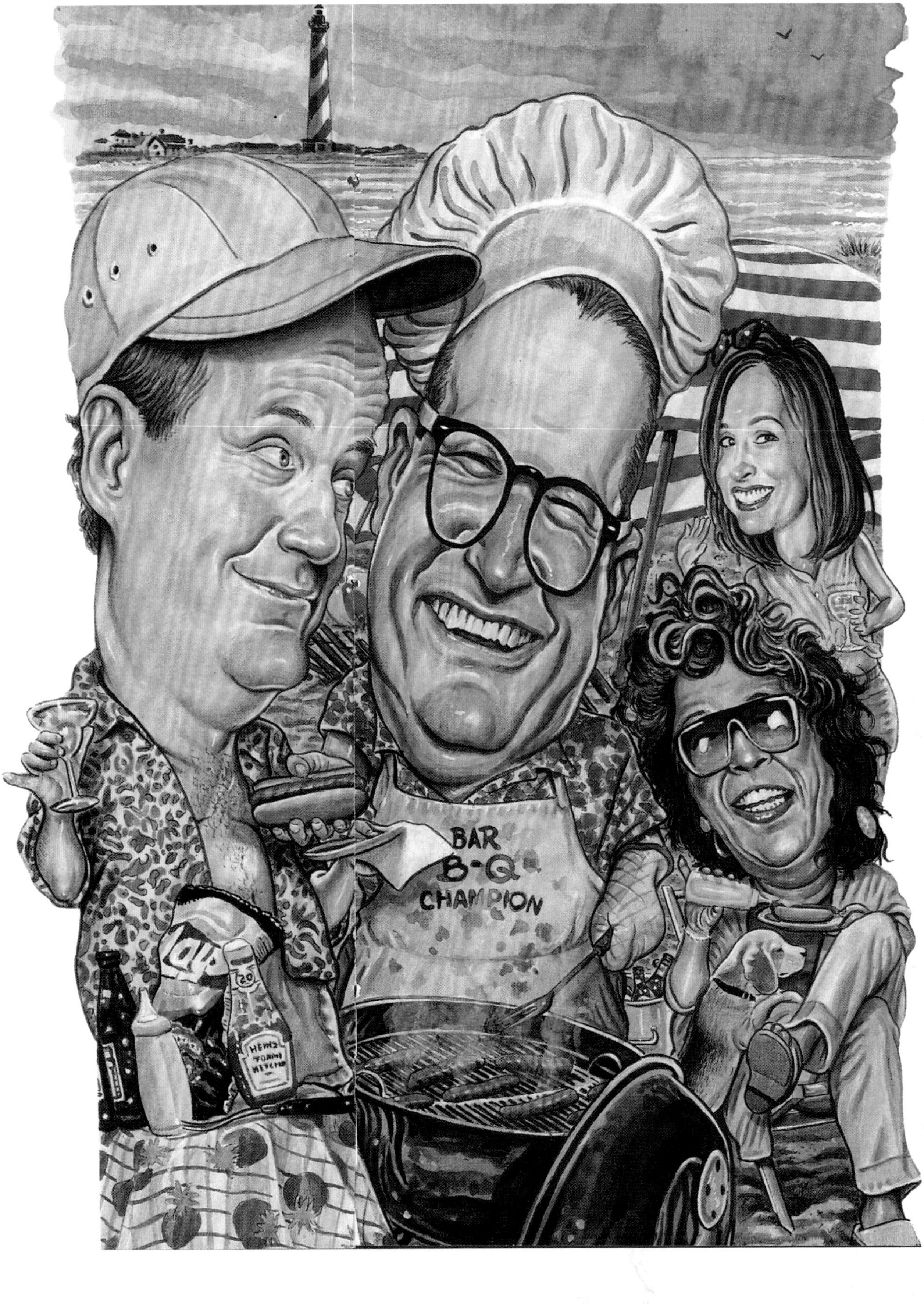
BAR
B-Q
CHAMPION

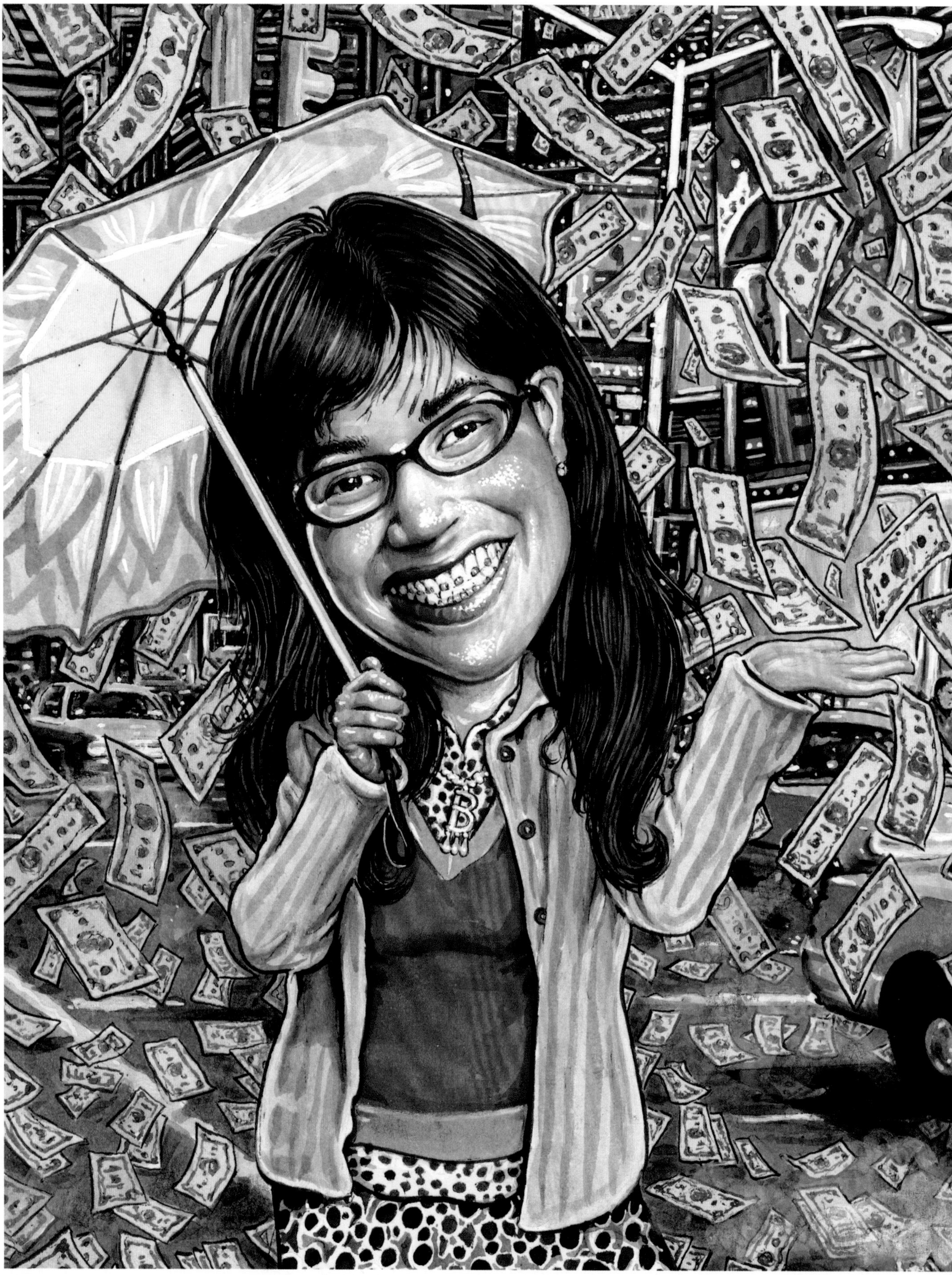

"IT'S RAINING MONEY."

EMMY MAGAZINE

"Why it's cheaper to film television series in New York."

America Ferrera as Ugly Betty.

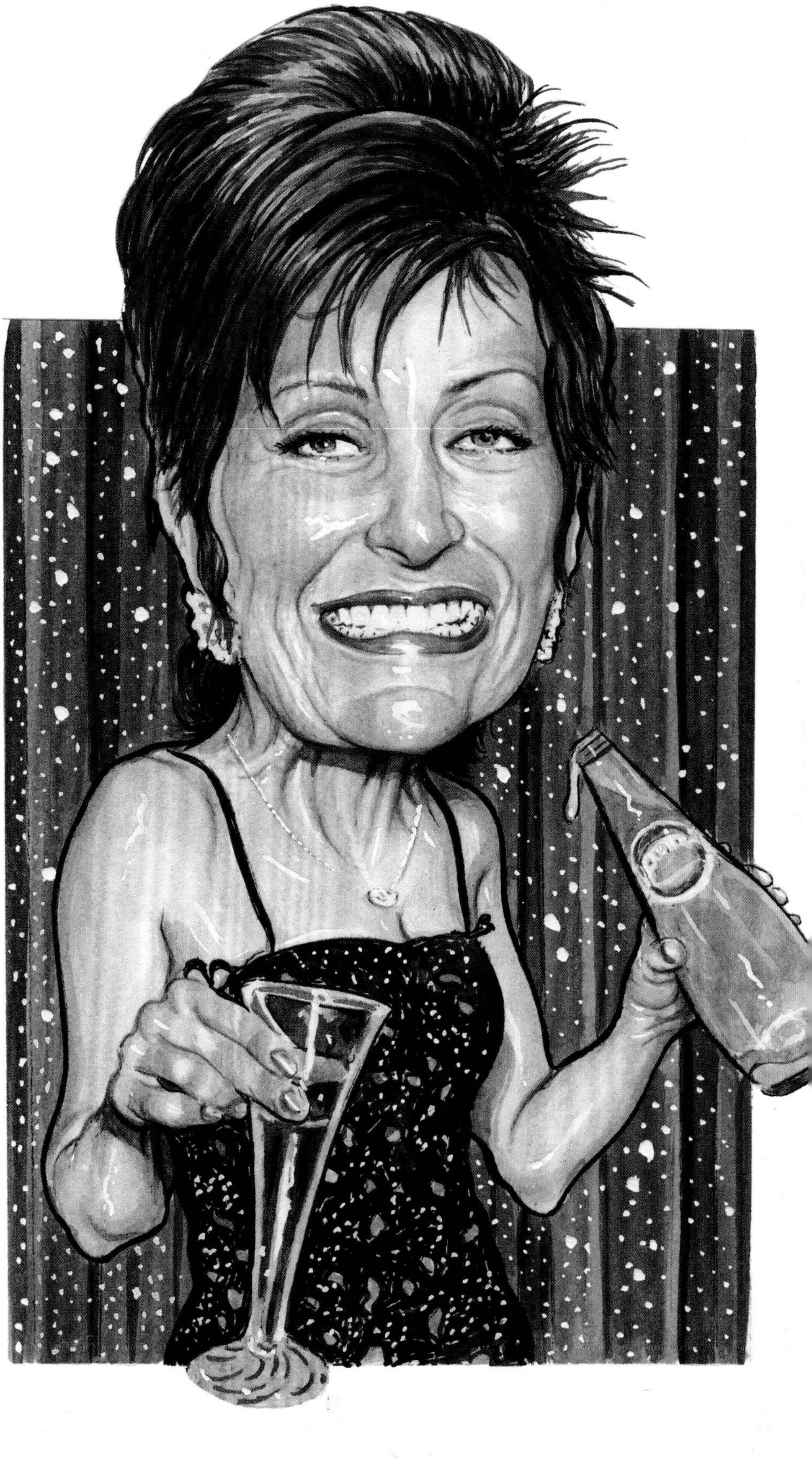

"...SHARON OSBOURNE HOSTS, AND THE PERRIER WILL SURELY BE FLOWING."

LOS ANGELES

"OPRAH."

THE WEEKLY STANDARD

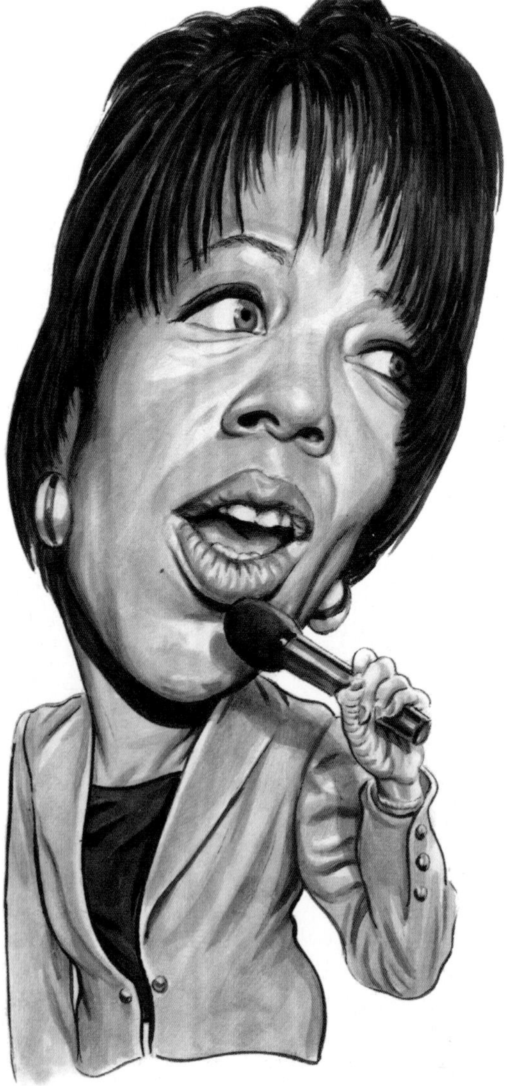

"SPRINGTIME FOR OPRAH."

THE NEW REPUBLIC (cover)

When the Queen of Daytime Talk goes to Auschwitz.

A parody of ***O: The Oprah Magazine*** cover featuring **Oprah Winfrey** posing in front of the gates of Auschwitz, which she was getting ready to visit.

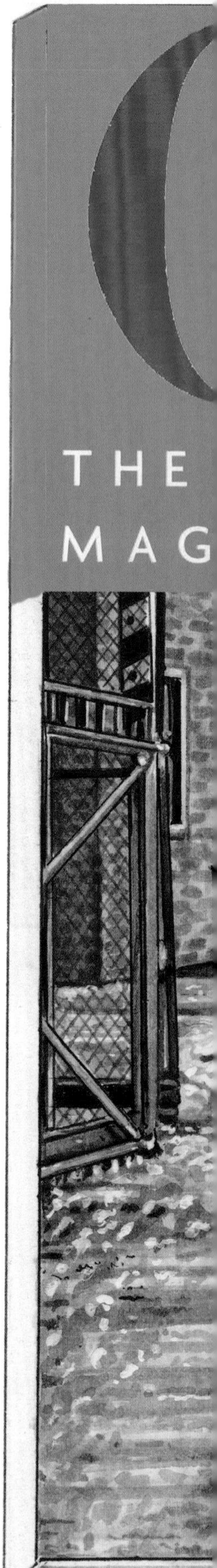
THE
MAG

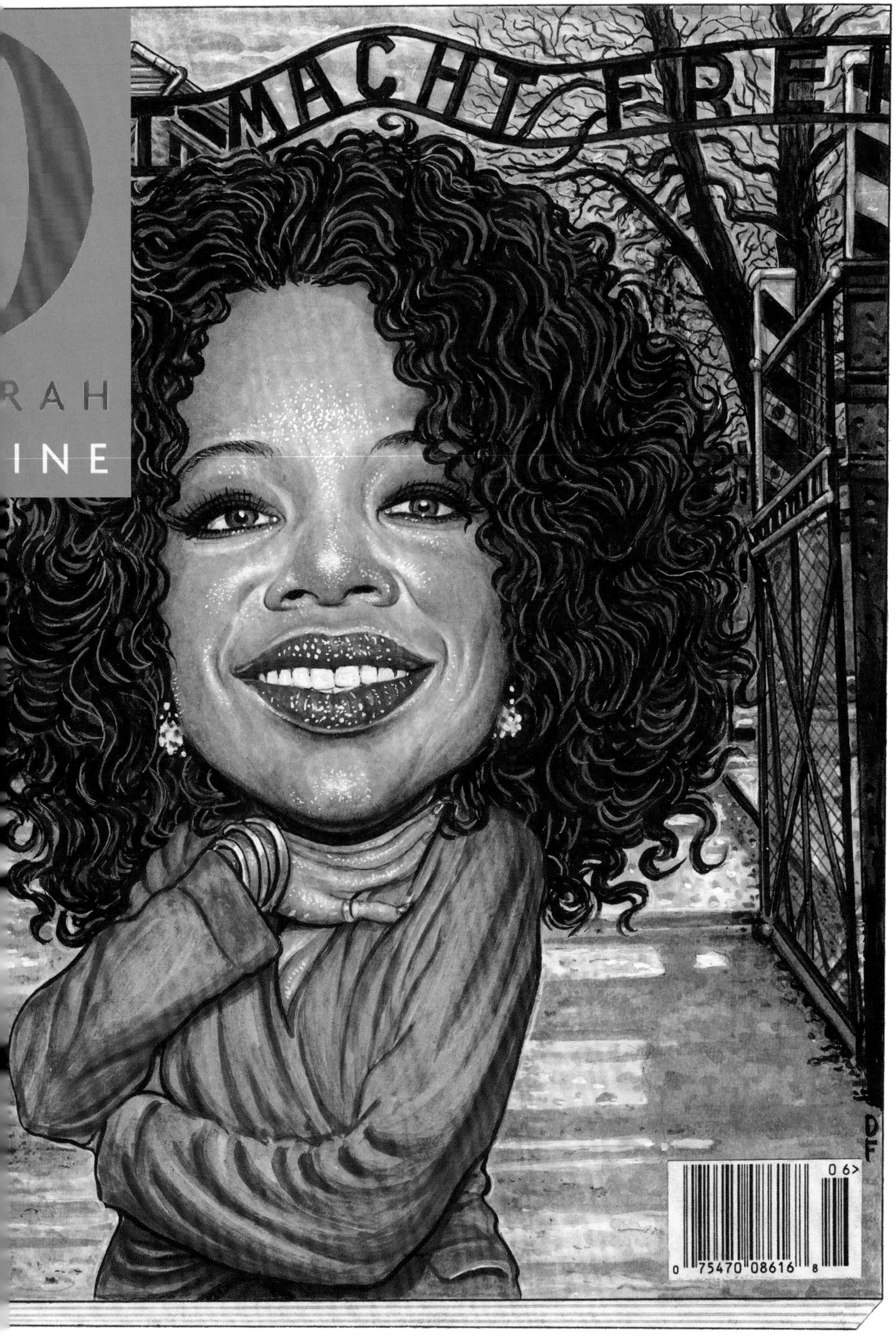
MACHT FRE
RAH
INE
DF
0 6>
0 75470 08616 8

"OH JOHNNY, AIN'T YOU THE ONE."

EMMY

Jay Leno, Johnny Carson, David Letterman, Conan O'Brien. Let the sucking-up commence. Who will be the late night heir to Johnny Carson?… Who cares?

"HEADS OF COMEDY."

Poster created for the 2000 U.S. Comedy Arts Festival in Aspen. Guests included (clockwise from bottom left) **Elaine May, Mike Nichols, Jerry Lewis, Homer Simpson** (via video), **Barry Levinson, Dickie Smothers, Tommy Smothers**, and **Robin Williams**. (*Lettering by Phil Felix.*)

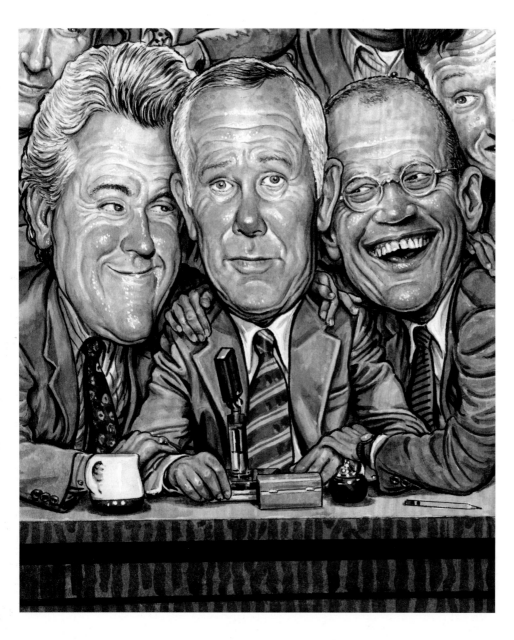

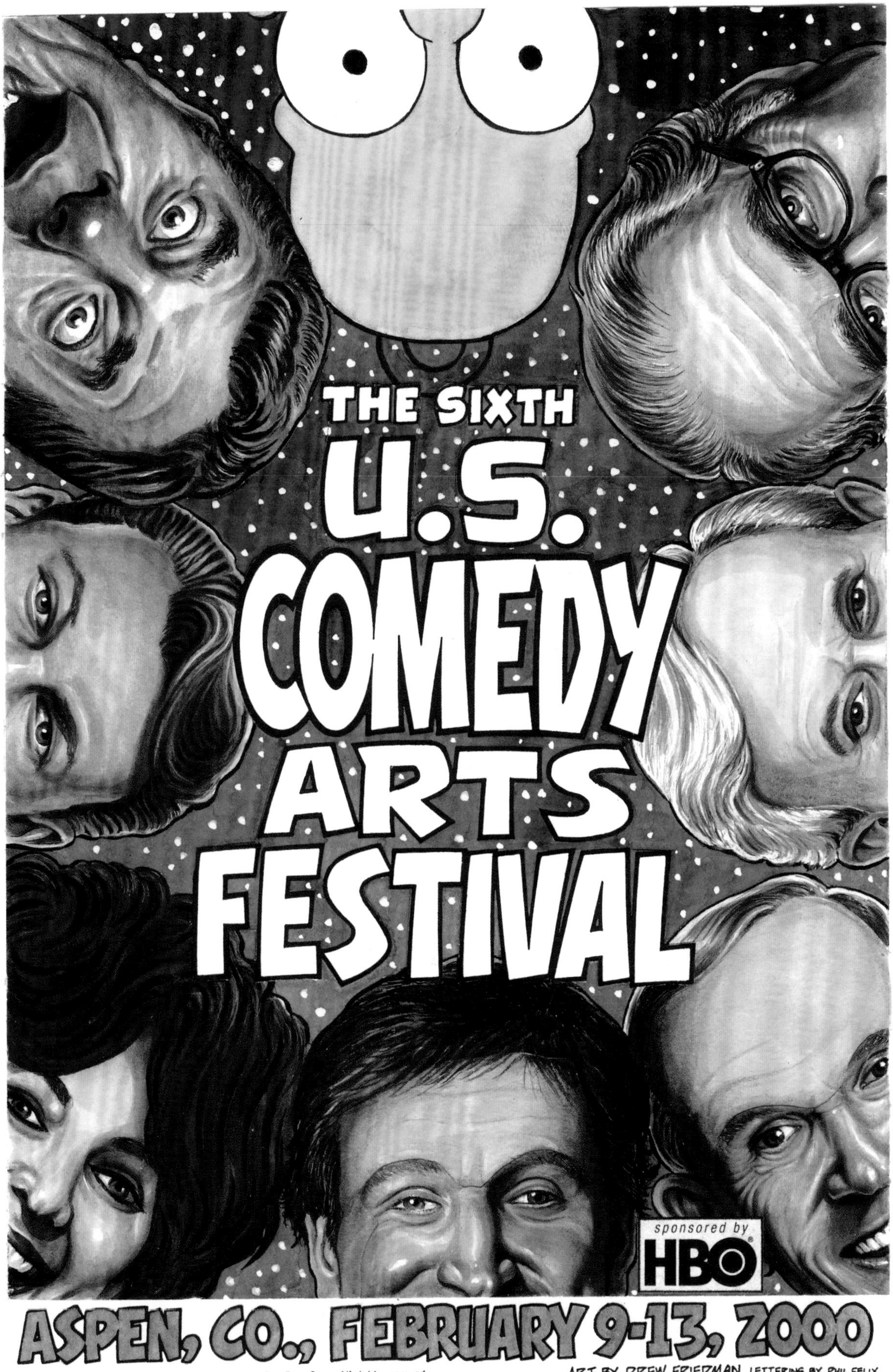
THE SIXTH
U.S.
COMEDY
ARTS
FESTIVAL
sponsored by
HBO
ASPEN, CO., FEBRUARY 9-13, 2000

ART BY DREW FRIEDMAN LETTERING BY PHIL FELIX

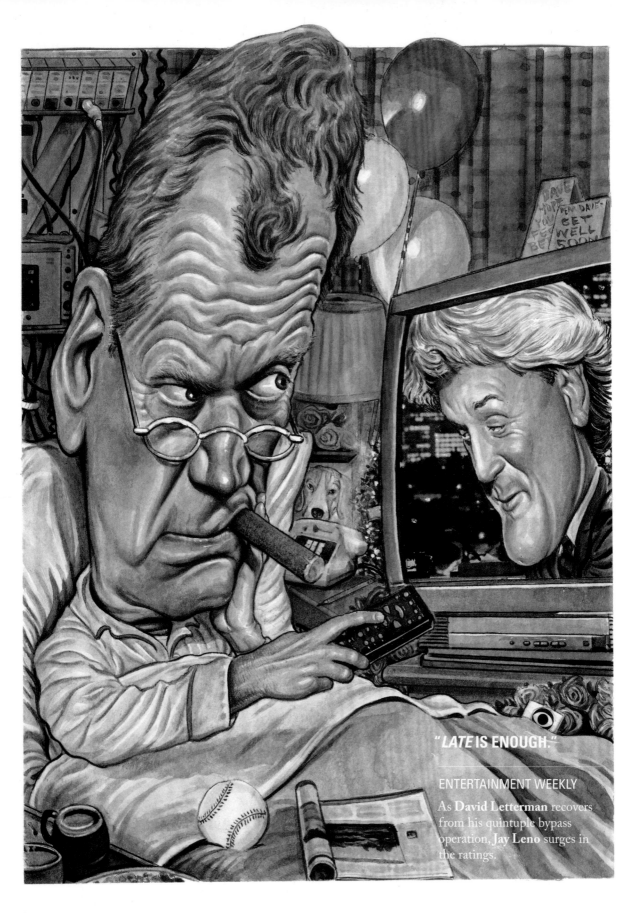

"*LATE* IS ENOUGH."

ENTERTAINMENT WEEKLY

As **David Letterman** recovers from his quintuple bypass operation, **Jay Leno** surges in the ratings.

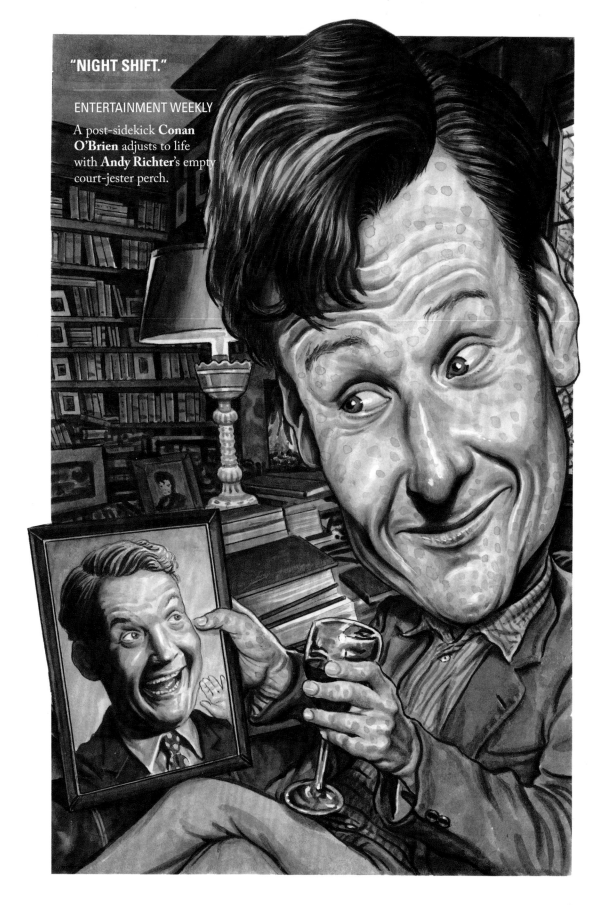

"NIGHT SHIFT."

ENTERTAINMENT WEEKLY

A post-sidekick **Conan O'Brien** adjusts to life with **Andy Richter**'s empty court-jester perch.

"GOOD EVENING, LADIES AND GERMS."

LOS ANGELES MAGAZINE

LA Magazine's special Comedy issue, featuring master of ceremonies, **Ellen DeGeneres**, who also posed for the cover. Ellen would enlarge this image and show it on her day-time talk show, pointing out that the mic looked more like a "cheese grater." I totally agreed.

"ARE WE OBNOXIOUS ENOUGH?"

EMMY MAGAZINE

Potential **"reality show" contestants**, auditioning for **the producers**.

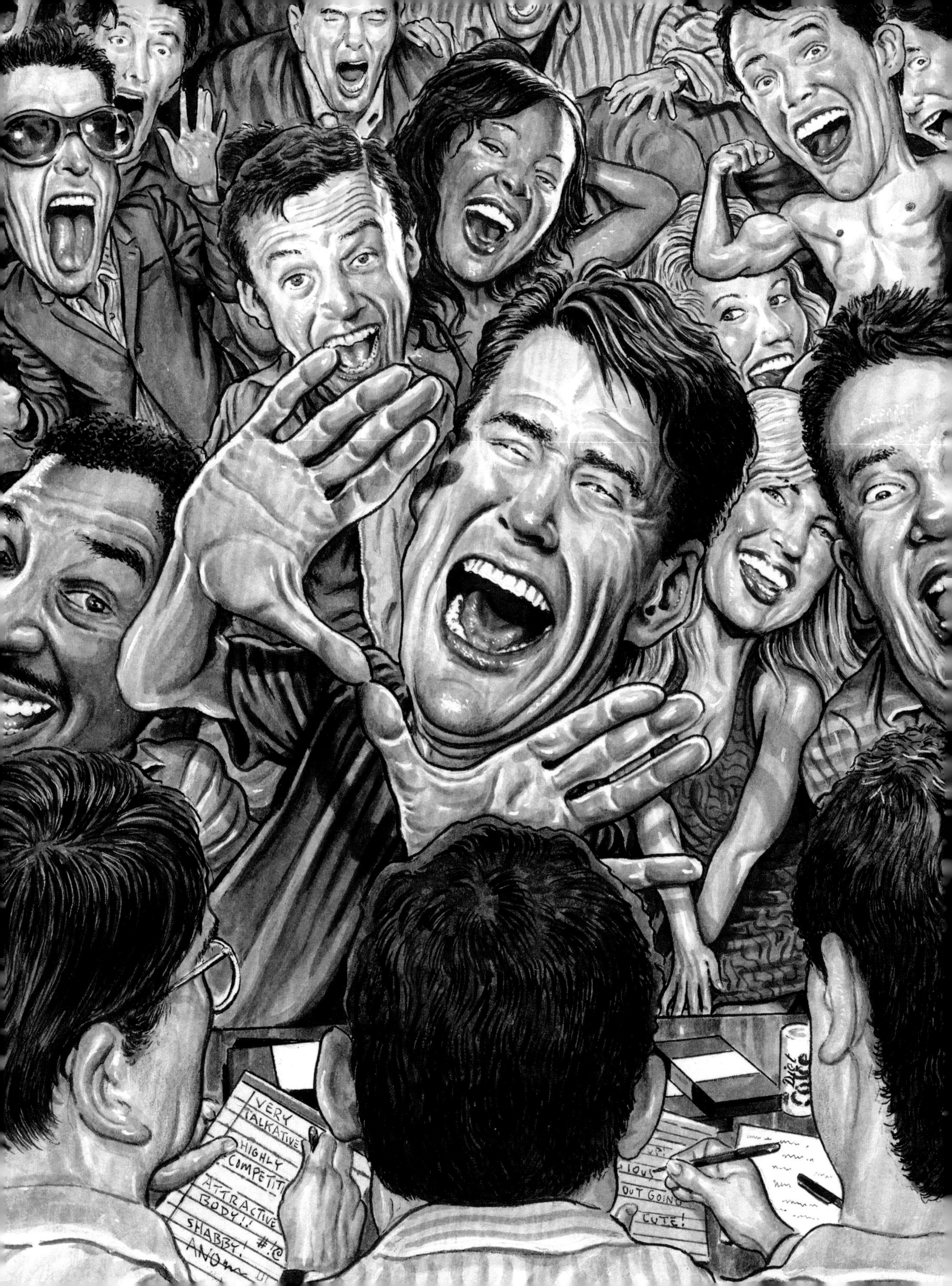
VERY
TALKATIVE
HIGHLY
COMPETITI
ATTRACTIVE
BODY!!
SHABBY!
#!@
OUT GOING
CUTE!
Diet Coke

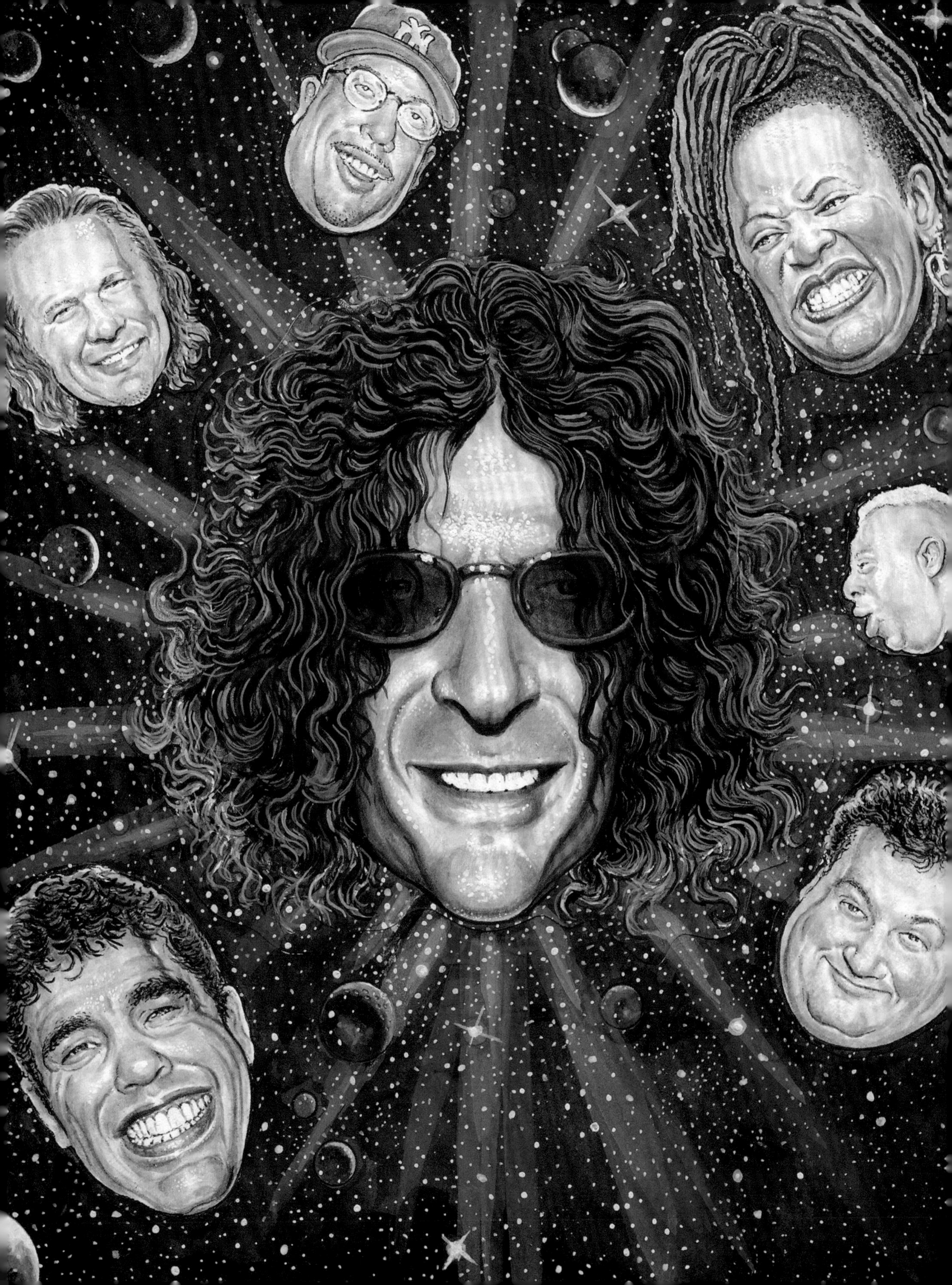

"HOWARD STERN'S BIG BANG."

GQ MAGAZINE

On the eve of the **Howard Stern** Show, moving to satellite radio, a *Howard Stern Show* primer for the uninitiated. Clockwise from bottom left: **Gary Del'abate, Fred Norris, "High Pitch" Eric, Robin Quivers, "Beetle-juice," Artie Lange.**

"BIG SCREAM."

LAS VEGAS WEEKLY (cover)

A tribute to comedian **Sam Kinison** on the 10th anniversary of his death.

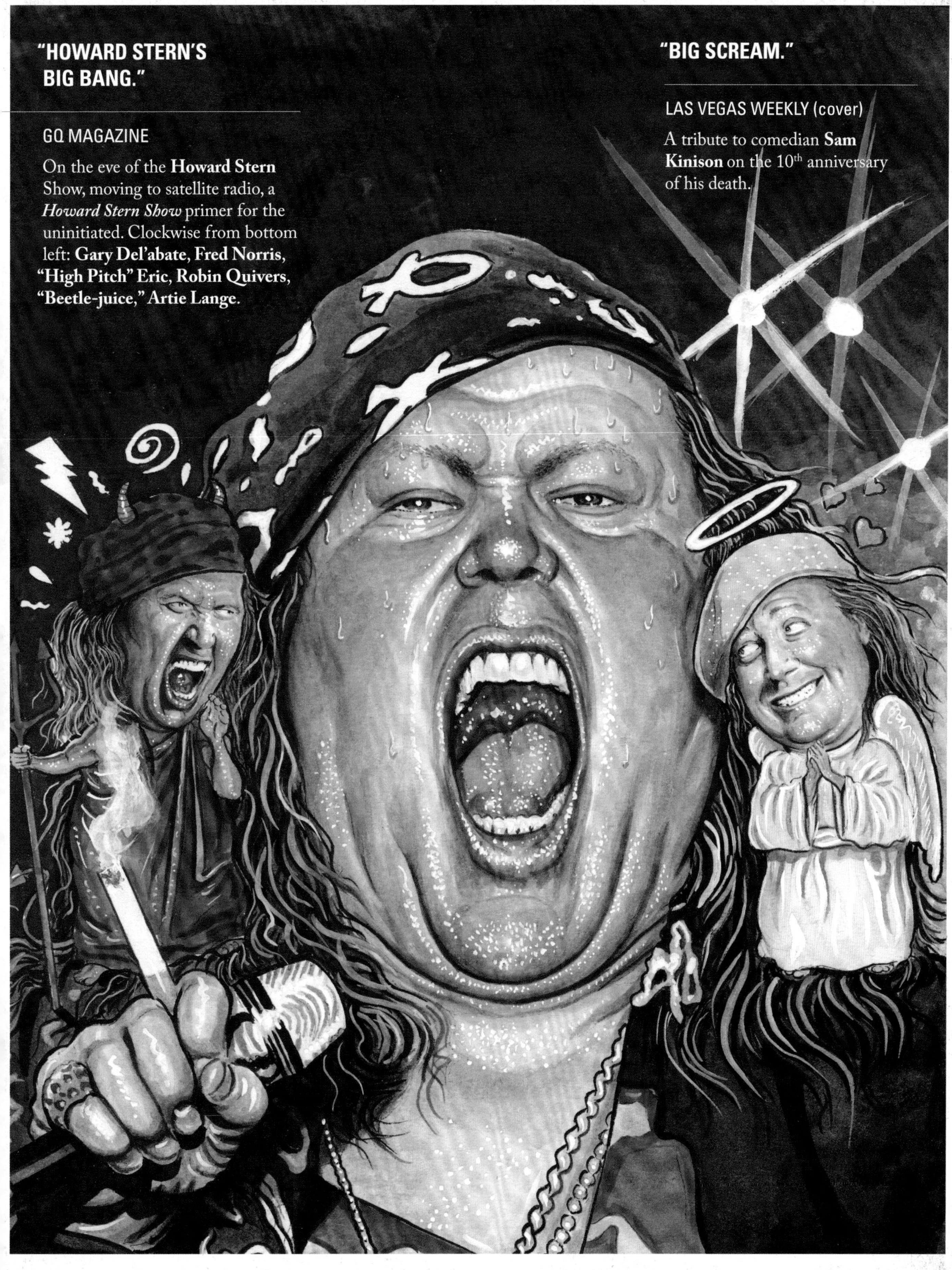

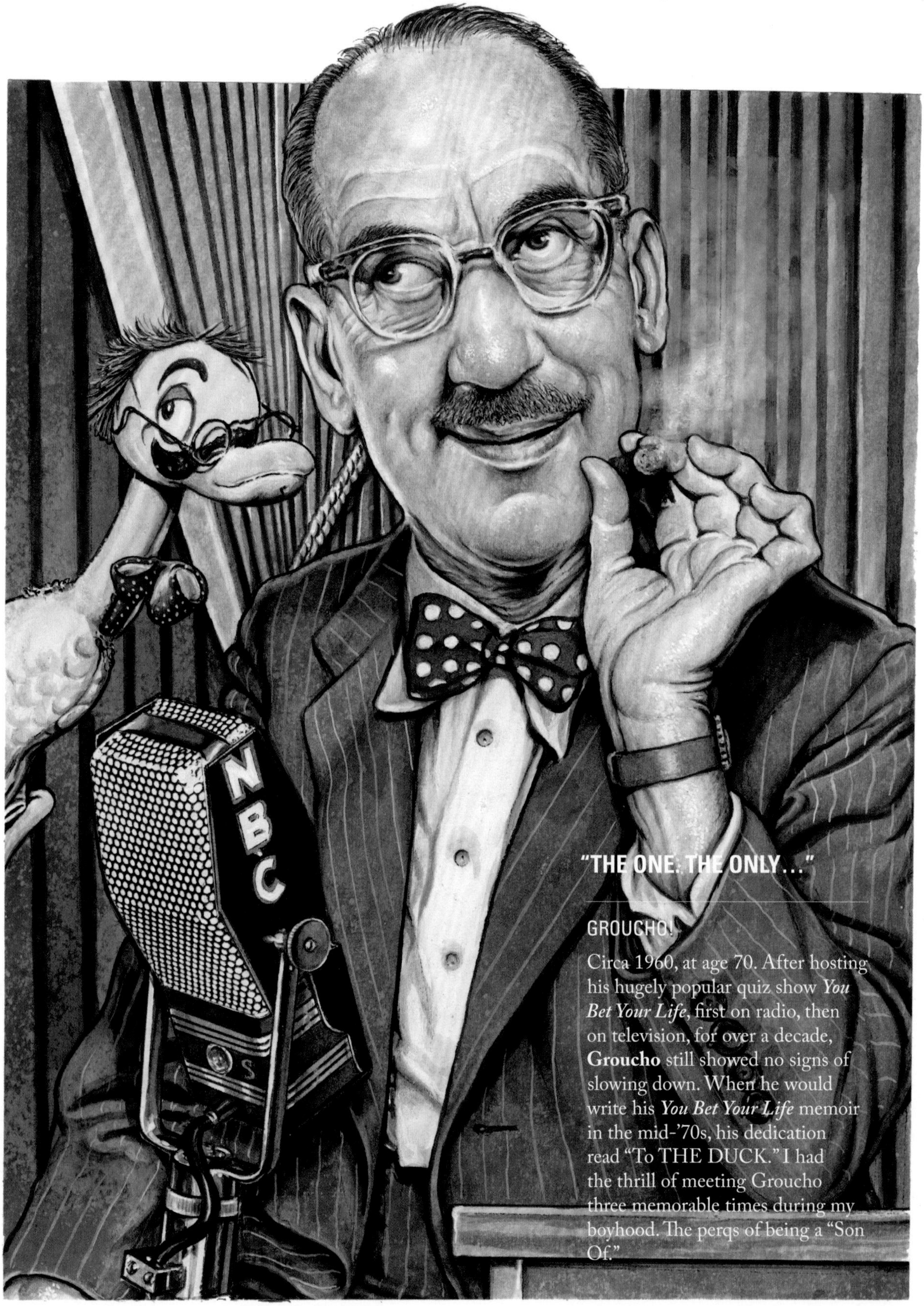
NBC

"THE ONE, THE ONLY…"

GROUCHO!

Circa 1960, at age 70. After hosting his hugely popular quiz show *You Bet Your Life*, first on radio, then on television, for over a decade, **Groucho** still showed no signs of slowing down. When he would write his *You Bet Your Life* memoir in the mid-'70s, his dedication read "To THE DUCK." I had the thrill of meeting Groucho three memorable times during my boyhood. The perqs of being a "Son Of."

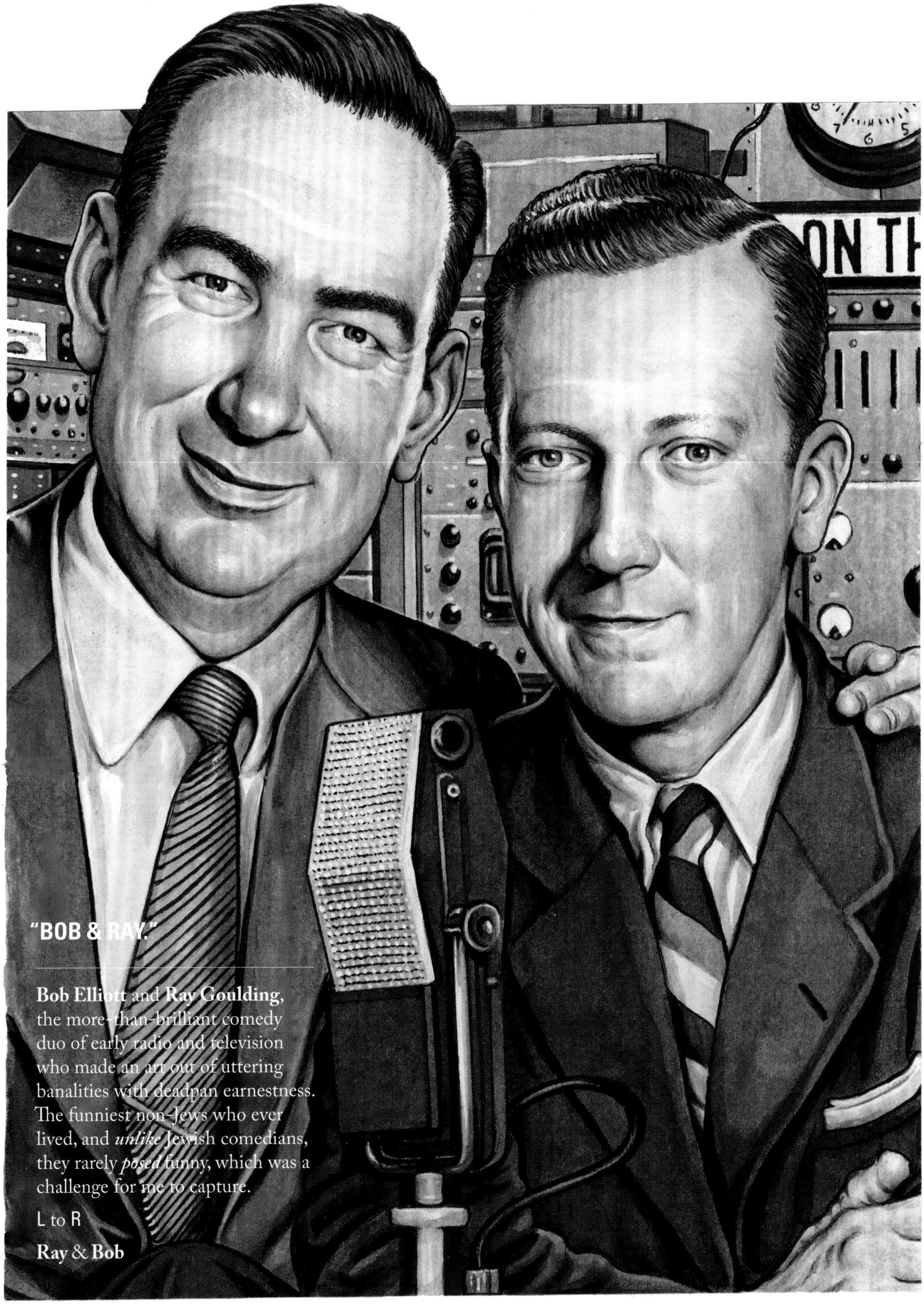

"BOB & RAY."

Bob Elliott and **Ray Goulding**, the more-than-brilliant comedy duo of early radio and television who made an art out of uttering banalities with deadpan earnestness. The funniest non-Jews who ever lived, and *unlike* Jewish comedians, they rarely *posed* funny, which was a challenge for me to capture.

L to R

Ray & **Bob**

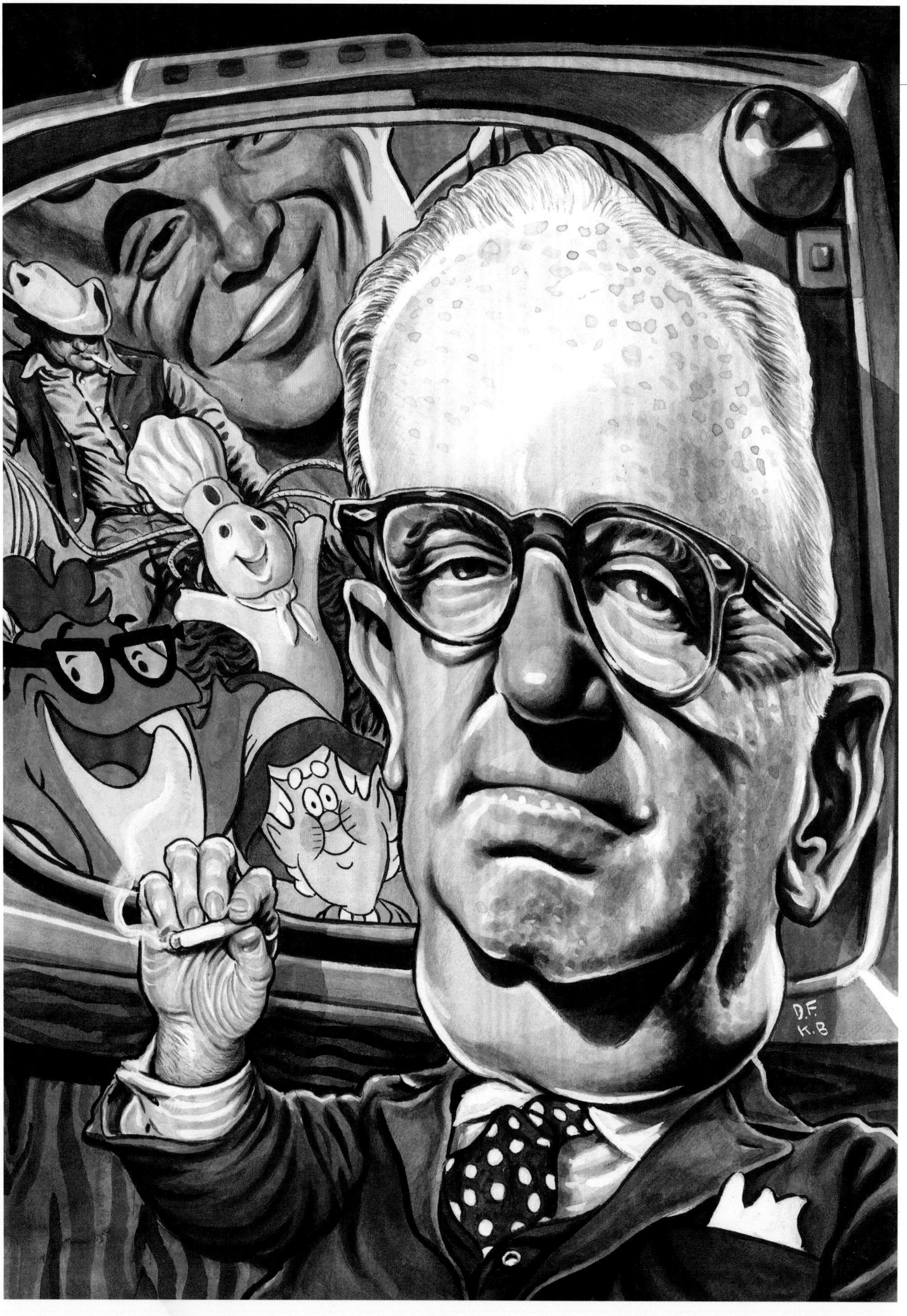
D.F.
K.B

"SULTAN OF SELL."

TIME

For the *"TIME 100"* series, the most influential people of the 20th century, I was asked to draw **Leo Burnett**, "ad guru," creator of "The Jolly Green Giant," the "Marlboro Man," "Tony the Tiger," among many others.

"JACK, WE HARDLY KNEW YE."

GEORGE

Jack Valenti, 78-year-old president of the motion picture association of America, former lobbyist and "special assistant" to LBJ, finally retires, waving good-bye in the "Wall of Fame."

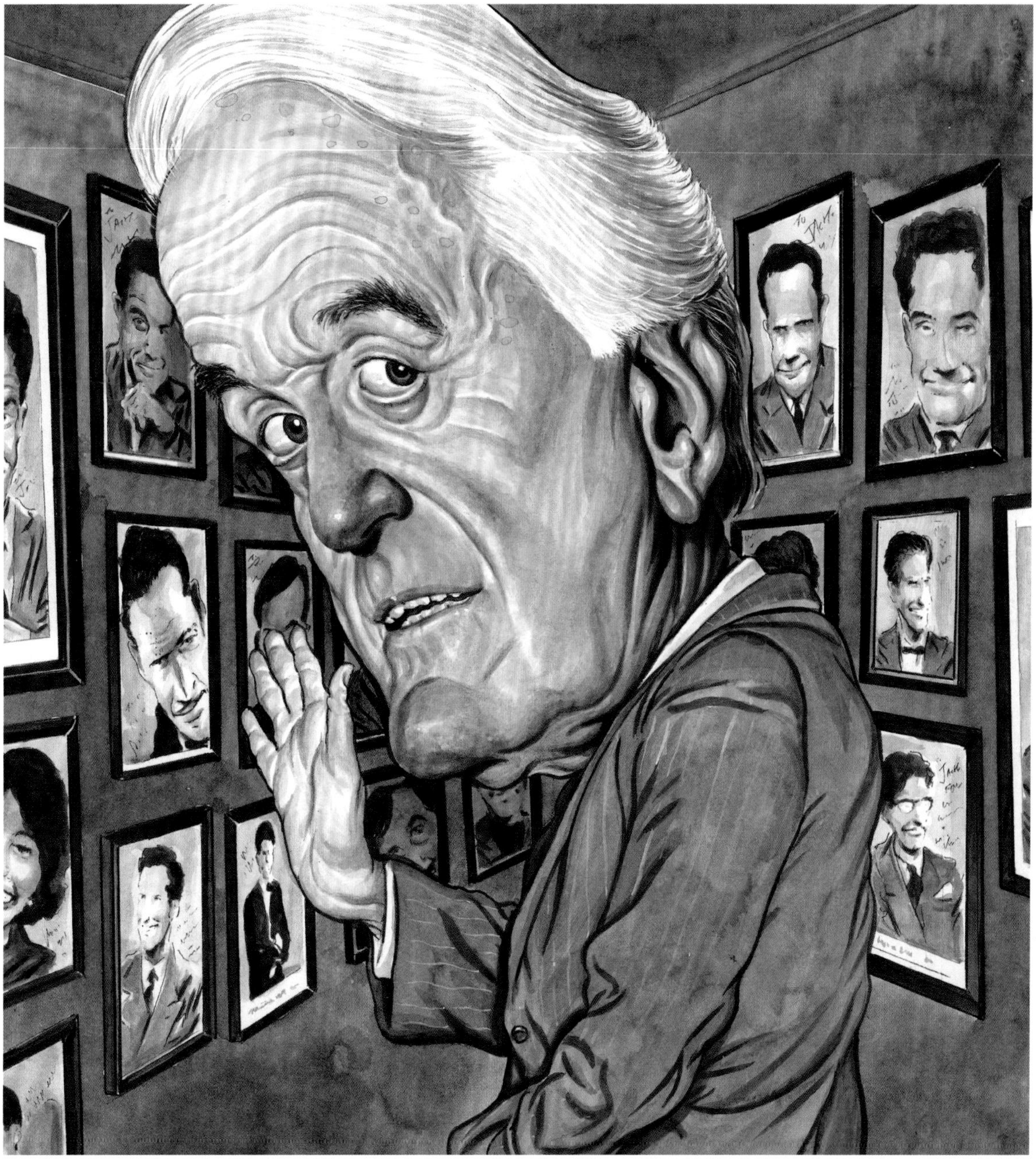

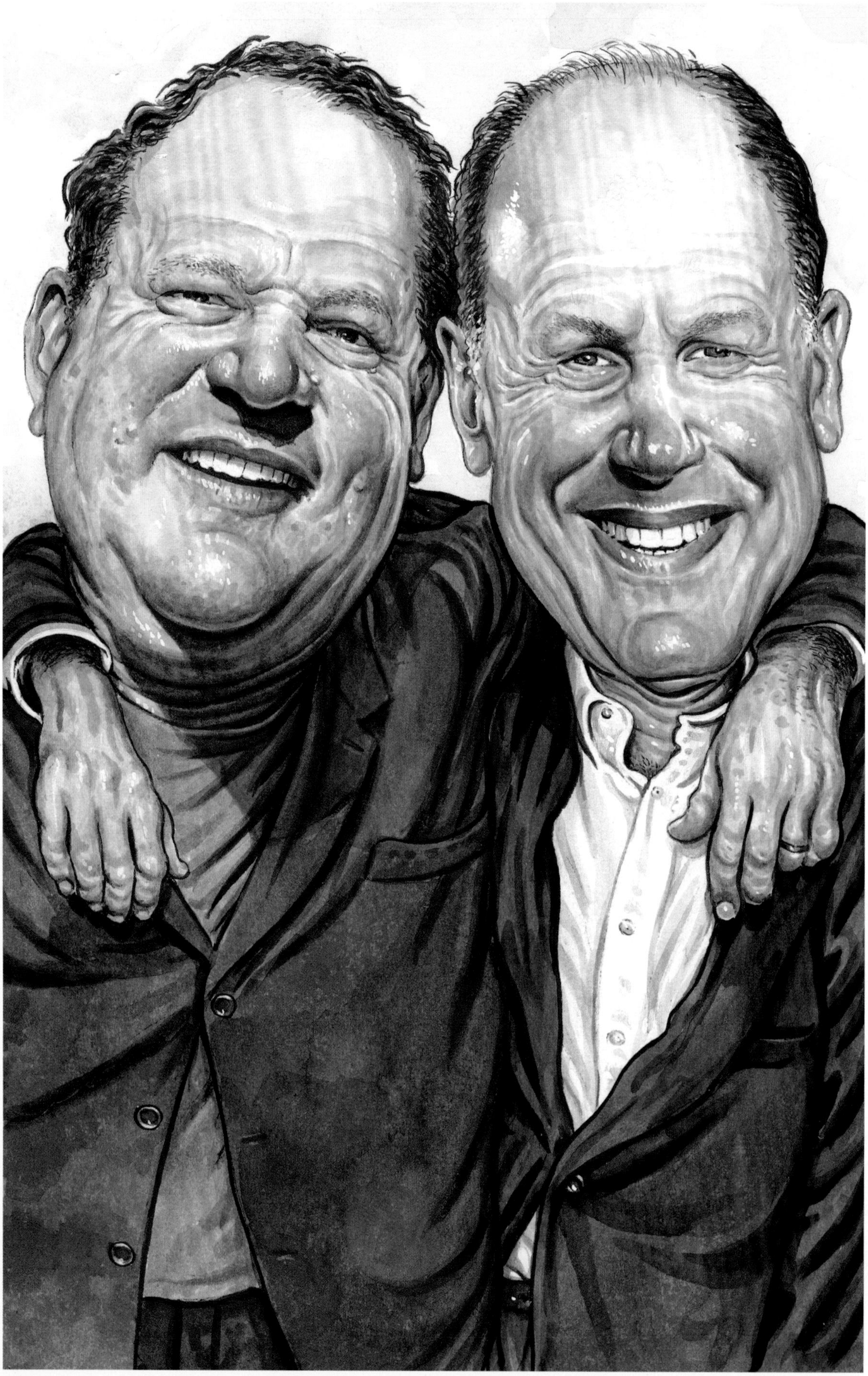

"HARVEY & MICHAEL, THE BESTEST FRIENDS EVER!"

VARIETY

"What feud?"

Miramax chairman **Harvey Weinstein** and Disney Chairman **Michael Eisner**, forever friends, buddies and pals!

"THE INCREDIBLE BULK"

ENTERTAINMENT WEEKLY

For *EW's* "Power Issue." Miramax producers **Bob Weinstein** as Bruce Banner and brother **Harvey Weinstein** as The Incredible Hulk. I've drawn Harvey several times over the years, one of my favorite subjects. Harvey obviously has a good sense of humor, buying several of the originals.

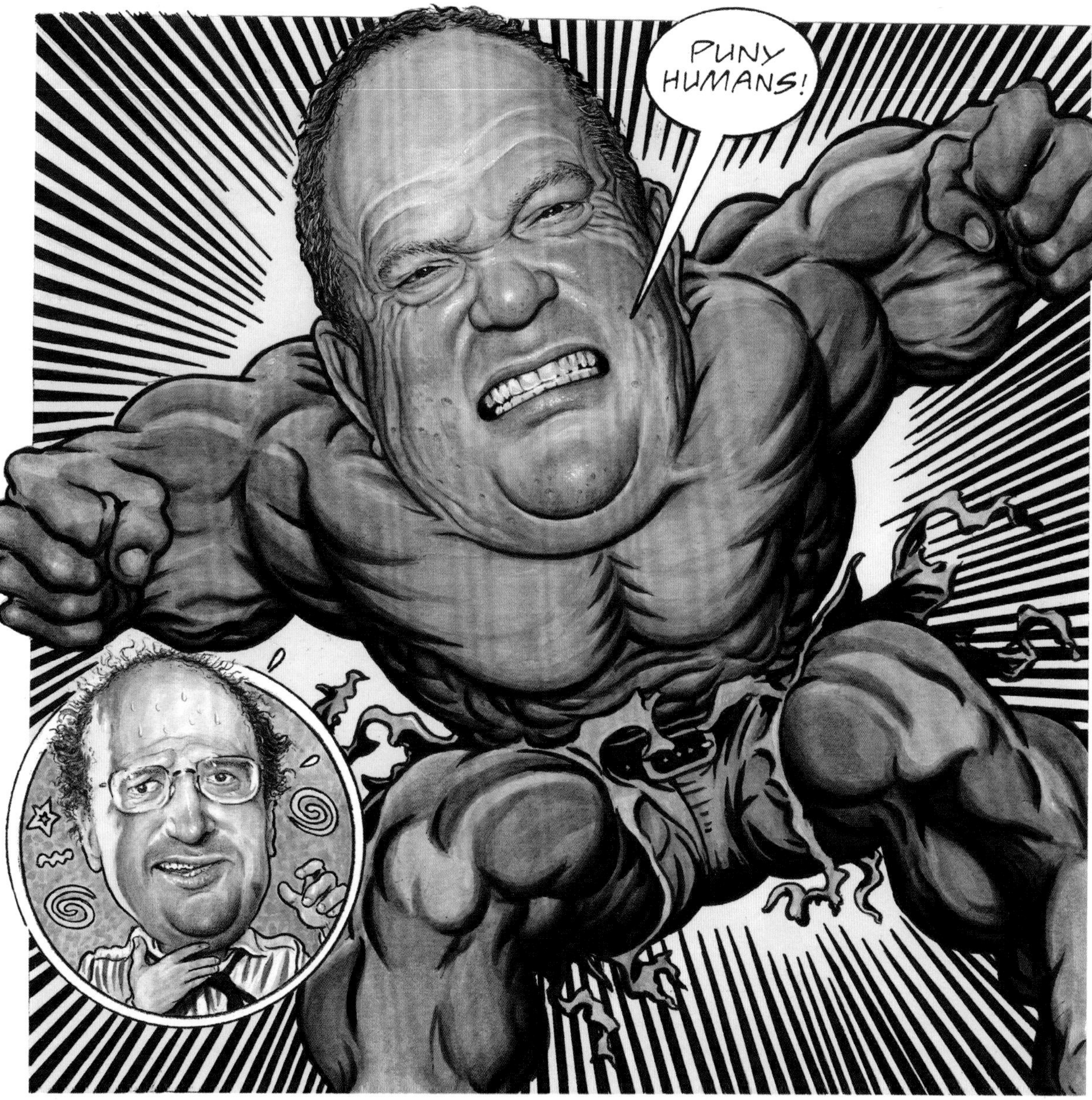
PUNY HUMANS!

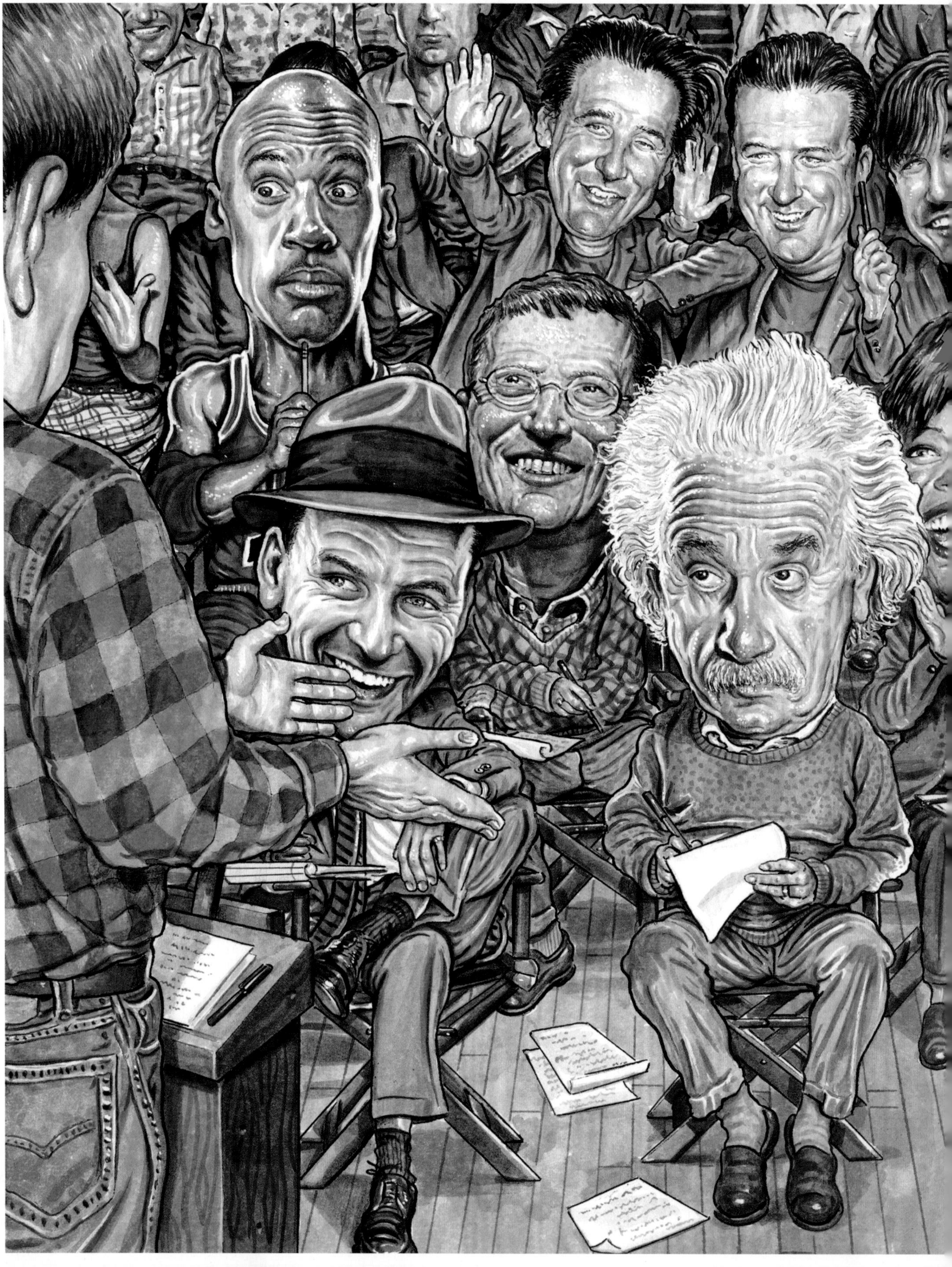

"TEACH ME TONIGHT."

UNLIMITED

...was an (ironically) short-lived magazine dedicated to "living life to its fullest" sponsored by Phillip Morris—makers of... Marlboro Cigarettes. I think this piece was about celebrities from past and present getting advice from an "everyday guy."

Back row: **Michael Jordan, three Baldwin brothers, Madonna, William Shakespeare.**

Front row: **Frank Sinatra, Bill Gates, Albert Einstein, Oprah Winfrey, Mahatma Gandhi.**

"YOU TALKIN' TO ME?"

THE WALL STREET JOURNAL

Barry Diller, chairman of Expedia, has words with **John Malone**, chairman of Liberty Media.

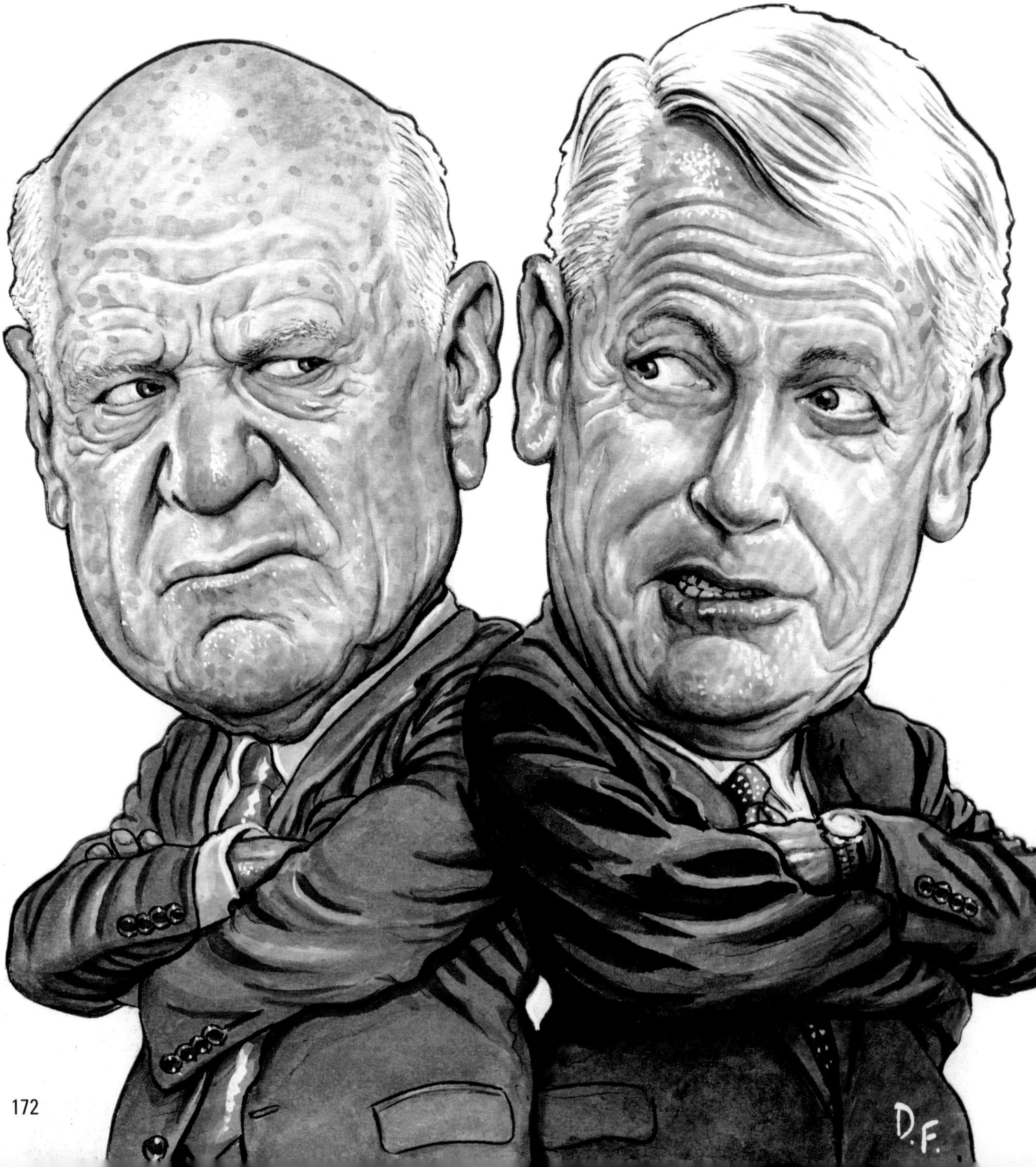
D.F.

"BILL GATES MAKEOVER."

20/20 MAGAZINE

I was hired by this eyeglass magazine, sponsored by Bausch & Lomb, to depict celebrities with suggested eye-glass makeovers. Here's **Bill Gates** in this lovely yellow-glassed number.

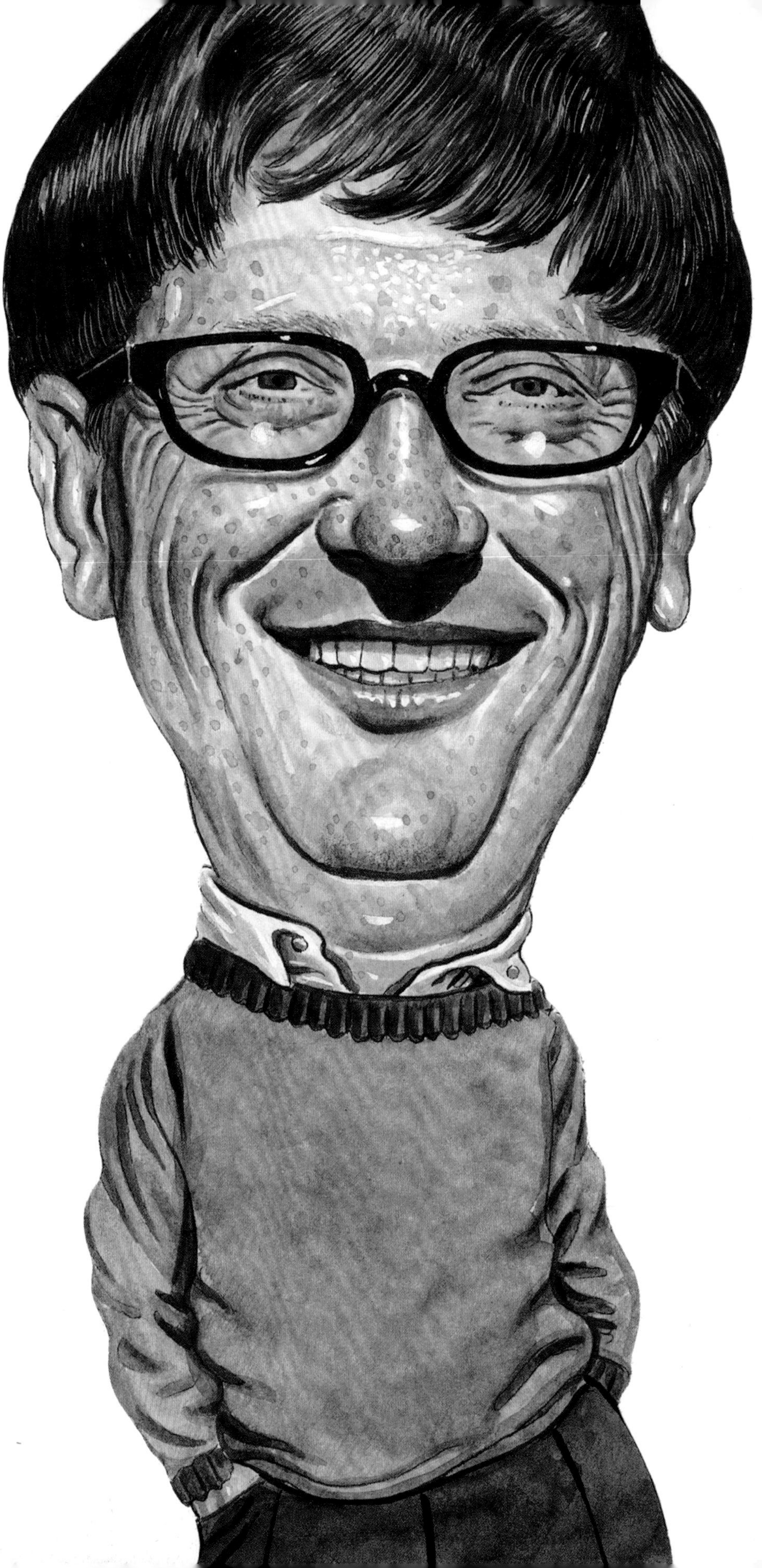

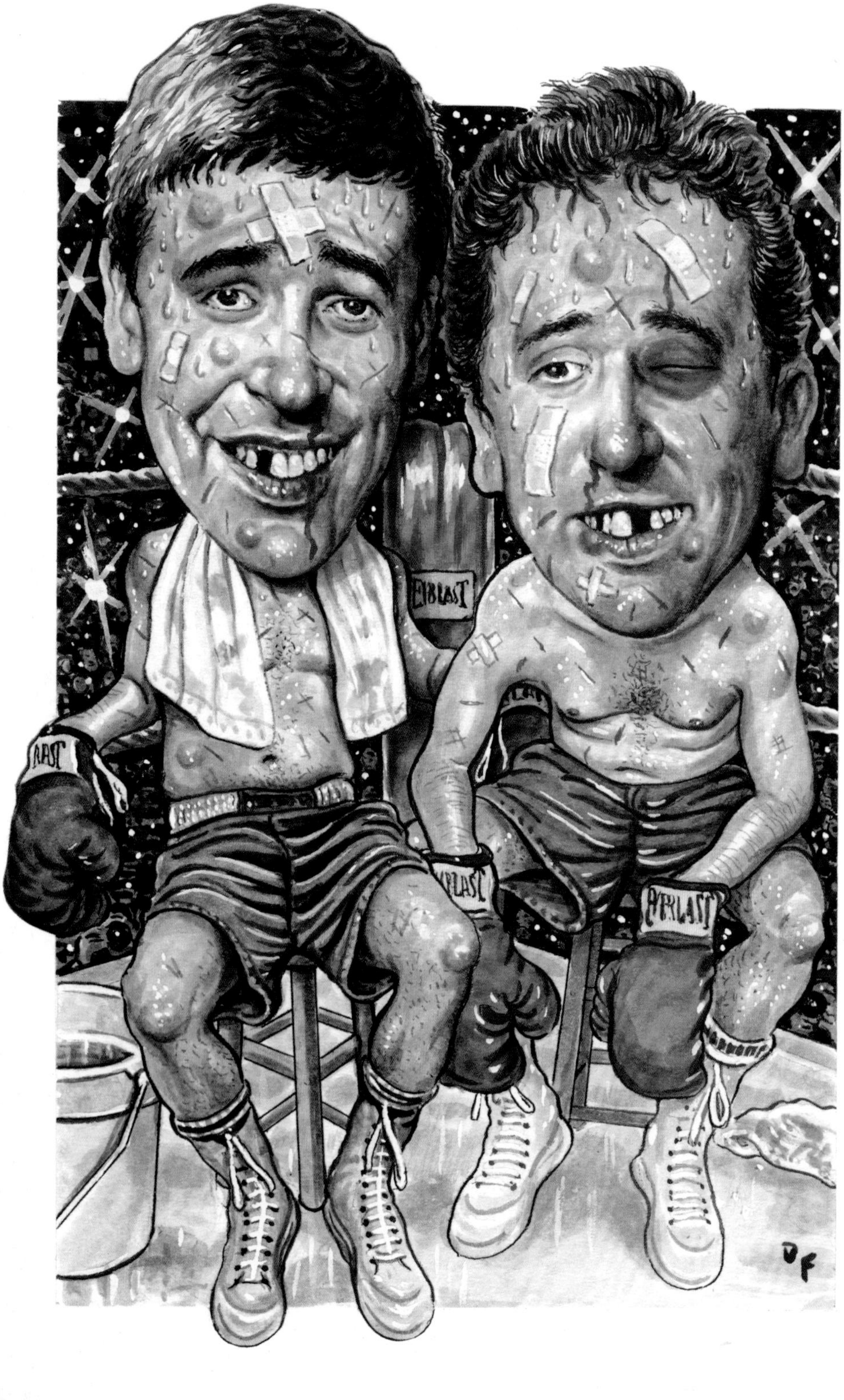

"NO LOVE LOST FOR GOOGLE."

FORTUNE

Its feisty founders have taken a beating lately, but we haven't even begun to see what this company can do. Google founders **Sergey Brin** and **Larry Page**, on the ropes.

"UNCLE SAM IS SICKO."

THE NATION (cover)

Upon the release of *Sicko*, **Michael Moore** examines a sickly **Uncle Sam**.

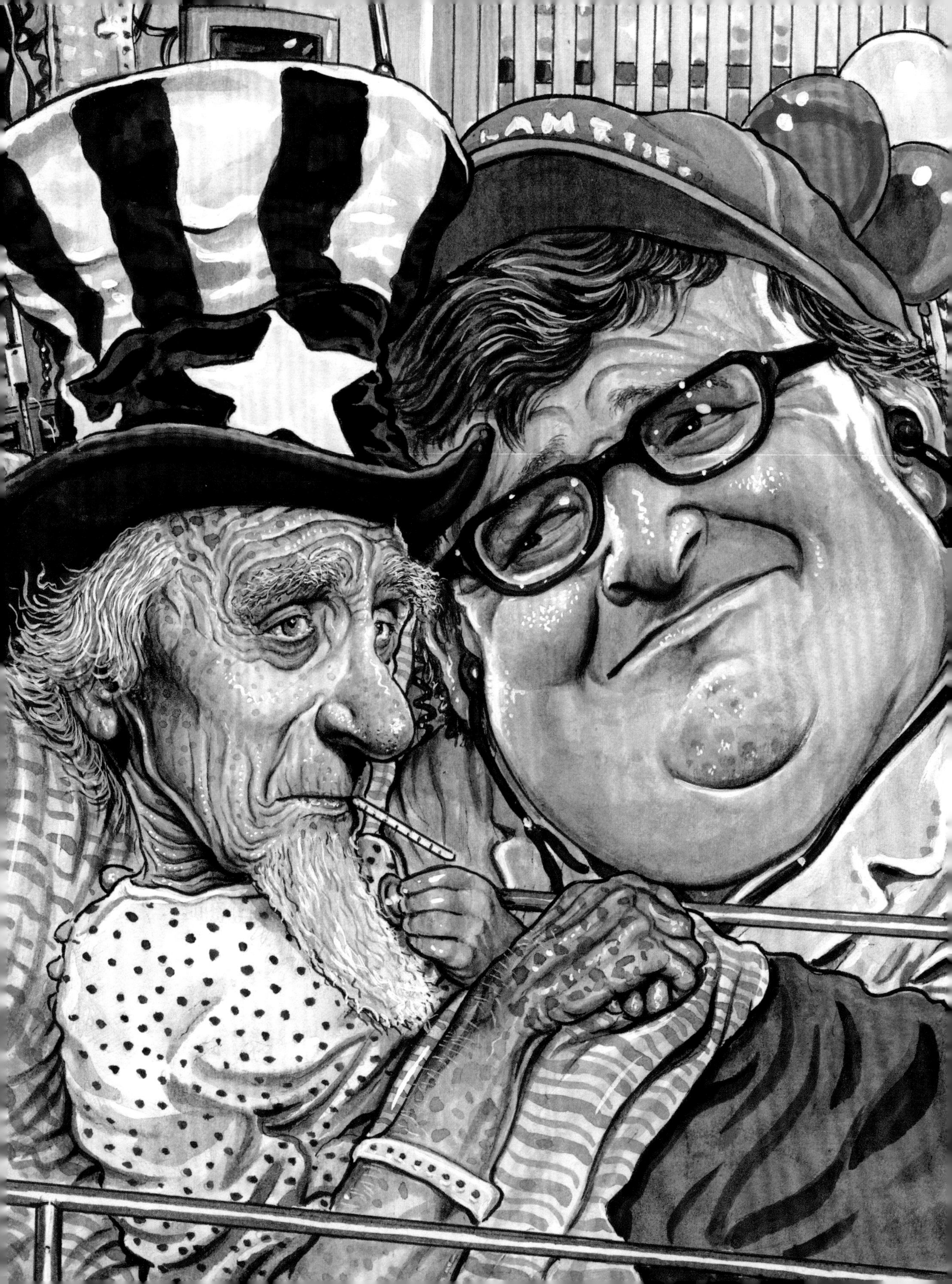

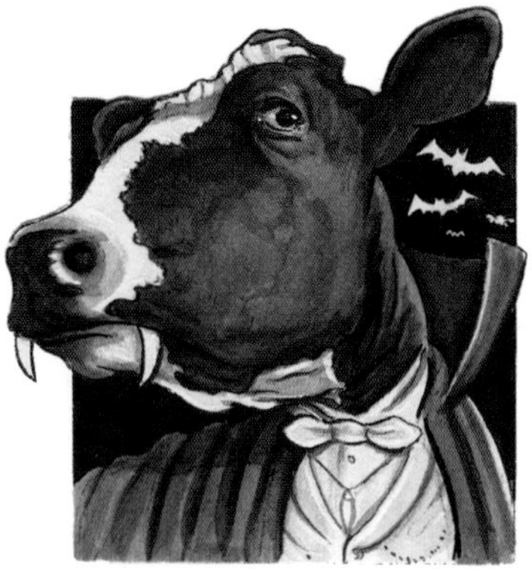

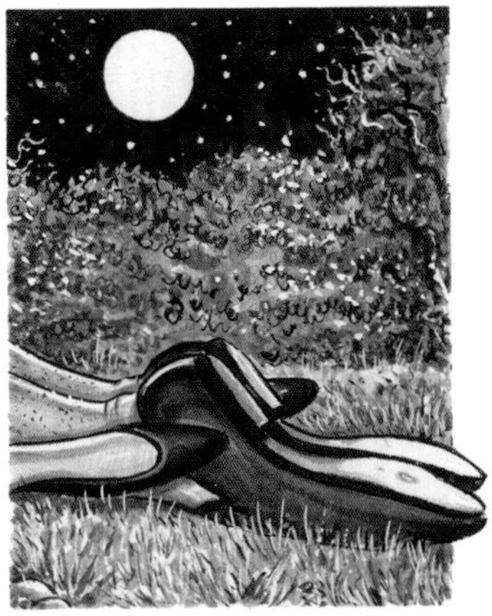

Vampire Cows.

How to have sex in the woods.

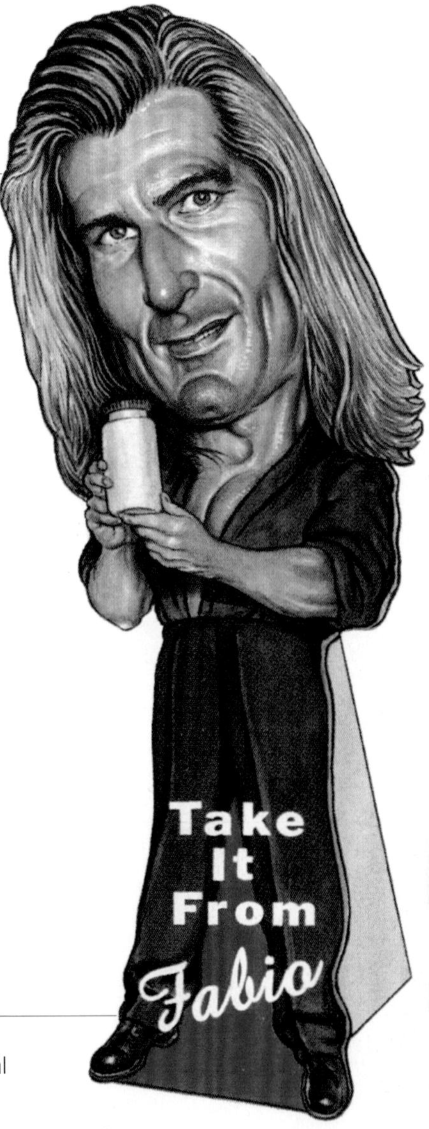
Take It From Fabio

"**PHARM AID**." FABIO'S placard shills for weight-loss supplements.

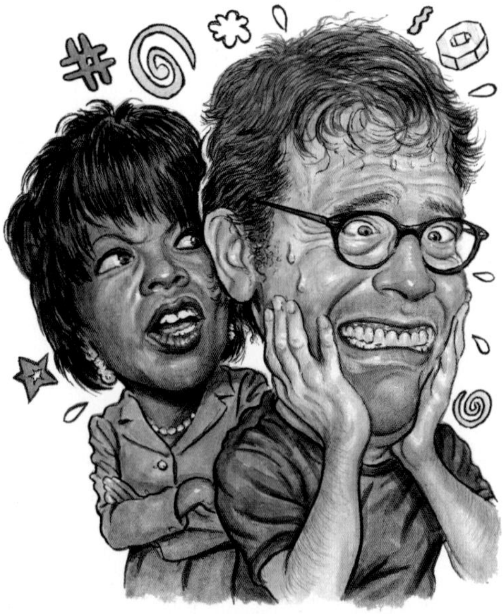

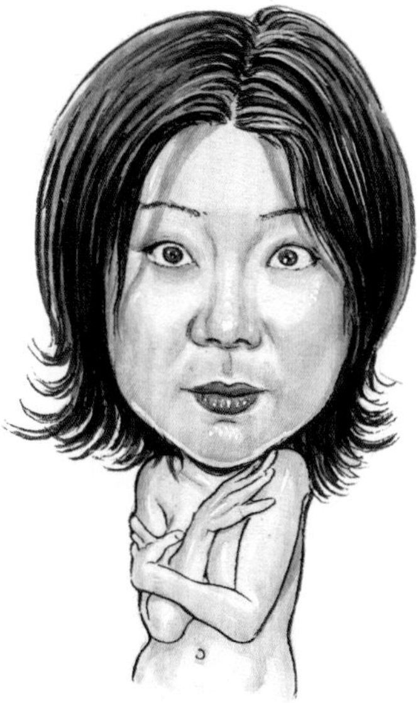

"**HE'S BECOME UNGLUED**." What happens when a man doesn't want to belong to a club that will have him as a member? OPRAH WINFREY berates JONATHAN FRANZEN.

MARGARET CHO, writing a young-adult novel dealing with body image and sexual orientation.

"SUMMER SMACKDOWN."

BOSTON GLOBE MAGAZINE (cover)

Settling some of the best Boston arguments. **Tracy Chapman** vs. **Joan Baez**, Harvard Chairman **Larry Summers** vs. plagiarizing author **Kaavya Viswanathan, a stone duck** vs. **Curious George, Julia Child** vs. **Fannie Farmer,** Red Sox **Alex Gonzalez** vs. New England Patriot **Tom Brady, Ben Affleck** vs. **Matt Damon,** *Cheers* barmaids **Kirstie Alley** vs. **Shelley Long**.

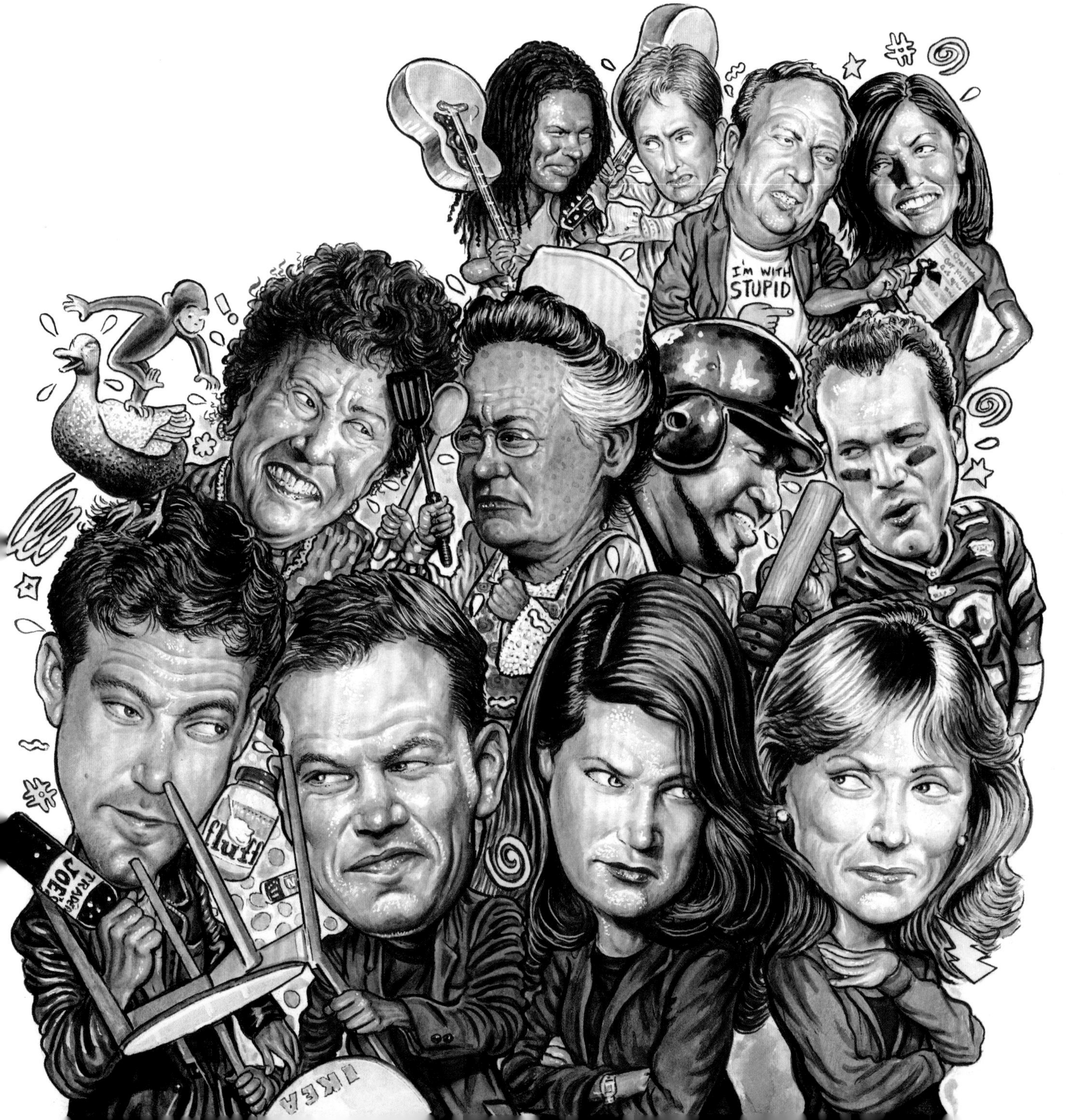
I'M WITH
STUPID
fluff

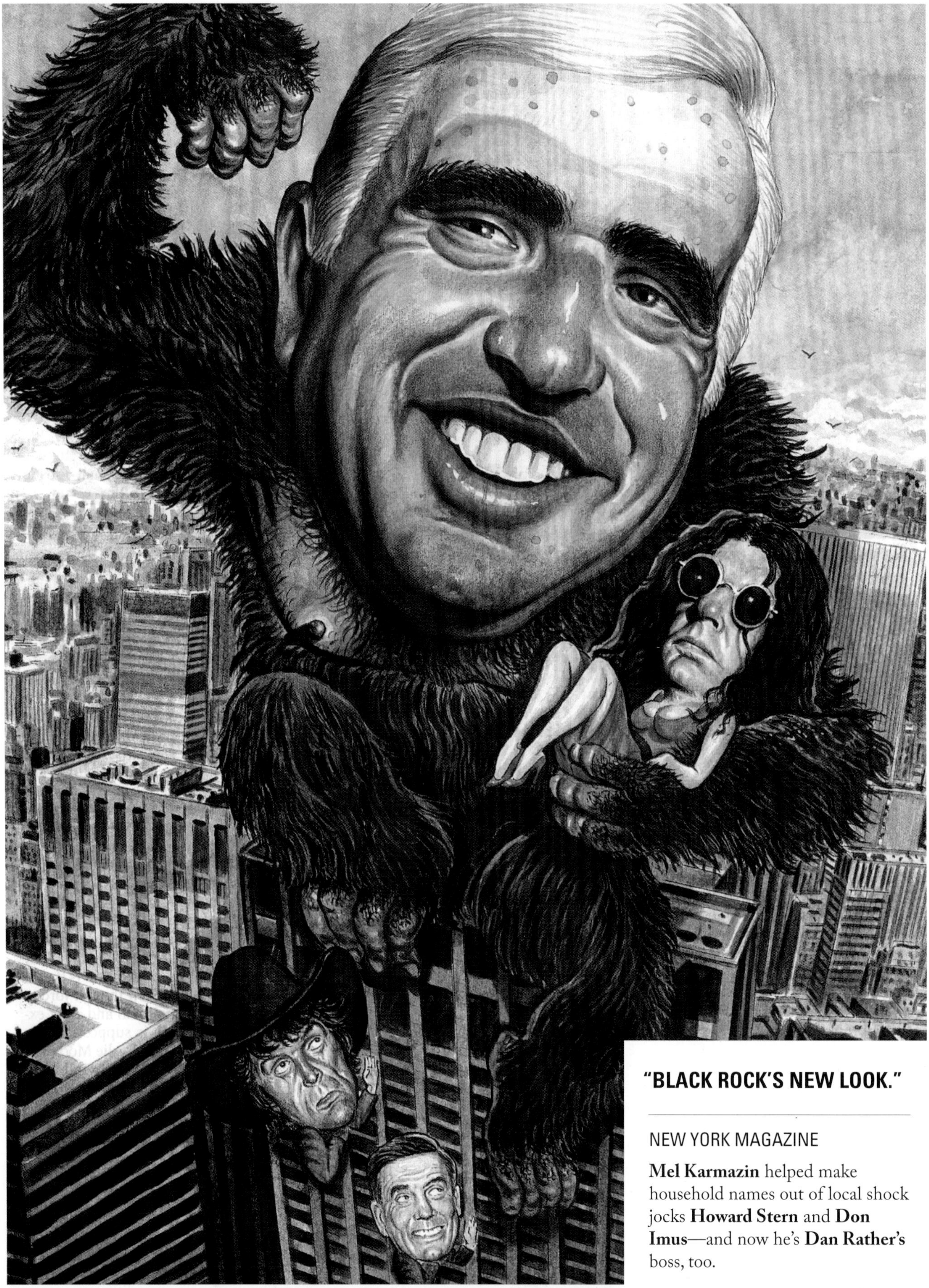

"BLACK ROCK'S NEW LOOK."

NEW YORK MAGAZINE

Mel Karmazin helped make household names out of local shock jocks **Howard Stern** and **Don Imus**—and now he's **Dan Rather's** boss, too.

"YOU BELONG TO ME."

TIME

"After a whopping $70 billion merger between Viacom and CBS, **Sumner Redstone** is the patriarch of a media family so huge, **Dan Rather** and Comedy Central's *South Park* kids are in-laws. Can they get along?"

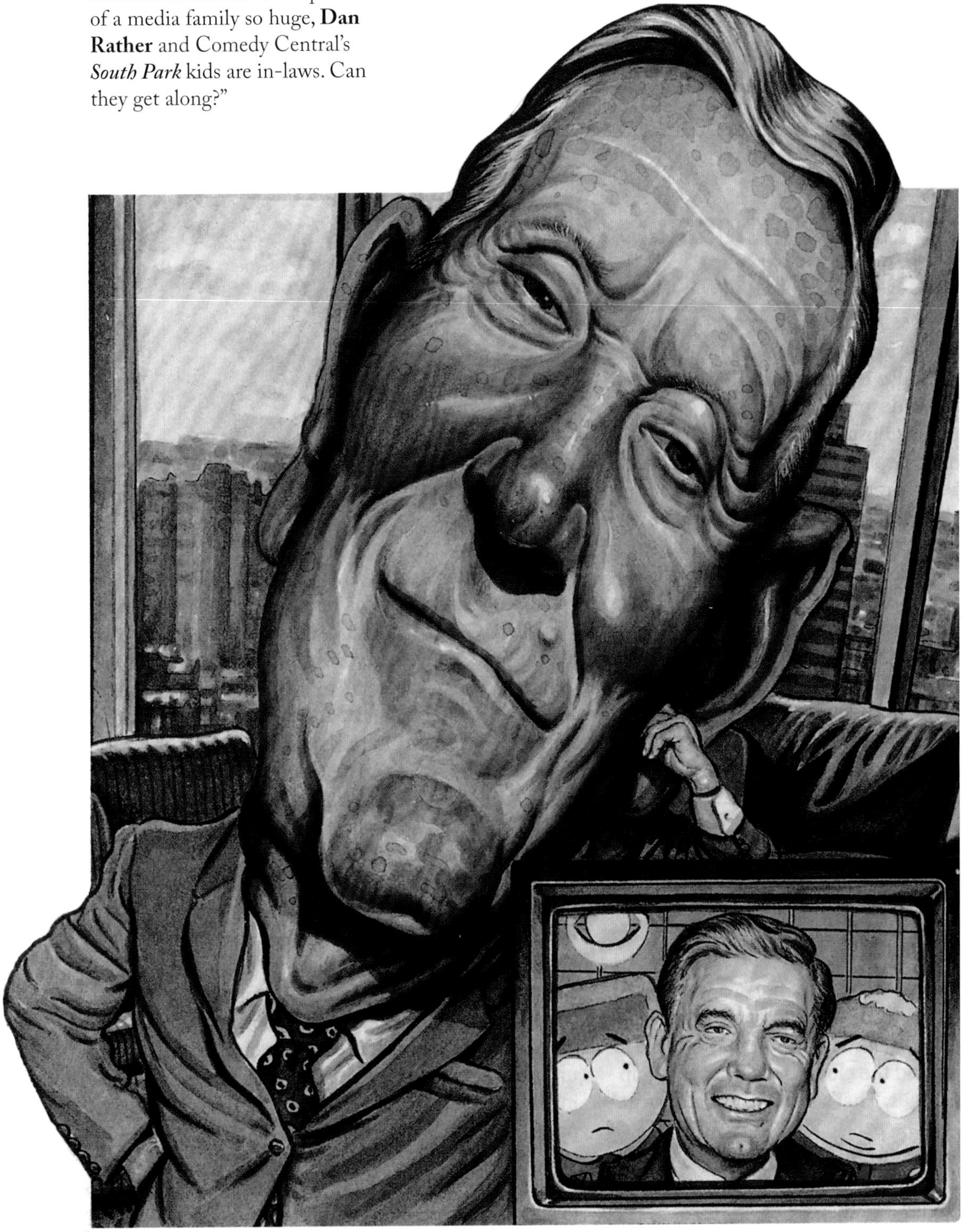

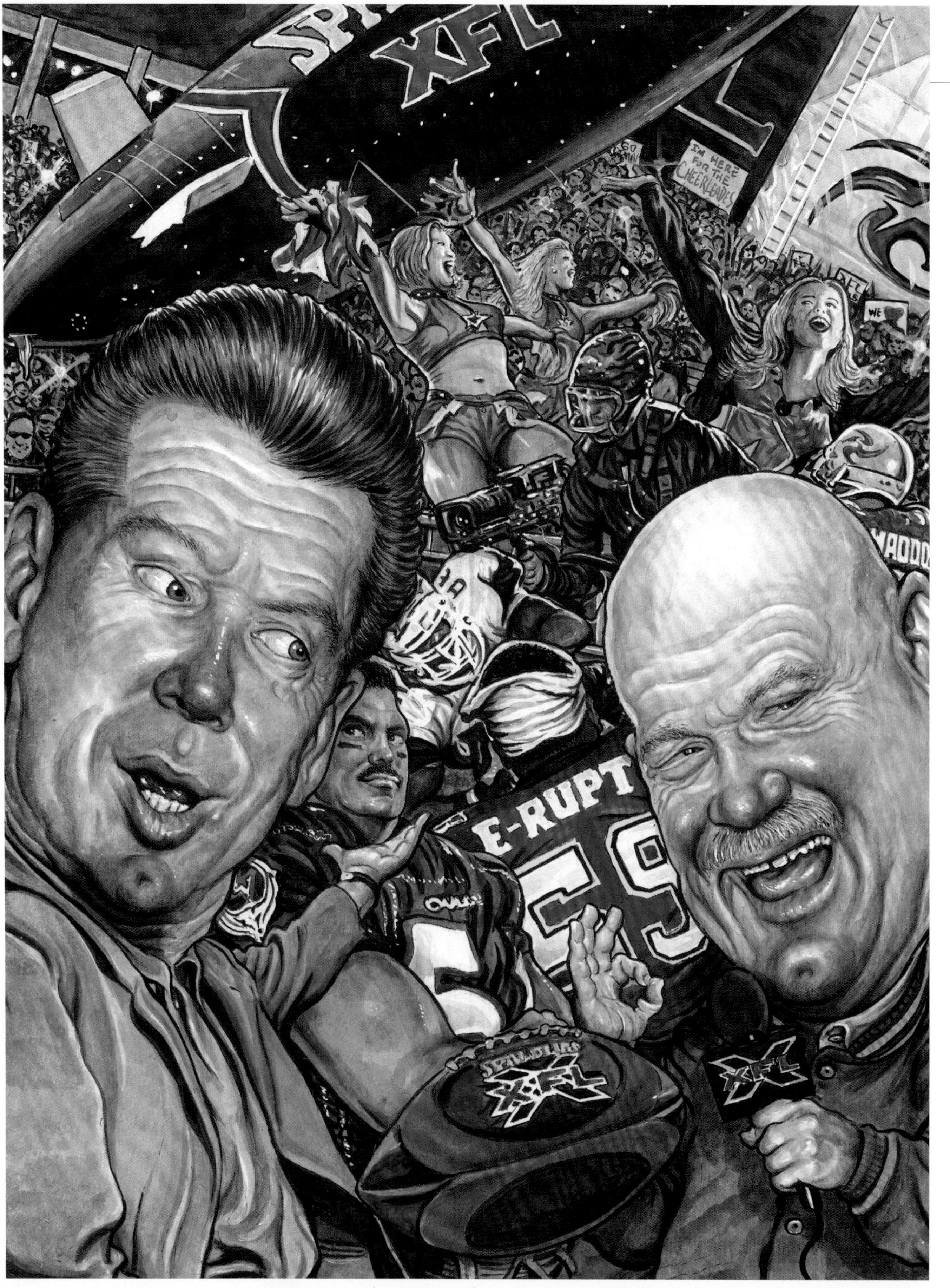
XFL
E-RUPT
XFL
XFL

"FOOTBALLAMANIA."

SPORTS ILLUSTRATED

Wrestling promoter **Vince McMahon** announced *XFL*, his American football league with great fanfare, along with governor **Jesse Ventura** in tow as announcer. Inevitably, it folded after just one season.

"KNOCK WOOD(S)."

SPORTS ILLUSTRATED

Comparing **Mike Tyson's** bad boy image to **Tiger Woods's** squeaky-clean image. My, how times have changed.

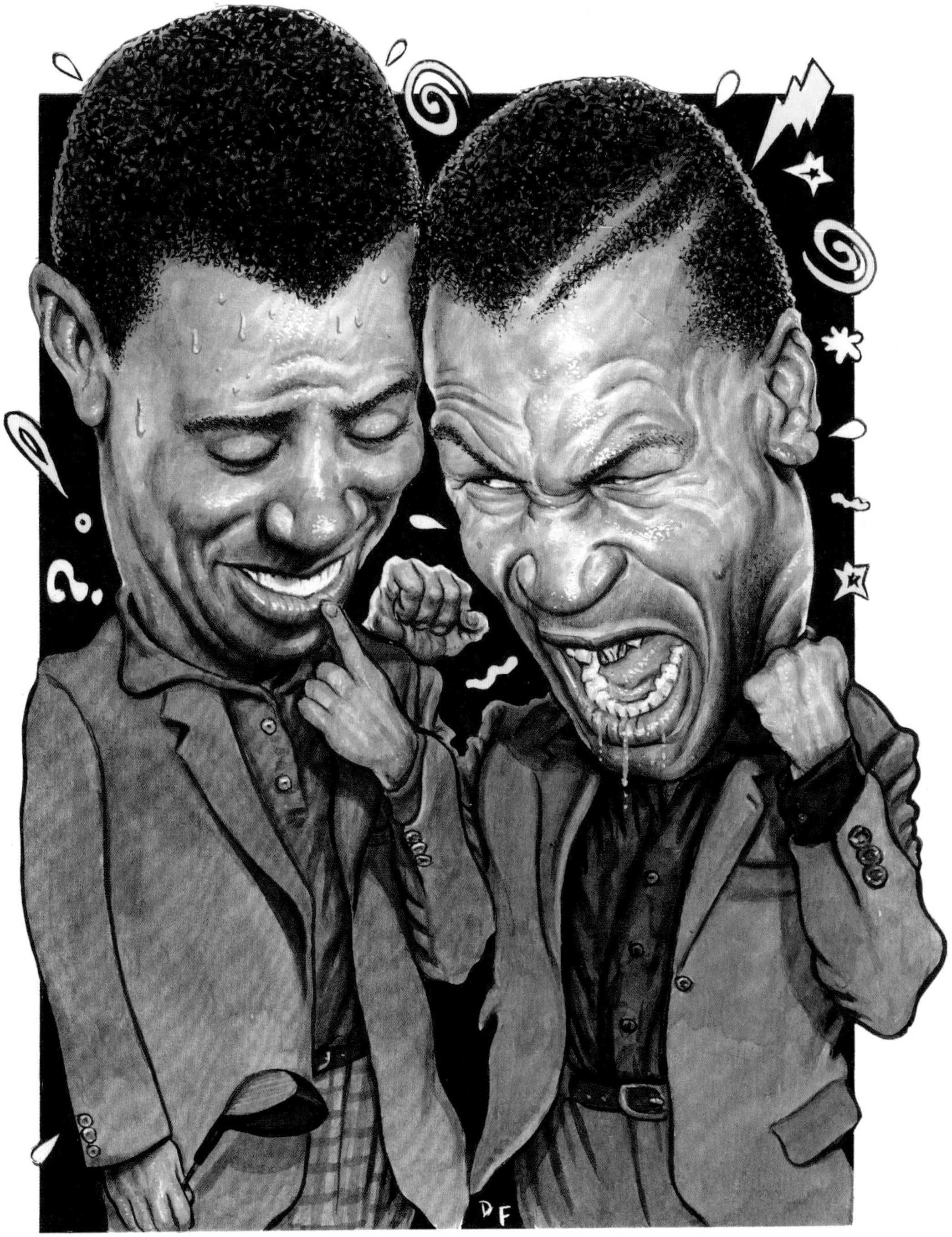

"LATE CARTOONISTS."

ENTERTAINMENT WEEEKLY

For several years, I was asked by *EW* to illustrate cartoonists and animators who had died that year for their "In Memoriam" issue. I always wondered how they'd have handled it if *I* suddenly died?

Graffiti artists: **Hank Ketcham**, **Bill Hanna**, **George Gately**, **Herblock**, **Fred Lasswell**.

After this appeared, someone pointed out that that was ***not*** George Gately—the creator of *Heathcliff*. Turns out the photo editor had sent me the wronge photo. To this day, I still have no idea who this guy is?

The real George Gately:

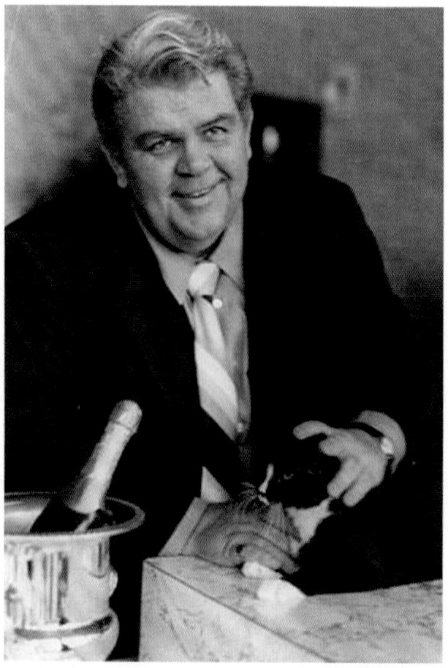

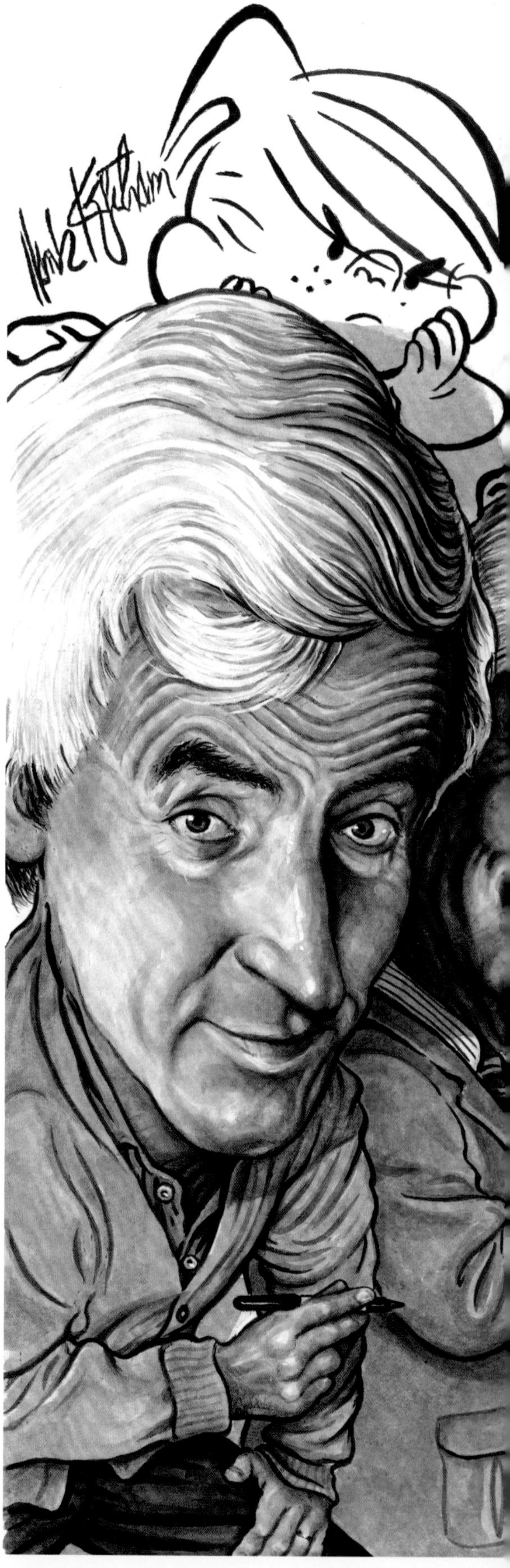

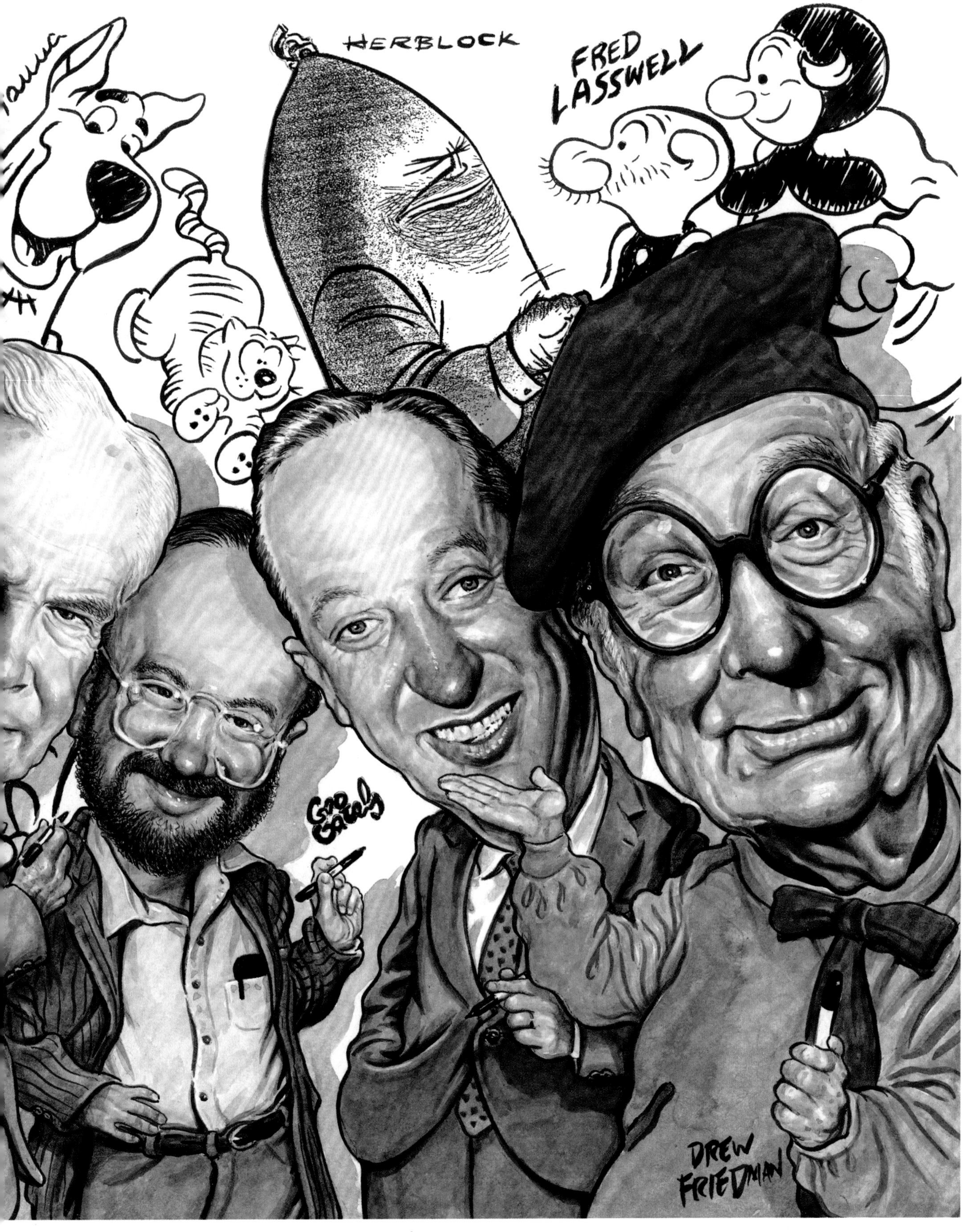
HERBLOCK
FRED LASSWELL
DREW FRIEDMAN

"THIS ONE AND THAT ONE."

ENTERTAINMENT WEEKLY

Leonard Nimoy, Vulcan shutterbug.

Ayn Rand—a star is born.

Anne Rice as a mustached five-o'clock-shadowed baby.

FAST COMPANY

Former CEO **Jack Welch's** secret diary.

LOS ANGELES MAGAZINE

Author **Salman Rushdie.**

MEN'S HEALTH

Gunslinger **G. Gordon Liddy.**

"WHAT SCARES STEPHEN KING?"

NEW YORK MAGAZINE

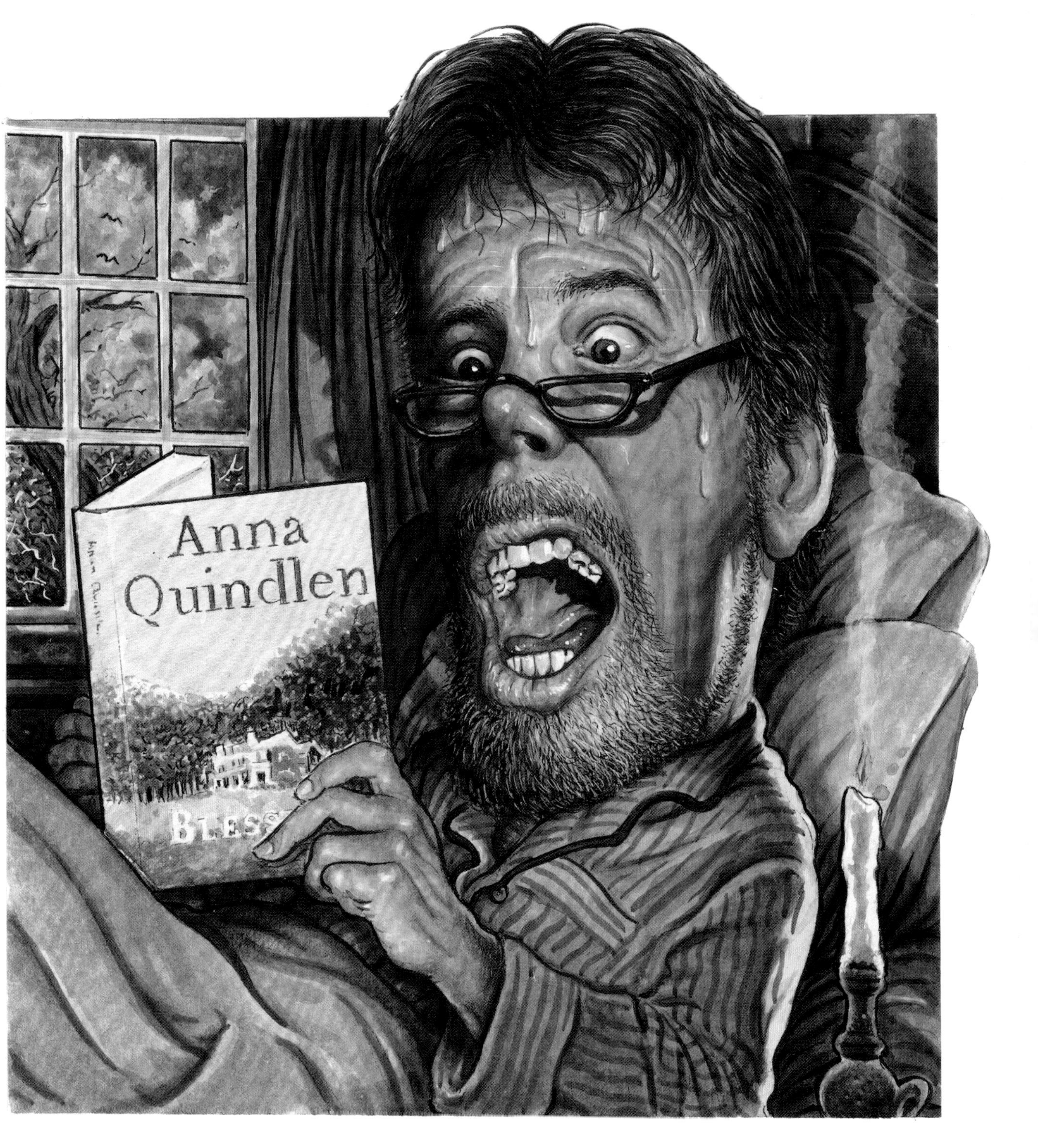
Anna
Quindlen
BLESS

"SAM FULLER'S LAST YARN."

THE LOS ANGELES TIMES
BOOK REVIEW (cover)

A portrait of the rowdy filmmaker for a review of his posthumously published memoir *A Third Face*.

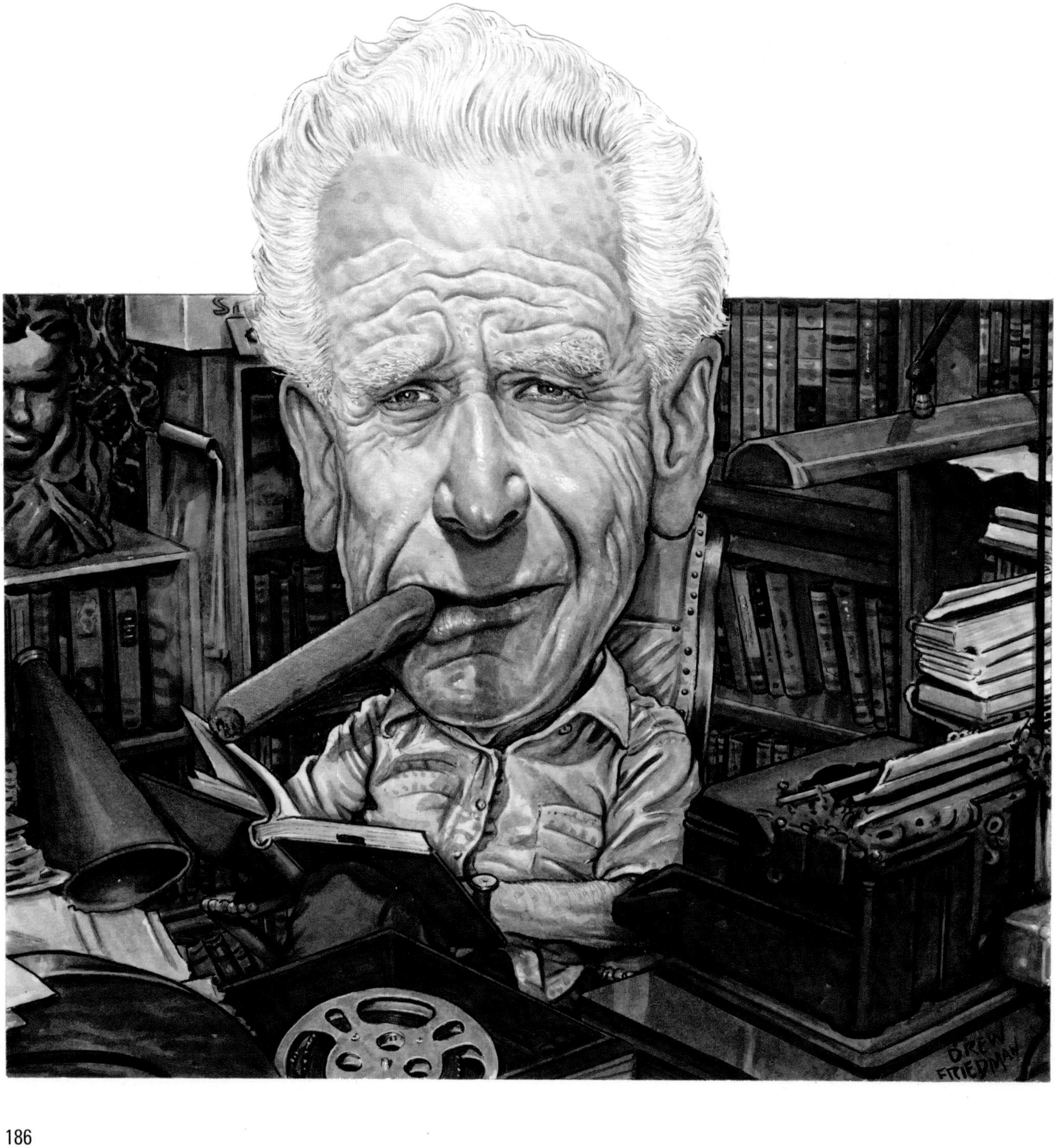
DREW FRIEDMAN

"SCHLITZIE."

...was born with microcephaly, endowing him with a small brain and skull, and reaching adulthood, the cognizance of a 3-year-old. He was dressed in colorful "muumuus" due to his incontinence, leaving the impression with many that he was female. Schlitzie was one of the most beloved sideshow freaks in history, and his infectious personality was memorably captured in Tod Browning's classic film ***Freaks***, depicted here. Inspiration for Bill Griffith's Zippy.

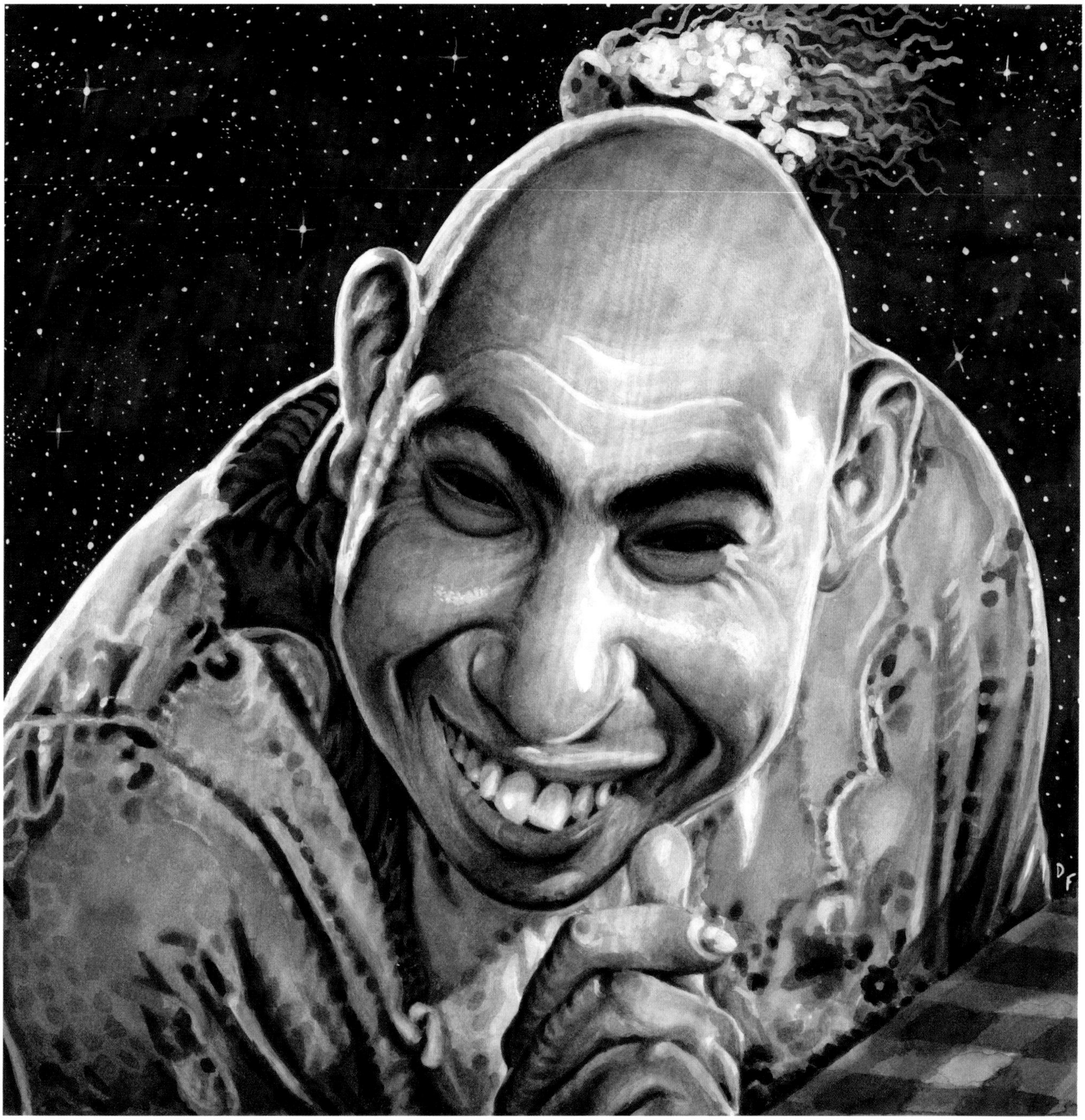
DF

"THE OLD CODGER."

COURTNEY T. EDISON

...is a radio broadcaster and a 78 RPM record archivist popularly known as "The Old Codger," His age is... "ageless. He taunts WFMU listeners by sneering, 'I've got shoes older than you.'" He's notorious for his on-air come-ons to female admirers, crooning that he loves "younger women, age 45–50—but ain't messin' with no 40-year-old jail bait!"

(Information provided by Irwin Chusid.)

"JUDSON FOUNTAIN."

...has been called "The Ed Wood of radio dramas." He produced original, gothic-tinged dramas (such as "the old woman of haunted house"), in the style of old-time radio theatre, assisted by his trusted announcer, **Sandor Weisberger**. That he lacked training, technology, staff and a budget did not deter him.

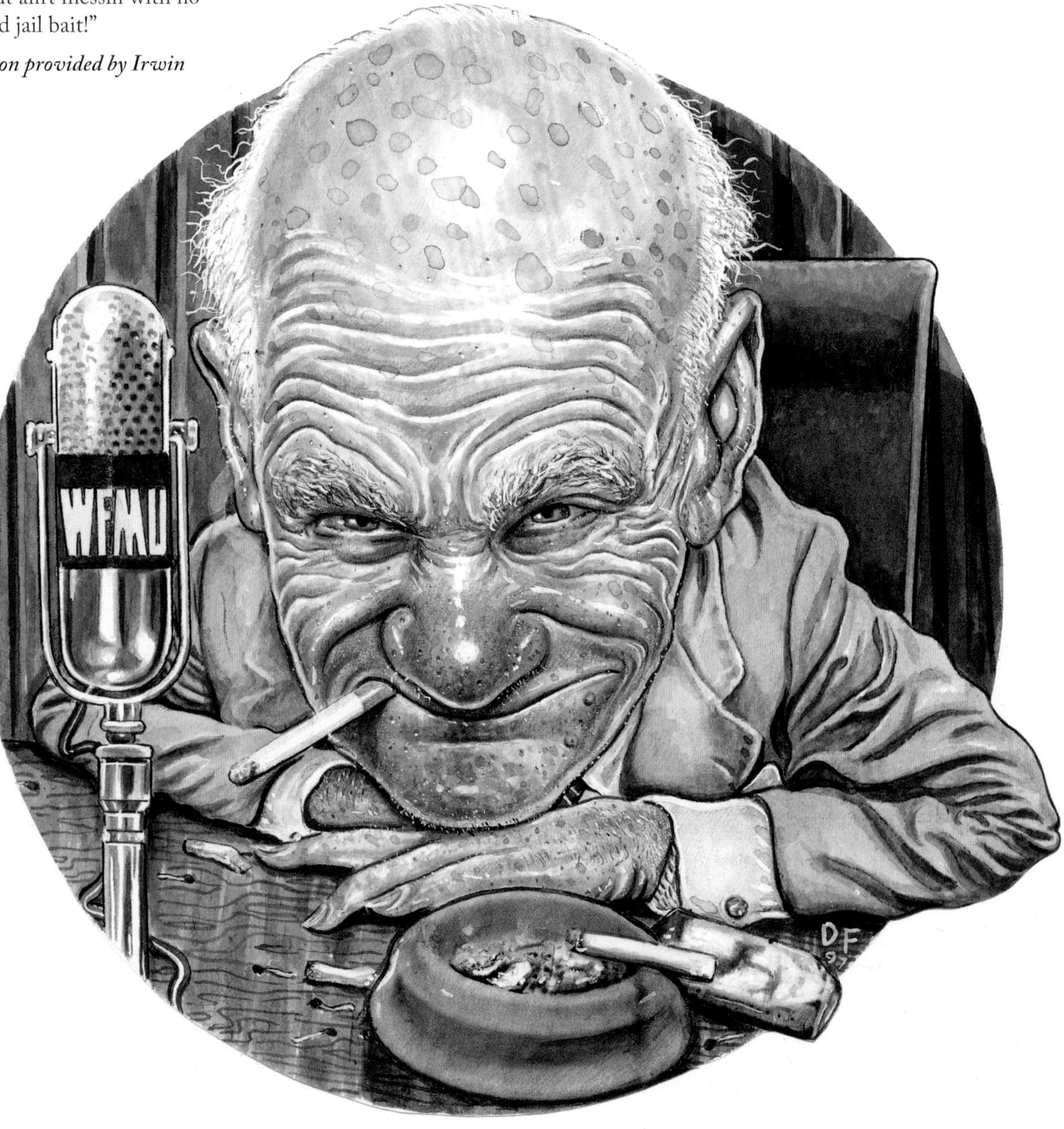
WFMU
DF

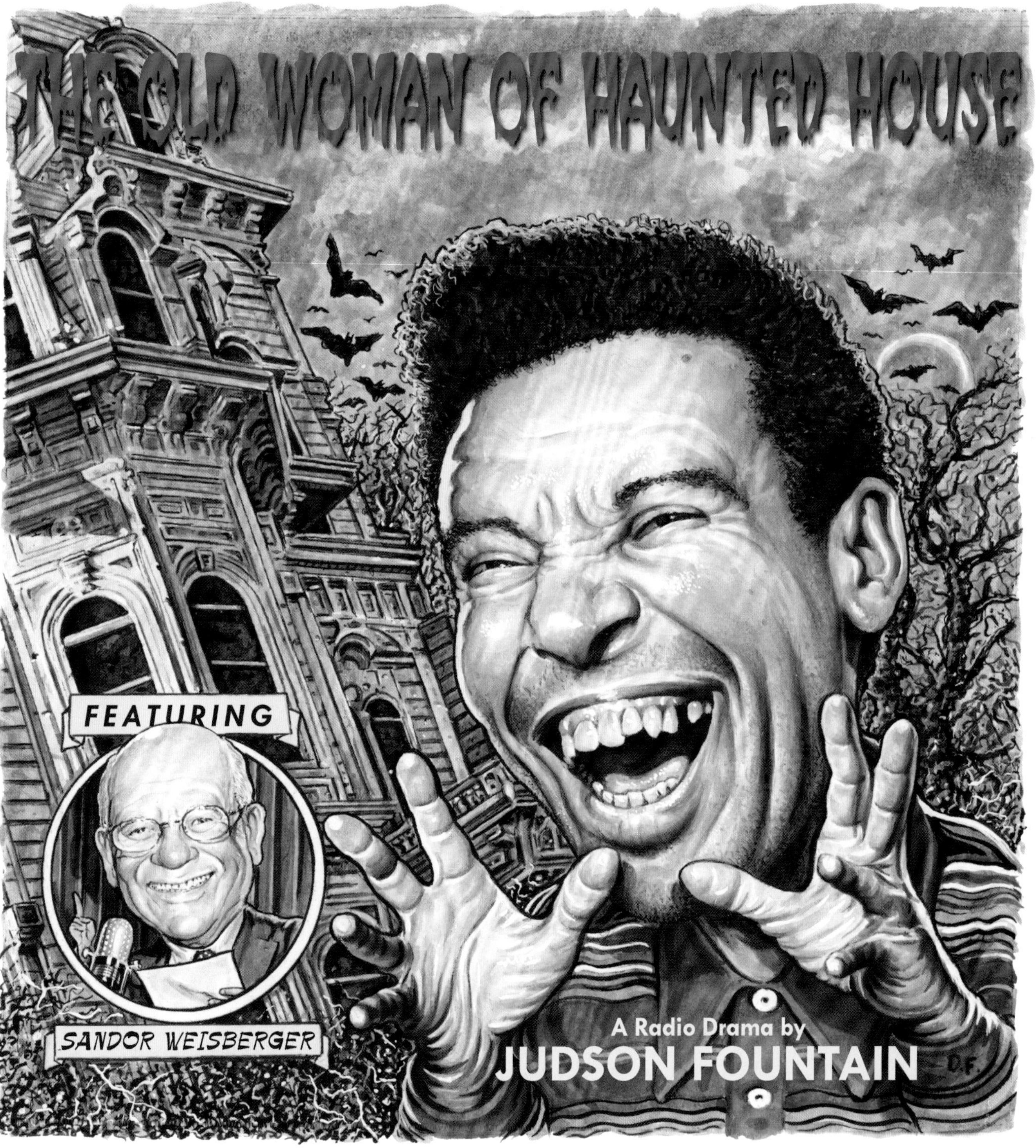
THE OLD WOMAN OF HAUNTED HOUSE
FEATURING
SANDOR WEISBERGER
A Radio Drama by
JUDSON FOUNTAIN
D.F.

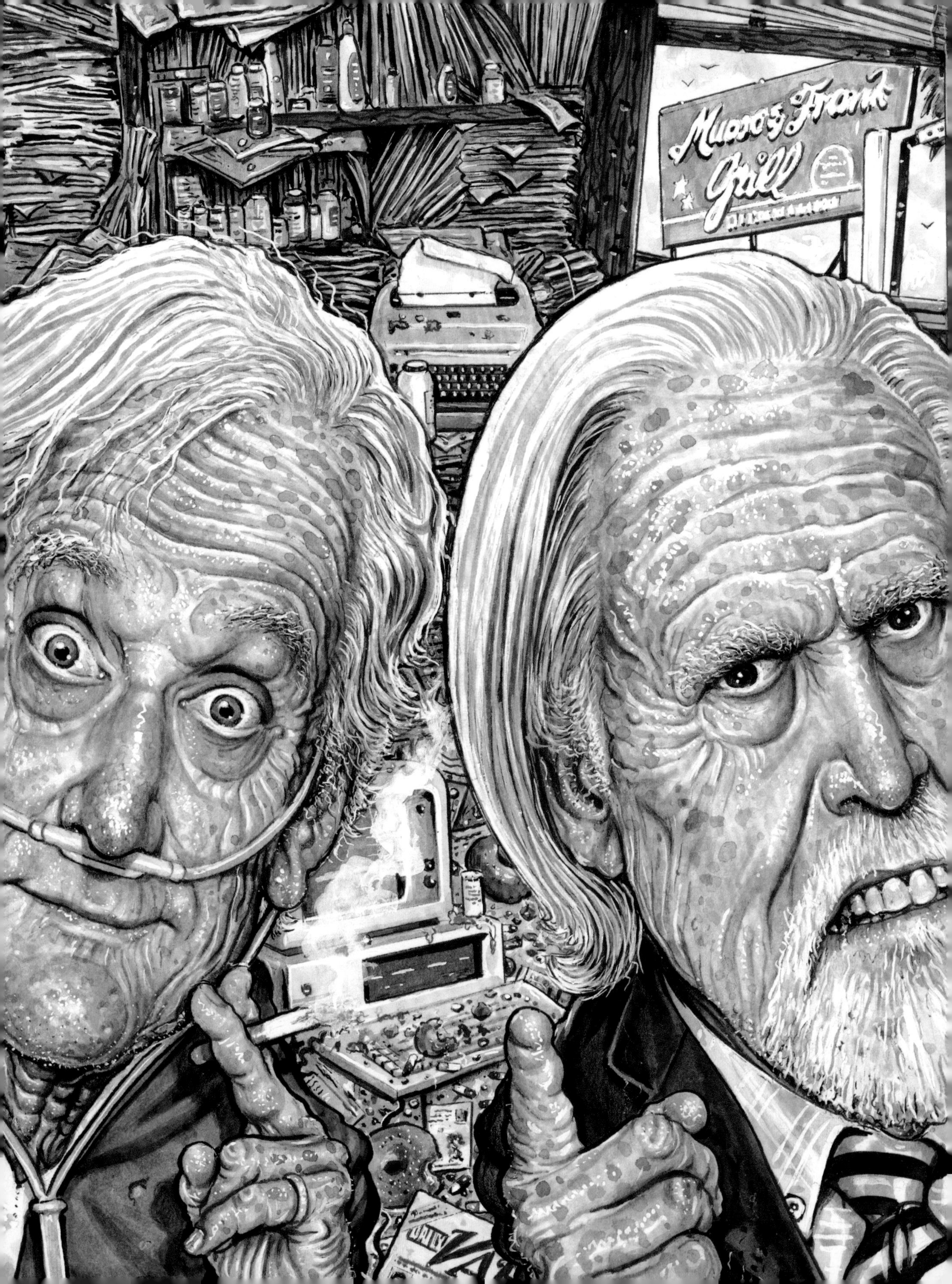
Musso & Frank
Grill

"MILT & MARTY."

COVER ART created for
MILT & MARTY

...The story of the "longest lasting and least successful comedy writing team in showbiz history," by Tom Leopold and Bob Sand.

Milt Wagonman and **Marty** "The X is Silent!" **Sloyxne**.

"SHOW BUSINESS."

BLAB!

This rare ad, found in the back of the long-forgotten rag *Crap for Men*, is all that remains of the legacy of one **Kippy Spagenbusch**, back-stabbing agent, relentless self-promoter, failed philanderer, cheap-suit haranguer. To quote B'way Moe Weingarten on Kippy: "The guy's running out of barrels to scrape the bottom of."

(Information provided by Irwin Chusid.)

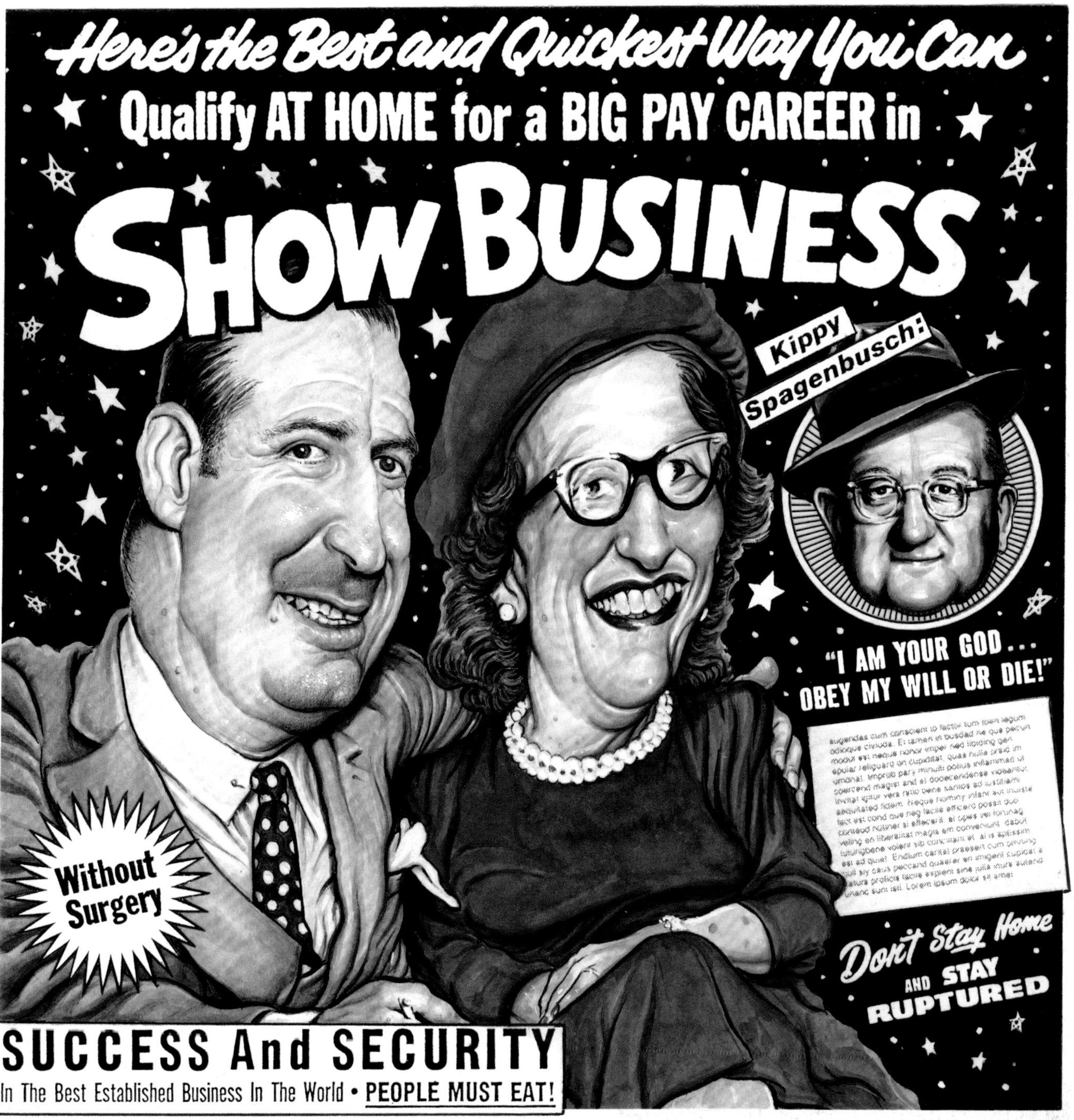

Here's the Best and Quickest Way You Can
Qualify AT HOME for a BIG PAY CAREER in
SHOW BUSINESS
Kippy Spagenbusch:
"I AM YOUR GOD... OBEY MY WILL OR DIE!"
Without Surgery
Don't Stay Home AND STAY RUPTURED
SUCCESS And SECURITY
In The Best Established Business In The World • PEOPLE MUST EAT!

INDEX

OTHER BOOKS BY DREW FRIEDMAN
AVAILABLE FROM FANTAGRAPHICS:

**ANY SIMILARITY TO PERSONS
LIVING OR DEAD IS PURELY COINCIDENTAL**
(co-written by Josh Alan Friedman)
(1986 and 1997—out of print,
25th anniversary edition coming in 2011)

WARTS & ALL
(co-written by Josh Alan Friedman)
(Penguin, 1990, re-issued by Fantagraphics Books, 1994)

OLD JEWISH COMEDIANS
(2006)

THE FUN NEVER STOPS!
(2007)

MORE OLD JEWISH COMEDIANS
 (2008)

EVEN MORE OLD JEWISH COMEDIANS
(coming Spring 2011)

FRIEDMAN ON THE WEB

To purchase limited-edition
prints, visit:

WWW.DREWFRIEDMAN.NET

To see Drew's latest work and
to follow his blog, head to:

WWW.DRAWGER.COM

To purchase Drew's other books,
and to shop for comics, graphic
novels, and other visual delights:

WWW.FANTAGRAPHICS.COM